THE COLOR OF KINK

SEXUAL CULTURES

General Editors: Ann Pellegrini, Tavia Nyong'o, and Joshua Chambers-Letson

Founding Editors: José Esteban Muñoz and Ann Pellegrini

Titles in the series include:

For a complete list of books in the series, see www.nyupress.org.

The Color of Kink

Black Women, BDSM, and Pornography

Ariane Cruz

NEW YORK UNIVERSITY PRESS

New York

NEW YORK UNIVERSITY PRESS
New York
www.nyupress.org

References to Internet websites (URLs) were accurate at the time of writing.
Neither the author nor New York University Press is responsible for URLs that may have
expired or changed since the manuscript was prepared.

Library of Congress Cataloging-in-Publication Data
Names: Cruz, Ariane, author.
Title: The color of kink : black women, BDSM, and pornography / Ariane Cruz.
Description: New York : New York University Press, 2016. | Series: Sexual cultures |
Includes bibliographical references and index.
Identifiers: LCCN 2016017049| ISBN 978-1-4798-0928-8 (hbk : alk. paper) |
ISBN 978-1-4798-2746-6 (pbk : alk. paper)
Subjects: LCSH: Bondage (Sexual behavior) | Sadomasochism. | Pornography. | Women,
Black—Sexual behavior.
Classification: LCC HQ79 .C78 2016 | DDC 306.77/5—dc23
LC record available at https://lccn.loc.gov/2016017049

New York University Press books are printed on acid-free paper, and their binding materials
are chosen for strength and durability. We strive to use environmentally responsible suppli-
ers and materials to the greatest extent possible in publishing our books.

Manufactured in the United States of America

10 9 8 7 6 5 4 3 2 1

Also available as an ebook

For Florence, Bertie, and especially for Derek

CONTENTS

ACKNOWLEDGMENTS

This project materialized with the support and encouragement of many people. Over many years and through multiple and meandering routes, it has received funding from sources such as the Ford Foundation, the UC Berkeley Center for the Study of Sexual Culture, and the Penn State Institute for the Arts and Humanities. This book was partially funded by a fellowship and grant from the Africana Research Center at the Pennsylvania State University. I thank these institutions for their support. I would also like to thank the University of California, Berkeley and the Pennsylvania State University for providing institutional homes for this project and for enabling me to meet a number of wonderful colleagues and friends. From my time at UC Berkeley, I would like to thank Percy Hintzen, Patricia Penn Hilden, Leigh Raiford, and a host of other individuals, including Ula Taylor, Robert Allen, Paola Bacchetta, Lindsey Herbert, and, last but not least, the late, great VèVè Amasasa Clark, an awesome mentor and an early voice of honesty and confidence.

The incredible faculty and staff of the Department of Women's, Gender, and Sexuality Studies at Penn State is a beacon of support and a rich intellectual community. I am especially thankful to a number of colleagues and friends at Penn State for their support for this manuscript, including Gabeba Baderoon, Robert Bernasconi, Lovalerie King, Carolyn Sachs, Nancy Tuana, Melissa Wright, "The Doctor Sisters," and my "Homegirls" writing (and more) group. I would also like to thank Irina Aristarkhova for her conversations and continued support through this journey.

I am grateful to the light numerous scholars have shed in the field of racialized sexuality, a few of whom have especially offered their support: Matt Richardson, L. H. Stallings, Marlon Bailey, Jennifer Nash, and in particular Mireille Miller-Young, whose trailblazing work on black women in pornography has carved the space for this manuscript.

New York University Press has been instrumental in the materialization of this project. I am thankful to Eric Zinner and Alicia Nadkarni for their labor and support. I am especially thankful to the Sexual Cultures series editors, Joshua Takano Chambers-Letson, Tavia Nyong'o, and Ann Pellegrini, for their encouragement, guidance, and vision. I am honored to be a part of such a wonderful series. Two anonymous readers have strengthened this work with their keen critique and encouragement. I am also thankful to Cecelia Cancellaro for her careful editing of select chapters of this book. I would be remiss if I did not thank the black women on and from whom this project draws. These women generously offered their knowledge, time, and stories and continue to teach me so much.

I express my deepest gratitude to my friends and family. Christine DeHart's "off the mat" pedagogy breathed energy, strength, flow, and balance into the body, mind, and spirit of this book. Elizabeth Adam, Alyssa Garcia, Deirdre Conroy, Malene Welch, and Jasmine Cobb continue to listen in profound ways. I thank Rob Ferguson, an enthusiastic, tireless, and patient supporter whose perpetual optimism and faith matters. Finally my "treasures of the heart," Barbara, John, and Justin Cruz and Donna Snow, have blessed me with a level of love and support I do not have words for. I cannot thank them enough.

Introduction

Speaking the Unspeakable

In many cases, desire lies like a bodily boundary between
the everyday and the unspeakable.
—Samuel R. Delany[1]

Home*coming*

Black female visual artist crystal am nelson's *Building Me a Home* (2009),
an eight-minute, three channel video, engages the unspeakable pleasures of black female sexuality that anchor this book, an exploration of
black women, BDSM, and pornography that presents BDSM as a stage
for analyzing black women's sexuality and its representation in order to
unveil the complex desires and self-making practices of black women
subjects.[2] Moreover, it signals queerness, interraciality, and technology as vibrant motifs that galvanize my discussion of racialized BDSM
as a critical site for reinvigorating debates about pleasure, domination,
and perversion in the context of black female sexuality. In the video,
we look at various parts of nelson's body bound in intricate knots by
Mistress Heart, a celebrated San Francisco Bay Area dom, model, and
community activist. Both nelson and Heart were instrumental members
of the Bay Area Women of Color Photo Project, a photography collective formed by Heart and fetish photographer Andrew Morgan in 2003
to document local women of color BDSM practitioners.[3] Its mission was
"to expand the aesthetic and cultural perception of the BDSM community by promoting artistically tasteful photographic images of Women
of Color in BDSM."[4] According to queer feminist photographer Shilo
McCabe, one of several photographers on the project, it was an intervention to increase the visibility and belonging of women of color in the
BDSM community.[5] McCabe explains the project's mission: "The goal

Figure I.1. crystal am nelson, *Portrait of crystal, suburban born, daughter of Valerie and James, State of Rhode Island and Providence Plantations–full frontal* [from *Untitled (Bound)* series], 2007, ~4x5" giclée print. Image courtesy of artist.

of the project was to increase the visibility of women of color in erotic/fetish images in order to make women of color feel like they belonged in those communities."[6] Although nelson's *Building Me a Home* presents this politics of visibility, it also explores the complexities of black women's navigation of BDSM space.

While nelson recognizes BDSM as a "hot-button" issue, she acknowledges that its inflammatory power is compounded by race—specifically the black female body's legacy of sexual trauma.[7] She refers to "a compacted body doing things that are very loaded with history and historical trauma that haven't been resolved."[8] nelson says that her goal "is to try to cultivate a vocabulary but also to try to help people shift their perspective."[9] *Building Me a Home* functions as a visual vocabulary to critically intervene in our reading of black female sexuality—one that recognizes the pleasure and power some black female subjects experience in sexual performances scripted by the memory of slavery.

Because it deftly engages the multiple contradictions that cohere in the performance of BDSM, *Building Me a Home* is the entry point I have chosen for this book. Like nelson, I am interested in what BDSM and black female sexuality "means for someone in [her] body." I interrogate our contested libidinal investments in "the residuals of trauma" as evinced by black women's representations and performances within BDSM and in contemporary American pornography from the 1930s to the present.[10] I read performances of black female sexual aggression, domination, humiliation, and submission in pornography and BDSM as critical modes of black women's pleasure, power, and agency. *The Color of Kink* also explores the multiple and contradictory fantasies that animate black women's practice of BDSM, placing them in the context of long-standing debates and controversies about the representation of race, gender, and sexuality. How do we rethink the formative links between black female sexuality and violence? Like nelson, I explore how domination and submission are not just mechanisms of power but also modes of pleasure. I argue that BDSM is a productive space from which to consider the complexity and diverseness of black women's sexual practice and the mutability of black female sexuality. I also illustrate how BDSM illuminates the queerness of blackness and how blackness brings into focus the queerness of BDSM.

As a BDSM apparatus and tool of bondage, the rope functions not just as a technology of pleasure and pain, but also race. In *Building Me a Home*, a rope bit gag is slipped in between nelson's parted lips and fastened around the back of her head. Another knot forms beneath her breasts at the base of her breastbone. Her wrists are thickly shackled with coils of rope. The white rope contrasts with the color of her skin and the black frame of the triptych video. The scene is a BDSM fantasy of black female sexuality shaped by the memory of chattel slavery. In one image, the indentations of the rope form a visible pattern of small ripples on nelson's stomach. While these flesh imprints manifest the black female's bodily memory of slavery, they are also impressions of pain and pleasure. While the rope elicits whiteness in order to fetishize whites' violent domination in the primal scene of slavery, it also marks the pleasure in this queer encounter of black female intimacy. In her art, nelson recognizes the salience of what she terms the "black/white dichotomy" and the magnetism of its pull while at the same time, she works to place black subjectivity beyond this binary.[11] She states, "The work I was doing is really about asserting black subjectivity and subjectivity that's not necessarily wrapped up in how my body or my experience is related to the white body or the white experience."[12] Though whiteness is corporeally absent from the powerful piece, its symbolic presence is strong. Whiteness becomes personified in ways that perhaps contradict its absence from this bodily encounter to assert itself in this particular staging of black female subjectivity and within the scene of black female BDSM performance more broadly. While the artist did not include a white performer, whiteness haunts the scene nonetheless.

The metaphoric residue of whiteness resonates with this book's assertion that interraciality is a necessary optic when considering kink. As a symbol of whiteness, the white ropes encasing nelson's brown flesh visualize the intimate relationship of whiteness and blackness that I argue is salient in black women's enactment of BDSM erotic fantasy. *Building Me a Home* instantiates the presence of whiteness in the sexual scene of black women's domination and submission, a grip nelson is aware of, as evidenced by her desire to disentangle black female subjectivity from whiteness in this provocative piece. The work is one of physically and metaphorically wrapping and unwrapping. In drawing on the symbolic yoking of black female BDSM sexuality to the memory of transatlantic slavery, the work invokes whiteness. If BDSM becomes a map for sketching out black female sexuality, whiteness stands as a signpost, a point of reference that often intrudes on the erotic scene to highlight its enactment of pleasure, power, and pain. In racialized BDSM performance and its dynamic representation in pornography, interraciality signals the political stakes for black women.

If the rope is an ambivalent signifier of race, it is also an equivocal marker of pleasure and pain, empowerment and captivity, and past and present. The tightly pulled diagonal line of rope guides our eyes to the central image of nelson's bound figure. But it also serves as a (color/time) line, marking black female sexuality in relation to the moorings of queerness (figured here as a mode of complicit blackness), the remembrance of slavery, and the somatically absent but symbolically present whiteness, creating an erotic threshold that is vital to the performances I interpret in this book. At the same time that the rope leads our gaze to nelson and Heart's hands, it also directs our eyes to the unsettled space outside the frame—a willing canvas for our own imaginary. The tension of the rope emanates from its physical tautness and from what it metaphorically represents of what lies between black women's historic captivity under chattel slavery and the "erotic macramé" of contemporary BDSM bondage.[13] nelson conveys the imbrication of pleasure and power that BDSM performance may engender for black women: "The work is about empowerment through pleasure. I do think that pleasure is a source of empowerment and I think also that when you are able to empower yourself that's also a feeling of bliss. I think that's a reciprocal relationship."[14] nelson asks us to critically rethink power—not only what it feels like but also what it looks like and what it *can* look like as enacted by the black female body specifically. She states, "I am really interested in BDSM and particularly what it means for someone in my body."[15] Her work represents an attempt "to reconfigure both the understanding of how individuals in certain situations empower themselves and how they assert their will."[16]

The subjects in *Building Me a Home* do not speak. Sound becomes a further challenge to this digital fantasy of pleasure, power, and will. In the absence of dialogue, a looped soundtrack heightens the complexity of racialized pleasure in the landscape of domination/submission. The audio accompaniment is an electronic tinny static—a soft metallic rattling sound overlaid by wind or perhaps by distant crashing waves—interspersed with a soft humming. Though we are unable to conclude if the humming is a diegetic or extradiegetic sound, the impression is that it comes from Mistress Heart (nelson's mouth is bound) as a kind of soundtrack to her labor. The humming amplifies the slow methodical care with which she binds and unbinds nelson's body. The effect of this chorus of sounds is almost soothing, amplified by the hazy repetitive white noise. This calm contrasts with the inescapable violence of this scene of black female captivity. Yet the humming also becomes an audible instantiation of queer black female pleasure. The sonic thus collaborates with the visual in elucidating how producing blackness is bound to domination, submission, and queerness and their intricate pleasures. In its artful play with the dynamics of speechlessness and sound, *Building Me a Home* presents BDSM as a mode of speaking the unspeakable of and for black female sexuality.

Figure I.2. crystal am nelson, *Portrait of crystal, suburban born daughter of Valerie and James, State of Rhode Island and Providence Plantations—womb* [from *Untitled (Bound)* series], 2007, ~4x5" giclée print. Image courtesy of the artist.

In rendering tangible the tethering of black female sexuality to the history of chattel slavery, the rope connects the past to the present, but it also reveals the past as the present (and future). Does the visual image of the bound flesh of the captive black female body necessitate such a psychic return? Is this homing to the mythologized site of transatlantic slavery ineluctable? nelson articulates the work's querying and queering of linear time: "At what point do historical readings of the black figure end and black female desire and subjectivity begin, if at all?"[17] Yet a couple of minutes into the piece, this fettering, like many aspects of *Building Me a Home*, is complicated as it becomes clear that the work is a process of doing and undoing, building and deconstructing. Heart's hands enwrap nelson's body and free her from the rope's constraints. At times it is difficult to ascertain which is happening—tying or untying. This linear ambiguity compounds the complexity of the piece while disrupting the idea of slavery as in the past. The work narrates a process, a movement forward and backward, that belies linear time.

Mirroring this lapse between past and present, doing and undoing, the three simultaneous viewing frames of *Building Me a Home* facilitate multiple temporal and spatial vantage points. This pastiche of temporal frames mirrors the slippage of present and past, of modern BDSM and chattel slavery, pleasure and pain, subject and object. nelson is interested in precisely these slippages and how we, as spectators of her work, read them; she and her work ask: "What is that fine line between a representation of a contemporary space that is consensual and a representation of historical spaces or historical traumas that were non-consensual and is it possible to kind of make that leap from a historical reading to a more contemporary reading?"[18] The negative space between the frames reinforces the tension of the spatiotemporal leaps nelson describes. The fragmentation of frames reflects that of the black female body itself. We never see nelson's full body in one frame, only isolated pieces of it as the camera pans up from her rope-shackled bare feet to her thighs, to a cluster of white knots nestled in her dark pubic hair like a floral arrangement adorning her pubis, to the flesh of the belly gently nudg-

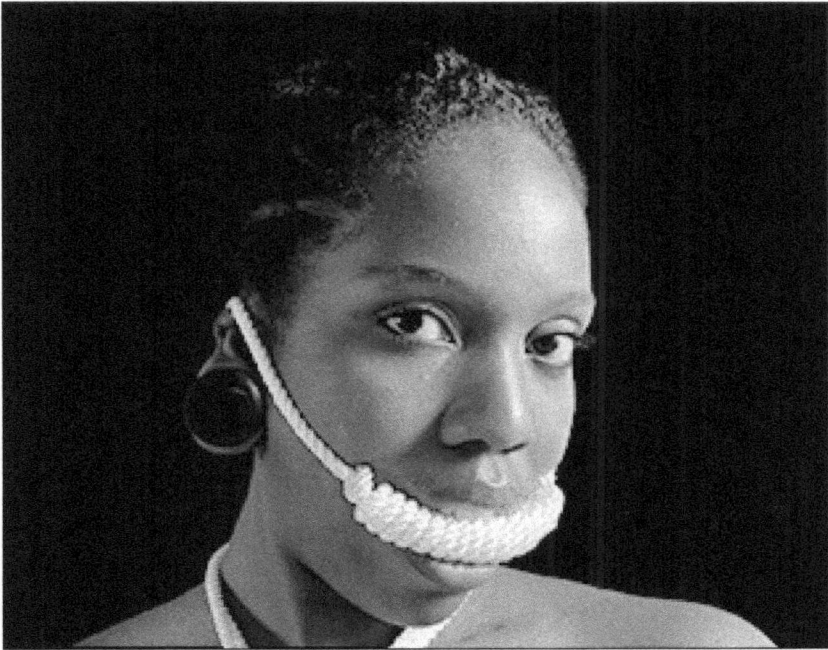

Figure I.3. crystal am nelson, *Portrait of crystal, suburban born daughter of Valerie and James, State of Rhode Island and Providence Plantations–semi-profile* [from *Untitled (Bound)* series], 2007, ~4x5" giclée print. Image courtesy of the artist.

ing through spaces between the rings of tight rope that form a bustier around her stomach region and encircle her breasts, to a group of knots at the base of her sternum, to her face. At times her eyes are closed, at others she gazes directly at the camera, confronting our own gaze and challenging an understanding of her as passive, undesirous, and submissive.

Occupying both the central frame and the periphery in this video triptych, the black female body plays an essential role in *Building Me a Home* and in nelson's work more generally. As in much of nelson's art where she doubles as both artist and model, the line between subject and object is blurred here. The black female body is doing the building and the unbuilding and is itself the site of this complex architectural project. Art historian Huey Copeland has explored contemporary black artists' critical aesthetic engagement with transatlantic slavery. By disrupting the privileging of the body as a medium for this artistic engagement, Copeland discusses the limitations of the figure as a vehicle for the visual rendering of slavery.[19] Hitching an artistic engagement of slavery to the body, Copeland argues, individualizes the memory of transatlantic slavery, foreclosing our recognition of the vast material instantiations of its aftermath. He writes: "These artists took the meaning of slavery out of the figure and made it a function of the viewer's relationship to the world."[20] By *not* relying on the figure, these artists depersonalize the legacy of slavery, imploring us to see slavery everywhere, etched in both the flesh of the black body and in our material landscape. I would argue that while nelson anchors slavery's meaning in the figure, her use of the rope effects a more comprehensive viewing of the material embodiment of slavery—one that conveys both its structural and psychic logic and the collision of the two.[21] nelson's work, like much of the BDSM and pornography performance I discuss here, is fundamentally a distinctly embodied encounter with the history of slavery.

Drawing on feminist and queer theory, critical race theory, and media studies, *The Color of Kink* contributes to the growing scholarship on pornography and racialized sexuality. This interdisciplinary analysis makes a number of theoretical and scholarly interventions. First, it complicates the traditional androcentric, heteronormative, and narrow framing of the question of violence in pornography discourse. As a result of critical feminist interventions during the "sex wars" of the late 1970s and early 1980s, violence is usually conceptualized as men enacting violence toward women and is usually framed as harmful and unproductive.[22] I am interested in how violence and aggression become a source of sexual pleasure and possibility for women and how women are active agents of violence and domination rather than passive victims. This research reinvigorates important debates in feminist sexual politics in the arena of BDSM and pornography dating back to the "sex wars" in the United States, in which, as I reveal in the book, women of color, though marginalized, played a significant role. Second, linked to this question of violence is the legacy of sexual violence for black women and how this history, which is so constitutive (but not solely productive) of black female sexuality and its representations, informs these performances. Third, this book, like nelson's *Building Me a Home* and the Bay Area Women of Color Photo Project, interrogates the deracialization of BDSM. Illuminating the cross-pollination of black sexuality and BDSM, *The Color of Kink* argues that BDSM is an apt lens through which to consider black sexuality and its performance in pornography. Finally, this project pays special attention to issues of technology. I interrogate the entwinement of various technologies— the technologies of gender, race, and sexuality with the technologies of sexual pleasure (for example, the "fucking machines" I analyze in chapter 4). My interest in technology extends beyond cyberspace as a site for the performance and laboring of black female sexuality to include the technologies of pleasure women employ in pornographic BDSM performances.

BDSM is currently a hot topic in popular culture, most notably evidenced by E. L. James's bestselling book *50 Shades of Grey* (2011) and the film adaptation.[23] Films such as *Kink* (2013, dir. Christina Voros) and *About Cherry* (2012, dir. Stephen Elliott), which both focus on the BDSM pornography company kink.com (whose work I analyze in chapter 4), also testify to the popularity of BDSM within the public sphere. In addition to films, countless television talk shows and articles in newspapers and magazines and on websites attest to the current interest in BDSM. Scholars such as Margot Weiss have critiqued this mainstreaming, arguing that the increased representation and visibility of BDSM in contemporary popular culture fail to challenge the hegemony and privilege of "normative" sexuality, often reinforcing the perceived binary between normal and aberrant, privileged and marginalized, and protected and policed.[24] What scholars have not adequately analyzed is how this mainstream popularity perpetuates an understanding of BDSM that fails to consider how it is deeply informed by racialized sexual politics. Race is marginalized in both the scholarly literature and popular media about BDSM, contributing to the impression that it is not something black people do, or should do, and/or that race is not a salient factor in the power dynamics so essential to the practice. In these public, popular visual representations of BDSM, racialized bodies are typically absent or are peripheral, contributing to a long-standing imagining of BDSM as a kind of Anglo phenomenon. nelson's *Building Me a Home is a* response to this impression. Inspired by what I term the politics of perversion, this book seeks to disrupt the politics of visibility and respectability that police nonheteronormative black female sexualities in order to encourage a depathologization of both BDSM and black female sexuality.

Problematizing a Politics of Perversion

The title of this book, *The Color of Kink*, references its foregrounding of black female sexuality in the landscape of BDSM and pornography and its revisiting of a politics of perversion as a springboard for thinking through the intersection of perversion with black female sexuality. Elsewhere I have advocated a politics of perversion as a disruptive shift in black feminist studies in order to critically analyze the entanglements of pleasure and power through the consumption, performance, and production of pornography.[25] Here I revisit, refine, and reanimate this critical framework, not as a rehearsal of the queer theory truism that perversion maintains disruptive and productive politics or to reinforce the disavowal of race in these critiques of the queer currency of perversion but rather to map the critical interchange between perversion and black female sexuality. Elucidating the many ways that black female sexuality influences the dynamics of power and pleasure that undergird kink, *The Color of Kink* analyzes and explores larger questions of the relationship between perversion and the queer limits and potentials of non-"normative" sexual desires and practices for black women. For example, in what ways can perversion open up new modes of being in the world for black women while at the same time accounting for the historical bondage (literally and symbolically) associated with black women's bodies?

My conjuring of a politics of perversion relies on the plural and polymorphous resonance of the term "perversion."[26] The politics of perversion recognizes the subversive, transformative power of perversion as the alteration of something from its original course and the *kink*—the sexual deviance—that perversion evokes. In theorizing the politics of perversion, I explore the multivalence of the word "pervert," which the *New Oxford American Dictionary* defines in its verb form as "to alter (something) from its original course, meaning, or state to a distortion or corruption of what was first intended; lead (someone) away from what is considered right, natural, or acceptable" and in its noun form as "a person whose sexual behavior is regarded as abnormal and unacceptable."[27] Such a politics of perversion might be understood as a kind of queering that enables us to see "sexual pleasure as a feminist choice" and the ways that pornography continues to inform the pivotal nexus of black women's power and pleasure.[28] Though my development of the politics of perversion is imagined in contradistinction to "the politics of respectability," both function as critical strategies of black female sexuality and its continued negotiation of history.[29]

The politics of perversion represents a critical kink in a reading of the entangled performances of race, gender, and sexuality that not only signals their perversions or "unusual sexual preference[s]" but also exposes the multiple kinks, the "sharp twist[s] or curve[s] in something that is otherwise straight" that are so central to these performances.[30] Throughout this book I am invested in undertaking a critical kink—highlighting the color of kink to reveal BDSM as an overlooked site for the performance of black female sexuality while reading the multiple deviations from straightness that are integral to these performances. This kinked black feminist critique seeks to unveil the unspeakable perverse pleasures in and of pornography and BDSM to consider how pornography informs both black women's erotic subjectivities and the resonance of BDSM for black sexuality.

I am informed by Freud's use of the term "polymorphous perversion." Freud's understanding of polymorphous perversity is useful here because it signals BDSM's degenitalization of erotic pleasure, the perverse inclination as natural rather than aberrant, and the multiple shapes—both symbolic and material—that perversion manifests in performances of black female sexuality.[31] He argues that "the disposition to perversions is itself of no great rarity but must form a part of what passes as the normal constitution."[32] Contradicting his sexology forefathers, Freud's contention of the normality and fundamentality of perversion (i.e., that it is not deviant but standard) was nonetheless mediated by a kind of hierarchy or classification, however ambiguous, of perversions that reinforced a sexological tradition of defining sexual perversion as contradicting *the* purpose of the human sexual instinct: reproduction.[33] Freud believed that a perversion becomes pathological if and when it supplants the normal "sexual aim" ("the act towards which the instinct tends") and "sexual object" ("the person from whom sexual attraction proceeds").[34] The subjective social, cultural, and moral foundation that anchors the purportedly scientific sexual perversion renders perversion a useful theoretical tool for illuminating the use of sexuality as a technique of power.

Perversion in psychoanalytic discourse is linked with transgression and the destabilization of social hierarchies and epistemologies.[35] Inspired by a Foucauldian tradition that revealed perversion as instrumental in the discursive production of sexuality some feminists, sex radicals, and queer theorists have embraced the "insurrectionary nature" of perversion.[36] Though Foucault did not identify perversion as transgressive but rather as part of the biopolitical relations of power that discursively produce sexuality, the theoretical lure of perversion emanates from its perceived subversiveness in spotlighting and dismantling the "nature" of sexuality and its punitive heteronormative standards. That is, perversion as a "real product of the encroachment of a type of power on bodies and their pleasures" directs our attention to the conditionality, labor, and unnaturalness of sexual normativity.[37] For example, Adrienne Rich's celebrated feminist theory of "compulsory heterosexuality" spotlights heteronormative coercion in order to refute the oppressive binaries of sexuality and contest the nature of (hetero)sexuality.[38] Also illuminating the relationship between perversion and norms, Gayle Rubin's theory of radical sexuality is one that accounts for the ways that perversion forms the basis of hierarchies of erotic pleasure that are oppressively policed by law.[39]

Within queer theory, perversion performs as a kind of theoretical metonymic mascot for queerness—gesturing toward a prolific and unstable range of sexualities that the assumed norm of heterosexuality marginalizes. Perversion demands a rethinking of pleasure beyond the domain of heteronormative sex to facilitate a queer critique of what Michael Warner terms "the regime of normal."[40] Warner illuminates how a politics of perversion becomes not merely a question of pleasure but also a matter of queer sexual autonomy and self-elaboration.[41] More specifically, Lauren Berlant and Warner consider the queer cultivation of perversions, or "criminal intimacies," as practices of belonging.[42] Illuminating perversion as a kind of queer "counter intimacy," they exemplify a line of queer thought that (re)aligns perversion in a way that queers—lays bare and denaturalizes—the discursive mechanisms of sexuality as a technology of power to contest the terms of intimacy. Yet what is less fleshed out in these engagements with the politics of perversion is how race directs notions of perversion within queer theory. Race is not merely a lacuna in this theoretical body. The lack of critical analysis of race, specifically black female sexuality, unsettles the disruption that perversion potentially has to change the rules of the "game of powers and pleasures" that both BDSM and race play.[43] As I discuss at length in the following chapter, black female sexuality complicates the narratives of subversion, pleasure, and power that underline BDSM.

I want to call our attention to the ways that what might seem like the absence of black female sexuality in these important discussions of perversion functions not so much as an empty void but instead an influencing, gravitational presence in what I see as the still-dynamic energetic field of the politics of perversion. How does black female sexuality effect and affect the "region of space" in which it is so often (dis)located?[44] Using the allegory of a black hole to theorize black female sexuality and the reading practices that have consistently failed it, Evelynn Hammonds calls for an alternate conceptual framework that challenges the paradigms of (in)visibility that characterize the discourse of black female sexuality.[45] Yet, as Hammonds suggests, the metaphoric currency of the black hole lies not within its power to reveal the repletion of what appears to be vacant space but in its prompting of an alternate conceptual geometry with which to rethink perversion. Black female sexuality offers an important critique of what Hammond calls the dichotomous "axis of normal and perverse."[46] Hence, problematizing the politics of perversion uncovers new vistas for considering the intersection of race and "perverse" sexuality to intervene in a "genealogy of black female sexuality," that as Hammonds argues, recognizes black women's silence and excision but not the multiplicity of their desires and the polyvalence of their pleasures.[47]

Black feminist scholar Cathy Cohen, a critical voice of intervention in this genealogy, has suggested that we, as scholars, shift our critical gaze away from the conventionally respectable to read deviance as kind of black political strategy. Indeed, deviance is where Cohen locates the "radical potential of queer politics."[48] She argues that "intentional deviance" can function as an important stratagem of resistance and agency, albeit restricted, for marginalized subjects who reside outside the disciplined limits that are policed by normative white heteropatriarchy. Cohen is in conversation with Warner, who unveils respectability politics as a kind of "false ethics" of queer sexuality, asking: "What kind of politics could be based in such a refusal to behave properly?"[49] The politics of perversion is inspired by Warner's query and Cohen's push to read deviance not as pathology but as a mode of "oppositional politics" that might enable us to see power, agency, and resistance as well as pleasure differently.[50] Hence my return to the vexed site of perversion is not intended to platitudinize the fruitfulness of queer theory's exploration of perversion and unsettlement of the coherence of heterosexuality; instead, I want to push toward a more nuanced critical crossing of perversion with black female sexuality. Black female sexuality informs and further queers the dynamics of subversion, reproduction, power, and pleasure that undergird kink.

In scholarly theory, BDSM enjoys a complicated and ambiguous relationship with the term "perversion." I use the term "enjoy" quite deliberately to capture the eroticization of aberrancy that the "perversion" of BDSM evinces. Though BDSM, in practice and theory, is anchored in the literary foundation of Marquis de Sade and Leopold von Sacher-Masoch, in the nineteenth century, people began to see sadism and masochism as psychosexual perversions.[51] In *Psychopathia Sexualis* (1886), Richard von Krafft-Ebing not only coins the terms but also inaugurates them within the moralizing pathologizing impulse of psycho-analysis as sexual perversions. Krafft-Ebing's description of "cerebral neuroses" was divided into four types of paraesthesia, or "perversions of the sexual instinct": sadism, masochism, fetishism, and "antipathetic sexuality" (essentially homosexuality, or sexual inversion).[52] While classical theories of BDSM are grounded in perversion, they remain divided over the relationship between sadism and masochism; they are theorized as radically opposed, interrelated, or more "complementary," as sexologist Havelock Ellis deems them.[53] While Krafft-Ebing considered sadism and masochism to be distinct entities, Freud viewed them as linked—two simultaneous perversions in the same individual. Adopting a psychoanalytic literary methodology, Gilles Deleuze radically challenges Freud's reading of masochism on multiple fronts, arguing that masochism and sadism are independent of each other and are fundamentally different.[54]

Although many classic scholars identify BDSM as a perverse pathology, they also argue for its gendered existence in "normal" sexuality, contending that sadism and masochism are evidence of the atavism and primitivity of sexuality itself.[55] Like Krafft-Ebing, Freud believed that BDSM tendencies were manifest in "the normal individual."[56] Krafft-Ebing writes, "Modern civilized man, insofar as he is untainted, may exhibit a weak and rudimentary association between lust and cruelty."[57] Similarly, Freud states that "the history of civilization shows beyond any doubt that there is an intimate connection between cruelty and the sexual instinct."[58] Despite more recent work in the field of BDSM that approaches the practice from a standpoint that it is not pathological, BDSM remains tainted by its psychopathological roots.[59] Though the most recent edition American Psychological Association's *Diagnostic and Statistical Manual of Mental Disorders* (DSM-5) has taken steps toward depathologizing sexual sadism and masochism and distinguishes between aberrant sexual interest and sexual practices that threaten disorder, it still locates the "paraphilias" of sadism and masochism within the bedrock of psychiatric disorders.[60] As Gayle Rubin acutely acknowledged some twenty years ago: "Sexualities keep marching out of the *Diagnostic and Statistical Manual* and on to the pages of sexual history."[61] BDSM delimits the shaky boundaries of perversion and how it relates to so-called normal sexuality.

Perversion maintains an intimate relationship with the concept of "normal" as its point of deviation. As Kaja Silverman argues in her sharp analysis of masochism and male sexuality, perversion "always represents some kind of response to what it repudiates, and is always organized to some degree by what it subverts."[62] Silverman identifies the profound tension in perversion, its "double nature" as a simultaneous movement of surrender and rebellion, "capitulation and revolt."[63] She is, however, largely focused on the latter—how perversion, specifically masochism, fundamentally contests sexual difference, to radically disrupt ideologies and performances of gender and gendered social binaries. As I argue throughout this book, BDSM, as both an invention and a rejection of the social symbolic system, maintains an ambivalent relationship to the many binaries (including reproduction/subversion) it labors so dynamically to erect and erotically transgress. Like Silverman, I am interested in unveiling the "politics," not merely gendered, but also racialized, that inform BDSM's "libidinal deviations."[64] That is, how might "the theoretical interest of perversion exten[d] beyond the disruptive force it brings to bear upon gender" to kink race?[65]

Heeding the politics of perversion highlights perversion as a technology of power deployed in the discursive production of sexuality. In his analysis of "consensual sadomasochistic perversions," psychoanalyst Robert Stoller critically problematizes the term "perversion" as determined by the "moral order" of psychoanalysis to argue psychosexual perversions such as BDSM are heterogeneous and should be depathologized.[66] Stoller identifies three central components of perversion. First, hostility is central to the meaning of perversion; it is an "essential interplay between hostility and desire."[67] Second, perversion is a discipline: its threatening moralizing force is used to separate the abnormal from the normal (the "unperverse").[68] Third, perversion "reflects the need of individuals in society to keep from recognizing their own perverse tendencies by providing scapegoats who liberate the rest of us in that they serve as the objects of our own acceptable and projected perverse tendencies."[69] Encouraging us to see the perversion of *all* erotic fantasy, Stoller contends: "When (the psychoanalyst's great advantage) one gets into people's heads and they allow one access to their fantasies, all erotic desires are aberrant. We should legislate (diagnose) not on the basis of the engaged anatomy or the positions taken during an act, but on what behaviors mean to actors."[70] Contextualizing sexual fantasies, desires, and performances from the viewpoint of the "actors" is critical in gaining both a more cohesive, holistic understanding of sexuality and one that has the potential to temper the moralizing psychoanalytic force behind perversions. Therefore, when possible, throughout this book I have relied on interviews to supplement my readings of the performances. I remain inspired by Stoller's push to unveil erotic fantasy as perverse and by his move to expunge the word "normal" from our lexicon of sexuality.[71]

In shifting our reading of perversions, the politics of perversion queers our conceptualization of normalcy. Deconstructing the perverse "social construction of sadomasochism" requires a deconstruction of normal.[72] We might be more inclined to pathologize "normal," to give it the meaning it lacks in the context of fantasy, according to Stoller.[73] Pathologizing normal is different from recognizing the existence of perversions such as sadism and masochism in our "normal," quotidian sexuality, as sexologists from Krafft-Ebing to Freud to Gebhard have done in various ways, arguing that sadomasochistic tendencies, such as aggression, passivity, humiliation, dominance and/or submission, are both natural and sociocultural facets of masculinity and/or femininity. The politics of perversion works to queer "normal," to unveil its kinks, disclose its ethical foundation, and destabilize its privileged zenith on a hierarchy of sexuality. In a Freudian tradition wherein sexual perversions represent that which contests the authority of heterosexual genital penetration as the purportedly "true" and "correct" form of sex, to pervert *is* to queer. The politics of perversion reflects this queering power of perversion. This book discusses queer sexual performances and works to queer black female sexuality, using a queer theoretical framework to read marginal sexual desires and practices while illuminating the many binaries that these sexual performances engage and deconstruct.

I initially used the politics of perversion to critically interrogate the historically contentious relationship between black feminism and pornography. It served as a valuable analytical tool in my personal attempt to reconcile black feminism and pornography as a black feminist scholar of pornography who does not view it as wholly oppressive, inimical, and definitively at odds with a kind of black feminist political agenda. Such a perspective has distanced me from a number of seminal black feminist scholars, whose work I deeply respect, who have argued against pornography. For example, in an honest, incisive story of an intimate encounter with pornography, Alice Walker condemns pornography as "Poor: Ignorant: Sleazy: Depressing," deeming it an impossible tool of sexual intimacy.[74] She objects to pornography's animalistic and scatological treatment of the black female body.[75] Walker's analysis identifies black women as "the roots of modern pornography."[76] Patricia Hill Collins argues that black women are a "key pillar on which contemporary pornography rests," as a medium that treats black women as sex objects, relies on violence as an implicit or explicit theme, and champions motifs of female passivity.[77] Jewel D. Amoah argues that pornography is particularly detrimental for black women in its double-jeopardy effect of combining racism and sexism.[78] According to both Collins and Amoah, black women are especially vulnerable to the dangers of pornography because they must contend with both its sexual and racial politics—sexism and racism.[79] Tracey A. Gardner reaffirms the sociohistorical salience of racism to contemporary American pornography. First presented at a conference on feminist perspectives on pornography in 1978, Gardner's attack against pornography is deeply personal. She states: "I want you to understand that when a person of color is used in pornography it's not the physical appearance of that person which makes it racist. Rather it's how pornography capitalizes on the underlying history and myths surrounding and oppressing people of color in this country."[80] Similarly, Luisah Teish posits the unique harm that pornography wreaks on black women because of their historical legacies of violence (sexual violence in particular): "The pornography industry's exploitation of the black woman's body is qualitatively different from that of the white woman."[81] Last but not least, Audre Lorde, in her groundbreaking conceptualization of the erotic as a "life force of women," considers pornography as antithetical to the erotic.[82]

Though these scholars have done important work to bring pornography into the discourse of black feminism and to consider its unique sociohistorical, cultural, and political relationship with black women, the substratum of racism, sexism, exploitation, and victimization that buttresses this body of work prevents a more nuanced, radical analysis of the polyvalence of pornography, of its vital narration of the complexities of black female sexuality, and of its productive opportunities for black female sexual pleasure and power. The separation of pornography and black feminism is an ideological wedge that distances elements that profoundly inform one another, ultimately preventing a radical analysis of black female sexuality. Pornography and black feminism maintain a critical, if volatile, relationship with one another.

Rather than viewing this relationship as inherently incompatible, we need to understand porn and black feminism as pushing, not policing, each other in productive directions that elucidate black female sexuality as "simultaneously a domain of restriction, repression, and danger as well as a domain of exploration, pleasure and agency."[83] Jennifer Nash has done indispensable work to explicate this clash between black feminism and pornography. She explores the peculiar alliance between antipornography feminism and black feminism, arguing that the relationship hinges upon the figure of the so-called Hottentot Venus—a problematic analytic tool of both scholarly political projects.[84] According to Nash, her work highlights the sexual conservatism of black feminism and the narrow analysis of racial imagery in pornography that does not account for changes in historical and technological specificity and the complex dynamics of black pleasure.

Although my understanding of this productive and pleasurable potential of pornography for black women has distanced me from these seminal black feminist scholars, it has aligned me with a burgeoning generation of black feminist scholars who study pornography. Mireille Miller-Young is a pioneer in this field. Her groundbreaking archival and ethnographic research has both solidified the academic field of racial pornographics and illuminated the political, symbolic, and, ideological labor of black women's sexual performances in pornography and the materialities of this labor. Dynamically contesting a black feminist tradition that views black women as oppressed and victimized within pornography, Miller-Young considers how black women performers and producers autonomously negotiate the landscape of pornography, analyzing porn as a critical arena for black women's labor, pleasure, and self-representation. Illuminating the intricacies of black female sexual politics, Miller-Young reveals how black women, as sexual subjects, engage in "illicit erotic economies" in ways that demonstrate their professional autonomy, financial independence, and self-determination.[85] While she exposes pornography as a unique site of resistance in the arena of black female sexuality, she does not imagine a utopian promise of pornography. On the contrary, Miller-Young shows how black women's history of racial-sexual violence and "exploitation" nuances their labor in pornography, a visual domain in which they are "ambivalently mythologized as sources of both fascination and disgust in a system organized around the marking and marketing of their absolute difference."[86] Conveying this ambivalence "illicit eroticism" encompasses how black women capitalize on their "mythic racialized hypersexuality in the sexual economy."[87]

Asking difficult questions about the entanglement between sexual pleasure and exploitation, labor and agency, self-authorship and self-representation, and desire and anxiety, Miller-Young has undertaken trailblazing work to deepen our understanding of the entanglement of power and pleasure for black women. She paved the way for other black feminist scholars, such as myself and Jennifer Nash, to articulate a modern black feminist reading of pornography that departs from its anti-pornography roots. This book approaches pornography and BDSM from a black feminist standpoint to demonstrate the power, agency, and pleasure, albeit highly conflicted, that they engender for black women. Focusing on black women's performances in hard-core pornographic films from the 1970s and 1980s, Nash's recent work reconciles pornography and black feminism around the concepts of black women's pleasure and agency. In doing so, she relies on a method of black feminist analysis she calls "racial iconography," an innovative critical practice of reading performances of black female sexuality in moving-image pornography in ways that foreground black women's pleasure rather than their exploitation, oppression, and trauma.[88] Nash uses "racial iconography" to problematize a tradition of black feminist criticism anchored in a foundation of damage—the black female body's purported harm by both pornography and visual culture at large. BDSM always already performs a kind of practice and theory of racial iconography—"moments of racialized excitement, . . . instances of surprising pleasures in racialization, and . . . hyperbolic performances of race that poke fun at the very project of race."[89] BDSM both creates and necessitates a reading that considers the complex interplay of black women's pleasure and pain in the collaborative performance—the dynamic play—of race and sex. Like Nash, my work puts the question of black women's pleasure at the center of my analysis; however, my work focuses on the unspeakable pleasures in and of black female abjection as a mode of racialization. Such pleasures coalesce in *race play*—a BDSM practice that explicitly plays with race—which, as I argue, is not a peripheral sexual practice relegated to the perverse margins of BDSM and pornography but is rather a powerful metaphor of black female sexuality that evinces its constitutive interplay of race, pleasure, trauma, and abjection.

My work differs from these two paramount scholars' analysis of the black female body in contemporary American pornography in multiple ways—most significantly in its focus on BDSM and its reading of a recent pornographic archive. Because of this attention to BDSM and its discussion of heretofore untheorized work, *The Color of Kink* offers new breadth to the burgeoning field of racial pornographics. If historical black feminist criticism evidences a privileging of pornography's "injury" over its pleasure, it has similarly approached the topic of BDSM from a foundation of harm.[90] Pornography and BDSM have both been objects of vehement feminist critique since the sex wars as cultural products that both purportedly reflected and perpetuated heteropatriarchy and, perhaps more dangerously, signaled women's complicity in their own gendered, racialized, and sexualized oppression. As I demonstrate in chapter 1, these black feminist discussions of BDSM are fiercely political and polar, most arguing, unsurprisingly, against BDSM and black women's nuanced practice of it. In antipornography feminism, as in anti-BDSM feminist discourse, we see analogous arguments about women's pleasure as problematically circumscribed by patriarchal domination. However, BDSM is an apt site for a contemporary analysis of black female sexuality that is grounded in "racial iconography" to foreground questions of black female pleasure, demand a recognition of the complexities of this pleasure, and highlight the stakes of black female sexual politics. I use BDSM as a critical aperture for elucidating the dynamics of racialized shame, humiliation, and pleasure that undergird the genre of commercial contemporary interracial pornography in the United States.

Toward a Methodology of Perversion

The politics of perversion informs the standpoint from which I have researched and written this book. It describes the critical practice with which I read the many performances of black female sexuality that constitute this text to foreground questions of black women's power, pleasure, and agency. The politics of perversion also inspires this book's unique, mixed methodology. Using a variety of innovative source materials including personal interviews, visual and textual analysis, and archival research, I reveal BDSM and pornography as critical sites from which to rethink the enmeshment of black female sexuality and violence. This work contextualizes particular historic and contemporary debates and analyzes pornographic film, videos, and websites. I draw upon the interviews I conducted for additional context. In each of these tasks, I aim to pervert, but ultimately enrich, our reading practices. Analyses of pornography must not be confined to the space of representation or the ethnographic: the perverse overlaps and interstices illuminate new perspectives for considering the intersection of race, gender, and sexuality. Though I am inspired by a tradition of feminist studies of pornography, inaugurated by Linda Williams's formative analysis of pornography in the late 1980s, I engage the intersections of race and violence.[91] While many feminist scholars of pornography, including Williams, have analyzed the question of race, its constitutive imbrication with eroticized violence and abjection remains undertheorized.[92] Similarly, as I discuss in chapter 1, recent scholarship on BDSM has not offered a thorough discussion of how race and the gradations of racialized sexuality beget the practice. Unlike these texts, *The Color of Kink* contextualizes black women's BDSM performance in important historical and contemporary debates and reads its representation in modern pornography. I argue that the unique historical legacies of black female sexual violence necessitate a more nuanced reading of black women's BDSM performance, particularly race play.

Throughout the book I draw from open-ended interviews I conducted with black femdoms, pornography performers, and producers. I also use published interviews in trade publications in the adult entertainment industry, mainstream magazines and websites, personal websites, and blogs. These interviews irradiate the marginalized voices of black women in pornography and BDSM. In line with the depathologizing impetus of the politics of perversion, my inclusion of personal testimonies from these sites reflects my interest in illuminating black women's agency and diverse pleasures in pornography and BDSM. Attending the voices of black women who narrate their own sexual experiences of domination, submission, and erotic power exchange in BDSM and pornography—their pleasures, limits, pains, fantasies, histories, conflicts, and boundaries—brings us closer to a more comprehensive understanding of these performances. Indeed, part of the feminist intervention of this book is a destigmatization of varied and transgressive black women's sexual pleasures such as BDSM. Marshaling the diverse voices of black women self-narrating their sexuality, *The Color of Kink* disrupts monolithic views of black female sexuality as anchored in a bedrock of normativity and silence. Yet these voices do more than simply function as intervening utterances in a politics of speechlessness; they form the basis for my central claims regarding the theoretical entanglement of BDSM, race, and sexuality. Despite my reliance on interviews, unlike many recent studies of BDSM communities and sites of labor (which I discuss in the following chapter) *The Color of Kink* is neither an ethnography nor a systematic historical study of black women in the field of BDSM or the broad, nebulous kink community. While such projects are greatly needed endeavors, my interest is largely in reading performances and visual representations of racialized sexuality in the arenas of pornography and BDSM and how the categories of race, sexuality, and gender are revealed as performances via these sites. Informed by a critical genealogy of scholars who study performance as a site of the entangled identities of race, sexuality, and gender, interviews supplement and deepen my close readings of the texts and of the sexual performances *as* texts.[93]

I read a series of visual and written texts across disciplines, media technologies, and historical periods. What unites these diverse texts is their engagement with the question of unspeakable pleasures—in the enactment of racialized abjection, in the history of chattel slavery, and in blackness as a site of trauma and rapture. Though I focus on more recent work of the early twenty-first century to interrogate the imbrication of black female sexual pleasure and violence, I make leaps (to recall nelson) across the convergent pornography landscape—the stag genre, the golden age, and the video age—to present a historical context in which to read this entanglement in contemporary American pornography. These leaps are both temporal and technological jumps. This book reads across disciplinary perspectives as it journeys across the media landscape in its analysis of the black female body's representation in different types of pornography from the late 1930s to today: film, video, and Internet. From the Kinsey Institute's historical stag collection to kink.com's twenty-first-century Fucking Machines video archive and from mainstream to amateur to independent to underground, I draw from a heterogeneous pornographic archive. This chronologically and technologically diverse archive facilitates my reading of the complex imbrication of black female sexual pleasure and violence: I argue that the black female body is an ambivalent site of absence and presence in the genre.

Organization of the Book

Chapter 1, "The Dark Side of Desire: Racial-Sexual Alterity and the Play of Race," examines black women's participation in BDSM and how these performances illustrate a complex and contradictory brokering of pain, pleasure, and power for the black female performer. I reveal BDSM as a critical site for reconsidering the entanglement of black female sexuality and violence. Within BDSM, violence becomes both a mode of pleasure and a vehicle for accessing and contesting power. This book reinvigorates important debates in feminist sexual politics in the arena of BDSM and pornography dating back to the sex wars in which women of color played a significant role. The chapter begins with a brief section that frames black women practitioners of BDSM in the context of still very vigorous feminist dialogues surrounding sexuality, violence, and BDSM. Here, I am interested in staging the unique theoretical and practical challenges of the unspeakable pleasures aroused in racial submission and domination that BDSM presents to black women specifically. I examine race play as a particularly problematic yet powerful BDSM practice for black women, one that unveils the contradictory dynamics of racialized pleasure and power via the eroticization of racism and what I term *racial-sexual alterity*. As I explicate in chapter 2, this term synthesizes the simultaneity of racial and sexual difference in the performance of black female sexuality—a difference that pornography and BDSM reveal to be profoundly tentative. *The Color of Kink* intersects with historical and recent public debates regarding black women's controversial practice of race play. I argue that race play unsettles the dichotomies of transgression/compliance, subversion/reproduction, mind/body, and fantasy/reality that buttress BDSM. This chapter unveils performances of black female sexual domination and submission in BDSM as critical modes for and of black women's pleasure, power, and agency.

Chapter 2, "Pornography's Play(ing) of Race," reads black women's diverse performance of race play in contemporary American pornography, focusing on three sites of analysis. First, I discuss the performance of black female/white male humiliation in the BDSM femdom website of a veteran black female performer/pornographer, Vanessa Blue, arguing that race is a critical technology of interracial BDSM pornography. Next, I read a performance of black female submission staged as a historical reenactment of chattel slavery in hard-core mainstream race-play pornography. This type of pornography evinces the hold this history maintains over our erotic imaginary. Then, I turn to amateur Internet race-play pornography to analyze queer race-play performance in porn. Personal interviews with a producer inform a more comprehensive reading of the work and shed light on the dynamics of amateur race-play pornography production. From amateur to high budget, mainstream to margins, and across the shifting racial and gender dynamics of production and positions of domination and submission, pornographic performances of race play exhibit an unfaltering racial hyperbole and eroticization of black female racial-sexual alterity and its anxiety. Though I demonstrate the salience of race play in the pornographic imaginary, I analyze race play as a comprehensive performance with a more universal sociocultural currency and relevance. Far from being a liminal sexual practice, race play delineates the performance of racialized sexuality more generally. Thus, this chapter reveals that another critical tension in race play is the tension between the quotidian and the spectacular, the pornographic and the mainstream.

Turning my analysis toward the adult entertainment industry niche of interracial pornography, chapter 3, "Interracial Iterations and Internet In(ter)ventions," continues the discussion of (inter)racial aggression in pornography. I argue that BDSM becomes a critical lens for elucidating the dynamics of racialized shame, humiliation, and pleasure that undergird interracial pornography, a profitable genre of commercial American pornography that is deeply invested in the miscegenation taboo. The lens of BDSM enacts a critical queering of interracial "heterosexual" pornography in order to read across the gendered and racialized subject positions of pleasure, power, and desire and to analyze homoerotic desire, pleasure, and anxiety as working in tandem with the genre's eroticization of racial-sexual alterity. I discuss pornography as a historic site of racial-sexual revenge—a contemporary staging of racialized sexualized violence in which the retaliatory rhetoric of interracial aggression is enacted. Though I focus on contemporary Internet pornography, this chapter reads across the convergent pornography landscape—the stag genre, the golden age, and the video age—to provide a contextual frame for reading performances of black-white interracial intimacy in pornography and tracing the black female body as an ambivalent site of absence and presence in the genre. This chapter concludes with an exploration of how a contemporary black queer feminist pornographer uses new media to intervene in heteronormative, hegemonic representations of the black female body and interrupt long-standing pornographic scripts of black female sexuality in pornography.

Finally, in chapter 4, "Techno-Kink: Fucking Machines and Racialized Technologies of Desire," I interrogate the simultaneity of the "technologies" of sexuality, race, gender, pleasure, and visuality. Focusing my analysis on one popular contemporary U.S. hard-core BDSM pornography website, kink.com, and its use of so-called fucking machines (mechanized phallic devices), I analyze performances of racialized sexuality staged through multimodal intimate points of encounter—between human and machine; black and white; "man," "woman," and cyborg; self and other. I argue that such places are rich sites for reading the collaborative laboring of technologies—sexuality, race, gender, pleasure, and visuality—as they delineate the material and symbolic ontological boundaries of the black female body and black women's erotic subjectivity. While the machines most explicitly labor as technologies of pleasure, they also operate as technologies of race that reveal race as a technology. I read the fucking-machine performances as imbricated technologies of racialization, sexualization, gendering, visuality, and pleasure in the context of theories of race and/as technology and "new media" discourses of race in cyberspace. Fuckingmachines.com exhibits complex technologies of racialization performed at multiple, overlapping sites:

machines, performers, and spectators. These obscene machines effect a powerful oscillation that animates the fantastic slippage between pleasure and pain that characterizes BDSM. Illuminating the racialized and gendered corporealization of sex and sexual pleasure, these fucking machines and their sexual performances reveal the interlocking systems of race, gender, and sexuality as not only mechanized but also as mechanisms of power.

Together these chapters increase our understanding of the relationship between sex, race, and the politics of pleasure. I use BDSM as a site for exploring broader questions of the relationship between perversion and the queer margins and possibilities of black female sexual desires and practices. Just as *Building Me a Home* portrays a queer rendering of black female sexuality that engages the black female body's contested visibility in this space, the *Color of Kink* reveals the ways that BDSM unveils the queerness of blackness and blackness unearths the queerness of BDSM. This study explores how racialized fantasies of abjection, power, and pleasure are not just essential to BDSM practices and their representation in contemporary American pornography, they are also vital in shaping the experiences of racialized sexuality, particularly black female sexuality. Racialized BDSM play is a critical site for reinvigorating debates about pleasure, domination, and perversion and a paradigmatic mode of black female erotic subjectivity

1

The Dark Side of Desire

Racial-Sexual Alterity and the Play of Race

I have been the meaning of rape
I have been the problem everyone seeks to
eliminate by forced
penetrations with or without the evidence of slime and/
but let this be unmistakable in this poem
is not consent I do not consent
—June Jordan[1]

Sketching the Negress

While June Jordan speaks the unspeakable, black female visual artist Kara Walker helps us both see the unspeakable and consider how this ineffability becomes strategically evoked and used by those we might not expect to articulate such utterances. In her art Walker actively engages the subject of sexual violence and the black female body.[2] Her signature black cutout silhouettes, at once mythical, grotesque, erotic, and alarming, function as shadows of the past that evoke the history of sexual violence against black women. Walker's subject matter, style, media, and even reception have generated much controversy and critique from the art world and beyond. Fellow African American female artist Betye Saar's epistolary censure of Walker's work is one of many critiques black artists have made of Walker's provocative art, largely on the grounds that it replicates "derogatory" stereotypical images of black people, uses racial caricatures, and depicts black abjection.[3] Beyond the images themselves, Saar and others objected to the eager reception, indeed "raves," such imagery generated within majority-white systems of patronage, such as galleries, museums, curators, collectors, and critics.[4] Prominent black cultural figures such as Henry Louis Gates Jr. expressed support for Walker's work. Viewing her art as a critique rather

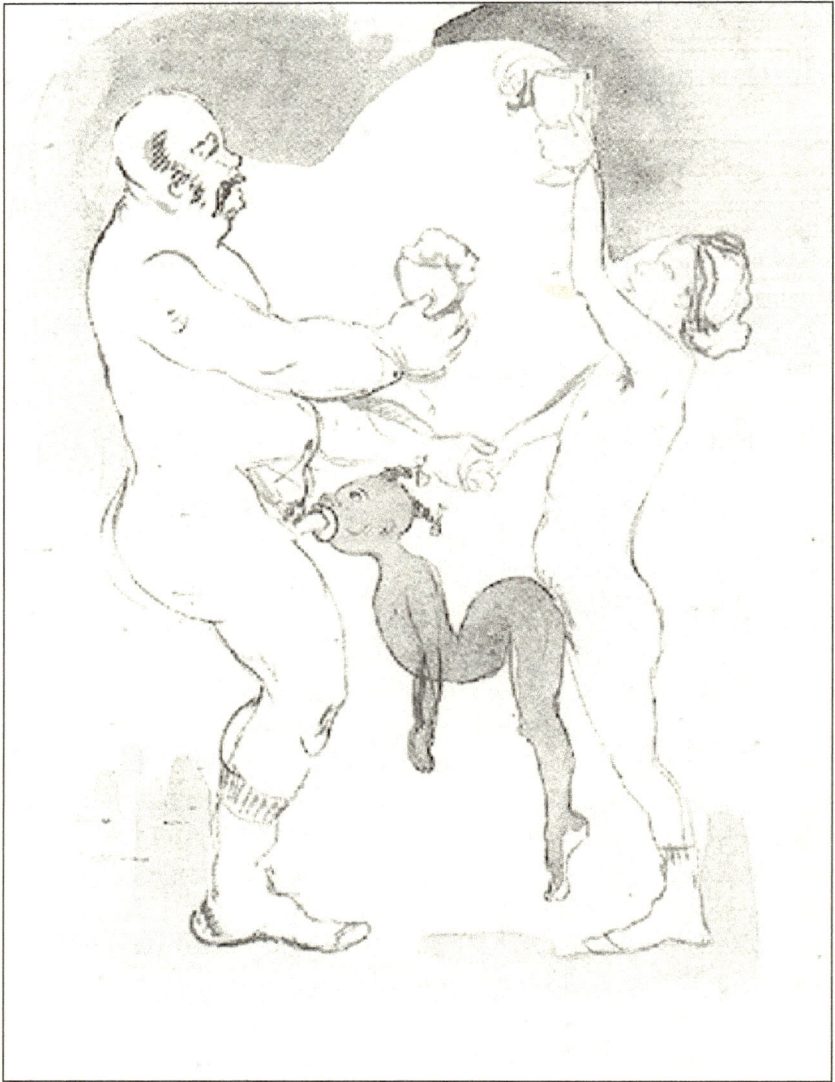

Figure 1.1. Kara Walker, *Negress Notes* (Brown Follies) (1996–1997)

than a rehabilitation of stereotypes, Gates, (re)citing his own theory of signifying, slammed Walker's detractors for their failure to recognize a pomo parody when they see it.[5] Similarly, in her recent incisive analysis of Walker's schismatic trading in "monstrous intimacies," the racialized, sexualized violence of slavery, Christina Sharpe contends that Walker's "work is not simply the recycling of stereotypes."[6] Rather, it emblematizes the constitutivity of this repetition for black female sexuality and subjectivity—the "signifying power of slavery" in the present, "a violent past that it not yet past."[7]

If the questions of the stereotype, racist imagery, and its critical reception in black art were compelling, it was because the stereotype is a preferred medium for many black artists—Ellen Gallagher, Gary Simmons, Fred Wilson, Carrie Mae Weems, Betye Saar, and Robert Colescott. The seeming deadlock among those who critique Walker's art about whether it reproduces or subverts stereotypes resembles the conversation surrounding black women's current practice of race play— "the peculiar deed" this chapter explores.[8] Beyond her use of the racial stereotype, Walker's work centers on an entanglement of race, sex, violence, and desire convened in, around, and on the black female body. Like black women BDSM practitioners who perform race play, Walker forces us to reckon with what happens when such stereotypes are the stimulus of sexual fantasy and the conduits of sexual desire and with black women's complicity in this unspeakable pleasure. Walker's work, an aesthetic articulation of abjection, and the critical discourse in response to it produce a tension similar to that surrounding black women's participation in BDSM: not merely arousal from violent images or enacting scenes of racial-sexual aggression, but pleasure from a type of violence, steeped in a historical tradition of trauma that forms and informs modern black female consciousness, representation, sexuality, and subjectivity.

Like black women BDSMers, in particular those who engage in race play, Kara Walker navigates an if not forbidden then certainly conflicted violent topography of gender, race, and sexuality. Walker's watercolor sketch of a young black female slave being doubly penetrated serves as a clear example.[9] The striking image is part of a series titled *Negress Notes (Brown Follies)* (1996–97). These small paintings—awash with sepia, blue, yellow, and sometimes black—are softer in color, line, and aura than her hallmark bold black-white silhouettes yet are none-theless searing in subject matter. Similar imagery abounds in her work across media and decades. These loaded images do more than "engage our pleasure centers," jog our historical memories, and stimulate a collective unconscious.[10] They trip the live wires of memory carried in the mind and etched in the flesh. Black women writers such as Hortense Spillers and Elizabeth Alexander speak of this idea of corporeal traumatic memory, of trauma that comes to reside in the flesh as forms of memory that are reactivated and articulated at moments of collective spectatorship."[11] Kara Walker actively withdraws from this epidermal bank. Simultaneously a scathing historical critique of our nation's public consumption of the black female body in pain and a spectacle of this same pain for public consumption, Walker's work offers an optimum entrance point for this chapter.

The Evidence of Slime Not Seen

A form of slime itself, slavery remains an active stage for the production of black female sexuality and its representations.[12] The impact of chattel slavery and the pervasive rape of black female slaves on modern constructions and representations of black women has been well theorized, in particular by a number of black feminist scholars and historians who have ruptured what Darlene Clark Hine terms "the culture of dissemblance," the politics of silence shrouding expressions of black female sexuality.[13] While the antebellum legacy of sexual violence on black female subjectivity and on representations of the black female body is substantive, how black women deliberately use the shadows of slavery and engage antebellum sexual politics—aesthetically, rhetorically, and symbolically—in the delivery and/or receiving of sexual pleasure has not been adequately considered.[14] I am interested in how the evidence of slime—a staining sludge of pain and violence—becomes a lubricant to stimulate sexual fantasies, heighten sexual desire, and provide access to sexual rapture.

In this chapter I explore how black women negotiate a complex and contradictory world of pain, pleasure, and power in their performances in the fetish realm of BDSM. Situating my analysis in the context of the controversial praxis of race play, I argue that BDSM is a critical site from which to reimagine the formative links between black female sexuality and violence. Race play is a BDSM practice that explicitly uses race to script power exchange and the dynamics of domination and submission. Most commonly an interracial erotic play, race play uses racism as a tool of practice, often involving the exchange of racist language, role play, and the construction of scenes of racial degradation. As I reveal here, race play is deeply controversial and contradictory within BDSM communities and beyond. Informed by statements of black women BDSMers about their varied lived experiences with race play, I explore the myriad tensions that animate the practice and its discourse.

I begin with a brief section that frames black women practitioners of BDSM as in conversation with the still-vigorous feminist dialogues surrounding sexuality, violence, and BDSM. Here I am interested in sketching the unique theoretical and practical challenges of the unspeakable pleasures of racial subordination and domination that BDSM presents to black women. I contextualize important debates regarding BDSM's eroticization of race against those of its equally contentious eroticization of Nazism and fascism. Finally, I examine race play as a particularly problematic yet powerful BDSM practice for black women that highlights the contradictory dynamics of racialized pleasure and power through eroticizing racism and racial-sexual alterity. Women experience the practice in a variety of ways. Assembling these heterogeneous voices, I aim to destigmatize black women's non-"normative" sexual practices.

I use the term "racial-sexual alterity" to describe the perceived entangled racial and sexual otherness that characterizes the lived experience of black womanhood. Historically, this alterity has been produced (pseudo) scientifically, theoretically, and aesthetically, and it has been inscribed corporeally as well as psychically. The term speaks to the imbrication—the mutually constitutive nature—of racialization and sexualization in the construction of black femininity. Racial-sexual alterity signifies the ways black womanhood is constituted, but *not* produced solely, through a dynamic invention of racial and sexual otherness. It does not signify a fixed core. Rather, it expresses the importance of both race and sexuality as complex social constructions that are imposed on and enacted by the black female body. It designates a particular, though neither static nor essential, sociocultural experience of subjectivity—one in which sexual categories of difference are always linked to systems of power and social hierarchies. As I argue throughout this book and as pornography makes clear, such otherness is highly ambivalent, oscillating between threat and necessity, desire and derision, sameness and otherness.

Performances of black female sexual aggression, domination, humiliation, and submission in BDSM are critical modes for and of black women's pleasure, power, and agency. Drawing from textual analysis, archival research, and interviews, I reveal how violence for black female performers in BDSM becomes not just a vehicle of intense pleasure but also a mode of accessing and critiquing power. This work is engaged in deconstructing the "culture of dissemblance" and opening up the dialogue surrounding black women's diverse sexuality.[15] The voices showcased here do more than merely de-silence those of marginalized sexualities or instantiate the discursive production of sexuality, they also constitute the foundation of my claim that race is central to an understanding of BDSM and that BDSM serves as a critical paradigm for racialized sexuality. I use these voices to articulate BDSM as a mode of speaking the unspeakable in black female sexuality. Not heeding the "don't go there" attitude that often quashes discussions of black women, sexual violence, and sexual pleasure, this chapter follows the unorthodox lead of its subjects and is invested in a type of work that is aligned with what Hortense Spillers might call "the retrieval of mutilated bodies."[16]

Negresses Divided: Introducing the BDSM Debate

A consideration of black women's performances in BDSM necessitates an inquiry into the important feminist debates that such research revisits and reignites. The perspectives of two queer black women writers on BDSM set up the debate about specifically what is at stake for black women. Audre Lorde and Tina Portillo, critical and pioneering voices in black feminist sexual politics, present polarized views on the issue of BDSM, reflecting the enduring binaries that frame the practice. Their voices contest the notion that black queer womanhood was peripheral in the early feminist debates about BDSM, signaling the racialized stakes that continue to frame the practice and how the legacies of black female sexual violence pervade black women's negotiation of BDSM. For Lorde BDSM is not divorced from but rather operates in tandem with social, cultural, economic, and political patterns of domination and submission. She argues that BDSM perpetuates the inevitability of social domination and subordination,

> Sadomasochism is an institutionalized celebration of dominant/subordinate relationships. And, it *prepares* us to either accept subordination or dominance. *Even in play*, to affirm that the exertion of power over powerlessness is erotic, is empowering, is to set the emotional and social stage for the continuation of that relationship, politically, socially and economically.[17]

Lorde's conceptualization of BDSM echoes that of American sexologist Paul H. Gebhard, who posits that "sadomasochism is embedded in our culture since our culture operates on the basis of dominance-submission relationships and aggression is socially valued."[18] Lorde contends that the same problematic "linkage of passion to dominance/subordination" undergirds both BDSM and pornography.[19]

In her radical black feminist conceptualization of the erotic as a "life force of women," Lorde imagines the erotic as not necessarily sexual, but "a considered source of power and information," "a resource" of "nonrational knowledge" located within a "deeply female and spiritual plane."[20] However, she argues because the erotic has been suppressed by a hetero-patriarchal power, it "has often been misnamed by men and used against women."[21] Her erotic, gendered as woman's autonomy and power, is antithetical to the pornographic, which she sees as a disavowal of erotic power and a "suppression of true feeling."[22] This view of the erotic further complicates the already conflicted territory between black feminism and pornography. Citing pornography as a "direct denial of the power of the erotic," Lorde's "Uses of the Erotic" sets the stage for a black feminist critique of pornography, conceptualized as a monolithic cultural entity, that closes off critical consideration of pornography's erotic potential.[23]

Though Lorde's critique of BDSM is not necessarily propelled by black women's unique location within the practice—for Lorde BDSM is a problem for *everyone*—her understanding of difference as "the prototypical justification of all relationships of oppression" clearly informs her critique, as it does her later exegesis of the erotic itself.[24]

Difference, specifically "the learned intolerance of differences," is a technique of hierarchical power that Lorde argues must be radically envisioned outside a "superior/inferior mold" as a way to bring women together, not keep them apart.[25] Still, her identification as a black woman who is intimately aware of difference amplifies her firm anti-BDSM position. She states, "As a minority woman, I know dominance and subordination are not bedroom issues. In the same way rape is not about sex, s/m is not about sex but about how we use power."[26] Lorde's writing conveys the ways BDSM becomes an especially stigmatized sexual practice for black women.

In contrast, black female BDSM practitioner and writer Tina Portillo celebrates her "sadomasochistic soul," an identity that she does not see as at odds with her claiming of black womanhood.[27] Portillo is aware of what she terms the "politically incorrect" nature of black female bottoms playing with white tops. She writes, "As for S/M being politically incorrect, especially for me as a *Black woman* who plays with *white tops* (occasionally a white *male* top), people say that because of history I shouldn't be enjoying this, let alone wanting it."[28] Nevertheless, despite the "history" of violence and imbalanced power relations between white and black, specifically white men's sexual domination of black women, she attains sexual pleasure through BDSM narratives that recite these historical scripts. In contrast to Lorde, Portillo names pleasure and desire in distinctly different terms: "If someone desires a scenario such as plantation slave and master or cowboy and Indian, as long as it is mutual and done in a loving spirit that's all that matters and all I care about."[29] For Portillo, mutually consensual pleasure in the moment *is* what matters, regardless of whether that rapture is linked to the internalization and/or perpetuation (consciously, unconsciously, or subconsciously) of oppressive white heteropatriarchal supremacist structures and values (past, present, and future). As I discuss later, similar notions of pleasure resonate in the current dialogues animating black women's involvement in BDSM, specifically race play.

The divergence between Lorde and Portillo's conceptualizations of BDSM becomes a productive space in which this chapter intervenes. That is, how might performances of BDSM function not, as Lorde states, as a "celebration" or "continuation" of dominant/subordinate relationships but as an interruptive critique that evinces the utter performativity of such relationships? How can rituals of domination and subordination in BDSM reveal such positions as not necessarily unstable but rather as unnatural, socially constructed, continually re(produced), and hence possibly deconstructed and reconstructed? How do we acknowledge what *matters*—the historical, social, and political contexts that script slave/master and Indian/cowboy scenarios while accessing pleasure in their staging? Finally, how can we push beyond the subversion/reproduction binary framing of such inquiries to see black women's performance in BDSM as more than an either/or articulation of power to challenge, as Margot Weiss writes, "a political reading of SM as a formal dichotomy between transgression and reification of social hierarchies," and how can we instead see it as one that makes possible multiple, shifting, contextual, and simultaneously conflicting conceptualizations of the practice?[30] Though dated, Lorde and Portillo's voices remain relevant; they express not only active philosophical and ethical concerns about black women's engagement with BDSM but also a critical discourse about black female sexual politics. Beyond encapsulating the vibrant BDSM debate, Lorde and Portillo speak to broader issues of black female sexual autonomy and agency; the self- and other policing of black female sexuality; the complicated dynamics of black women's pleasure, power, and violence; and the historically contentious relationship of black feminism to nontraditional, nonconservative, and often nonheteronormative practices of black female sexuality (such as BDSM and pornography). Audible in their commentary are the larger feminist debates of the so-called sex wars of the 1970s and 1980s that surround BDSM and its recitation of historical violence and patriarchy.

During that time there was an active debate concerning BDSM (then it was typically referred to as S & M). Groups such as SAMOIS represented one side of what has been problematically framed as an entirely dichotomous argument.[31] Formed in the late 1970s, SAMOIS, a small San Francisco–based collective of lesbian feminist BDSM practitioners, contended that BDSM was not antithetical to being a lesbian or a feminist.[32] They argued that BDSM was a productive and pleasurable sexual expression, offering a critique of heteropatriarchy and its naturalization of gendered hierarchies of power that saw men as dominant, violent, and aggressive and women as submissive, passive, and nonviolent.[33] Opponents of BDSM did not view it as way to theorize gendered and sexualized power outside the rigid binary of male/female relationships. Instead, they claimed that it replicated patriarchal, heterosexist modes of oppression and sexuality. In particular, BDSM among lesbians challenged the authority of heterosexuality and was, as Sheila Jeffreys argued, a form of "lesbian heresy."[34]

Feminist women of color in particular took offense to the fact that SAMOIS proclaimed themselves an "oppressed sexual minority" and to their attempt to align politically with Third World oppression and the oppression of minorities in the United States. Many felt that this claim mocked the lived realities of women of color. In an interview published in *Against Sadomasochism* (1982), Karen Sims and Rose Mason exposed what they saw as racism and privilege among BDSM practitioners. Sims in particular objected to BDSM's erotic ritualization of the master/slave dialectic while Rose communicated what she viewed as BDSM promoters' exploitation of the minority identity, particularly in the face of her struggles daily against oppression as a black lesbian in the white majority of the women's movement.[35] Ironically, though they began with the premise that BDSM is a "white woman's issue," the interview brought race to the forefront of both the BDSM debate and the second-wave feminist movement in the United States.[36]

Like Lorde, Alice Walker evaluates BDSM as a detrimental eroticization of dominance and submission that runs the risk of trivializing the history of black women's actual enslavement and falsely perpetuating black women's contentment with and consent to such captivity. In a story entitled "A Letter of the Times, or Should This Sado-Masochism Be Saved?" Walker, writing as the character Susan Marie, a black female teacher, describes her horror at watching a television report on the phenomenon of BDSM featuring a black and white interracial lesbian couple, mistress and slave.[37] The image wreaks havoc on her personally and on her efforts, as a black feminist scholar, to teach about the conditions of black female enslavement:

> All I had been teaching was subverted by that one image, and I was incensed to think of the hard struggle of my students to rid themselves of stereotype, to combat prejudice, to put themselves into enslaved women's skins, and then to see their struggle mocked, and the actual enslaved *condition* of literally millions of our mothers trivialized—because two igno-

rant women insisted on their right to act out publically a "fantasy" that still strikes terror in black women's hearts.[38]

In the clip the black female "slave" dons a chain around her neck for which her white mistress possesses the key. The black woman sub is further disciplined by the power of speech—the force of silence.[39] Walker asserts, "Regardless of the 'slave' on television, black women do not want to be slaves. They never wanted to be slaves."[40] Repudiating the possibility of the enslaved black women's consent and desire, Walker is in opposition to Kara Walker, whose infamous inflammatory remark that "all black people in America want to be slaves just a little bit" invokes the unspeakable pleasures of black women's submission.[41]

Alice Walker interprets the image as a devastating reenactment of black female sexual vulnerability during chattel slavery.[42] Ironically, in the story, she uses precisely this "image" of enslavement to teach her students to reject racist stereotypes, challenge notions of consent, and renounce myths of black female slave passivity.[43] In order to "teach [her] students what it felt like to be captured and enslaved," each "student was required to imagine herself a 'slave,' a mistress or a master, and to come to terms, in imagination and feeling, with what it meant."[44] This exercise requires the same "playing" of race that Walker denounces in BDSM. The complex divergence in intent, reception, (re)contextualization, and meaning of both enactments of black female enslavement—one seemingly motivated by didactic enlightenment (perhaps even empathy) and the other by carnal pleasures—gestures to the political stakes in black women's harnessing of such histories. Her exegesis of the scene illustrates how, as Anne McClintock argues, the material appendages of BDSM fetish role playing carry the vestiges of chattel slavery itself. For McClintock, "the fetish slave-band, mimicking the metal collars worn by Black slaves in the homes of the imperial bourgeoisie, enacts the history of industrial capital as haunted by the traumatic and ineradicable memory of slave imperialism."[45] The women's voices I marshal here expose how the rich historical symbolic capital of the BDSM "slave" fantasy maintains not just a deeply erotic currency but also the power to induce disgust.

Isaac Julien identifies this ambivalence in the icon of the slave band, a BDSM accessory that symbolizes our erotic fettering to slavery. Noting BDSM's fetishistic appropriation, indeed transformation, of collars, whips, and chains heisted from a colonial repertoire, Julien calls for a queer reading of this kind of recontextualization that recognizes the "unspeakable masochistic desire for sexual domination" and black queer consent. He insists that "surely in this postcolonial moment, black queers should have the choice of acting out the roles of 'slaves' or 'masters' in the realm of desire and sexual fantasy."[46] For Julien, such a queer reading challenges "the popular 'black,' 'straight' reading that tries to use the signs of s/m (whips and chains) for a neo-colonial racist/sexual practice [a]s an attempt to 'fix' these images in time, perpetuating white power and domination. It is thus reductionist, a misreading of the 'theatre of s/m' based on politically correct notions of sexual practices from a work devoid of fantasy."[47] Julien's short film *The Attendant* (1993) performs this queer reading. It is the story of a black gay male museum attendant in a BDSM encounter with a white male patron inside the gallery against the backdrop of François-Auguste Biard's abolitionist painting *Scene on the Coast of Africa* (circa 1840), which illustrates the brutality of the transatlantic slave trade. The film boldly engages, while queering and exposing as queer, the erotic memory of chattel slavery as a continued site of production for black queer sexuality. It also uses BDSM as an apposite stage for this production. Identifying the power of consent and fantasy that I identify as integral to black women's involvement with race play, Julien speaks to and with these feminist debates *and* to an analogous historical dispute about BDSM's other unspeakable, particularly in the realm of queer sexuality.

Whips and Chains May . . . but Swastikas Will: BDSM's Embattled Iconicity

If, to recall McClintock, the fetishized metal slave collar summons the "memory of slave imperialism" the "whips chains, racks, shackles, and other instruments of torture [that] are our inheritance—passed down through history" also evoke the memory of the Holocaust, as many feminist scholars have discussed.[48] While the dialogue about race and BDSM was sparse, reflecting both the marginalization of black women's voices in the contemporary feminist discourse of sexual politics and the in(visibility) of black women in BDSM communities at the time, conversations about lesbian and gay BDSM and its relationship to fascism and Nazism were prevalent. Such dialogues, which more often were heated debates in the arena of feminist sexual ethics, reflect similar tensions surrounding the historical legacies of violence and the entanglement of violence and pleasure in our intimate lives. Concerns about BDSM and its reciting of Nazi and fascist imagery, themes, and aesthetics inform concerns about black women's participation in BDSM and their eroticization of the history of chattel slavery through BDSM performance. Though clearly divergent in terms of the vastly differing histories these practices draw from, both similarly mine racialized violence and power hierarchies to stage the paradigms of domination and submission. The discussions about such practices provide useful insight into the underexamined practice of contemporary race play and its critical elucidation of black female sexual politics. The complicated dynamics of reproduction, subversion, and transgression characterize BDSM stagings of slavery, Nazism, and fascism.

Susan Sontag's "Fascinating Fascism," first published in 1975, years before the 1980s wave of lesbian feminist critiques of BDSM's "erotic cult of fascism," reviewed BDSM's eroticization of fascistic violence.[49] Both a critique of the sociocultural "rehabilitation" of German filmmaker Leni Reifenstahl and an exploration of fascist aesthetics in the contemporary pornographic imagination and BDSM, Sontag's essay examines the aesthetic and sexual decontextualization of facism, which she considers to be kind of a neutralization of it.[50] Musing on the enduring presence of Hitler's *Schutzstaffel* in the erotic imaginary, Sontag credits not just the organization's epic violence and totalitarian power but also its aestheticism; she sees it as a "supremely violent but also supremely beautiful" force.[51] Beyond the highly subjective "utopian aesthetics" of "physical perfection" that Sontag identifies as the source of the intense erotic charge of fascism, I am most interested in the sexualization of racialized violence that is premised on the eroticized crossing of racial boundaries, something Sontag does not explicitly address.[52]

Inspired by Jean Genet, Sontag theorizes a "natural link" between fascism and BDSM.[53] While BDSM, as Sontag and many others have contended, is a theatrical staging of sexuality, it is also a theatrical enactment of race.[54] BDSM, specifically race play, is a site that brings into sharp relief the complex and often contradictory modes in which racial identities are performatively constructed. Sontag's much-critiqued article was a pioneer in a wave of feminist critiques that condemned the marriage of BDSM and fascism, only some of which considered anti-black racism and the parallels between BDSM's eroticization of racialized violence in the context of both the Holocaust and chattel slavery in the Americas.[55]

Irene Reti, for example, criticizes BDSM's co-optation of the "the technology and scenarios of both slavery and the Holocaust," arguing that slavery and the Holocaust analogously functioned as exploited erotic wellsprings in the making of modern BDSM sexual fantasies.[56] For Reti, it is not just the "uniform of militarism"—army fatigues, military paraphernalia, weaponry, and so forth—but also the "rituals of militarism" that have problematically pervaded lesbian BDSM.[57] Linking practices such as "excremental assault" (a Nazi tactic of humiliating victims with their own feces and that of others) to modern-day accounts of coprophagy in the lesbian BDSM anthology *Coming to Power*, Reti argues that the specific techniques of punishment, discipline, and humiliation used in BDSM are directly imported from Nazi practices.[58] Like Audre Lorde and Alice Walker, Reti contends that BDSM reproduces the dynamics of violent heteropatriarchy to paint a flawed picture of suffering as redemptive, romantic, and volitional. She states, "To play masochist in bed is to endorse the Nazi picture of reality in which there are sadistic torturers who believe their victims enjoy being punished."[59]

Susan Griffin offers another scathing critique that includes a cursory reference to chattel slavery and the black body. Like Reti, Griffin sees parallels between Nazi aesthetics, ideology, and practice and the pornographic "sadomasochistic mind," arguing that "in every detail, the concentration camp resembled and enacted pornographic fantasy."[60] But it is through the concept of the "racial *ideal*" that Griffin elicits blackness, positing that "the same polarity" of hierarchical human value frames the relationship between anti-Semite and Jew and white southern slave owner and black slave.[61] Careful to differentiate between the "sufferings of black people in a racist society [and] Jewish people under anti-Semite[s]," Griffin argues that a pornographic, racist, and "chauvinist" mind undergirds both oppressions.[62] Notwithstanding Griffin's firm anti-pornography stance and one-dimensional view of pornography as "tragedy" (very much reflective of the second-wave feminist campaign against pornography at the time), she critically educes the power of the miscegenation taboo in our erotic imaginary.[63] Race play both reflects and perpetuates a "specter of miscegenation."[64]

Many critiques of BDSM's recital of historical violence focus on the iconography of anti-Semitism, specifically the swastika, and its controversial appropriation in BDSM sexuality. Susan Leigh Star, for example, argues that despite the fact that the swastika was already de/re/contextualized before members of the BDSM community co-opted it, it remains inseparable from its association with the Third Reich and death.[65] For Star, among "symbols of whips, dog collars, and 'slave collars' and chains, the swastika is the most powerful exemplar."[66] Because she maintains that symbols such as the swastika simply cannot "be amputated from their historical and social context," she rejects the claims of BDSM "advocates" that they have recontextualized, indeed resignified, the swastika through the parameters of mutual consent, scene, self-determination, control, and pleasure.[67]

Of course debates over the swastika's use in the BDSM community were not relegated to lesbian practice, nor was the use of the controversial symbol itself. Many lesbian objections to the swastika at the time viewed the symbol as not only a vexed inheritance from a painful moment in history but also as a problematic patrimony of the gay male leather community.[68] Critiques such as that of writer and activist Arnie Kantrowitz, who wonders why "a persistent Germanophilia pervades the [gay male] leather subculture," are as heated as those emanating from the lesbian feminist community.[69] While many of the latter were steeped in the politics of sexual ethics, Kantrowitz's consideration of the quandary of sexual morality is situated within "the kink ethics" of the leather community.[70] He believes that the swastika and other Nazi aesthetics contravene the core values of "good," "true" BDSM.[71] He acknowledges "the menace of [the] swastika," its formidable transgressive erotic charge, in practices of "bad" BDSM.[72] Unsure whether or not he has "betrayed [his] moral and political values by having sex with a Nazi" (a man who has a poster of Hitler on his wall), Kantrowitz avows that "'politically correct' sex rarely leads to orgasm."[73] Perhaps a grim commentary about the human sexual response cycle, this remark touches on the force of taboo in sexual pleasure that is axiomatic within BDSM. As such it foreshadows black women's testimony about their own sexual pleasure within the politically incorrect sexual-social scripts of race play.

While the critiques of the incorporation of Nazi symbolism, iconography, and narrative were more numerous (and more vociferous) than those in defense of such practices, Linda Wayne's essay published in SAMOIS's publication *The Second Coming: A Leatherdyke Reader* is an important rebuttal. Her short, powerful piece functions equally as a critique of the feminist censures of lesbian BDSM's eroticization of Nazism and a narration of the slippages in representation itself. Such slippages, Wayne argues, propel subgroups to translate dominant imagery and propel history into the present, thereby obscuring hierarchies of power and histories of oppression. Wayne writes, "Within such a reductive economy of visual self-evidence, it is assumed that, through proximity and resemblance, the dominant figuration of evil and subgroup symbol are actually the same thing.[74] Still, while I recognize the ambiguous potentiality of signs and the complexity of their signification—something semiotic theorists such as Saussure and Peirce have long revealed—I think we need to be careful of interpreting, as Wayne does, "dominant" imagery such as the swastika and metal slave collars as "empty effig[ies] of the past operating in the present," even while we recognize that "it is exactly this prior significance of a historically specific dominant order that makes the appropriation of these symbols powerful."[75] Indeed, the debate synthesized here and its audible reincarnation in the voices of black women BDSMers showcased later in this chapter attest to the richness of such icons. Wayne's analysis prompts us to interrogate the work of representation to as great a degree as we do the sexual labors themselves. As Christina Sharpe astutely notes, "The whips and chains in slavery do look a lot like the whips and chains in s/m. Playing it straight, fixing those images and meanings in time is perhaps less a (black) world devoid of fantasy than one in which narrative, fantasy, and representation each has a cause-and-effect correlation to material reality."[76] Nudging this matter outside of a moral corral facilitates a critical depathologization of those who seek such unspeakable pleasures. How might we amplify the theoretical politics of representation in these conversations in a way that does not mute the volume of ethical politics but instead tunes the debate?

Pat Califia, a primary advocate in the U.S. lesbian sadomasochism movement, situates BDSM's eroticization of racial difference and power under the rubric of satire, arguing that "SM is more a parody of the hidden nature of fascism than it is a worship of or acquiescence to it."[77] Califia, like many BDSM practitioners, claims the debate is misinformed—that BDSM has been decontextualized from its spheres of practice.[78] This decontextualization is one, according to Califia, that moves BDSM out of the realm of fantasy in which it is situated for many practitioners. In addition, as I argue here, we need to listen to women articulate their own sexual practices and narrate their individual sexual desires, motivations, and experiences. There is a core of fantasy, ritual, and play that epitomizes the practice and its representation. BDSM "players," as some identify, are engaged in a volitional erotic relationship involving role play, power exchange, and the often-elaborate staging of "scenes." Narratives, which are typically scripted by each player, direct these consensual scenes or encounters.

While Lorde and Walker question whether black women can indeed consent to racialized sexual play, black women BDSMers suggest that this consent is not only possible but also pleasurable and affectively empowering. Amplifying the complexity of sexual consent itself, race play evidences what Biman Basu calls the "crucial but constrained" nature of consent within BDSM sexuality.[79] Basu, who analyzes the vexed but vital relationship between domination, submission, and desire that animates the slave and neoslave narrative, conveys how these "texts" evince "the ambiguity of consent and represent the nuances of (non)consensual desire. They remind us that consent everywhere is constrained in both libidinal and political economies."[80] The dynamics of domination and submission, particularly when stratified by the processes of racialization, disrupt understandings and enactments of an already complicated sexual consent.[81]

BDSM highlights the moral compass of the slippery, often neoliberal, politics of consent and its operation as a mode of validating, legalizing, and hierarchizing sexuality. Gayle Rubin has exposed how consent becomes a valuable conceptual tool in revealing the oppressive cultural, social, political, and legal regimes of sexuality. Problematizing the discursive political rhetoric of consent, Rubin argues that feminist critiques of sexual consent are misdirected.[82] Instead of focusing on the social structures and institutions that constrain or even negate consent, she urges us to recognize the power of consent, or lack thereof, in laws and practices regarding sex. In the modern Western system of legal and extralegal imposition of sex, consent collapses, failing to protect those at the bottom of the "erotic pyramid," sexual minorities and "perverts" whose sexual acts, such as sodomy or BDSM, cannot be understood as autonomous but rather as further substantiation of a kind of inherent lechery.[83] Consent is not a universal principle; it does not have the same valence for everyone. We must be cautious about adopting consent as our primary determinant of sexual freedom because it often buttresses normative sexualities and sexual hierarchies.

In Rubin's critical lineage, scholars have interrogated the role of consent as a tool of power, reflecting and reinforcing sexual hierarchies. Yet as I demonstrate here, black female sexuality and the legacy of black female sexual violence complicates notions of consent and the already complex dynamics of power surrounding consent. In his analysis of the relationship between consent and marginalized sexuality, Joseph Fischel offers a trenchant critique that demonstrates how sexual consent functions as a political tool of morality and state regulation, manipulation, policing, and violence that can actually impede sexual justice.[84] *Regina v. Brown* (1993), the so-called Spanner case, in which a group of gay men were convicted for bodily injury incurred during consensual BDSM, serves as a stellar example of how consent collapses under the coercive power of state law (and its ideological underpinnings) in the context of BDSM and homosexual sex acts.[85] With the exception of rape law, Rubin argues, sex law has not distinguished historically between consensual and coercive sexual practice. While she fails to theoretically take rape law to task for its categorical failure to protect enslaved black women (on the contrary, rape law reflected the state's economic and political interest in their sexuality), she problematizes the discourse of consent and its legal privilege.[86] The June Jordan poem in the epigraph articulates the importance of consent in relationship to black female sexuality, long an extralegal site in U.S. history. While BDSM reinforces how consent maintains an ambivalent, nonetheless vital, space within our sexual regime, race further enriches our critical consideration of the value and limitations of sexual consent.

Black female sexuality raises the theoretical stakes of both consent and its praxis. Desire and consent encode the history of violent domination, or that which consent may conceal.[87] But consent, as black women BDSMers articulate, can also operate to reveal histories of violent domination. Christina Sharpe's stunning recent study of the enduring sexual horrors and pleasures—the "monstrous intimacies"—of chattel slavery that continue to mold the postslavery subject illuminates the profound ambivalence of sexual consent. While Sharpe questions the possibility of sexual consent for the enslaved—"as much as an enslaved person can be said to participate in nonconsensual sexual acts"—she confronts this fraught subject and its continuing relevance as conflicted territory for postslavery subjects.[88] Sharpe engages with the enslaved subject's sexual desire, arguing that indeed, as black women who perform race play also express, "sadomasochistic desire might be a place from which to exercise power and to exorcise it through the repetition of particular power relations."[89] She argues that in the murky realm of sexual ethics, "the distinction between public good and private harm and the effects of violence in these supposedly distinct realms is maintained by erasing the ways that in be(com)ing a subject one is called on continually to consent to violence."[90] Mirroring the complexity of the multitude of binaries that characterize BDSM, consent is rarely ever a simple yes/no binary.

Reflecting the abiding motto of the kink community, SSC (safe sane consensual) and its more recent permutation, RACK (risk aware consensual kink), consent operates as a principal feature of BDSM practice.[91] The binary between consensual and nonconsensual becomes another slippery slope in the terrain of BDSM. While Staci Newmahr notes that consent serves to distinguish BDSM from nonconsensual, immoral, and even criminal acts of violence; internally police the dynamics of play; and act as a "conceptual tool for achieving understanding and acceptance" for members of the BDSM community, Melanie A. Beres problematizes the function of consent as "an agent of moral transformation" because of the ways it assumes a coercive understanding of sexual relations and the ambiguity, subjectivity, and hegemony of a moral framework that it presumably alters.[92] Yet what kinds of violence might the construct of consent and its neoliberal rendering not only obfuscate but also effect? Weiss problematizes the dichotomy between consensual and nonconsensual, arguing that in "requiring *nonconsensual* social inequality and power differentials for erotic charge, but also the fantasy of a subject free to choose and perform in such scenes without social consequence, SM's unstable and ambivalent relations between consent and nonconsent highlight social tensions between agency and coercion."[93]

Consent in BDSM paradoxically performs a certain rhetorical, if not also symbolic, violence. In the Western neoliberal imagination, consent simultaneously obscures the violence from which it seeks to detach itself. The severing of fantasy from reality that consent implies can obscure, recode, or even excuse certain types of violence, and thus consent can itself, paradoxically, constitute a form of violence.

Consent is thus an important part of BDSM's artful negotiation of the mercurial divide between fantasy and reality that is so salient to race play. This disconnect has been challenged by critics of BDSM such as Judith Butler who argues that consent can serve to obviate personal responsibility in and for our sexual fantasies and practices while "exaggerating the autonomy and intelligence of desire" itself.[94] For critics and proponents of BDSM, the fantasy/reality binary is problematic.[95] Race play reveals the profound paradox of this enduring fantasy/reality dialectic: even as these practices recite, indeed require "real, shared world" historical and political references, such play can be imagined, enacted, and narrated as pure fantasy.[96] This is a profound tension at the heart of race play.

The rhetoric of fantasy and play ought not to belie the seriousness of the practice. BDSM is an organized, structured, and trained practice for those who are earnestly devoted to it as not only a practice but often also as a lifestyle. BDSM scholarship confirms the diversity of the practice, the salience of power exchange, and the engendering of sexual pleasure as key motivations for practicing BDSM.[97] This important work has forged an understanding of the misunderstood "subculture" of BDSM and detached it from its roots in psychopathology, as studied by sexologists such as German psychiatrist Richard von Krafft-Ebing in his seminal text *Psychopathia Sexualis* (1886) and later by Freud, Havelock Ellis, Paul Gebhard, and others. Still, BDSM remains tainted as a psychosexual pathology despite its recent reform in the DSM-5 as a paraphilia with no "sufficient condition for having a paraphilic disorder"; that is, no necessarily diagnosable mental illness.[98]

However, BDSM remains a marginalized sexual practice, and its aberrance is compounded by race. Though condemnatory, the dialogue black feminist writers such as Audre Lorde and Alice Walker began in the early 1980s about BDSM is one that brought race into the foreground and needs to be revisited in the context of black women's diverse modern-day enactment of BDSM. Recent literature exploring BDSM maintains a tradition of white hegemony and marginalization of the voices of people of color.[99] Black women's experience with the practice remains undertheorized. Both Staci Newmahr and Margot Weiss mobilize iterations of what I call the *racial caveat*: a polite jettisoning of race in order to refer to or theorize it in its absence.[100] Citing the rarity of people of color in the BDSM community she studied and the need to protect their privacy, Newmahr regrets that she "was not able to be as inclusive as [she] would have liked" with respect to race and sexual orientation.[101] She writes, "I make no mention at all of respondents' race or ethnicity anywhere in this book, because people of color are so underrepresented in the community that to do otherwise would itself constitute a breach of confidentiality."[102] Unlike Newmahr, Weiss maintains an interest in race and engages in an illuminative discussion of the racial dynamics of BDSM and white privilege that mark the BDSM community. However, she experiences similar obstacles: "Although racial dynamics within the SM community were a central interest for me, and I made an effort to interview nonwhite practitioners, the vast majority of my interviews were white."[103] In these studies, the black body is paradoxically evoked as a site of disappearance. While their racial caveats affirm these scholars' investment in methodological soundness and their interest in undertaking comprehensive, intersectional analysis, they perform a kind of rhetorical expunction that translates into a violent, albeit familiar, act of racial disavowal. Mobilizing the diverse voices of black women BDSMers reveals how BDSM becomes an effective tool in destabilizing articulations of black female sexuality that are anchored in the tenacious ground of degradation, disempowerment, exploitation, normativity, oppression, policing, and silence. Listening to these voices is an important step in moving us toward an urgently needed depathologization of black female sexual practices, such as race play, that perform a fantasy of racialized abjection.

All Fun and Games? Black Women's Performance of Race Play

Outspoken race play practitioner Mollena Williams, aka The Perverted Negress, was Ms. San Francisco Leather 2009 and International Ms. Leather 2010. She is also a BDSM educator and writer who identifies race play as a form of BDSM play that "openly embraces and explores the (either 'real' or 'assumed') racial identity of the players," often using racism as a primary mode of titillation.[104] Williams's nom de plume, The Perverted Negress, recalls Kara Walker's fantastic alter ego, the Negress. The two women share more than a name: both dare to publically navigate the schismatic terrain of pleasure and racism. According to Williams, "Race play can include the fetishization of a specific racial feature (skin color, hair texture, facial features, etc.)[,] it might incorporate an assumption of supremacy based on race, and it sometimes even delves into troubling aspects of bigotry and privilege manifested in base racial slurs and exploitative scenarios."[105] Also referred to as "slave play," "nigger play," or "cultural trauma play," race play typically uses racist epithets, role playing, scenes (for example, the antebellum slave auction), tools, and props that stage and eroticize racial difference and histories of racialized exploitation. Scott Daddy, a columnist for *Edge Magazine*, defines race play as "erotic play that explores power exchange within the dynamics of cultural, ethnic, socio-economic, religious/and or racial differences."[106] Like other BDSM practices, race play relies on the simultaneous observance and violation of conventional sociocultural taboos. In race play, the taboos of racism and interracial intimacy fuel the transgressive pleasure practitioners experience.

Yet it is not just racism that is eroticized, but also a vibrantly imagined racial difference in which the color line between black and white is *played* with—constantly smudged, re-delineated, and traversed. Performances of racial-sexual alterity are therefore essential in race play. Race play reveals how narratives of racialized sexual violence hinge on historical offense and how racial transgression scripts performances of black-white interracial intimacy in BDSM. The practice of race play is not limited to black and white racial dynamics. Online race play discussion groups such as "Racial Name Calling, And Racist Fantasies" provide evidence of the inclusive spirit of fetishized racial play; it cheekily advertises that "this group is for all of the Honkies, Niggers, Spics, Gooks, Chinks, Dago Wops, Bogs, Canucks, Flips, Heebs, Hymies, Japs, Krauts, and Polaks, and any other derogatory named group, who have racist sexual fantasies."[107] I focus on black-white bodily intimacy as what Sharon Holland calls the "primal scene of racist practice." She urges us to "rethink the black/white binary and its hold upon exemplary epistemologies."[108] This discussion exposes but does not resolve the paradoxes of race play related to its performance, theorization, representation, and spectatorship. Offering a complicated reading, not a firm conclusion, I consider the multitude of contradictions at work within the practice of race play and its encircling discourse. The diverse lived experiences of black women BDSMers, specifically black female dominatrices (or femdoms) reveals the ambivalence that underlines the practice. Race play means different things to those who enact it at different times in their lives. Different women encounter the practice differently. I draw upon these voices to facilitate a resistance to theorizing race play in a way that further pathologizes both BDSM and black female sexuality.

Still considered "on the edge of edgy sex" by many in the BDSM community, race play is a popular topic on BDSM social networking websites and is becoming increasingly prevalent in hard-core fetish pornography.[109] Discussion groups in online BDSM communities evidence an interest in the controversial practice of fetishized race play. One popular social network houses groups such as "Black women Who Love to Be Called Names during Race Play" (1,598 members), "Race Play" (1,471 members), "Cyber Race Play" (268 members), "Lesbians and Bisexual Women into Race Play" (218 members), "Black Cum Whores for White Masters" (1,898 members), and "Racial Name Calling and Racist Fantasies" (747 members).[110] Like other arenas of BDSM, race play is a consensual and trained practice. Many established BDSM trainers such as Midori, a well-known Japanese American sexuality educator, recommend it only for "advanced" players. Midori's race play pedagogy includes reconstructing scenes of antebellum plantation auction blocks; in such scenes, she plays the white mistress inspecting the black male slave prior to purchasing his body.[111] Her enactment of a U.S. chattel slavery scene speaks both to the complex racial landscape of doms, submissives, and trainers and to the erotic power of the black/white binary. Indeed, some have suggested that the black/white binary is critical to the success of a race play scene. Weiss recognizes the affective power of the black/white binary as a most "effective scene" for BDSM enactment.[112] Describing what she perceives as the ineffectiveness of a mugging scene with a Latino male and a black woman that she saw as part of a race-play demonstration at a BDSM workshop, Weiss argues that "effective race play, in other words, generates a complex circuit between affective response, erotic attachment, and national imaginaries, tapping into complex veins of shame and desire—the 'charge' that animates national belonging."[113] Contemporary American pornography has also long recognized, indeed exploited, the vast erotic potential of the black/white binary. In *playing* race, Midori, like Kara Walker, uses as "her setting the greatest of American interracial sex factories, the antebellum plantation."[114] Not just BDSM but pornography too draws upon the erotic potential of chattel slavery.

Those who practice race play acknowledge that it is sensitive, demands a certain level of experience with BDSM, and is not recommended for dilettantes. One professional black femdom attests to the edginess of race play as a taboo within a taboo. She typically relegates race play to the realm of cyberspace, where identities might be somewhat protected and play can be experienced as anonymous.[115] Another professional black dom tells me that race play isn't as commonly requested as other BDSM acts and is often a practice that is built up to. According to her, "most guys prefer garden variety humiliation and they don't dip their toe into racial humiliation until they can tell me a little bit."[116] While most serious practitioners of BDSM, both professional and nonprofessional, recommend the importance of training, technical skill, discipline, and practice, setting race play apart from other "garden variety humiliation" on a kind of hierarchy of bodily practices reveals the currency that race brings into already proscribed BDSM performances. These experienced professional doms consider race play to be special. Similarly in BDSM guides such as *The New Bottoming Book*, psychotherapist Dossie Easton and sexuality educator Janet Hardy "suggest extreme care in negotiating and enacting" race-play scenes, although they propose that "the darkest corners of BDSM can bring the greatest illumination."[117]

Beyond the binary of black/white, race play is policed by a racialized and gendered code of sexual ethics and animated by a number of entangled dichotomies such as fantasy/reality and mind/body. Viola Johnson, an active figure in the BDSM community since the mid-1970s, articulates such tensions in her fundamental exegesis of race play, which was published almost a decade before Mollena Williams and others launched race play into the popular sphere.[118] Indeed, if black BDSMers such as Williams (the now poster child for race play) and others are able to speak out publicly in defense of the practice, it is because of "Old Guard

Slave" and "Leather Mother" Viola Johnson. [119] In her powerful piece, Johnson interrogates the fantasy/reality divide in BDSM and reconciles her own fraught practice of race play. Recounting her personal conflict about being aroused by the word "nigger" while playing with her mistress, she describes the profound conflict of arousal and degradation that race play both reflects and engenders:

> Alone in the darkness of my quarters my mind is reliving the scene of a few nights ago. I can feel my Mistress's body beneath me. I can feel her voice, raspy and sexual, in my ear. 'Fuck, Niggah. That's what I bought you for.' With little if any mechanical aid I cum. My orgasm is sudden, and powerful. For a brief second I am exhausted and happy. But in only a moment there is a little voice creeping into the back of my consciousness (You shouldn't be turned on to the word NIGGER).[120]

For Johnson, race play is not only pleasurable but also empowering. She asks, "Why is it that we, as Leathermen and women of color, can't accept the possibility that to some of us, Nigger may be empowering?"[121] In her honest account of her long struggles as a black woman in the BDSM community, she describes the moralizing force of political correctness that polices sexuality, the often blurred yet fundamental binary between fantasy/reality and mind/body, and the pleasure and power of racialized abjection through race play. Yet she also implores us to recognize the racial axis of BDSM's fundamental master/slave dialectic: "As a tribe we have come to accept the slave-master relationship, while ignoring (for the most part) its racial origin."[122] Johnson describes slavery as both a part of our past and a part of our present.[123]

Johnson outlines how race informs the power relations of the masochist contract, queers its historically heterosexual model, and articulates how consent is imperative in its practice. Her 1981 "Contract of Slavery," written for one of her longtime mistresses and "owners" is a modern instantiation of Deleuze's theorization of the masochist contract. Indeed, we might trace the theoretical lineage of consent within BDSM, as Deleuze does, to its literary root: Leopold von Sacher-Masoch's *Venus in Furs* (1870). After reading about Sacher-Masoch's multiple "love-contracts," Deleuze theorized the masochist contract as central to masochism. Deleuze distinguishes between sadism and masochism, arguing that while sadism is disordered and institutional, masochism is formal and contractual, its relations governed by a contract between consenting partners that delineates the rules and roles of a dramatized romance.[124] It is the contract that binds, not the collars, cuffs, or chains of BDSM. Consent, the crux of the masochistic contract, informs the dynamics of the encounter between subject (male masochist) and "sovereign lady" (mistress), between slave and master. Yet the masochistic contract scripts the dynamics of power in ways that challenge the master-slave relationship. In conferring power upon the master only through the authority of the slave, it represents a kind of subversion of power relations. The first-person voice of Johnson's "Contract," which begins with "I, Viola Mary Johnson (also known as Slave Viola), do hereby accept the servitude of slavery and, in accepting this servitude, do bind myself to Mistress who will henceforth be my owner," reaffirms that the power of the slave is not lost in the masochist contract. Rather, the power of the slave is enacted.[125] The contract articulates the power of the bottom—"his ability to persuade, and his pedagogical and judicial efforts to train his torturer."[126] As Johnson illustrates, the masochist contract is far from an archaic theoretical or literary apparatus. A symbolic conferment of power, it is a document that provides the blueprint for fantasy.

The concept of fantasy is vital to how black women conceptualize their sexual performances in BDSM, specifically race play, which is often seen as a chimerical act that takes place outside the realm of reality. A dialectic exists between the fantasy world of BDSM, as it is typically imagined by those who practice it, and the "real" world. For some, there is the perception that what one does while she is *playing* is somehow removed from her everyday existence. Many BDSM scholars have revealed how fantasy is essential to BDSM encounters. According to Thomas S. Weinberg, fantasy both shapes particular BDSM scenarios and serves as a scapegoat for the guilt participants may feel while enjoying the enactment of taboo sexual experiences.[127] In race play, the rhetoric of play belies the sociohistorical gravity of racism and its contemporary utterances. Much more than mere play, race play requires its participants to undertake a unique physical and psychic labor. This work demonstrates just how much sexual desire and pleasure are products of both fantasy and reality and mind and body, how they are socially constructed through myriad social exchanges.

Race further lubricates the already slippery negotiation of BDSM's fantasy/reality binary. Adopting a "performative materialist methodology" in her ethnography of a large San Francisco Bay Area BDSM scene, Weiss describes the social, cultural, political, and economic complexity of the BDSM community. She describes BDSM performance as charged by various "circuits," "connections [that] are created between realms that are imagined as isolated and opposed."[128] The "fantasized split between the real (social inequality, norms, oppression, politics—the public) and the scene (radicalness, transgression, equality, desire—the private)" functions to reinscribe and exonerate white privilege.[129] Weiss's astute analysis situates her primarily white subjects and herself, a white female "queer, SM-friendly practitioner" scholar, within the terrain of privilege and identifies the "violence of whiteness."[130] For Weiss, race play might become an intervention into such privilege: by "challeng[ing] a narrative of historical progress, where we (urban, progressive, alternative white people) are beyond race, along with America—instead showing that we remain affectively and erotically bound to precisely the forms of difference that we might wish to overcome."[131] However, this fantasy/reality binary engenders a certain type of disavowal as well: "The fantasy of the scene as separate, as set off or bracketed from the real world, acts as an alibi that enables practitioners to dramatize—while also disavowing—social hierarchies and institutional systems of domination, especially those of race, class, gender, sexuality, and imperialism."[132] While I agree that this tension between fantasy and reality becomes a productive dichotomy in the labor of BDSM (its enactment, theorization, and spectatorship), for me, race play does not exhibit a disavowal of racial hierarchies or material institutionalizations of racial domination; it recognizes them.

Instead, race play, as a performative enactment and affective engagement with the history of racial domination, signals an acknowledgement of that history. Citing disavowal does two things. First, it serves to reinforce the "white privilege and racism" that Weiss's incisive critique works so hard to deconstruct.[133] Like Kara Walker, black women race-play practitioners refuse to "disavow the monstrous pleasures" that linger from the institution of chattel slavery.[134] Second, it works to dangerously obscure elements of pleasure, particularly its complexity and social construction.[135] What would happen if we understood the fantasy/reality divide as enabling not a disavowal of racial hierarchies and the power of racism but rather a rapture in them? I advocate reading race play as a way to fuck and fuck *with* racism: a potential parody or mimetic reiteration that exposes the fabrication of race and challenges and reifies racial-sexual alterity and racism *and* a sexual relationship with these "racialisms"—a pleasure in their enactment, a getting off on, a fucking.[136] Read this way, race play may be less of a neoliberal "fantasy of an escape from racism" and more of an escape in it or to it.[137]

While it is easy to interpret black women's testimonies from the early 1980s to today as evidence of the impossibility of disavowing racism, I wonder if resisting this interpretation might be important in contesting the white neoliberal mythology of race play that Weiss exposes. That mythology obscures the racial undertones of BDSM and exempts "well-meaning white people" from "the politics of SM racial projects" and from responsibility for larger structures of race and racism.[138] I am aware of the tension between the desire to showcase black women's voices in the tempestuous terrain of race play and the knowledge that this recognition might further marginalize these voices and increase their responsibility for being "the bearers of race and racism."[139] The magical spectacles through which to behold race and racism continue to rest heavily on black women's faces. Ultimately, I believe such voices need to be heard because they can facilitate both an intervention into "how whiteness is produced as a universal for the scene" and a depathologization of black women's unspeakable pleasures.[140]

Rejecting claims that people who participate in race play are/must be racist, the black dominatrix known as the Black Fuhrer illuminates this tension between fantasy/reality and inside/outside:

> I mean if we are going to try to make parallels between the world outside of fetish and inside of fetish and claiming that people who engage in racial type play are racist, then we are going to have to bring in domestic violence, assault and battery, verbal abuse, gay bashing, civil liberties. So we let some of this stuff go because no will bat an eye to a guy being caned, or nipple clamps, or labia clamps being put on someone, yet you know the use of certain words in racial context gets people up in arms.

Figure 1.2. The Black Fuhrer

> So you know, you have to be consistent, if race play is off limits then so is
> impact play, breath play, forced bi or any other sorts of things that aren't
> kosher outside of fetish.[141]

Inside the realm of fetish, what would be outside the boundaries of
conventional social mores and political correctness is not merely sanc-
tioned but eroticized. As conceptualized by the Black Fuhrer, racism
and domestic violence transform into something else when practiced
within the fantasy domain of BDSM. Playing with race in a fetish space
inhabited by consenting adults cannot be read as racism, according to
the Black Fuhrer:

> You know these are adults here and we're on a fetish, you know, site or
> scene or place or whatever. I mean use your common fucking sense. You

know they are not really racists. They would be at a clan rally or a skin-head meeting right now if that's what they really wanted to do. But they are here, you know, playing amongst people who they thought were sane enough to say hey you know this is race play. . . . For some reason race play is a very hot topic.[142]

What I find so compelling about these remarks is that even as she is calling for an "inside of fetish" reading of race play that positions it on par with other BDSM play, she is simultaneously recognizing race's unique power to incite and performatively enact the very inconsistency she interrogates, illustrating the fundamental challenge race poses to the fantasy/reality divide. As the Black Fuhrer elucidates, BDSM, not just race play, centers on an illicit eroticization of violence and power. She cautions us not to forget the foundations of BDSM as always already an enactment of taboo sexual fantasies in which "you kind of have to understand that you know whatever is being said is probably being played out as somebody's fantasy. It's somebody's fetish. You can't take it literally."[143] Though this is an important reminder about the practice—"you know, emphasis on the word *play*"—seeing race play as parallel to other BDSM role playing such as "daddy–baby girl dynamic[s]" (which she contrasts to pedophilia "outside of fetish") risks undervaluing race as a critical tool of human difference and power. The Black Fuhrer's name and martial image contravenes such an undervaluing, evoking not just the domination that she performs as a black femdom but also the sexual-political discourse surrounding BDSM's (and pornography's) controversial eroticization of Nazism and fascism. Her name facilitates a link between race play and other types of cultural trauma play such as Nazi play.

While many scripts that explore the possibilities of consensual bodily practices such as parent-child, boss-secretary, teacher-student, doctor-patient, priest-penitent, and warden-prisoner rely on an eroticized transgression of societal hierarchies (such as gender, race, class, sexuality, body, and age), lumping these taboos together conceals their historical specificity. Race uniquely augments this eroticization. Race play evinces how historically loaded black/interracial sex still is. As historian Kevin Mumford notes, black-white sex is always "more than just sex": "always extraordinary," black-white sexual intimacy in American society is necessarily informed by a national history of sexual racism.[144] Importing "real"-world racism and racial scripts into the "fantasy" world of fetish reveals just how permeable, albeit vital, the line between fantasy and reality, inside and outside, is here. While the importation of such scripts does not undermine the fantasy/reality binary many black women cite in the context of race play, it impels us to recognize that sexual fantasy, desire, pleasure, and practice—indeed, sexuality—are profoundly sociocultural. Similarly, if, as Mumford argues, black-white interracial sex is always "more than just sex," then BDSM practiced among black and white partners is always a kind of race play. Mollena Williams's statement that "I do race play whether or not I want to" is relevant here.[145] It touches upon the resonance of race play for the theory and praxis of black female sexuality beyond the temporal and spatial limits of BDSM. Her words testify to the always alreadyness and perdurability of race play for black women—the fact that we may be involved in race play whether or not we want to be—while critically expanding the scope and stage of race play. I am invested in this project of opening up the critical theoretical frame of race play. The daily presence of racism in black women's lives contrasts with the ephemerality of race play for white men, who, as Weiss notes, know that "when the scene is done, 'it[']s done." "This means that he can play with the erotics of such a scene without 'promoting racial violence' or 'disrespecting' black people or the history of slavery."[146] The contrast between black women's and white men's experiences with race play attests to the gradations of race and gender, if not privileges, that are enacted in the practice.

Playing with the Labor of Race/ Fucking (with) Black Abjection

Play is central to the concept of fantasy. While play in BDSM contexts is complex, demanding emotional, physical, and psychological labor and requiring preparation, training, and education, race further complicates the dynamics of play and the transgression, pleasure, and power exchange play facilitates. Andrea Beckman identifies play as a critical part of consensual BDSM practice in a transgressive space of "exploration," "choice," and experimentation with positions of subjecthood and power. She argues that "these 'bodily practices' allow 'lived bodies' to experiment within the spaces of subject-and object-position to which they are usually assigned by the apparatuses of domination."[147] Though she does not explicitly mention race play, it is in the context of a discussion of BDSM play that she summons race, citing the testimony of a black gay male interviewee, "Anthony," to illustrate her argument about the power dynamics of play and its potential for experimentation and sociopolitical transformation. For Anthony, BDSM provides a shame-free space for him to play with race, test limits, and express his taboo desires related to the history of chattel slavery. He states that "'S/M' actually provides that place to play out what I want to play out without feeling guilty. As a black person, there's a lot of issues around slavery and bondage—black experience—dealing with those issues."[148] Anthony's testimony of race play reiterates black women's expression of BDSM as a critical site for a psychological and physical play with the unspeakable racial-sexual horrors and pleasures of chattel slavery.

Race play lays bare the labor and play of race. Recognizing the labor and recreation of sexuality, Weiss conceptualizes BDSM as "working at play": a kind of fluid movement "between the registers of work (productive labor) and play (as creative recombination)."[149] Race play highlights Newmahr's understanding of BDSM play as "the joint boundary transgression of personal boundaries between people, of hegemonic social and ethical boundaries, and often of physical and physiological boundaries."[150] However, I would like us to consider that black women who participate in race play are not only playing with race (and the myriad boundaries it relies upon), but also demonstrating the *play* of race—how we *play* race and even how race *plays* us. That is, race play allows for the eroticized transgression of racial boundaries, enables a dramatization of race that irradiates the performativity of race as a social identity and a category of power, and speaks to the ways race *plays* us. As an African American urban colloquialism, the word "play" is often used as both a synonym for sexual action and a term to describe a kind of exploitation, misuse, deceit, or delusion. I elicit this sense of play here to signal the multiple complex and contradictory ways race is riddled with paradoxes, despite its function as a primary disciplining principle of humankind.

My thinking about how race *plays* us and the dynamic paradoxes of racialization is indebted to Robert Bernasconi's recent work on race as a "border concept."[151] Revealing the myriad contradictions within the volatile landscape of racial borders, Bernasconi exposes how sexual transgression is historically constitutive of race and its conceptualization.[152] Arguing that the racial borders are the places where we best assess the dynamic, sociohistorical, political, and culturally evolving processes of racialization, racial difference, and the operation of racism, Bernasconi disrupts deep-seated narratives of racial essentialism to expose race as a profoundly "relational concept" that is (re)produced in and through the continual delineation of porous, often-transgressed, yet formidably systemic racial boundaries.[153] Echoing Abdul JanMohamed's point that the systematic violation of the racial-sexual border is one if its "most blatant contradictions," Bernasconi sees the racial-sexual border as an ambivalent yet critical site for a "hermeneutics of racialization."[154] In race play, it is precisely this site that is staged and eroticized as the domain of play.

Race play illuminates race as a border concept, "a dynamic fluid concept whose core lies not at the center but at its edges" while simultaneously enacting the paradox involved with traversing the sexual border, that in order "to map the racial borders, the borders must be crossed."[155] In race play, racial boundaries are delineated only to be crossed. Like the line between fantasy and reality, the racial border is marked by its "selective permeability."[156] Race play elucidates how race *plays* us in multiple ways. Race is imagined as a stable, sovereign truth, when in fact, it is a dynamic and fluid site of demarcation. It embodies what Sharon Holland calls the "lie of difference"; it masquerades as a fundamental marker of difference and separation, while actually it is an emblem of relation and intimacy. Racial borders, as race play evinces, are marked by an erotically charged crossing.[157] Yet it is, as race play so vibrantly illustrates, the eroticized, highly dramatized traversing of the constructed racial binary that reifies racial categories. That is, though fluid and continually shifting, race and racial boundaries are upheld in and through their sexual transgression. Race play heightens the practice of "the drawing and redrawing of the racial boundaries" because BDSM is always already a practice of delineating personal sexual limits, a practice of setting, pushing against, and retracting the physical and psychic borders of the "play territory."[158] In race play, racial boundaries collide with psychosexual and physical boundaries in an unresolved melodrama animated by racism, eroticism, racial-sexual alterity,

power, pleasure, pain, and the unsettled dichotomies of transgression/
compliance, subversion/reproduction, black/white, fantasy/reality, and
mind/body.

Like the carefully constructed dichotomy between inside/outside and
fantasy/reality, the body/mind split offers a critical, if conflicted, space for
black women to reconcile their feelings about race play. This split is exemplified by Mollena Williams's statement that "my vagina isn't really interested in uplifting the race. What pussy wants is fucked up stuff, really dark
scenarios to test the boundaries and cut with an exhilarating level of danger."[159] Her comment underscores the tension of race play; she endows
her pussy with the very intellect she disavows in effecting the dissociation
between mind and body. This privileging of pussy is undercut by her description of race play as an exercise in a kind of racial pedagogy. She states
that "the prime motive in a 'Race Play' scene is to underscore and investigate the challenges of racial or cultural differences."[160] Williams outlines
the contradictions, complexities, and darkness of sexual pleasure itself,
echoing Kantrowitz's confession that "'politically correct' sex rarely leads
to orgasm," Pat Califia's distinction between "what really gets us wet" and
"what we think should get us wet," and Simone de Beauvoir's comment
that "no aphrodisiac is so potent as deviance of the Good."[161] And if we
agree with Leonore Tiefer that "it's the symbolic investment that makes
sex ecstatic," then we might see race play as revealing our symbolic erotic
investment in racism and the history of chattel slavery.[162]

However, many black women BDSMers assert that it is the body
that is aroused by racist fantasies rather than the mind. This disassociation is fascinating because it allows for an important reconciliation
of feelings about race play. Some black women participants in BDSM
express that while it's not necessarily "cool" to like being called, or to
call one's partner, a "nigger whore," a "nigger cunt," a "nigger slave slut,"
or a "tar monkey nigger cunt," they can rationalize that a) it's only fantasy, only play; and b) it's not my mind that is stimulated by this, in fact
my mind knows better, it is my body that is aroused.[163] The names of
Kara Walker's fantasy personas, the "Negress" and "Nigger Wench," illustrate a similar volatile juxtaposition of fantasy and reality, reiteration
and resignification.

Other black women express a kind of therapeutic, restorative quality in race play, echoing what recent scholars have written about

BDSM practice. However Mollena Williams offers a warning about this benefit: "Kink can be therapeutic, but it isn't therapy."[164] Heeding the lived experience of BDSMers, scholars have revealed the affective psychological and physical therapy that BDSM engenders for many of its practitioners.[165] In her ethnographic study of one BDSM community, Beckman notes the therapeutic potentiality of BDSM play in working through the pain of the past, wherein play becomes a kind of performance of catharsis. She writes of

> "play" with formerly painful and threatening situations which can be "relived" and "re-experienced" within the trusting and safe, because controlled, context of consensual "S/M" appears to have therapeutic effects for some practitioners. The experiential transformation of traumatic experiences allows for a process of rememorising and my observations suggest that it increases self-confidence and assertiveness for many practitioners.[166]

Beckman observes that in the "safe" setting of consensual, negotiated BDSM erotic play, (re)memory may operate to transform trauma into both pleasure and a kind of healing and self-recovery.[167] Her analysis substantiates the notion that sexuality is a vital site for enacting "the rememorising" of the history of chattel slavery.[168]

The practice of rape play, a consensual BDSM sexual practice of performed rape, is an example of BDSM's therapeutic possibility.[169] Exploring sexual assault and rape survivors' engagement in rape play, Corie Hammers examines BDSM's therapeutic power, arguing that rape play becomes an important psychosomatic intervention into sexual trauma that facilitates "corporeal and psychic shifts" in and for the sexually traumatized bodies of its practitioners.[170] Beyond engendering pleasure in the sex act and alleviating the physical and mental pain of sexual encounters, rape play enables some women survivors to reconnect with their bodies and experience feelings of empowerment that often exceed the temporal and spatial limits of the rape-play scene. Here the therapeutic potential of BDSM lies in its recuperation of both desire and power and as a kind of affective reclamation of the body.[171] Through reenactment of past sexual trauma on their own terms, these women become agents of their own sexual pleasure and pain; their performance of rape play is a mode of what Hammers terms "bodily becoming."[172] One interviewee, Sheila, explains: "In re-enacting my rape I'm doing it on my own terms. Trying to explain what it does . . . is very difficult. I own my own power, my body with SM in my rape play. With kink, the pain is no longer there. The pain I felt physically is more or less gone. I am loose, present, in my body. . . . I lost this with the rape. I have reclaimed myself."[173] Marshaling the oral testimonies of women rape-play practitioners, Hammers evinces the keen sense of authorship and ownership of their own sexuality these women experience in performing rape play—reinforced here by the use of the possessive pronoun "my."

These narratives of agency are echoed by those who practice race play, imagining it as a psychological and physical intervention into the subjective state of black abjection, a spectacular fucking with both the memory of slavery and the continued domination of black womanhood. Witnesses are central to this transformation of corporeal sexual trauma through rape play. That is, it is not just the enactment of consent that allows these women to rescript and control their own experiences of sexual trauma through its performative reenactment ("sculpting the scar"); spectatorship by another is also crucial.[174] Hammers argues that "BDSM disrupts this silencing and the atomizing experience of trauma through public witnessing. BDSM rape play is a public witnessing, a sharing of the unbearable, and it is through this sharing—this witnessing—that the trauma is spoken in both verbal and extra-verbal ways."[175] Similarly, Theodore Reik has argued that spectatorship is necessary for the construction of the masochist.[176] I want to be clear that in making this parallel between rape play and race play, I am not asserting that the historical legacies of sexual trauma—the "monstrous intimacies"—haunting black female sexual subjectivity are equivalent to the trauma experienced by present-day survivors of rape and sexual assault. However, in drawing on the erotic experiences of women practicing rape play and the theorization of their narratives, I seek to illuminate the complex dynamics of pain, pleasure, and power, hinged on consent, that suffuse the practice of race play. Race play and rape play, both of which are performative renditions of past trauma, represent a critical recoding of what Hortense Spillers calls "the hieroglyphics of the flesh" in ways that engender feelings of pleasure and control.[177] In narrating their performance of rape play and race play, women describe a renegotiation of their relationships with their past and signal a kind of becoming or remaking of the future. Such a future might be paradoxically accessed through a mythical return to and repetition of—a replaying of—the past.[178]

Both rape play and race play reinforce how important consent and agency are for any kind of pain play. Darren Langdridge reveals how consent operates as a form of agency to rescript the "terms" of violence in order "to maximize the possibility of violent acts being understood in the participant's own terms, providing an opening-up of meaning."[179] Bringing us toward a critical understanding of "the paradox" of BDSM pain play, Langdridge contends that "most critically[,] pain play appears to involve a way of experiencing the limits of one's material-semiotic subjectivity through the exploration of agency and subjection."[180] As black women BDSMers convey, consent within BDSM functions to transform the quotidian physical and psychic pain of black abjection into the realm of rapture and affective agency within the "safe" playground of kink.[181]

Race profoundly shapes the currency of BDSM interventions. In her groundbreaking ethnographic study of professional dominatrices that explores how professional erotic dominance sheds light on the everyday "normative" societal dynamics of power, Danielle Lindemann briefly visits the practice of race play. Though she does not make the same kind of racial caveat that Weiss and Newmahr did, Lindemann notes that race play is not common in her majority-white subject population of professional dominatrices, who also have predominately white male clients.[182] Considering the racial dynamics of BDSM's therapeutic potential, Lindemann identifies race play "as a mechanism through which clients could negotiate their anxiety by reproducing traumatic experiences on their own terms."[183] Her theory differs from Weiss's argument that while race play unveils the white hegemony and privilege of the BDSM community (and national belonging more generally), it might contest such racialized power dynamics.[184] Lindeman argues that in race play, clients either reproduce or subvert broader racial hierarchies.[185] Though this either/or posture flattens out the distinctions between these two moments—reproduction and subversion—obfuscating a spectrum of possibilities, it is through this manipulation that racial hierarchies are revealed as performative and unnatural. Hence, the therapeutic potentiality of race play for black women may lie in the choice to be subjugated, a kind of exercising of one's own conscious experience of racialized oppression and aggression: Williams states "I like my violence consensual." Just as significant, there is also potential in recognizing one's role as an actor in the making and performance of racial hierarchies.[186]

Still, the antidotal and analeptic capacity of shame and humiliation is fundamentally complicated by race. Lindeman finds that the process of shaming is restorative because of its ephemerality: it "confirms that which the client is *not*—that is 'You are no longer a pig or a dog or whatever.'"[187] Describing his experience playing top with Mollena Williams in a race-play demonstration, white male BDSM and sex educator Graydancer expressed a similar logic of identity: "That's part of the lesson of race play, for me. It's a reminder of what I'm not, of what we have been, and of what we have to constantly fight becoming."[188] However, as a state that one typically cannot effortlessly slip in and out of, blackness problematizes this perception. Can one no longer be a nigger in the same way she is no longer a pig, a slave, or a whore? Fanon's statement, "Against all the arguments I have just cited, I come back to one fact: Wherever he goes: The Negro remains a Negro," captures "the *fact* of Blackness," the endurance of black abjection.[189] Outside the dungeon, the bedroom, or the stage, one may very well remain a nigger.

Race play confronts black women with a set of paradoxical limits. First, it reveals a temporal and spatial extension of the frontier of black women's racial-sexual "play" outside the boundaries of BDSM (recall Mollena Williams' statement, "I do race play whether or not I want to"). Second, it reveals the challenges that blackness poses to BDSM's destabilization of identity categories and hierarchies of power. Race extends the field of play while constraining its potential for subversion. I envision race play as presenting a different kind of conflict for BDSM's therapeutic discourse than the one Lindemann has outlined. Lindemann argues that race play presents pro-doms with a moral quandary that complicates their therapeutic role: "A final wrinkle in the therapeutic discourse is that, in identifying as therapists, some pro-dommes felt that they were absolving clients of conduct with which they personally did not agree."[190] While for Lindemann it is the ethical dilemma of "well-educated white liberal" women that undercuts BDSM's therapeutic potential, I argue that race, the "fact of Blackness," is what ultimately problematizes a therapeutic rendering of BDSM.[191] Pat Califia has suggested that there are limits to BDSM play with respect to race: "If you don't like being a top or a bottom, you switch your keys. Try doing that with your race our socioeconomic status."[192] We might, then, think of race play as play with a certain type of fixity of race, not necessarily its fluidity. Race play complicates the theorization of BDSM play, challenging arguments that play rearranges power hierarchies.[193]

Black women's testimony of race play signals the nuances race engenders in BDSM's therapeutic discourse while attesting to the possibility of a racialized salutary effect. While feminists debated BDSM's therapeutic potential at the height of the sex wars in the early 1980s, contemporary scholars of BDSM have recently problematized the therapeutic impetus that animates the practice.[194] For example, Meg Barker and Darren Langdridge remain conflicted over whether or not to include narratives of "healing" and the "therapeutic" in their scholarship.[195] While Barker believes that such narratives should be incorporated because they attest to "lived experiences" and are aligned with the methodological commitment of feminist researchers to "giving people a voice, not silencing people," Langdridge worries about the potential these healing narratives have to be perverted by mainstream culture.[196] He contends that the therapeutic discourse underlining BDSM practice is at odds with scholarly efforts to disengage BDSM from the psychiatric profession and will have dangerous repercussions for the BDSM community. Analysis of BDSM as a healing practices, Langdridge argues, encourages the pathologization of BDSM through two implications: "first, that SMers have a need for healing and second, that once 'cured[,]' people will stop doing SM. It seems a pretty negative way of storying SM."[197] Similarly, Barker, Gupta, and Iantaffi contend that such healing narratives and cultural representations of the practice are "extremely value-laden" and can reify rather than reject the pathologizing impetus toward BDSM of the medical and psychotherapy industries.[198] Consequently, BDSM healing narratives can be "read as both empowering and problematic" in their shoring up of a moral discourse that constructs a "good BDSMer" (i.e., one who practices for the 'right' reasons of healing her/himself). This "good BDSMer" can also idealize particular experiences and narratives of practice over others.[199] However, Barker, Langdridge, Gupta, and Iantaffi do not consider how race further complicates BDSM's therapeutic potential and/or how the problems of pathologization for the "minority community" of BDSM might be compounded by the minoritized racialized body.

While Williams effects a Cartesian disassociation in order to enjoy race play, other black women BDSMers are unable to do so. Though she does not get many requests for it, professional femdom Goddess Sonya does not do race play because she does not enjoy it.[200] While comfortable and skilled in diverse acts of edge play and humiliation, ranging from golden showers to corporal punishment, Sonya expresses that her own fantasies and pleasure are tantamount to her domination. Hence, she does not engage in race play. Furthermore as a black femdom with primarily white submissive male clients, she does not often get requests for "nigger play." Her statement that "there is nothing really racially charged in calling a white man a honky" attests to race play's grounding in a particular white heteropatriarchal rendering of American racism and its reliance on a specific (and very familiar) hierarchy of race and racial embodiment.[201] Her comment prompts us to consider how race play's erotic current ebbs and flows with the shifting racial and gender dynamics of racial abjection performed.

Black female dominatrices such as Goddess Sonya and the Black Fuhrer navigate a complex economy of sexual labor. Though scholars have recently analyzed female dominatrices, they have not theorized their representation in pornography, especially that of black women. Lindeman suggests that professional domination sheds light on professionalism within the service industry more generally.[202] For example, Goddess Sonya and the Black Fuhrer mirror a common professional trajectory that Lindemann identifies of transitioning from larger houses to becoming independent doms. Claims to professionalism, training, and skill are vital to the type of labor women perform in commercial BDSM, including the dynamics of the dom/sub fantasy and the more material aspects of work that is often framed as more skilled and specialized than other types of erotic labor.[203] Such assertions of professionalism use a discourse of authenticity wherein the "real" BDSM dom is professional, rigorously trained, and experienced.[204] Authenticity is, as Lindemann suggests, a form of cultural capital for pro-doms. What begs consideration is how this authenticity collides with racial authenticity and the myriad ways race impacts the cultural capital of femdoms.

The elaborate labor of race is inextricable from the multiplex erotic labor of BDSM, both physical and psychic. Race is another aspect of the labor BDSM performs. While the question of race and its labor in commercial BDSM remains undertheorized in recent literature, black feminist scholars have examined the critical ways race informs sex work. In her ethnographic study of black and Latina strippers in New York City and the San Francisco Bay Area, Siobhan Brooks documents the ways that race affects the institutional and symbolic erotic capital of dancers. Brooks uses the term "racialized erotic capital" to delineate how black women navigate a hierarchy of power wherein blackness is devalued. This affects hiring practices, digital marketing, pay, safety, the work environment, and more.[205] Miller-Young describes black women's devaluation within pornography, a domain where white women reign as "stars."[206] She documents the complex auxiliary labor demanded of black female performers in the face of this racial hierarchy as they navigate the structural racism of the industry and contend with wage inequality, labor segregation, and the more insidious, multifaceted "*work of racial fantasy.*"[207] Like black women in the porn industry who strategically "'play up' race," black female dominatrices engage the drama of race in their erotic labor.[208]

Goddess Sonya's sentiment suggests the limits of subversion through race play that I previously discussed in the context of race's playing of us. If, as Goddess Sonya and others say, calling a white man a honkey lacks the same "charge" as calling a black woman a nigger, race play's potential for racial subversion is circumscribed by race and gender and ultimately disciplined by white heteropatriarchy, seemingly a powerful, stable force both inside and outside the world of fetish. Furthermore, assigning power to a particular mode or position of domination or submission encourages a problematic moral of reading race play (i.e., some practices can be "good" while others are "bad") and facilitates a failure to recognize that both oppressor and oppressed, top and bottom, are tethered to the same history.

Linked to the body/mind split is the contradictory undercurrent of political correctness that informs race play. For example, certain scenarios such as black dom/white slave are often deemed more "palatable," "acceptable," and "less racist" than black slave/white master. This protocol reflects a common but flawed understanding of power

Figure 1.3. Goddess Sonya at play

and racism as top down and does not recognize that it is a more fluid exchange dependent upon relationality, resistance, and (power) exchange between master/slave, oppressor/oppressed, and dom/sub. Affirming Foucault's contention that power "comes from below," BDSM has long challenged a top-down understanding of power, revealing how positions that are conventionally imagined as subordinate (i.e., bottom and submissive) enact power, exert control, and deploy influence.[209] Leo Bersani argues that the locations of top and bottom "can never be just a question of physical position."[210] Many black women BDSMers also question a static logic of power within the moral framework of race play. They express their desire to play sub to a white dom and their belief that this type of partnership is an acceptable and immensely pleasurable one. Williams, for example, challenges the idea that it is "OK if the Black person is dominant, but [she's] not 'UPLIFTING THE RACE!!!' if she's submissive," joking, "Yes. Payback, you see. We aren't getting reparations, so go beat up some White [person] and get yours."[211] Like many black women who have been censured for their race play, especially in the submissive role, Williams vocalizes the double standards that energize ethical charges against the practice.[212] Her statement accentuates the intense ambivalence of race play and reiterates how changes in how it is received and policed are dependent upon the racial and gender dynamics of racialized abjection that are performed. She elucidates how race play concretizes the charged, complex, and contradictory relationship between racism and rapture. I advocate reading these women's commentary as a critical testament of sexual autonomy, a kind of claiming of sexual pleasure on their own terms. Their words outline the stakes of black female sexual politics. Black women's participation in BDSM, especially race play, is fraught with contradictions, complicated by racialized and gendered sociohistorical subtexts and positionalities of domination and submission that are animated by the enacted binaries of fantasy/reality, mind/body, and black/white.

Coda

In a 1982 interview, Foucault, a theorist and practitioner of BDSM, stated that "the idea that S&M is related to a deep violence, that S&M practice is a way of liberating this violence, this aggression, is stupid. We know very well that what those people are doing is not aggressive; they are inventing new possibilities of pleasure with strange parts of their body—through the eroticization of the body."[213] Foucault recognized the productive potential of BDSM in creating novel pleasure but he rejected the psychological and somatic historical registers of BDSM—the premise that it is linked to an "uncovering of S & M tendencies deep within our unconscious."[214] Following in this Foucauldian stream of thought, we might consider BDSM a practice that is uninformed by the black female's psychic and bodily memory of trauma and the constitutive links between black female sexuality and violence. Accordingly, BDSM cannot be about working out, in, or through a black female (un)consciousness occupied by a history of sexual violence because it is not, as Foucault suggests, about the "deep" psychic past of historical trauma and/or memory but rather about the creative future of bodily pleasures. However, marshaling the voices of black women BDSMers, I argue that it can be both. These women provide evidence that their pleasure, though highly conflicted, *is* informed by the histories of chattel slavery and racism, interracial sexual violence, racialized exchanges of power and it is also about finding innovative new modes of accessing pleasure. While BDSM might not heal a historical wound and/or allow for the enactment of some kind of redress—actual or symbolic—for black women, it might serve as a stage, or better yet a ring, for re*playing* primordial scenes of black-white sexual intimacy and the imbrications of pleasure, power, race, and sex. Perhaps such narratives of black-white interracial sexual aggression speak not only about the psychic past but also about felt blackness in the present—the sentience of the black body.

African American writer Gary Fisher poignantly and painfully elucidates this sentiment in *Gary in Your Pocket: Stories and Notebooks of Gary Fisher* (1996), a work that expresses the complexities of racism, pleasure, and pain within the context of gay interracial intimacy. Fischer candidly shares his interest in race play and racial humiliation, specifically his desire to play the "nigger" sub worshipping the "whiteness" of his male dom.[215] Proudly relishing his role as "nigger cocksucker," physically and metaphorically genuflecting for the white male body, Fisher articulates the tangle of arousal and degradation that race play engenders with his statement that "piss and sperm nourish the nigger body and feed his Black soul."[216] Fisher envisions such acts as a sacrament that ritualizes arousal and empowerment through black abjection. Uncannily echoing "Leather Mother" Viola Johnson, Fisher writes, "The nigger takes his hot sacrament from the cocks of men who know where a nigger should be, why he should be, how he should be and find pleasure in reaffirming that I AM PROUD TO BE A NIGGER."[217] Fisher speaks to the dynamic ways that differently raced and gendered bodies experience the epistemic violence and pleasure of race (play) in different ways. He articulates the contradictions and complexities race play encompasses and our use of race and racism as technologies of sexual pleasure and power enacted in scenes of black-white interracial intimacy. For Fisher, race play becomes an elixir for the frustration of race—the vexation of blackness through a state of what Darieck Scott might call "extravagant abjection."[218] Fisher states:

> Blackness is a state of frustration. There's no way out of this racial depression (I don't feel the frustration personally, but as a part of a people I

know that I am being fucked, abused). Sexually I want (desire, fantasize myself) to be (being) used. I want to be a slave, sexually and perhaps otherwise.[219]

Playing into his seemingly inexorable "racial depression" offers an affective agency—an awareness of one's own responsibility in the performativity of race and a kind of vital rhapsody, however fleeting. His testimony illuminates the performance of abjection as a means not merely of pleasure but also of perception. Beyond pleasure, race play perhaps becomes a kind of critical negotiation for the abject black body—a way of working not through the past, but perhaps in and through the present.

This chapter has illustrated how black women's performances in BDSM are shaped by the sociopolitical and cultural histories related to black women, sexuality, and violence. I have argued that BDSM is a critical site for rethinking the enmeshment of black female sexuality and violence. In the context of BDSM, violence becomes not just a vehicle of desire and pleasure but also a mode of accessing and contesting power. Deconstructing the uniquely problematic nature of black women's involvement in BDSM, I amplify black women's voicing of a complex and contradictory negotiation of pain, pleasure, and power. Black women BDSMers engage in an elaborate play of race in the pursuit of sexual pleasure, empowerment, and autonomy. BDSM is a productive space from which to consider the multiplicity of black women's sexual practice and the multiplicity of black female sexuality. It is simultaneously an arena of pleasure, power, danger, and agency.[220] It is my hope that this exploration, in addition to challenging androcentric and narrow conceptualizations of sexual violence and pleasure, will move us toward a necessary destigmatization of black women's unconventional sexual practices. Race play illuminates not only the erotic play of race but also the enduring erotic power of the black/white binary, the history of slavery, and racism itself.

2

Pornography's Play(ing) of Race

Intimacy Interventions

In April 2013, a corner of the Internet was set ablaze by the spark of controversy. The words of Abiola Abrams, black female pornographer turned sex, love, life and relationship guru, provoked the firestorm.[1] In her online advice column "Intimacy Intervention" in *Essence Magazine*, Abrams responded to the letter of a distraught reader. An anonymous African American woman, writing under the nom de plume "Black and Proud" described her revulsion at her new white husband's use of racial slurs during sex. She wrote, "My man keeps calling me a 'nigger bitch' during sex and I hate it."[2] "Black and Proud" described how his use of the n-word and explicit eroticization of blackness—he called her pubic hair a "negro bush" and himself a "nigger lover"—shattered her "picture perfect fantasy life."[3] The racial slurs her husband used during sex left her "completely turned off."[4]

In Abrams's response, she wrote that there is nothing "normal" about the use of racialized names, which she deemed "verbally abusive and emotionally harmful."[5] She referred to race-play "expert" Mollena Williams to make the case that such racial slurs are indeed not race play because they lack the fundamental BDSM mandate of consent. Abrams's identification of race play as something black women must "sign up for" contrasts with Williams's statement that black women experience race play every day without consent; recall her statement that "I do 'race play' whether or not I want to."[6]

Abrams's response went viral. Almost 600 readers, most of whom were disgusted by the husband's behavior, posted comments on essence. com, and a series of follow-up articles were written about the exchange and the controversial phenomenon of race play. Commenting on the fallout, Mollena Williams discussed the importance of "open and honest communication" about sexuality with one's spouse, awareness of the often-divergent sexual backgrounds of interracial partners, and the need for consent when playing the precarious erotic game of race.[7] Inspired by the controversy and by letters from her own readers, Christelyn D. Karazin, publisher and editor-in-chief of beyondblackwhite.com, brought Abrams and Williams together for a podcast conversation about the controversial letter; that conversation also highlighted the issue of consent.[8] Writing for the grio.com, Alexis Garrett Stodghill argued that race play is "a curious fringe realm of sexuality" and used the opportunity to "underscore the need to honestly and openly communicate one's true sexual needs as essential to the success of any sexual partnership."[9] Lastly, *Clutch* magazine ran a story, "Racial Slurs, and 4 Other Things You Shouldn't Say During Sex," that ranked racial slurs at the top of their list of sexual faux pas.[10]

Abrams's "Intimacy Intervention" and the letter that inspired it speak to a continuing rage for race play and its multiple spheres of performance. This intimacy intervention and the online responses it generated are part of a flurry of recent web stories about the practice.[11] Most of these media stories drew from the words of race-play "representative" Mollena Williams and highlight the controversial aspects of race play, reflecting the same polarized sexual ethics that marked discussions of black women's participation in BDSM.[12] In *Ebony* magazine's article "Race Play Ain't for Everyone," Feminist Jones rhetorically asked, "How far is too far? Where do we draw the line between what we consider freedom of expression and hate speech? Is there ever a time when 'race play' can be enjoyable and rewarding, or is it an absolute non-no in any situation?"[13] Lori Adelman's report on grio.com sought to dispel common misconceptions about the practice.[14] Kirsten West Savali's article on HelloBeautiful.com featured an interactive reader poll that revealed that most readers find race play disgusting and would not engage it.[15] Chauncey Devega, black cultural critic and author of the blog We Are Respectable Negroes, repudiated race play: "I could not engage in such types of role-playing. My personal politics would not allow it; my libido would not respond."[16] Nevertheless, he wrote of a theoretical interest in "how individuals negotiate white supremacy and Power."[17] Even when these cyber critiques rejected race play, they cited a titillation that belies repudiation, echoing the tensions black women BDSMers express. In this personal distancing of themselves from race play, these authors implicitly labeled race play perverse, a characterization some seemed to want to refute.

Because the majority of these pieces were published in black media outlets, these dialogues resituated race play as a black problem. Ownership of race "problems" is a burden black women are familiar with. This responsibility engenders a paradoxical punishment of the black female body as a fomenter of racism. As Sarah Ahmed has noted, "Given that racism recedes from social consciousness, it appears as if the ones who 'bring it up' are bringing it into existence."[18] The articles written in response to Abrams's "Intimacy Intervention" generated much comment from readers, transforming each piece from static piece into an ongoing collective dialogue about race play. These cyber commentaries speak to the dynamic representation of race play, a contested space in which this chapter hovers as it explores the representation of race play in contemporary America pornography. Pornography acts as an "intimacy intervention" into race play, mediating its performances, fantasies, and desires. In making visible the race-play fantasy, pornography is a critical venue of and for race-play performance. It is an important site of race-play analysis because of the dynamic ways it highlights both the fantasy/reality tension and the interracial dynamics that are so salient to the practice. It also brings into relief the perverse pleasures of race play—specifically as I reveal here, the queer valence of its performance.

In this chapter I analyze black women's diverse performance of race play in contemporary American pornography. First, I look at the practice of black female/white male humiliation on the BDSM femdom website of a veteran black female pornographer, Vanessa Blue, to illuminate how race is a critical technology of interracial BDSM practice. Next, I read a performance of black female submission staged as a historical reenactment of chattel slavery in hard-core mainstream race-play pornography—a production that recites not only the history of slavery but also cinematic spectacles of that history in contemporary popular culture. Finally, I look at interracial lesbian domination in amateur-race play pornography that facilitates a queer reading of race-play performance in pornography and illuminates the production of race-play porn. Leaving the realm of pornography, I conclude with an analysis of a comic rendition of race play that also draws upon the erotic storehouse of slavery. Even as I argue that pornography is an optimal space for race play because it is imagined as a fantasy realm of sexuality, I analyze race play as a comprehensive performance with a more universal sociocultural currency and relevance. This chapter reveals several critical tensions in race play: between the quotidian and the spectacular, the pornographic and the mainstream.

Staging the Field of Play

As the work I analyze here demonstrates, a lot has changed in the field of BDSM pornography since Linda Williams's pioneering discussion of sadomasochistic film pornography. Since the eighteenth century, pornography has vividly engaged the taboo of violence and pain.[19] Sadistic pornography's "spectacle of suffering" prevailed in the nineteenth century, when depictions of flagellation were common.[20] Modern discussions of violence in pornography are often motivated by question of harm—the potential harm performers might experience and the harm incurred through witnessing such violence.[21] In the l980s when Williams was writing the canonical book *Hardcore*, the issue of violence in pornography was at the forefront of social discourse animated by anti-porn feminist activism, inquiry by the federal government, and scholarship.[22]

Reorienting the question of harm, Williams argues that BDSM perverts the question of violence in pornography. She contends that sadomasochistic pornography exhibits two types of perversions: "a perversion of cinema"—a perversion of a Bazinian cinematic "noble realism"—and "cinema *as* perversion in itself as an economic, technical, social, and symbolic system."[23] "Cinema as perversion" is less concerned with literal acts of violence and instead focuses on the broader "implant[ations]" within the discourse of cinema as "sadistic, masochistic, voyeuristic, and fetishizing."[24] Steered by a politics of perversion, I maintain in interest in the ways that BDSM unearths the perverse queer pleasures of "heterosexual" interracial pornographic desire and pleasure.

Reflecting anti-porn feminists' assertion that the heterosexist patriarchy is itself sadomasochistic, feminist film theorists have critiqued the concept of "cinema as perversion," illuminating the sadomasochistic quality of the cinematic male gaze.[25] Most famously, Laura Mulvey's influential theorization of fetishistic scopophilia, the fetishistic erotic pleasure in looking, of cinema exists in contradistinction to what she identifies as the voyeuristic sadism of film spectatorship.[26] Mulvey argues that both speak to the problem of female sexual difference, that both are strategies of the male unconscious for coping with castration anxiety. Many scholars have critiqued Mulvey. Gaylyn Studlar, for example, argues that masochism, not sadism, is what is salient for the perverse pleasures of film spectatorship.[27] For Williams, however, sadism is an inadequate explanation for the multifaceted perversion of hard core pornographic cinema because that explanation ultimately disavows the power she argues is essential to pleasure itself.[28] Williams elucidates how even in the volatile BDSM domain of unthinkable, unspeakable pleasure, power is what makes such pleasure possible: "There can be no pleasure, in other words, without some power."[29] Williams's analysis reinforces what BDSM advocates and practitioners, such as SAMOIS, have argued for some time—that there is power at the bottom.[30]

Williams offers a typology of three categories of heterosexual hardcore sadomasochistic film and video pornography. The first and most extreme, *amateur sadomasochism*, features prolonged scenes of bondage and discipline. Often shot in video, it contains highly ritualized forms of violence and domination and has a low production value reminiscent of stag films, which I discuss in the following chapter.[31] In the second and most common type, *sadie-max*, violence is not fundamental to the film's narrative but rather becomes a kind of "spice" to enhance pleasure. Such films typically depict domination, light bondage, anal penetration, and a kind of phantasmatic "exaggerated paraphernalia" of BDSM.[32] The final category, *aesthetic sadomasochism*, refers to pornography's aestheticization of violence. These works "situate themselves within an elitist sadomasochistic literary tradition" that casts violence as art.[33] Williams argues that the fantasy of female, not male, submission dominates BDSM pornography. This gender dynamic, according to Williams, contests "real-life heterosexual sadomasochistic practice" wherein male submissives are the majority.[34] Even if these categories did not reify a heteronormative BDSM fantasy that the debates I discussed in the previous chapter belie or reflect a complete absence of race, they no longer typify the field of BDSM pornography.

The question of race is integral to BDSM pornography while the dynamic of passive, submissive female/dominant male no longer epitomizes BDSM pornographic fantasy, if it ever did. A politics of perversion illumines the range of BDSM pornography to bring into relief the perverse collusions between race, BDSM, and queerness in the pornographic scene. More recently, scholars have reanimated the question of violence and pornography. While Natalie Purcell does not analyze BDSM pornography in her recent study of violence in pornography, she argues that sadism is the foundation of pornography's sexual arousal.[35] However, she is careful to distinguish sadism within pornography from its interpretation within BDSM. She argues that the sadism that is so integral to pleasure in mainstream pornography is an "absolute dominance," a suffering that must be legible to viewers "*as* suffering," not a mutually consensual, pleasurable encounter and power exchange, as it is in a BDSM scene.[36]

While race play has received recent coverage in popular and scholarly media, race-play pornography, particularly that which focuses on black women's performances, has received little scholarly attention. Darieck Scott and Tim Dean both discuss race-play pornography within the context of black-white gay male sexuality.[37] Though he explicitly mentions the term only twice in *Extravagant Abjection*, Scott offers a stunning analysis of the phenomenon of race play in literary pornography.[38] For Scott, race play illustrates what he calls "blackness in/and abjection," a phrase that speaks to the historical constitution of blackness as abjection through domination. Scott asserts that blackness and abjection are mutually constitutive and that abjection offers the black male body unique opportunities for black power. Reading power, and not just pleasure, as an important product of black women's racial sexual abjection within BDSM, I am inspired by Scott's foundational project of redefining the relationship between power, blackness, and sexuality.

Tim Dean examines race play in gay male bareback moving-image pornography as part of a multifaceted process of fetishization within the genre. Dean interrogates how pornography labors to make visible that which is invisible, and fetishization is a central issue of his analysis.[39] Focusing his analysis on one gay male bareback video, *Niggas' Revenge* (dir. Dick Wadd, 2001), he argues that race-play fantasy enables the imagination of other, less perceptible modes of transgression, most notably HIV transmission through bareback sex. In *Niggas' Revenge*, gay black porn star Bobby Blake and a group of black men seek revenge on a band of white neo-Nazis in a bout of fucking, urination, bondage, fisting, and more. He reads the video's violent inter(racial) sexual domination as "conjur[ing] the transgressive charge of unprotected anal sex among gay men."[40] Because I seek to unveil and destigmatize black women's practice of BDSM, I am encouraged by Dean's innovative reading of fetishism as an instrument of "erotic creativity" within sexual subcultures and as a possible instrument for disrupting sexual hegemonies.[41] Conceptualizing fetishism in BDSM as a mode of erotic innovation, à la Foucault, is in line with the critical depathologization of race play that I endeavor in this book. Nevertheless, I am wary of Dean's reading of race and racial fetishism within the context of a number of fetishes within bareback pornography. The fact of blackness poses a serious challenge to the disruption of sociocultural hierarchies of power, specifically racial hierarchies.

I disagree with Dean when he argues that "desire is not determined by difference" in order to contest theories of racial fetishism anchored in an anxiety of racial difference.[42] Critiquing Frantz Fanon's and Dwight A. McBride's readings of racial fetishism, Dean argues they inaccurately condemn racial fetishism as dehumanizing and neglect "the fundamental psychoanalytic insight that the vagaries of desire are determined by neither identity nor difference."[43] In the same piece that Dean singles out, McBride circumvents Dean's critique: "One of the dominant claims of that discourse [queer theory] is that attempts such as mine to politicize desire are tantamount to policing desire."[44] I find Dean's underestimation, if not repudiation, of racial difference strange, particularly when reading a race-play porn video like *Niggas' Revenge*. Bobby Blake, the adult entertainment industry legend, names *Niggas' Revenge* as "the most powerful movie of [his] career" and points to the salience of racial difference in the fetishistic imaginary; indeed, he cites this difference as being responsible for his successful career as porn star.[45] Blake recounts, "My persona, which had brought me so much success, was that of a certain type of black man, an aggressive, masculine top."[46] Similarly, David Savran argues that the eroticization and spectacularization of racial difference in BDSM pornography "unequivocally remains the product of an imperialist fantasmatic and often appeals (like most pornography and, more significant, like most American cultural productions) to racial and ethnic differences in constructing its erotic scenarios."[47]

Dean's important reading of racial fetishism in race-play pornography does not fully consider the relationship of race and disavowal so vital to racial fetishism as contested and as an affirmation *and* denial of difference.[48] Race-play pornography facilitates an ambivalent play of racial difference—a difference at once hyperbolized, mocked, dismantled, and profoundly played with—in which the fetishization of black corporeality is prominent.

Beyond Black and Blue: Vanessa Blue, FemdomX.com, and White Male Humiliation

Femdomx.com, which launched in 2004, is a hard-core BDSM website owned and operated by Vanessa Blue. The site presents a complex and contradictory negotiation of pain, pleasure, and power for the black female performer.[49] Blue and the performers on her website navigate a conflicted, violent terrain of gender, race, and sexuality, traversing antebellum legacies of black women's sexual violence and the feminist (largely lesbian feminist-led) debates about BDSM stemming from the late 1970s and early 1980s in which women of color, though marginalized, played a significant part. Blue is a veteran, highly accomplished black female porn performer whose websites feature primarily women of color.[50] In addition to performing on her website, she also directs and films much of the material herself. As Mireille Miller-Young notes, Blue's entrepreneurial role as a pornographer creates critical opportunities for self-authorship, "produc[ing] a space for black eroticism beyond the framework of stereotyped black sexuality in dominant porn."[51] In addition, Blue is candid and outspoken about racial discrimination in the industry, specifically the unique hardships black women face.

Femdomx.com is a progressive enterprise in terms of its expansion of roles for black women in the industry.[52] Blue "will never shoot a scene where the girl is anything less than in a position of power. There is enough product like that already."[53] She maintains that her femdom vision is about allowing "the girls to fuck back."[54] When speaking of her role as director/performer, Blue states, "I wanted to totally dig in on the girl power. I was able to take all of my ladies and empower them to fuck the way that they have been getting fucked in previous movies."[55] She seems to posit that BDSM performance is self-empowering and fosters sexual agency for black women. Yet despite championing what she calls the "power of the pussy," Blue says that she is not "interested in pushing any type of pro-black feminine agendas."[56] There is a curious inconsistency here. Firmly sited in the genre of black porn, employing predominately black women performers on her site, vocal about the discrimination of black women in the industry, and enunciating a seemingly feminist "fuck back" philosophy, Blue is not willing to "push any type of pro-black feminine agendas."[57] Her remark communicates an important ambivalence with regard to race that mirrors the industry's equivocal stance toward black women as simultaneously desired and disavowed. It also reflects Blue's careful and strategic negotiation of race within such an industry.

Femdomx.com features videos that range in severity from being invited to smoke a cigarette with partially clothed Blue as she reclines in bed to watching another black female performer get tickled to more elaborate and more violent scenes of domination, submission, fire play, and white male humiliation.[58] Larry Townsend, author of the pioneer BDSM guidebook *The Leatherman's Handbook* (1972), defines humiliation, a core element of BDSM practice, as "[a] conscious humbling of one partner by the other."[59] Humiliation is "the psychological counterpart to physical pain."[60] Practices of humiliation in BDSM include debased physical acts and verbal indignity. On Femdomx.com, race is a critical tool in the act of humiliation: the humiliation scenes on Blue's website can be categorized as a type of race play, though they are not explicitly marketed as such.

For example, in *Door 2 Door*, a seemingly inane video about a white insurance man named Major who is disconcerted by a scantily-clad horny woman (played by Blue) during a site visit, the story shifts quickly and dramatically to an incisive account of black-white interracial anxiety, aggression, and desire, specifically the ambivalent desirability of the black female body under the white heterosexual male gaze. The elaborately scripted scene includes two characters only: Blue and an unidentified middle-aged white male performer who plays Major, a novice insurance man whose agency has sent him to Blue's home to update her insurance policy. Blue plays an anonymous widow with a suspicious past (her last two houses have caught on fire and her husband died mysteriously after she took out a life insurance policy on him).

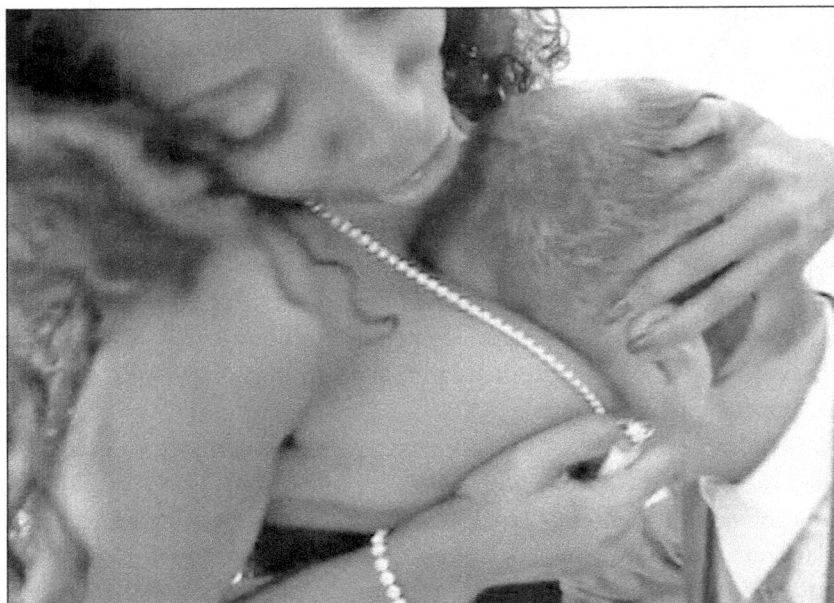

Figure 2.1. A scene from *Door 2 Door*

In the video, Blue chastens her white male partner physically and verbally, choking him with various body parts (breasts and buttocks in particular), and ridiculing him with remarks about the insufficient size and skill of his penis. The black female body is a key weapon in this BDSM scene: she commands him to "choke between [her] big Black tits" while she violently squeezes her breasts around his face, suffocating him. Here, blackness, as Blue repeatedly says to Major, is "too much." The hyperembodiment and corporeal excess of the black female body is evinced through visual effects and with language: close-up camera angles allow Blue's body to fill the frame and Blue repeatedly refers to her body parts as "big" and to her "blackness" as "too much."

Steeped in stereotype and racial hyperbole, such humiliation scenes rest on a volatile substratum of racial-sexual alterity. Though the staging of *Door 2 Door* is elaborate and reveals scripted, albeit quasi-comical, characterizations and plot lines, race emerges victorious as the crux of the BDSM scene. While black female sexuality is configured as superabundance, imbued with the power to make one choke, white male sexuality, which is also registered largely somatically, is portrayed as lack. However, black female sexuality emerges ambivalently as both deficiency and excess—the black female body's lack of desirability under the white male gaze and its somatic and libidinal superfluity. Blue continually badgers her white male sub about his genital inadequacy, specifically in relation to her own body. In turn, this corporeal excess of black female sexuality is displayed against white masculinity and presented as utterly deficient. That is, while a small penis is universally an undesirable characteristic in mainstream pornography, Major's small penis is especially problematic when confronted with the black female body and black female sexuality rendered as cavernous and rapacious. Humiliation scenes such as those in *Door 2 Door* illuminate both the racialized dynamics of violence in mainstream interracial pornography and the ways that race is explicitly evoked and used as an implement or a technology of BDSM.

Blue jokes that "punishing young white boys" is one of her favorite things to do on femdomx.com.[61] For Blue, such punishment is not discriminatory; on the contrary, she jests, "it's not racist, it's about spreading the love."[62] When asked if she considers her BDSM work as "trying to avenge hundreds of years of oppression," she responds, "only when I am fucking them in the ass."[63] Blue's sardonic responses reveal her awareness of the racialized codings of sex acts and her recognition of the possible uses of BDSM to destabilize conventional hierarchies of power (particularly within the context of mainstream American pornography)—for example, a black female sodomizing a white male. Indicating the affective catharsis such role-playing permits "women of color," she states, "As far as girls, I just try to shoot beautiful women of color. Most of us have a lot of pent-up anger anyway. It's just a matter of getting her to the point where she's comfortable enough to release it."[64] Blue presents the act of delivering pain as a release for pain carried in the flesh.[65] Like Fisher, Blue "imagines an interracial desire in which white[ness]can be objectified" as a vehicle for black pleasure and power and as a perverse remedy for (black) pain.[66] The essential, essentialized anger she suggests that women of color carry suggests an intimate understanding of black women's ambivalent position in the U.S. adult entertainment industry.

Race becomes essential in this type of humiliation scene, in which racial difference is fundamentally and stereotypically established and eroticized. *Door 2 Door* illuminates the ways that Internet pornography vividly reaffirms that in cyberspace, race is not a utopian transcendent space where we can elide or ignore the categories of race and gender as critical categories of power. Internet pornography is a ripe place to interrogate how these categories and their power dynamics function in the virtual realm as critical markers of human difference. Femodomx. com reaffirms how representations of the body in cyber-pornography are deeply embedded in the sociopolitical, historical, and material conditions of everyday life. On femdomx.com, myths of black female sexuality are reinvigorated at the same time that they are challenged and their utter performativity and construction are made hyaline. In humiliation scenes such as in *Door 2 Door*, power is not radically redefined as it is still legible in the rubric of domination and submission. However, it may be reclaimed for the black female in the scene, who has the power to humiliate a white man and to vocalize an acerbic critique of both black women's racial-sexual alterity and the binary of lust/disgust that characterizes responses to black female sexuality, especially under the heteronormative white male gaze. These dynamics of reinvigoration and challenge, reproduction and subversion represent a vibrant leitmotif pulsing through black women's BDSM race-play performance. Blue's performance and her commentary speak to the fantasies about and enactments of racialized violence (mytho-historically conceived) that sexual performance across the color line makes possible, particularly within the realm of BDSM pornography.

"I've become a bit fond of master": Slavery's Tether in the Mainstream Pornographic Race-Play Fantasy

Producer/performer Kelly Madison's *Get My Belt*, which was released on May 22, 2013, is a four-hour BDSM-themed hard-core pornography DVD that won BDSM Release of the Year at the 2014 XBIZ awards.[67] The DVD consists of four diverse BDSM vignettes starring four well-known female performers, all partnered with Ryan Madison, a performer who is Kelly's husband and business partner. Here I analyze in detail the closing race-play slavery vignette titled "The Final Chapter." It stars Ryan Madison as "Master" and black female porn star Skin Diamond as "Slave." In the scene, he drags her to a small rustic cabin to ravish her. Each "chapter" of the video is organized by the same (and very familiar) mainstream pornographic narrative sequence: "Fade Up," "BlowJob," "Sex," and "Cumshots." The repetitiveness of Madison's performed BDSM repertoire of sexualized aggression—deep throating, belt asphyxiation, hard-pounding vaginal and anal sex, and play with water—combined with the long duration of the vignettes (each of which averages approximately 50 minutes) and lack of dialogue compounds this monotony and renders the video somewhat tedious. These repeated sequences of sex and violence coupled with Madison's sexual stamina lend a Sadean quality to *Get My Belt*. Though he plays the dominant in every chapter, the eponymous belt—the narrative device that loosely ties together these divergent and at times inchoate D/S fantasies—dominates Madison and his performance.

In the multiple plays at work—age, religion, and water fetish—race emerges as dominant. As the scene with the most developed mise-en-scène—a clear, highly developed narrative; travel; multiple sophisticated sets; strong characterization; costumes; music; and dialogue—"The Final Chapter" ruptures the routine of *Get My Belt*.[68] The final vignette reinforces the erotic magnetism of chattel slavery and the ambivalence of its memory in the pornographic imaginary. Scenes of black-white erotic domination/ submission in race-play pornography often employ the mise-en-scène of chattel slavery, whether a literal rendering, as in *Get My Belt*, or a more symbolic and rhetorical conjuring, as in the final example I discuss in this chapter.[69] In this section I first offer a discussion of the main performer, Skin Diamond, and the critical reception of *Get My Belt* to contextualize my reading of race play in the DVD. The binary of fantasy/reality continues to police race play performance in BDSM pornography, while the memory of chattel slavery is a salient narrative force in the drama.

Often referred to as an "exotic beauty" in the press, Skin, who is of Ethiopian, Danish, Czech, Yugoslavian, and German descent, has recently risen to new heights of mainstream hard-core pornography stardom. She was named the Female Performer of the Year at the Urban X Awards in 2012 and Adult Video News nominated her as Best New Starlet in 2012 and as Female Performer of the Year in 2013 and 2014.[70] Born Raylin Christensen in 1987 in Ventura, California, where she lived until she was four, Skin lived in a good portion of her life in Scotland before returning to California in her early twenties. Her account of her "accidental" entry into porn resonates with the tale of many a young woman's entry into the industry.[71] She cites an unquenchable libido, a fondness for sex, and "complete exhibitionist" tendencies as what motivated her career in the adult entertainment industry.[72] Skin credits her early work in fetish modeling and "immersion in the fetish scene" as gateways to her entrance into BDSM porn.[73] With this professional background and "a personal preference" for BDSM, hard-core BDSM porn was, as she saw it, "just the next step."[74] Since her debut in hard-core porn with Burning Angel, she has worked with top names in the industry such as Penthouse, Vivid, Evil Angel, Elegant Angel, Kelly Madison Productions, Kink.com, and more.[75] Skin has also been successful in mainstream performance and modeling outside the adult entertainment industry.[76]

Skin signals how pornography is important in BDSM's invention and negotiation of the critical binaries of inside/outside and fantasy/reality. As "a self-described masochist"[77] who states that she is "heavily into BDSM,"[78] it might seem strange that she apparently did not know when asked in a live interview what the acronym "BDSM" stands for.[79] We might read this stumble as indicative of Skin's questionable knowledge of the BDSM she performs as a porn star.[80] Instead, I'd like to resist the pejorative impulse of the critical framing of authenticity that scholars such as Newmahr have relied upon to differentiate "real" BDSM from its pornographic rendition. For Newmahr, "*pornographic* SM" problematically invites what she terms "gawkers and wankers" within the BDSM community: "the wankers (men who attend SM clubs to masturbate while watching scenes) most clearly represent the boundary between the SM community and outsiders."[81] Newmahr asserts that pornography does not accurately represent the BDSM community and she stages this inauthenticity at multiple levels. First, mainstream porn typically depicts BDSM as kind of "alternative sex," when, Newmahr argues, BDSM is not fundamentally about sexual intercourse, at least as we conventionally imagine it.[82] Second, as Skin recognizes, porn subscribes to a beauty and body ideal that repudiates the "defiant bodies" of the BDSM community, which are often overweight, "geeky," and do not conform to hegemonic gender roles.[83] Newmahr marshals the policing technique of authenticity to partition lifestyle BDSM from its ersatz, perverse, fantastical pornographic version.

However, I find that such demarcation creates a kind of damning moral hierarchy of access, involvement, and spectatorship vis-à-vis BDSM and a continued pathologization of pornography and moral policing of pornographic fantasy. Within this hierarchy, porn performs its familiar perversity—it distorts and misrepresents that which it endeavors to represent. I do not seek to undermine the import of the BDSM community by arguing that there is no difference between those who are committed to the practice and the "wankers and gawkers" who come to the club on the weekends to, as Newmahr writes, "ejaculate in their pants and leave."[84] Rather, informed by a politics of perversion, I use Skin's failure to identify what the abbreviation "BDSM" stands for to critique the policing power of authenticity that the fantasy/reality dichotomy mobilizes. Instead, I would like to signal the multiple levels of BDSM performance and take note of BDSM pornography's thorny relationship to BDSM. Cautioned by the unrelenting discipline of black authenticity, especially in the realm of black sexuality, I remain wary of the policing of BDSM on the grounds of authenticity.[85]

Skin's transcontinental personal history and mixed ethnicity bolster her sexual capital. She seems very aware of this currency as a black female performer within an industry still governed by white ideals of feminine beauty and bodies, one that is, as she says, "dominated by the normal porno look: blondes with big boobs."[86] This "normal porno look" even or perhaps especially when artificially created (i.e., through hair coloring and breast augmentation) signals the racialized, gendered, sexualized somatic codes of belonging that pornography both reveals and engenders. Blonde hair and large breasts represent not just a particular racialized beauty hierarchy but also a claim to normalcy and humanity. Scholars such as Richard Dyer argue that the invisibility of whiteness as a racial position makes it possible for whites to claim that they are "normal" humans.[87]

With dark skin, dark hair, and a modest bust, Skin locates herself outside the bounds of the industry's corporeal normality. However, countless interviewers have referred to her "unique look" in ways that overlook the racial difference that is responsible for its legibility.[88] For example, *Fetish Buzz* magazine writes that "her skin and look is [*sic*] quite different from other models in the alternative genre, and renders [*sic*] her hard to forget."[89] *Adult Video News* says that "the fascinating element of this exotic beauty's background" is her transcontinental upbringing.[90] Another interviewer ascribes Skin's ranking as "one of the hottest girls in the industry" to her "different looks."[91] Skin herself states that "there's not really any girls that look like me in the industry."[92] In these recognitions of difference, blackness is the ghost in the room, a shadow seemingly recalcitrant to naming. Such descriptions communicate the way her racial difference is recognized, exoticized, and eroticized at the same time that blackness is paradoxically elided. In a familiar way, blackness is disavowed but nevertheless produces a racialized, sexualized difference. Skin recognizes, articulates, and strategically performs this difference in multiple arenas, perhaps beginning with her name.

Skin states she chose her name because it had a "really nice ring." However, I suggest that there is more behind such self-naming than sound.[93] The name "Skin" facilitates an exegesis of the dynamics of racial representation in pornography to elucidate both the strategic racial-sexual alterity she performs and the memory of racial-sexual violence of black womanhood that her BDSM pornographic performances engage.[94] Race play often involves a fetishization of the skin and other bodily features. Skin's name not only capitalizes on this fetishization but also effects a kind of race play, enacting a critical yet playful labor of racial difference.[95] Indeed, the names of black female porn stars have often performed this kind of racialized labor.[96]

The designation "Skin" signals the problematic logic of race that pornography maintains. Fanon reveals how skin color, specifically blackness, serves as a visual racial referent that marks one as black in an anti-black world. For Fanon, the skin is in a sense a trap, a violation of (black) humanity, and under its "racial epidermal schema" the black (male) body is "overdetermined from without"; black skin bears the psychic and somatic "distort[ions]" of anti-black racism.[97] Echoing Fanon, Homi Bhabha identifies the central and "common knowledge" role of skin in the quotidian postcolonial "racial drama" of otherness. Kobena Mercer similarly calls black skin "the most visible signifier of racial difference."[98] Skin's self-naming suggests that she is not only aware of the black body-as-object effected by the racial epidermal schema but also that she strategically mines and markets her embodiment of this objectification.

Skin signals the complex currency of black female sexual difference in pornography. While Fanon recognizes skin as a principal marker of blackness and of "lived experience," Paul Gilroy argues against such "dermo-politics."[99] Gilroy asserts that "today skin is no longer privileged as the threshold of either identity or particularity."[100] However, if, as Gilroy posits, "the boundaries of 'race' have moved across the threshold of the skin," contemporary mainstream pornography, as Skin's name epitomizes, might seem to disagree.[101] Skin's name and performance in *Get My Belt* illustrate pornography's continued fetishization of black skin as an erotic threshold to be delineated and crossed. While Skin's skin evinces a history of European colonialism and empire, her performance in *Get My Belt* portrays a distinctly American romance of coloniality. As I discuss further in the following chapter, since the stag genre of the early- to-mid-1900s, pornography has been deeply invested in representing transgressions of this "threshold of the skin," trespassing and mining the perceived boundary of black and white as a seemingly endless repository of eroticism.

The tension between Fanon's and Gilroy's theories of skin and race reflect larger historical shifts in epistemologies of race dating back to the transition in the seventeenth century from geography to skin color as a primary classification of race.[102] Unveiling the "economies of visibility" that are embedded in constructs of race and gender, Robyn Weigman elucidates the definition of race based on skin color as a technique of white supremacist ideology, analyzing how the visual "marks an epidermal hierarchy as the domain of natural difference."[103] Weigman contends that through the "visible taxonomy of the skin" we may witness the shifting disciplining of race itself.[104] Samira Kawash argues that skin is an ambivalent but salient marker of racial classification: "Race is on the skin, but the skin is the sign of something deeper, something hidden in the invisible interior of the organism (as organic or ontological). To see racial difference is therefore to see the bodily sign of race but also to see more than this sign, to see the interior difference it stands for."[105] S/skin limns the convergence of interior and exterior in the technique of racialization.[106] As an erotic racial fetish, skin articulates what is visible and what cannot be visible. Indeed, the racialization of skin is informed by the inside/outside binary that energizes BDSM.

Beyond challenging the racialized hegemonies of beauty and body that permeate the adult entertainment industry and conveying the epidermal technology of race, Skin's name contests the universality of whiteness within BDSM. The name stakes a particular claim for her as a black female performer within this space. While many public BDSM practitioners of color have exposed the marginalization and (in)visibility of people of color in the BDSM community, Weiss has recently analyzed how whiteness operates in the BDSM community as more than "a demographic issue." She sees it as "a nonracial, universal subject position in relation to the visibility of raced—nonwhite—practitioners" and argues that this universality perpetuates the multifaceted exclusion of people of color from the scene.[107]

If Skin's stage name signals the performativity of her own racial exoticism, it also summons the history of racial and sexual violence against black women, a history that her performance in *Get My Belt* recites. The name connotes the function of skin as a vehicle of history—a "principal medium that has carried the past into the present."[108] James Roach notes that skin simultaneously signifies a difference that is only "skin deep" and an essential "deep skin" that contradicts such difference.[109] Black women writers have documented this depth of skin—its existence as a site of memory, particularly the memory of the trauma of chattel slavery. Spillers considers this memory to be pain etched in the archives of flesh.[110] Toi Derricotte's statement that "the body has memory," resounds here, reverberating with Toni Morrison's concept of "skin memory."[111] Morrison describes skin as a site that chronicles the remembrance of pain and "the body's recollection of pleasure."[112] For Morrison, skin memory is distinctly sexual; the flesh is a palimpsest of sexual impression, "accumulating its own sexual memories like tattoos."[113]

The term "skin memory" encapsulates BDSM as a carnal-psychic index of pain and pleasure. Lynda Hart situates BDSM performance "between the body and the flesh." For Hart, the body and the flesh are two illusions that buttress the fantasy/reality cornerstone of BDSM. If the body is an invention of stability, an "anchor" in our quotidian realities, the flesh is a liminal site, an elusive, illusory "phantasmatic 'object' of our desire, as well as our longings for and resistances to merging the distinctions between the real and the phantasmatic."[114] Extending far deeper than the three layers of cells that constitute it, skin marks an ambiguous threshold of the body. Hart reads the flesh as a spatio-temporal entity that ambivalently mediates the already equivocal fantasy/reality divide that characterizes BDSM.[115] Deleuze argues that flesh is a central site of the masochist's subjection and practice. Drawing on this theoretical legacy, Amber Musser has recently revisited the flesh as representing the materiality of a difference that is neither fixed nor essential, but is rather in play. Like Skin, Musser spotlights the ways that flesh "oscillates between being a symptom of abjection and objectification and a territory ripe for reclamation."[116] Hence, the "ring" that attracted Skin to her stage name is indeed most sonorous. It resounds with the corporeality of BDSM, the complex epidermal logic of racialization, and the black female body's conflicted psychic and physical memory of the trauma of sexual violence under chattel slavery, all of which BDSM pornography dynamically engages, as *Get My Belt* illustrates.

History repeats itself. Debates waged about the alleged racism of *Get My Belt* in one online pornography community and shopping guide, Adult DVD Talk, uncannily reflect the feminist debates I discussed in the previous chapter surrounding whether BDSM reproduces or subverts racism. A forum on the site entitled "New Pornfidelity Scene a Bit Racist? Bad Taste?" discusses *Get My Belt*'s controversial race play, specifically its mining of the history of U.S. chattel slavery. Idlewild66 opens the conversation: "I know its just porn, but anyone else think this scene is a bit much."[117] The lack of a question mark punctuating this sentence facilitates its reading as a declarative statement of *Get My Belt*'s excess rather than a question about it. Ninja1 reconciles *Get My Belt*'s edginess with its technological sophistication, suggesting that the latter neutralizes the former: "It does seem over the line. But very impressive, technically. If all porn were this well-made I'd be spending lots more money on porn."[118] Reflecting the erotic forte of the black/white binary and the "sex factory" of chattel slavery, a9nostic states that "the slavery angle" is "too strong/juicy a taboo to let go."[119] The debate touches upon the embattled icons of BDSM and slavery—shackles and whips. Finally, one viewer compares *Get My Belt* to *The Night Porter* (dir. Liliana Cavani, 1974), drawing a parallel between BDSM's eroticization of Nazism and chattel slavery and posing the vexed yet persistent question of the black woman's unspeakable pleasure: "I mean could a black woman have a BDSM submitting fantasy?"[120]

Industry reviews of the video abound with advisories to those who sell and consume *Get My Belt*. The industry considered the video "different" and edgy for the Madisons, whose nearly decade-old hardcore porn website, Pornfidelty.com, is known for its "eclectic taste" but "lighthearted fare."[121] One review of *Get My Belt*, for example, encourages merchants to be careful about carrying the video and recommending it: "Be aware of your customer's sensibilities and stock and recommend accordingly."[122] Another warns, "This is some rough shit so viewer's [*sic*] beware!"[123] Others offered reassurances that the performers in *Get My Belt* consented willingly and experienced authentic pleasure. Kelly Madison Productions writes, "Get My Belt hits many controversial themes such as being held captive, struggles with desires of the flesh vs religion, Water BDSM, and slavery in which all the themes lead to one main theme, physical pleasure and sexual fulfillment of BOTH participants."[124] Such explications, as I discuss later, are familiar in the arena of hard-core BDSM porn. Yet it is not the "super rough sex," "extra-hard-hitting" scenes that "challeng[e] conventional limits of sexual relationships," or contentious themes such as religion and aggressive BDSM that such critical advisories attest to.[125] The cause célèbre here is race and its play in and with the memory of chattel slavery—a memory that is often evoked in the contemporary cinematic imaginary.

Indeed, the comeback Ed Guerrero predicted during a brief hiatus in the late 1980s following the 70-year reign of "the slavery motif and the plantation genre" in American narrative commercial cinema is upon us.[126] *Get My Belt* is evidence of pornography's long-established habit of borrowing from and parodying popular culture. Films such as *12 Years a Slave* (dir. Steve McQueen, 2013) and *Django Unchained* (dir. Tarantino, 2012) exemplify the renaissance of slavery as a theme in mainstream films. These recent films, particularly *Django*, boldly mimic the Blaxploitation genre and "attempt to recoup some of the cruder hegemonic manipulations and stereotypes depicted in the older films of the plantation genre."[127] Such stereotypes are vivid in films such as *Mandingo* (dir. Richard Fleischer, 1975) and *Passion Plantation* (dir. Mario Pinzauti, 1977), works that teeter on the lines between pornography, exploitation, and historical romance in their explicit depiction of interracial intimacy between blacks and whites in the context of an eroticized mise-en-scène of chattel slavery. Considering *Get My Belt* as plantation porn—an important extension of the plantation genre and not just indebted to it—reveals the already pornographic

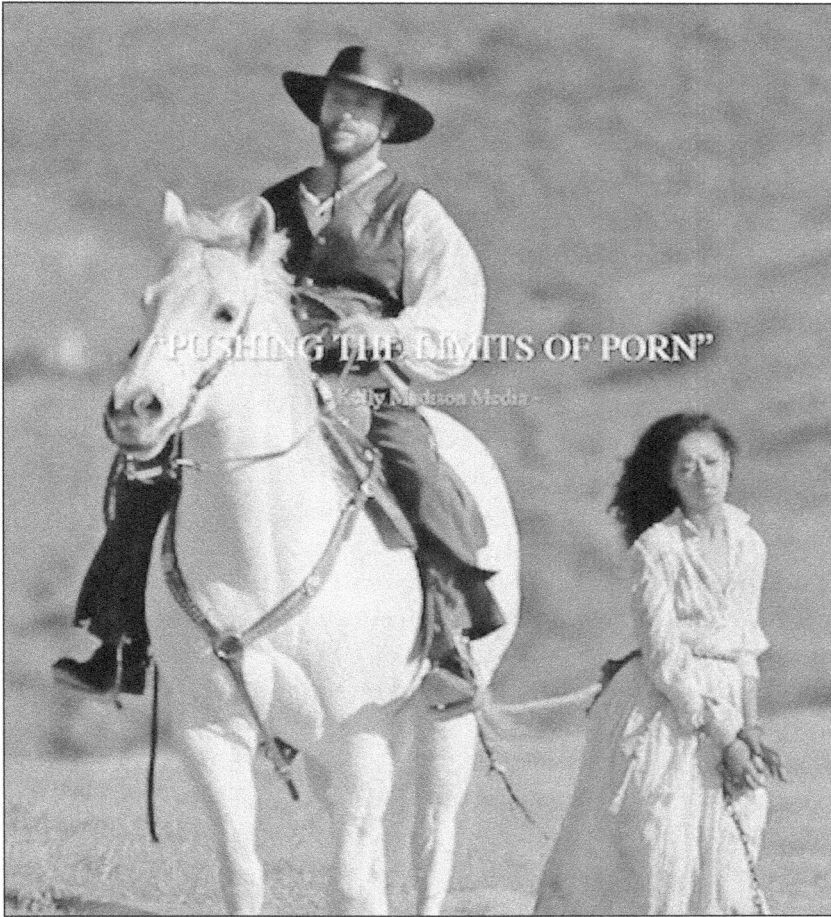

"PUSHING THE LIMITS OF PORN"

Figure 2.2. *Get My Belt*'s "Pushing the Limits of Porn"

place of slavery in the filmic imaginary. Pornography might be an ideal arena for staging slavery not only because of the erotic foundation or "sexual economy" of the peculiar, perpetual, institution but also because it is a genre less encumbered by the gaze of historical accuracy—the "fidelity to the truth of slavery"—that Jasmine Cobb has problematized in the neo-plantation genre.[128]

Get My Belt is part of the lineage of slavery films, most recently concluding with *Django*, a film it unabashedly appropriates in its aestheticization of chattel slavery, quasi-campy excess, melodrama, use of violence, racial hyperbole, and shocking revenge finale (which I will discuss in a moment). This mimicry is not lost on *Get My Belt*'s viewers, one of whom suggested an alternate title that humorously refers to this borrowing: "Djang-Ho Unchained."[129] *Get My Belt* is not the first porn film to explicitly borrow from Blaxploitation. Pornography maintains a fertile cross-pollination with the genre. *Lialeh* (dir. Barron Bericovichy, 1973), a film that many recognize as the first feature-length black hardcore film, stylistically, aesthetically, and thematically borrowed from the Blaxploitation genre. In turn, Blaxploitation offered vivid representations of a distinctly pornographic black sexuality to a mainstream cinematic audience, beginning in 1971 with Van Peebles's legendary *Sweet Sweetback's Baadasssss Song*, which was, in fact, made under the guise of a pornography film. Van Peebles recounts that "one of the security measures I had adopted was telling everyone I was making a nudie film."[130] Using the label of pornography, Van Peebles was able to employ non-union personnel and attract a certain type of actor who was willing to perform sexual acts in front of a camera and act in the nude. Peebles's language, "telling everyone I was making a nudie film," reveals that the alignment of porn and blaxploitation went beyond symbolic and/or ideological.

Get My Belt thematically, aesthetically and narratologically capitalizes on the slavery motif currently in vogue in American popular cinema, which is itself a realization of the erotic magnetism of this history.[131] Still, this is not Armond White's "torture porn," the condemnatory term the film critic uses to slam *12 Years a Slave* as a "shock fest" and "horror show."[132] White censors the film through the language of pornography and BDSM. Labeling it a work of "sadistic art" and "one-sided masochism," White scorns the entanglement of *12 Years* with violence and pleasure: "McQueen, Ridley and Gates' cast of existential victims won't do. Northup-renamed-Platt and especially the weeping mother Liza (Adepero Oduye) and multiply-abused Patsey (Lupita Nyong'o), are human whipping posts—beaten, humiliated, raped for our delectation just like Hirst's cut-up equine."[133] Similarly, in *Get My Belt*, pleasure and/in violence is instantiated on the body of the enslaved black female, Skin. White's rhetorical reliance on BDSM in his censure of the film is revealing: for him, BDSM is the reason for the film's "repugan[ce]" and "perversion." White signals, as *Get My Belt* exemplifies, that BDSM is a vibrant leitmotif within and vehicle for the performance of chattel slavery.

Part IV, "The Final Chapter," opens to a close-up of a tree trunk, then pans to display a rural western background—dry grass, rolling hills strewn with rocks, winding dirt paths, and low wiry shrubs that offer no cover from the glaring sun in a cloudless, cornflower-blue sky. The extra-diegetic sound of twangy guitar music punctuated by the hissing of rattlesnakes further stages the pastoral quality of the scene. Right away in this opening scene there seems to be some kind of slippage— aesthetic and aural—between plantation film and spaghetti western. In this mythological setting, *Get My Belt*'s imitation of *Django*, what Henry Louis Gates Jr. refers to as a "postmodern, slave-narrative Western," is clear.[134] If *Get My Belt* suffers from a kind of narratological confusion, it is impressive in its high production value, evidenced in crisp editing, aerial photography, soundtrack, elaborate sets, costumes, props, and so forth.[135]

Skin's voice immediately comes in to dominate this orchestra of sounds, as the two main characters, Skin and Madison, appear in the frame. At a slow gait, Madison, puffing a cigar and wearing a cowboy hat, a long-sleeved shirt, a vest, and leather riding chaps and boots, rides toward the camera on a white horse. The bright white of his shirt mirrors that of the horse's coat. Both glare in what looks to be a mid-day sun. He carries a long leather whip in his left hand; in his right, he holds a rope that leads to the waist of captive Skin, who trails behind him and his horse, wearing a loose faded dress and metal shackles at her hands and feet. In a voiceover, she states:

> We walked ten miles to Massa's new farm today. At first it was me and Zig but he fell too much and Master said he wouldn't be that much useful on the ranch if he couldn't walk. So we just left him there. I think he was just faking it so he could escape later. I should have done the same but I've become a bit fond of Master. At first it hurt a little, the lashes, but now I've grown to liking it.

This dialogue further differentiates this chapter of the DVD from the others, which are mostly dialogue free. It establishes Skin as "Slave" and

Ryan as her "Massa" and introduces the centrality of chattel slavery in *Get My Belt*'s race-play narrative.[136] This "grown-to-liking-it" casting of sex in the violent scene of domination/submission is familiar within multiple registers, including pornography. Anti-porn feminists have historically critiqued this framing of women's sexual pleasure using the concept of the rape myth, arguing that such rhetoric both reflects and perpetuates women's sexual abuse within the institution of hetero-sexist patriarchy.[137] In the antebellum milieu of racialized, sexualized domination and submission that the scene draws upon, this rape myth is forged differently, nuanced by the "sexual economy of slavery" in which the law's refusal to recognize the rape of an enslaved woman protected the social, political, and economic power of the plantation economy.[138] Reflecting this kind of historical impossibility of the enslaved black female's rape, Skin's language of "grown to liking it" articulates the profoundly ambiguous yet nonetheless critical labor of apparent consent that black women performed. As Saidiya Hartman argues, "The simulation of consent in the context of extreme domination was an orchestration intent upon making the captive body speak the master's truth as well as disproving the suffering of the enslaved."[139] Hartman argues that this simulation of not just consent but also of agency was central to the enslaved black body's constitutive function as "property of enjoyment," a vehicle of and for white pleasure.[140] Or, as Spillers puts it, "the captive body becomes the source of an irresistible, destructive sensuality."[141]

At the intersection of the pornographic and the antebellum, we can read Skin's "grown to liking it" as "speak[ing] the master's truth." However that reading does not necessarily account for the autonomy, albeit conflicted, of her pleasure and what *it* speaks, even as pleasure that problematically serves as a vehicle of consent. The possibility of her pleasure both complicates and is complicated by the negation of her will because of her status as "thing," as a slave.[142] Reenacting this antebellum "scene of subjection" in the twenty-first-century context of pornography brings into relief the vexed question of the enslaved black female's unspeakable pleasure and its messy entanglement with issues of consent, will, and agency. As Scott notes and as *Get My Belt* illustrates, such scenes "are consciously *spectacular* representations produced for the (sexual) excitement of those who consume them that call attention to, as *part* of the excitement, the historical processes of the production of racial difference through humiliation and domination."[143] BDSM pornography brings into relief the pornographic and sadomasochistic pleasures in racial difference to highlight the function of race as an eroticized technology of domination.[144]

Skin's articulation of her pleasure in race play echoes the voices of many black women BDSMers who express purportedly deviant desire. She states, "I feel like it gets me off more when it's so wrong."[145] Porn Fidelity discusses this conflicted pleasure in their description of *The Final Chapter*, writing that Skin is "tormented by the conflict of wanting to escape her abusive owner but loving the feel of his hard cock at the same time."[146] The taboo narrative of race play and the sheer physical aggressiveness of the scene heighten Skin's pleasure. Her statement that "I do really enjoy scenes that are more on the rough side" articulates the critical entanglement of pleasure and pain in her BDSM performance.[147] For her, pain seems to be about both bodily sexual pleasure and a kind of emotional gain or psychic triumph. She states, "But I get so much more satisfaction when I have to suffer through something and overcome it! It makes me feel strong and makes me realize how tough I am! Also, when you[r] body is experiencing that much pain, it releases a lot of endorphins which makes for more intense orgasms."[148] Skin communicates an understanding of race play that is not necessarily therapeutic, but one that encompasses a kind of redemptive suffering that engenders feelings of agency and power. Elaine Scarry has argued that agency is a physical experience of bodily pain.[149] In addition to articulating the effect of the physiological response to pain and its mimicry of sexual arousal through the release of endorphins, elevated blood pressure and pulse, muscular tautness, and increased breath rate, Skin articulates what Karen Halttunen terms the "pornography of pain," the entanglement of revulsion and arousal that marks the representation and experience of pain as taboo in modernity.[150] Revealing the ways that the civilizing project of humanitarian reform influenced the Anglo-American sociocultural construction of pain as "obscenely titillating," Halttunen argues that "the pornography of pain" emerged in the late nineteenth and early twentieth centuries as humanitarian reform that paradoxically produced the obscenity of pain that it morally policed in popular culture.[151]

Skin's voiceover prompts a flashback as we cut to an image of her nude body suspended by the arms from a tree as she enjoys the lashes of the whip. The camera zooms in on her bare breasts glistening with sweat. With every crack of the whip, she winces and moans. Her voiceover continues, now in direct, albeit conflicted, mediation of the enactment of eroticized violence. She says, "To be honest, I kind of like the things he does to me but that don't mean I wouldn't escape first chance I got." One review of *Get My Belt* fashions this statement as the Madisons' deliberate attempt to assert some kind of enslaved black female autonomy in amelioration of their explicit eroticization of slavery.[152] While this carefully scripted dialogue represents in part the Madisons' careful efforts to explicitly articulate Skin's pleasure in this play of race, her words also underline the ambivalence of pleasure, signal the complex and complicit libidinal and political economies in pornography's play of race, and set up the surprise ending of *Get My Belt*.

Following this whipping analepsis, Master drags Slave by a belt around her neck into a rustic wood cabin on a dude ranch, where the sex acts and most of the chapter take place, after the elaborate opening credits, which include an impressive montage of footage and an original musical score. Skin (who is now almost completely naked) is intricately bound to the wall by her arms and legs with various belts. Madison gets up from his seat at nearby table, where he tinkers angrily with metal tools and knives and commands Skin to meet his gaze: "Look at me!" When she will not, he raises his voice, yells at her again, then throws a knife into the wall, just missing the left side of her face. He pulls the knife out of the wall to trace the blade against her face, then begins to lick her face. His licking explicitly initiates what was up until now implicit yet clear—the "Massa's" sexual desire for his slave. He goes down on her, then violently unlashes her from the wall, only to bind her again with a long sisal rope to a wooden chair where the sex begins, after some whiskey-lubricated oral sex and finger penetration. Through many different sexual and spatial positions—from the chair to the floor to the bed and back to the floor, where the sex finishes—Madison's sexual repertory and dominant aggressive style of fucking is well established. He is both relentless and episodic: jackhammer fast at times, slow and deliberate at others.

When the sex begins, the storyline dwindles. There is no real dialogue for the remainder of "The Final Chapter." The play of race is less audio and more visual, staged, in the context of near-silence, by the mise-en-scène of the cabin.[153] Its wooden-planked interior is sparingly

Figure 2.3. Skin and Master inside the cabin

decorated with various accents to stage the imagined antebellum scene in which this coital encounter between Master and Slave is enacted—lanterns, horseshoes, a wooden bucket, a tattered woven rug, wood chips scattered on the wooden floor, and a small single bed. In this space, wearing no costumes but their skin(s), the bodies remain legible as Master and Slave.

The sex ends with them fucking frantically on the floor in missionary style with her head resting on the saddle. Apparently physically exhausted, Slave asks Master to "please come inside [her]," which he presumably does before dismounting, then crumbling, seemingly enervated, next to the bed. In a post-orgasmic stupor and with his back to her and the camera, Master is unable to defend himself when Slave grabs eponymous belt from the floor, puts it around his neck, and strangles him. The scourge is finally in the hands of the "other." Just as she grabs the belt, the music cuts in again, similar to the extra-diegetic twangy guitar that played in the opening scene, although here it is more adventurous, joined by an upbeat horn to sound a suitable anthem of avenge. Skin sits on the bed for a moment, smooths her hair as if to collect herself, then grabs his hat, dusts it off, and puts it on her head—an act which prompts another music change. She stands up, walks to the edge of the bed, and lifts her right leg to release a substantial amount of fluid from her vagina on his forehead. Then she spits on him, calls him an asshole, and walks outside the frame of the camera.

The next scene cuts outside to Skin, topless and gallantly galloping on Master's white horse as the rolling hills fade in the distance. Skin, a former equestrian vaulter in high school, is a skilled rider.[154] The freedom with which her bare breasts bounce mirror her newly gained liberation. The submissive becomes the dominant. Skin uses the master's tools to kill the master. The belt as a fetishistic object that symbolizes her eroticized submission is transformed into an object that facilitates her domination of her master. In this act, *Get My Belt* resembles *Django* and imitates the mercurial social hierarchies of the Blaxploitation and spaghetti western genres. It also reflects the fluidity of power roles such as top and bottom in BDSM.[155] After Skin rides out of the frame the screen goes black momentarily to showcase the pornfidelity.com logo before cutting back to Madison inside the cabin. His eyes dramatically flash open with the extra-diegetic sound of loud a keyboard note before the screen goes black again.

More than a campy horror-film-esque finale, *Get My Belt*'s dramatic revenge ending is a critical part of the play of race and a unique racialized rendition of the pornographic money shot.[156] Here the money shot is scripted by the reversal of the racialized dynamics of domination and submission, master and slave. I offer a more comprehensive reading of the money shot and female ejaculation in chapter 4, but for now, the money shot or cum shot, a salient spectacle in U.S. hard-core moving-image porn, provides visual evidence of the "truth" of conventionally male sexual pleasure.[157] While the money shot serves the function in pornography as "narrative closure," here it also is a critical theoretical aperture through which we see the complex dynamics of racialized and gendered pleasure and power at play in the film.[158] In this vengeance finale, both the conventional gender dynamics of the money shot (i.e., she "ejaculates" on his face) and the racialized power dynamics that script the master-slave encounter are reversed. Narratives of racialized revenge are central in interracial pornography, and BDSM is an apt lens through which to read these dramas.

Semi-clear and viscous, the fluid Skin releases onto Madison's face, whether her own ejaculate, his cum, or a combination of both, symbolizes racialized revenge. Like Blue's performance of racially charged domination, this performance is structured by a racial revenge that underscores the volatility of race play and the veering racial and gender dynamics of power that electrify its precarious boundaries. Here the money shot is both visual evidence of male and/or female pleasure and part of the narrative of racialized aggression between "Master" and "Slave." Read as female ejaculation, the act is a visual testimony of her unspeakable pleasure in the "monstrous intimacies" of racialized sexual domination and submission that have just taken place.[159] The fact that it takes place after the sex is over reflects Deleuze's theorization of masochism in which the orgasm—which is never the masochist's objective—is postponed.[160] We might read this finale as a triple murder. Madison's death (actual or attempted) is framed by "la petite mort" that precedes it: his and her orgasm. Read as a kind of regurgitation of his ejaculate in which she performs the money shot to make his pleasure visible to the audience, the act is a mediation and critical repudiation of his pleasure. Her rejection of his semen is a deed that rejects her body as the place of/ for his pleasure. Here, the ever-ringing words of June Jordan become a kind of alternative extra-diegetic soundtrack: "[she] [does] not consent." Skin's body will not carry the "evidence of slime."

Amateur Race-Play Pornography

Danny Sisko, the owner of Pudding Foot Productions, is an amateur independent black male race-play porn producer who specializes in black-white lesbian race play and (inter)racial domination, specifically black female humiliation. He has been producing and selling race-play video pornography since February 2012 and aims "to be the number one provider of black race play."[161] Sisko's own personal fetish of race play motivated his entrance into production; producing race-play pornography emerged as a solution to the difficulty of the "live" practice for him. Because of the forbidden quality of the practice, he struggled to find play partners and "decided to start making videos so I can enjoy the experience over and over again."[162] Though he began making the videos for his "own enjoyment" and consumption, high production costs led him to for-profit production. He states, "I always fantasized about creating a business that could make money at doing what I love to do."[163] Sisko, who is not professionally trained in videography, does "everything" at Pudding Foot Productions, including filming, writing, directing, and editing. The primary challenge for him is production: "It's very time consuming. I try to spend an hour a day on it." Sisko notes the difficulty of finding "avenues for marketing" his race play pornography because "many web sites and other social media outlets ban it or flag it and people get offended by it."[164] His account of these obstacles highlights the challenge race play presents to the device of fantasy and a particular moral code of sexuality. Because of what he calls the "taboo nature" of race play, he recognizes that "race play [porn] is an underserved niche."[165]

Sisko imagines himself as capitalizing on the sociocultural proscription of race play. He states, "And you know, so people who find me, they tend to be overjoyed that they have this content."[166] In addition to producing his own videos, Sisko makes custom race-play videos that cater to consumers' individual fantasies. He views custom video production as enabling him to bring to life the race-play fantasies of others and make a profit. His race-play videos, sold as clips or as full-length videos, are available on the popular pornography website clipsforsale.com. His eighteen race-play videos present a range of narratives, mise-en-scènes, video quality, performers, and duration.[167] What unites this diverse collection is the performance of black female racial-sexual abjection. Sisko's race-play pornography reflects his own "personal preference" for "black racial humiliation."[168]

Black female sexuality occupies the literal and figurative bottom in Sisko's race-play pornography: "My fetish videos feature interracial lesbian femdom domination. The femdoms I use are primarily white women, and the submissives are primarily black women. I also use other nationalities as femdoms such as Hispanic and Asian women, but I normally always use black women as the submissives."[169] His use of predominately white female tops with black female bottoms reifies the erotic magnetism of the black/white binary. These statements corroborate how black womanhood operates for Sisko and within his work as a seemingly stable signifier of racialized debasement and racial-sexual alterity.

As in Blue's femdomx.com, race here becomes a fundamental tool of BDSM. The racial-sexual currency of black womanhood heightens the level of humiliation, making the race play "extra erotic," in Sisko's words.[170] While Sisko notes that the racialized humiliation of black womanhood is very much a personal fetish, he believes that black female abjection appeals more universally, because of the history of chattel slavery and racism:

> I think I like to see the black woman on the bottom because I just think it intensifies the injustice and the cruelty of the, you know, the whole domination experience, you know. I just think there's something to do with, like I said, the cruelness of it all that, you know with slavery and the history of racism in this country and the injustices that have gone on. I think that it just kind of intensifies the humiliation factor in the whole paradigm.[171]

His statement reinforces the erotic currency of chattel slavery in the BDSM play of race. In referring to "slavery and the history of racism," Sisko complicates the rubric of fantasy in which he situates his race play pornography. Reading race play though a pornographic intermediary reveals familiar elements—the salience of the history of chattel slavery in our erotic imaginary, black women as representatives of this history, the enduring tension of the fantasy/reality binary, and the continued disciplining of black sexuality. Sisko's race-play pornography sketches the physical and metaphorical boundaries of race play to demonstrate how pornography's dynamic play of race is multifaceted and complex, encompassing more than the performances in front of the camera.

While *Get My Belt*'s race play is explicitly sexual (following the edicts of the genre of mainstream hard-core porn), Sisko's amateur race play is less sexually hard core and more explicit with regard to racial play, consistently using graphic racial language and stereotypes. Scott finds that "the more commercial and mainstream the black-white porn story (i.e. the more likely you can pick up a magazine from a rack in a store and read a porn story in it), the more muted such racial hyperbole is."[172] As I reveal here, this racial hyperbole is not without its anxiety and ambivalence. We might read this lack of explicit conventional "sex" and sexual pleasure as characteristic of masochism itself. Deleuze for example, separates sexual fulfillment and masochism, identifying it as a mode of suspense and delay, "a state of waiting."[173] He argues that "disavowal, suspense, waiting, fetishism, and fantasy together make up the specific constellation of masochism."[174] Similarly, Studlar contends that the "masochistic aesthetic" is comprised of the elements of "fantasy, disavowal, fetishism, and suspense."[175] Most of Sisko's race-play videos lack genital penetration and might be read as instantiating BDSM's polymorphous perversity and degenitalization of pleasure.

Sisko's videos begin with a textual warning and disclaimer. These seek to preempt the audience's assumption that the acts on screen reflect the racial politics of the producer and/or performers. The following two statements appear on a black screen in bold red and white letters:

Warning
This video contains hardcore racial humiliation with racial slurs, if you are offended by such content, do not watch this video.

Disclaimer
This video was made for those who have a fantasy race play fetish; the actors are only role playing and the action is simulated.

The makers of this video had no intention to degrade or offend any race, but cater to those who enjoy race play. Neither the actors nor the producers of this video are racist.

Such warnings are common in BDSM pornography and other types of extreme hard-core pornography.[176] Underlying these warnings is the long-standing question of whether pornography does harm to performers, to producers, and to viewers. Warnings preemptively serve to mediate this harm, which is especially a concern in the genre of bareback pornography and its potential to propagate HIV.[177] They are engendered by a desire to disclaim the belief that pornography might be accountable for shaping the behavior of viewers, even though it is this very belief such warnings seek to deny.[178] These warnings are thus predicated upon a kind of responsibility and denial performed through the construct of the fantasy/reality binary.

Like other black BDSMers who express their race-play fantasies, Sisko uses the rhetoric of fantasy to resituate race play within a (purportedly) insular, depoliticized, and protected space. Sisko's disclaimer that his work is fantasy attempts to mediate, if not mitigate, pornography's purported harm. First, it serves to block potentially offended viewers before they enter into the cyberworld of race play pornography. Second, it doubly exploits the rubric of fantasy with its assertion that the videos are both the product of fantasy and are produced for likeminded people who share that fantasy. Sisko's disclaimers originated from a space of personal fear:

> Honestly, when I put out my first video I was incredibly scared to do it. Because I felt that there'd be a big backlash and I thought the ACLU would come after me. And Jessie Jackson and everyone else would, you know, rise up against me. And I was incredibly scared of a backlash and the taboo nature of the whole subject, especially being a black man. So I felt I needed to put that disclaimer just so that people know that, you know, hey, this is just a sexual fantasy. It's nothing real about it. I don't mean any harm to any black woman or just any black people or anybody that is offended by this, by this content. I just am trying to fulfill a fantasy and that's all it is: a fantasy for people that have this fetish.[179]

Anxiously engaging the rhetoric of fantasy, this disclaimer manifests as a kind of self-policing that introduces the salient themes of the fantasy/reality divide and the racial-sexual discipline that charge the fraught play of race in Sisko's pornography.

Reverberating with long-standing debates about race play in the BDSM community, these warnings echo historical advisories in the context of live BDSM performance, pedagogy, and protocol. In 2004, prompted by the enduring controversy of race play, The Eulenspiegel Society (TES), which is recognized as the oldest BDSM community support and educational group in the United States (it was founded in 1971), issued a warning as part of their annual TES Fest Edge Play Track.[180] The programming chair, Lolita Wolf, was inundated with complaints about a race-play workshop entitled "Nigger Play: Free at Last!" that was led by black male BDSM educator and self-identified masochist Mike Bond.[181] The majority of these grievances objected to the use of the word "nigger" in the workshop's title.[182] In response, Wolf wrote she was reluctant to "censor" TES's use of the word "nigger" because of the organization's reputation for negotiating the vanguard of BDSM play.[183] To resolve this quandary Wolf instituted a warning that accompanied the TES Fest class schedules that year:

> WARNING: This track contains material that may be offensive or objectionable to some people. We respect your rights to make choices about which workshops you would like to attend. If you are uncomfortable or disturbed by any of these topics, please move on to something that does interest you and do not click on the links below for more information. Remember there are more than 65 other workshops at TES Fest 04.[184]

This warning speaks loudly about race in its silencing of race. That is, as in the exchanges regarding Skin Diamond's elusive difference, here blackness fails to be explicitly named. Indeed, the generality of this warning belies the centrality of race in the politics of BDSM pedagogy and practice. It is significant that more than three decades since the formation of TES, an organization known for charting the transgressive edges of BDSM, race was the issue that prompted such an advisory. Even as "nigger" is invited to the space of play, s/he is jettisoned from the scene. This demonstrates what Robert F. Reid-Pharr identifies as a paradox of Occidental modernity: that "the nigger is absent even and especially when his body is present."[185]

As reflected in Bond's incendiary workshop title "Nigger Play: Free at Last!," the word "nigger" is "central to the play" in delineating the specific type of play he teaches.[186] Nigger play refers to a particular submissive mode of eroticized black abjection, that, as he is clear to articulate, does not include the "black over white model, except to make this point: submissive white men have always had the freedom to engage in their form of 'affirmative action' race play at the hands of 'powerful black women.' It's considered cute and PC."[187] Bond argues that white male submissives enjoy a privilege in performing race play that black subs do not: "It's also considered cute for them to take it from a white mistress in the form of a 'big black dildo' or little white penis ridicule. Black slaves/submissives/bottoms on the other hand have traditionally been shackled by other people's political correctness in the exercise of our expression."[188] He illuminates the racialized and gendered power dynamics that discipline race play. In using the word "free" in the title, Bond refers not to the affective freedom race play potentially engenders but rather to the increased acceptance of race play in BDSM communities—"how the 'fetish' of nigger play has gained freedom in the last three years in BDSM circles around the country as reflected in all the classes myself and others have taught."[189] Bond envisions his nigger-play pedagogy as an urgent intervention into the marginalization and discrimination of black people in the BDSM community: "The whole point of this class and my contributions to the race play movement has been to ADVANCE black rights in BDSM."[190]

Similarly, for Sisko, the word "nigger"—although he codes it as a "racial slur" in his introductory warning—maintains an urgent presence in his race-play performance. In Sisko's work, the term "nigger" symbolically enacts the psychic and physical labor of a return to the traumatic past while highlighting the possibilities of pleasure in this history/present. It cues the simultaneous "degradation" and erotic zenith of black womanhood. Both Sisko and Bond maintain an investment in what Randall Kennedy, in his study of the "paradigmatic slur," terms "the most socially consequential racial insult."[191] Both cite the indispensable labor of this slur in the play of race. The word "nigger" is an utterance that sounds the entanglement of pain and pleasure that race play performs. It limns an ambivalent return to a painful history in which "the traumatic past is exacerbated as it is also soothed."[192]

The TES nigger controversy sheds light on the racialized and gendered politics of BDSM, illuminating the vital ways race informs the practice to expose how the purportedly universal creed of BDSM consent is not so generic and comprehensive as one might think. For black BDSMers, consent is often *not* a kind of neoliberal individual agreement, but a larger contract that includes a responsibility to some phantasmatic black community, allegiance to an invention of black authenticity, and homage to a particular recognition of history. Bond argues that indictments against the word "nigger" and nigger play reflect a "woeful misunderstanding of SSC—consent."[193] He asserts, "Consent is a kink doctrine that applies between BDSM player one, two or three. It is not a call for a player to seek the permission for whatever community claims him or her. . . . Why use consent to create special censorship rules for blacks?"[194] Blackness profoundly complicates the terms of BDSM, even as it lays them bare.

Perhaps mirroring the caveats that commence Sisko's pornography, in an effort to resist the pathologization of Sisko and his work and/or condemn his treatment of black women, I'd like to document more of his own conceptualization of his race play. He does not feel that such interracial domination is at odds with his affection or respect for black women, maintaining, "I don't hate black women."[195] Sisko proclaims:

> I am an artist at heart and I believe that it's coming through in my work and, you know, I just wanted to reiterate that, you know, I'm not trying to disrespect black women or, you know, or to hurt them in any way. It's just a fetish I have. I you know I love black women but at the same time I don't know why . . . it's just a humiliation factor that is the reason that I do this.[196]

In articulating that interracial domination and black female humiliation are fetishes for him, he signals the discipline of sexual pleasure and fantasy. His effort at etiology contradicts the kind of aberrancy he attempts to circumvent by citing his "love" for black women. The continuing need to explain purportedly abnormal pleasures by those who relish in practicing them and/or those who seek to scientifically asses them often reifies the deviance it seeks to dismantle, further strengthening the dichotomy of normal/abnormal. Aided by a politics of perversion, I seek not to explain race play but to elucidate the multiple ways it may be experienced and how it illuminates the experience of black female sexuality.

The prominence of the "humiliation factor" in Sisko's race-play pornography is exemplified in *Get Out of My Town* (dir. Danny Sisko, 2012), a video that stars Mistress Betty Sue and Slave Mabel. The story is loosely premised on Betty Sue's racist objection to the fact that Mabel is staying in the same motel as she is. When the KKK notifies her that there is a "nigger bitch" on the premises, Betty Sue visits Mabel's room to forcefully evict her. *Get Out of My Town* eroticizes the violent racial discipline of the black female body in the space of whiteness. Another one of his best-selling race play videos, *Nigger 911* (dir. Danny Sisko,

2012), a custom video, similarly depicts the sexualized policing of the black female body at the hands of the white female. In *Nigger 911*, Mistress Francheska plays a cop who visits the home of Slave Coco, whom she suspects is guilty of the recent crimes in the neighborhood. Shortly after interrogation, the punishment begins. Both videos speak to longstanding stereotypes about blackness, criminality, and contamination hinged on black female sexuality. Sisko's work signals the racial-sexual geography at work in race play, its eroticized demarcation and policing of racialized space. As is evident in Vanessa Blue's *Door 2 Door*, in *Get Out of My Town* race is integral to both the technique of BDSM and the pornographic narrative, indeed seeming to not only eclipse but also to *become* the narrative.

Get Out of My Town begins with a knock on a motel-room door. The room is small and modest, with bright blue walls, garish floral bedspreads, window curtains hanging off the track, and an old box television. Slave Mabel, a large-breasted black woman wearing a black halter chemise, answers the door. She asks, "Who is it?" When no one replies, she opens the door. An equally large-breasted white woman wearing a leopard-bra top and cut-off jean shorts stands in the doorway. She introduces herself as Mistress Betty Sue and immediately states the reason for her visit. In a poorly affected southern accent that will not endure the duration of the 37-minute video, she states, "The KKK told me there's a nigger bitch in our motel here, and we don't have nigger bitches in our hotel here and you look like a nigger bitch to me. You look like Aunt Jemima, by the way." Her acerbic words are belied her physical demeanor: smiling, batting her eyelashes, and flipping her dirty-blond hair, she is saucy. This incongruity evidences the *play* of race and the pleasure of its play.

Here, the nigger identity is contested even as it is embraced. Mabel retorts, "Well, you know this is one Aunt Jemima bitch that would taste good melted in your mouth." This statement is representative of the kind of sexualized race pride she initially asserts to counteract Betty Sue's debasement of black womanhood. That is, Mabel avows a kind of black sexual supremacy in response to Betty Sue's anti-black racism and shaming of black female sexuality. For example, she declares that would never have sex with "honkeys," that "once you go black you never go back," and that "the darker the berry, the sweeter the juice." Betty

Figure 2.4. *Get Out of My Town*

Sue becomes more aggressive in response to these rejoinders. She enters the hotel room, closes the door behind her, and restates her purpose: "We don't take niggers here. You need to go back, back to roots, back to the Kunta Kinte, back to the plantation houses. I think there's a place in Charleston waiting for you right now; I can book you flight real quick. Screw the flight. You're taking the bus!" Though Mabel holds her ground, replying, "I am not taking a bus. I am not taking a plane. I am not taking a train, because I am staying right here," Betty Sue grabs her by the neck, pushes her down onto one of the double beds, mounts her stomach, and slaps her face. This moment marks a turning point in the video: the physicality of the race play dominates the rest of the scene and the demeanor of both women changes. Betty Sue asserts her dominance becoming physically aggressive while Mabel becomes verbally and physically submissive.

The bed serves as the physical stage for the erotic play of race. Though there is no sex that would be legible in mainstream pornography (both leave on what little clothes they had on at the beginning of the video),except that Betty Sue forces Mabel to lick her toes, the scene is distinctly erotic because of the sexualized violence—physical and verbal—of race play. Betty Sue grabs Mabel's hair, pulls her head into her groin, and squeezes her thick thighs tightly around Mabel's head. She demands, "How close have you been to a white crotch? Have you ever been this close to a white crotch? Huh? I think you like this. You like this, Aunt Jemima!" Mabel moans, cries, and laughs alternatively while Betty Sue proceeds to pin her down on the bed in a variety of elaborate leg restraints that limit Mabel's mobility and at times restrict her airway, becoming a kind of breath play. Kicking, slapping, and stomping on various parts of Mabel's body, Betty Sue relies on a litany of trite stereotypes in her humiliation of Mabel. "Tar baby," "Aunt Jemima," "nappy," "little cocoa," and of course "nigger" assume their rotation in this racial-sexual drama. In their repetition, these erotic epithets are revealed to be performative utterances of black female racial-sexual alterity.

Race play illuminates the slippery mix of degradation and pleasure that these stereotypes elicit. Betty Sue explicitly acknowledges such pleasure: "I haven't had this much fun since we lassoed a bunch a niggers a few months ago, took 'em down to the rodeo, rode 'em like a bunch a bulls. It was lots of fun." Because of Mabel's limited dialogue after the first few minutes of video, we must attempt to "read" pleasure on the text of her body. While she does smile intermittently, it is difficult to interpret whether these smiles indicate enjoyment, nervous laughter at the audacity of Mabel's comments, or both. Furthermore, as is characteristic of top/bottom BDSM dynamics, Mabel's pleasure as a submissive is policed by Betty Sue as a dominant. When Mabel laughs, she is further punished. Straddling and ramming her breasts into Mabel's face, Betty Sue says, "Nigger bitch, nigger fucking bitch. Here, you want to laugh at something? I'll give you something to laugh at, then." If the question of whether Mabel is experiencing pleasure is unanswered, the erotic ebullience of racism is undeniable. Indeed, what is so incisive about this video is its ability to capture the profound tension in race play between seriousness and camp. *Get Out of My Town* demonstrates an uncanny ability to illuminate the delight of black female racial abjection within the context of race play, enacting malignant racism as light-hearted play. Mabel enacts this dialectic by grinning, laughing, and bouncing around the bed while simultaneously uttering "black nigger bitch ho!" with, at times, a chilling quietness.

This tension mirrors *Get Out of My Town*'s slippage between fantasy and reality, between acting, and authenticity, that Sisko identifies among his performers. He hires women who range from professional domina-trices and pornography performers to wrestlers to complete amateurs with respect to both pornography and BDSM performance, and the "taboo nature" of race play presents itself again because of how Sisko casts his videos. He explains he has to occasionally "limit the race play" because of some women's reluctance to perform it. For Sisko, whether or not his performers can successfully execute race play "depends on their acting skills." He states, "I mean, it kind of just depends if they're a natural or not. You know, as far as acting; it's all acting." Yet his un-stable delineation of "natural" versus "acting" betrays his assertion that race play is "all acting." His framework recalls the tension Mollena Wil-liams identifies between conscious, consensual race play and a more quotidian, automatic race play. On the surface, Sisko seems to be com-municating a common perception about acting—that "good" race-play performance, like successful acting, engenders a kind of natural effect. However, I would like to push us to consider this naturalness in the con-text of more than a performer's acting ability; I would like us to consider it in the context of racism itself.

Sisko's description of Betty Sue's race-play performance brings this critical tension between the natural and acting into high relief: "Betty Sue is a very experienced wrestler and dominatrix, so she pretty much came up with all the material on her own. She's a natural at coming up with the content and role play."[197] This tension between the idea of Betty Sue as "natural" and the idea that she is an experienced pro-fessional touches upon both the fantasy/realty dialectic of BDSM and the profound tension of race itself as both essential and socially con-structed. Race play, as Sisko narrates, elucidates the simultaneous natu-ralness and pedagogy of race and racism. To foster the production of this "naturalness," he does not typically write a script but instead allows the performers to ad lib: "I just give them like a theme and then a plot and I tell them to basically, you know, run with it."[198] Race play is a kind of "improvisation" whose success depends on the rehearsal of a repertoire of essential stereotypes that attempt to distill a quintessence of race even as they demand that it is fiction. Betty Sue's remarkable and energetic race play is a violent policing of the space of whiteness that invokes an impressive sampling of historic oppressive images of black womanhood that includes references to the KKK, *Roots*, and the antebellum plantation. These unscripted narratives of race play draw upon the scripts of black female abjection etched in our erotic imaginaries while gesturing toward the ways these texts must be tended, revisited, and anxiously re-played.

This tension is also evident in a recent post on Sisko's blog in which he describes his experience at a race-play shoot at the 2014 AVN Adult Entertainment Expo in Las Vegas and contrasts the race-play ability of two female performers, Cheyenne Jewel (white) and Astrokittie (Asian). Cheyenne demonstrates a familiarity and experience with race play that betrays Sisko's attempt to quantify it as "all acting." He writes, "Cheyenne Jewel . . . is no stranger to race play. She could degrade and racially humiliate Black people with the best of them. She was saying things that I wish I had thought of. She is an amazing actress with the ability to show no mercy or empathy for her submissives."[199] In contrast, Astrokittie, whom Sisko also describes as a talented actress, struggles with race play. He explains, "Astrokittie did a pretty good job, and is a great actress, but seemed a little gun shy with the race play. I think she was a little uncomfortable with it. She kept referring to Quida as 'Black girl'; I had to keep reminding her to refer to Quida as a 'Nigger, Ape, Monkey, or Gorilla,' which she eventually did."[200] Of course, the divergence between Cheyenne and Astrokittie's race-play proficiency are indications of the performer's personal preferences, pleasures, and limits with respect to racial-sexual play, but it fundamentally challenges an understanding of race play as either performance ("all acting") or "natural" ability. This bifurcation speaks to the paradox of race and racism as things that are learned but need to be perfected, effortless yet exceedingly difficult. Race play is a practice of race that brings these contradictions into sharp relief. Beyond registering and rousing a form of pleasure that documents the erotic currency of race and racism, we might read race-play pornography as a kind of pleasure pedagogy in and of race and racism.

Still, pleasure in *Get Out of My Town* is equivocal. This ambiguity compounds the queerness of this scene of interracial lesbian domination/submission. Here lesbian desire is fraught not just because it is scripted by a black male imaginary and coded within the scrambled cues of domination and submission, pleasure and constraint, erotics and violence, but also because it is disavowed within the narrative of the video. Nearly two minutes into the video, Mabel says, "I'm gonna stay loving me some black big dick." Role-playing banter aside, in referring to and idealizing the black male cock, the remark plays into the black male gaze of the author of *Get of My Town*. Although we might think about this disavowal of lesbianism as reflecting the fantasy/reality binary that characterizes race play and gesturing toward the "gay for pay" phenomenon in contemporary American pornography, I suggest that it must be read as reinforcing the queer currency of the race-play fantasy.[201] As I argue more in depth in the next chapter in the context of cuckold pornography, pornography's play of race is animated by queerness and its disavowal. That is, the pleasure of race play is a queer pleasure, although it is often denied as such.

Race play brings into focus the queerness of heterosexual desire in pornography. Sisko states, "I mean girl-boy would be, you know, sexy too, but I prefer girl-girl. Lesbian, woman on woman, is just a bigger turn-on to me and it's just my personal preference."[202] What strikes me about this scene of interracial lesbian race play mediated by the black male gaze is not that queerness occupies the nadir in a hierarchy of straight male desire. "Girl-girl" pornography that is authored by and directed toward the heterosexual male gaze is of course nothing new in pornography. Rather, this scene speaks to the ways that race play and its pleasures are rendered ambivalently queer. The different levels of performance—verbal and visual—further convolute lesbian desire. Mabel's oral allegiance to black manhood contradicts both her other comments that convey lesbian desire (e.g., the pleasure Betty Sue imagines Mabel experiences from being in proximity to her "white crotch" and the pleasure Mabel asserts Betty Sue would derive from the taste of her "melted" blackness) and the actions of the performers, which are ambiguous. For example, Mabel's moans indicate both pain and pleasure, while her laughter alternatively signals amusement and discomfort. The body is an unreliable index of desire here. However, while interracial lesbian desire is opaque, the *queerness* of the scene—its jumbling of binaries and dramatizing of the mercuriality of sexuality—is transparent.

Like *Get My Belt*, *Get Out of My Town* has an unexpected ending. It finishes with an exhausted Betty Sue taking a momentary break from punishing Mabel so she can grab a pie from the dresser, eat some, then smear some on her own feet in order to "feed the fucking nigger bitch." Slathering the pie's whipped cream topping on Mabel's forehead Betty Sue cries out, "Look, I am going to make you a white girl after all. Look at that, the KKK won't even know! You're a white supremacist after all. Look at that, you look just like me." A random, if not ludicrous prop in the narrative (how and why would Mabel be baking a pie in the confines of a small, shabby motel room with no kitchen?), the pie, as a maquillage of racial alchemy, is a gimmick of race play, an apparatus of racial absurdity that reifies and refutes the epidermal logic of race I discussed in the context of Skin's stage name. The pie highlights the hypervisibility and simulation of race—its opaque white renders blackness.

The fetishization of racial difference through skin color figures prominently in Sisko's race-play pornography. For example, in *Nigger 911*, as in *Get Out of My Town*, black skin serves as grounds for the white female's disciplining of the black female body. Mistress Francheska's statement to Slave Coco, "Did you look at yourself in the mirror lately? You see the difference; we don't have quite the same skin color," bespeaks the salience of difference that is often (as Skin Diamond reveals) configured through skin. "Skin/race" emerges as a vital trope in the pornographic imaginary's play of race, elucidating the entanglement of visibility, pleasure, power, and punishment that buttress the practice of race play.[203] In *Get Out of My Town*, the stark visual contrast of fluffy white whipped cream and Mabel's dark skin is a spectacle of eroticized racial difference, a moment when difference is not only overdeveloped but also mocked. Race play ridicules the hyperbole of race that it so anxiously enacts in order to disrupt the racialism it labors to fabricate. Here the ambivalence of black female racial-sexual alterity within the pornographic frame is brought into high relief as the viewers enjoy a pleasure not just in difference but also in sameness. The pie makes perceptible how race manifests as an accouterment of BDSM. Beyond race as the primary technique of humiliation, blackness is the source of shame, the reason for punishment. Finally, in the absence of a conventional money shot, this scene is a uniquely racialized proxy, offering not proof of sexual pleasure but a corroboration of race (and its representation in pornography) as at once essential and performed. Hence the pie functions not so much as a substitute for ejaculation but as a fetish for race itself and as an example of the dynamic mockery of race in pornography.

In addition to his videos, Sisko's Pudding Foot Video's Blog is another theatrical arena that narrates the libidinal and political economies of his race play. If in his unscripted race-play videos Sisko occupies a more remote, indistinct presence behind the camera, in the digital space of his blog, he appears as a main character. The blog provides general information about race play, updates about his projects, information about the performers he hires, and narrations of Sisko's "successes and failures running [his] business and supplying content to this niche market."[204] Though the blog's primary objective is to sell the content he produces (he writes that "I literally started the blog to promote and add value to my site to hopefully drive more traffic in customers"), it also serves as a site of research and development for his race-play porn production, where he solicits feedback.[205] The blog also functions as a site of pedagogy for aspiring amateur race-play pornography producers. Sisko states, "Like, you know, I did a blog on how to make their own videos and how to find girls and because it just depends when people contact me and have a certain interest request or question I'll blog about it."[206]

Yet the blog is very much a personal space where Sisko performs his own fetishization of race play. Reflecting upon his individual fantasies while introducing readers to the small underground niche of amateur race play pornography, he writes, "Consider me your race play tour guide. I will also share with you my inner most thoughts about this fetish, and what I hear from my fans, about this fetish. I sincerely hope that you will follow me on my blog journey."[207] As a site where he shares his "inner most" thoughts, the blog is a space where he reveals his own individual interest in black female humiliation. In this disclosure, the discipline of racial authenticity is pronounced. That is, here Sisko reveals his intimate fantasies and his racial identification. His fetishization of black female humiliation is prefaced by his confession that he is "a black man": he writes, "It may or may not shock you to know that I am a black man." This confession is testament to the policing of black BDSM sexuality that many black BDSMers have so vehemently contested. Confession remains a salient technology of the discursive production of sexuality and truth and its disciplining of bodies.[208] In an act of self-policing, Sisko preempts charges that he violates a code of black manhood (and black male pride) that would reject the notion of receiving pleasure from a purported defiling of black womanhood. Sisko believes that the transgression of this code could elicit "shock" from some of his customers. In our conversation, Sisko voiced this anxiety: "I'd just like to reiterate that I, you know, I don't hate myself as a Black man. I don't hate Black women." He thus articulated his negotiation of the gendered and racialized dynamics of policing not only race play but also blackness.

On his blog he further reiterates that he always uses black women submissives to perform black female racial-sexual abjection. Sisko registers this "fact" of black womanhood somatically, linking the function of black women as ideal submissives to racialized hierarchies of beauty. That is, black women become exemplary objects of humiliation because, Sisko believes, they occupy the nadir within such hierarchies. He writes, "Candidly, I must admit, that I find black women in general to be the least attractive of all the nationalities. . . . So ergo, that is the reason I like to see black women dominated by white women, because they are uglier, and it appeals to my sadomasochist nature." Intrigued by what I perceived as the Sisko "character" on his blog as a continuing space of race play, I was seduced by the very fantasy/reality binary I seek to recant:

> Okay, one thing I find that was really interesting about your blog is it seems like you're very much kind of in character or role-playing, like, so, the voice on your blog seems to be almost as if it was a voice from your filmmaking, so there's this really interesting synchronicity to me between the voice on your blog and your work. And I was wondering if you wanted to talk about that at all.

His reply serves as a corrective to my invocation of the fantasy/reality binary and an ambivalent, if ironic, assertion of the authenticity of his race play "fantasy." He responded, "What did you say, my voice? I am not sure what you're talking about. I'm just being me. I'm just being *real.*"[209] Sisko's insistence on "being real" belies the warnings that preface his videos and the "it's all acting" race-play philosophy that he describes when discussing his performers. He conveys the complex layers of reality and fantasy operating in the spectatorship, performance, and production of race-play pornography. More than an affirmation of his "authentic" voice, "being real" here reifies the profound tension between fantasy and reality that has animated my discussion of race play and its rendering in contemporary American pornography. Race-play pornography is at once simulation and documentary—a fictional invention of black female abjection made possible by the nonfictional legibility of black womanhood as abject.

Race Play: Out of Its BDSM and Pornographic Cages

What makes us laugh is just as vexed as what makes us wet. On August 15, 2013, Def Jam co-founder and media magnate Russell Simmons landed himself in hot water when his new youtube.com channel, All Def Digital, released the "Harriet Tubman Sex Tape," starring three established comedic actors. In the three-minute video parody, black female slave Harriet Tubman (Shanna Malcolm) conspires to seduce her white male "Massa" (Jason Horton) while a fellow slave/cameraman (DeStorm Power) films the event to use to blackmail their master in order to obtain their freedom. I read the parody as a critical iteration of race play that speaks to the sweeping range and depth of chattel slavery's repertoire in our erotic imaginary. I cite this example not to undermine the salience of BDSM and pornography as critical arenas for the performance of race play but to further signal the salience of race play in the mainstream popular imaginary. Closing "the leather door" on race play opens our gaze to its quotidian popular renderings.[210] As Nash has recently highlighted, because of its engagement with historical trauma, visual culture has long been a site for/of black feminist critique.[211] Evincing the visual (re)playing field of historical trauma, race play profoundly complicates a rendering of the visual as *only* suffering in order to foreground questions of pleasure, albeit highly conflicted.

The video opens to a worm's-eye view of the sky veiled through a curtain of silhouetted tree leaves and branches that fails to keep the sun's sharp rays from slicing through. The year "1851" is emblazoned on the screen in yellow font. An extra-diegetic harmonica plays for a moment before we cut inside to the small modest bedroom in which the caper ensues. Harriet (the actual historical Tubman would have been around thirty-one years old in 1851) and her fellow slave/cameraman plot before Massa enters the bedroom and the filming begins. With the camera tucked under his right arm, the slave/cameraman asks nervously, "Now you sure this gonna work, Ms. Harriet?" to which she resolutely responds, "This our only chance to gain freedoms!" He sneaks into the closet as Harriet adjusts her garments in preparation for Massa's arrival. Robed with a long apron over a dress and a headscarf, she channels mammy. She tells the cameraman, "Make sure you catches it all." He assures her: "I ain't gonna leave you hangin'." Upon uttering the word "hanging," he raises his arm as if to tug at an imaginary rope around his neck. The reference to lynching is perhaps ironic here as lynching was often punishment for the obverse of the scene about to unfold— that is, black-white racial intimacy purportedly initiated by black men. These two types of offenses—white men's sexual abuse and rape of black women and the accusation that black men raped or assaulted white women—have historically occupied very different spaces within the patriarchal politics of our collective imaginary.[212] Tubman, as mastermind here, is skilled in a sexual subterfuge that we can understand only as part of the "powerful ideological consequences" of chattel slavery.[213] Neither the spectacle of lynching nor the institutionalized rape of black women are off limits in this porno-comedic fantasy sex tape. However, the eroticization of both illuminates the fact that far from being a marginal practice in the "perverse" peripheral realms of pornography and BDSM, race play narrates the more quotidian dynamics of racialized sexuality and the fraught pleasures of the memory of chattel slavery for both black and white, and male and female.

Hiding in a dark closet with the door cracked to let in enough light to paint his face in chiaroscuro and enable him to film the sex in the nearby bed, slave/cameraman sings the chorus from "Wade in the Water." The irreverence of this classic Negro spiritual as soundtrack for Harriet Tubman's illicit sex tape is not lost on the viewers. Tubman, a leading figure in the abolitionist movement and one of the most recognized conductors of the Underground Railroad, used that song, which originally was written for the ritual of baptism, to signal to fugitive slaves that they should avoid terrestrial trails and instead "wade in the water" to avoid being tracked by the dogs of slave catchers.[214] The multiple layers of transgression heighten the power of the satire. Here in this sex-tape parody, the hymn serves sacrilegiously as the soundtrack for a more unconventional, albeit ignoble, path to liberty.[215]

Once Massa enters, Harriet grabs him by the lapels and pulls him toward the bed. He declares: "Harriet, I've never seen you be this frisky before." To quell his suspicion, she replies, "Oh Massa, all these years I been acting like I didn't love our special time together. Tonight, it's all gonna be different." She reclines on the bed, leading him in between her parted legs. Master replies, "This oughta be fun for the both of us, long as Mary don't find out." This verbal exchange signals the institutionalized rape of the enslaved of black female while animating the theme of ambivalent pleasure—the thorniness of the enslaved black female's pleasure. Massa's performative statement that "this outta be fun for the both of us" may be read as both a "speak[ing] the master's truth," to recall Hartman, wherein pleasure is a proxy for consent and complicity *and* an evincing of mutual pleasure.[216] Tubman assures him "Oh I's never gonna tell" before the video cuts back to the closet, where we watch the sex acts through the eyes of the camera, framed by the crack between the door and frame of the closet. The sex mimes the hyperbole of the parody. During the short sex scene in which the two remain fully clothed, Tubman is dominant, both physically and verbally. She aggressively rides her master in both the missionary and the doggie positions. Their joyous moans and comedic sexual utterances—Tubman exclaims "I'll set you free, I'll set your ass free" and demands, "Who's the Master now?!—mingle with the sound of reeling film from the camera inside the closet.

After coitus, Tubman is all business; her attitude and demeanor change dramatically from aggressive and fervent to disinterested and cold. As the two recline in bed, Harriet smokes the proverbial après sex cigarette and refutes Massa's confession of love, snapping, "Look, I don't give a damn about what you love." She reveals her ruse: "Look, Nigger, this is how it's gonna go. Well, Massa I'se got what you white folks like to call leverage and I'm gonna' be telling everybody about your negro love, including Mary." The reversal of master/slave power dynamics here recalls *Get My Belt*. With Harriet smiling smugly, the slave/cameraman slowly peeks the camera out of the closet to show Massa what she means. The screen quickly cuts to black and the harmonica floats back in, only to be interrupted by a nondiegetic voice saying "Get to work on that railroad, white nigga!" The parody concludes with an imitation History Channel logo that reads "History: The B Sides." This logo explicitly des-

ignates the sex-tape performance as an alternate history that encompasses both what Simmons perceives as "Harriet Tubman outwitting the
slave master" in perhaps more unconventional and unorthodox ways
than her work on the Underground Railroad *and* a kind of rewriting of
history that brazenly confronts the erotics of slavery in order to foreground the play of race.[217]

The *Harriet Tubman Sex Tape* reveals that humor, like sexuality, is
a prime arena in which to negotiate the manifold inheritances of chattel slavery. Black humor is a complex response to racism and the aftershocks of slavery. In her study of African American comedy, Glenda R.
Carpio argues that "far from being *only* a coping mechanism, or a means
of 'redress', African American humor has been and continues to be both
a bountiful source of creativity and pleasure and an energetic mode of
social and political critique."[218] A hyperbolic tale of ambivalent redress
set to the pulse of taboo black-white interracial desire, *The Harriet Tubman Sex Tape* foregrounds the topos of (inter)racial sexual revenge in
the context of contemporary American interracial pornography as a
symbolic site for the restitution for slavery. In its unabashed exploitation
of racial hyperbole and the erotic repository of chattel slavery, race-play
pornography brings into sharp relief the kinky narratives of black-white
intimacy that script mainstream interracial pornography. In the previous chapter, I argued that BDSM is limited both spatially and temporally
for black women in the context of its power to disrupt, destabilize and/
or subvert racialized power hierarchies. Here, I am suggesting that we
extend the theoretic aperture of race play to consider how the violent
pleasure of the play of race is enacted in the larger venue of popular
culture.

Only twenty-four hours after he uploaded what he initially considered a "hilarious" video, Simmons, pressured by a flurry of public outrage, including from his "buddies" at the NAACP, pulled *The Harriet
Tubman Sex Tape* from his channel and issued a formal apology.[219] In
a dizzying cacophony of online responses to the scandal and its media
coverage, comments ranged from outrage and offense at Simmons's in-
solence to reminders about the essential irreverent nature of comedy
itself to allegations of self-hatred and a disregard for history to further
indignation over what many regarded as the inadequacy of his apology.
Spike Lee, for example, tweeted "Just Saw Russell Simmons Produced

Skit "HARRIET TUBMAN SEXTAPE. I Ask Why Do We Desecrate Our Ancestors? Why Do We Hate Ourselves? QUESTION???"[220] These vociferous digital debates recall both the "intimacy interventions" with which I opened this chapter and the feminist debates of the late 1970s and early 1980s over the politics of BDSM. These recurrent debates speak to the slime of chattel slavery within our psyches and the continued policing of desire. We are still aroused by this history and we still keep getting in trouble for being titillated. The unspeakable keeps (be) speaking. Such is the continued grasp of slavery on our erotic imaginaries, past, present, and future.

3

Interracial Iterations and Internet In(ter)ventions

Does history die if you intentionally repeat it?
—Kara Walker[1]

History lays down a lush and troubling tapestry from which
you have the freedom to pluck the threads that intrigue, ap-
peal, terrify, hook, provoke and anger you, and weave them
into your own story. Yes, it is fucked up.
—Mollena Williams[2]

Pornography's Perverse Revenge

Since 2013, over two dozen states have passed legislation that provides for the prosecution of those who produce and purvey so-called
revenge porn. Many more states have bills in the works to criminalize
the posting of sexually explicit photographs or videos of another person without her/his consent. End Revenge Porn, an advocacy campaign
organized by the Cyber Civil Rights Initiative in 2012 to stop the prevalent phenomenon, defines revenge porn as "a form of sexual assault
that involves the distribution of nude/sexually explicit photos and/or
videos of an individual without their consent. Revenge porn is usually
posted by a scorned ex-lover or friend, in order to seek revenge after
a relationship has gone sour."[3] Revenge porn websites post sexually
explicit pirated photographs, sometimes with identifying information
and contact information about the victims, an estimated 90 percent of
whom are women.[4] Some revenge porn sites further abuse their victims by charging extortionate fees to remove material from the website.[5]
On the notorious, now-defunct popular revenge porn site isanybodyup.
com, users could upload explicit photographs, material purloined from
the Facebook pages of victims, and links to victims' Twitter accounts.
The website's founder, Hunter Moore, initially designed it as a site for
"public humiliation."[6] California attorney general Kamala Harris simi-

larly identifies "public humiliation" as constitutive of the phenomenon.[7] Lacking the consent that is imperative within BDSM (indeed eroticizing this absence), revenge porn is definitively not part of that practice. However, it traffics in the complex currency of the spectacle of eroticized humiliation, a practice this chapter revisits, analyzing pornography as a familiar, long-standing locus of fantasy revenge, particularly that of (inter)racialized sexual revenge.

This chapter continues the discussion of (inter)racial aggression in pornography as a primary representational trope of black female sexuality. I argue that BDSM becomes an apposite critical lens for elucidating the dynamics of racialized shame, humiliation, and pleasure that undergird interracial pornography, a profitable genre of American pornography that is deeply invested in the miscegenation taboo. Though I focus on contemporary Internet pornography, I also read across other genres of pornography—the stag genre, golden-age porn, and video-age porn—to provide a contextual frame for reading performances of black-white interracial intimacy in pornography and to argue that the black female body is an ambivalent site of absence and presence within pornography. Mapping a space from which to read the black female body's pornographic absence/presence requires spatio-temporal jumps—the "leaps" that artist crystal am nelson elegantly describes in this book's introduction. The chapter concludes with an exploration of how a contemporary black queer feminist pornographer uses new media to intervene in heteronormative, hegemonic representations of the black female body in order to interrupt long-standing scripts of black female sexuality within pornography.

Revenge porn has a rich historical tradition. In the golden-age pornography film classic *Behind the Green Door* (dir. Artie Mitchell and Jim Mitchell, 1972), renowned black male performer Johnny Keyes articulates an ambivalent fantasy of racialized sexualized revenge. Keyes is not the typical jilted or scorned lover evoked in contemporary narratives of revenge porn. His motives go much deeper into the rhizomatic memory of chattel slavery. While the golden age of porn is often deracialized in the historiography and memory of pornography, *Behind the Green Door* constitutes a salient moment not just in this important period but also in the history of interracial moving-image pornography: the moment when hard-core interracial sex was brought to the "mainscreen."[8]

In the 1970s, moving-image pornography enjoyed a more visible—though still liminal—space in American culture. Because of changes in obscenity laws, during the golden age of porn, the spaces where pornography was consumed changed, as did the genre itself. In order to abide by the Supreme Court ruling in *Miller v. California* (1973), pornography producers began making feature-length films with developed plots, original musical scores, special effects, and so forth in an attempt to imbue the films with "redeeming social value." Per *Miller*, the court was less likely to deem works with "serious literary, artistic, political, or scientific value" obscene. Though *Miller* restated that obscene material was not protected by the First Amendment, it effectively redefined obscenity in a way that opened loopholes for the production of pornography. Not just legal but also technological shifts continue to change pornography. After the golden age, the industry's shift to video technology in the early 1980s revolutionized pornography once more. The silver age of the 1980s catalyzed a democratization of pornography that made the development of black and interracial genres possible.[9] In the late 1990s, the digital age of pornography, which I examine in the next chapter, how pornography is produced and consumed changed dynamically, and through this transformation our experience and knowledge of racialized sexuality changed as well.

Behind the Green Door offers a transgressive sexual coupling of the black male, Keyes, and the white female, Marilyn Chambers. In its climactic scene, Keyes emerges from an illuminated green door on the otherwise dim stage wearing the arbitrary markers of an offensively generic Africanity or tribal quality—a long bone necklace, war paint on his forehead and surrounding his eyes, and white chap-like leggings that leave his penis exposed. Keyes wears a similar costume in the classic porn feature *Sexworld* (dir. Anthony Spinelli, 1978). The white of the fabric starkly contrasts with his dark skin to accentuate his large genitals. His martial face paint and pseudo-ethnic jewelry enforce his signification as a warrior and racial-sexual predator who symbolizes the imagined threat of black male sexuality to the cult of white womanhood, a trope pornography continues to creatively exploit. Slowly moving on stage toward Chambers against a soundtrack of trippy, tribal jazz music, Keyes is fashioned as walking primitivity. This display of racial-sexual alterity signals pornography's repetition of these stereotypes—its investment in the arousing artifice of hyperbolized blackness. Keyes exits the eponymous green door and enters the stage, where Chambers awaits, flocked by a crew of female courtiers. An anonymous male announcer warns the audience, both today's viewers and the 1971 on-screen audience in San Francisco's O'Farrell Theatre, where *Behind the Green Door* is set: "Ladies and gentlemen, you are about to witness the ravishment of a woman who has been abducted, a woman whose initial fear and anxiety has mellowed into curious expectation."

Behind the Green Door's manipulation of the taboo of black-white sex is intensified not merely by the "African" construction of Keyes, however inaccurate, but also by the casting of Chambers. Chambers's biography further contributes to the thrill of the racially delineated forbidden in the film. Chambers was once the face of Proctor and Gamble's advertisement campaign for Ivory Snow laundry detergent. The advertisements for the soap, which Proctor and Gamble continues to promote as 99.44 percent pure, depicted a familiar imagining of white femininity as naturally virtuous and pure. Chambers's blonde hair, blue eyes, and pale skin personified the wholesome image of Ivory Snow's campaign for purity and cleanliness. The packaging for the detergent featured Chambers cuddling a white infant. The campaign laid the groundwork for many layers of fetishization. It symbolized a U.S.-made domesticity, cleanliness (as a distinctly racial disinfectant), order, whiteness and the reproduction of whiteness. None of these are removed from the racialized, sexualized narratives of black masculinity and white femininity that pornography continues to replay. Here, the clichéd story of good girl gone very bad that is often narrated in pornography is uniquely circumscribed by a racially politicized dialectic of good, white sexuality versus bad, black sexuality that still fuels contemporary interracial American pornography. Underlined by an enactment of eroticized requital, shame, and humiliation, BDSM becomes a lens for viewing these dynamics of interracial sexuality as they are performed in pornography.

Beyond the framing of Keyes and Chambers, the actors' commentary about this pivotal pornographic performance of black-white sex unveils the essential narratives of reparation, redress, and revenge that script heterosexual black-white interracial pornography. Keyes explicitly articulated the force of historical retaliation and his own awareness of the historical script he drew upon in playing this role of "African": "I was fucking the hell out of this chick—I was acting like I was ten thousand Africans making up for that slavery shit. Here's this white woman that the African is fucking to get revenge on all those white motherfuckers that used to rape our mothers and aunts all those years ago, right? That's what I used as an incentive to fuck Marilyn Chambers."[10] Reflecting on the scene. Chambers stated: "I was still pretty nervous. The black-and-white sex thing—I knew this was a very big taboo, as it still is in our country. And I thought, 'Now my father's really going to kill me!' Ha, ha, ha!"[11] It is fascinating to consider their respective comments about this paramount interracial scene in a classic golden-age American pornography film. Both recognized that their sex act was highly politically charged from a definitively racial current. Whereas Chambers seemed to acknowledge and welcome the power of its shock value to both family (father) and nation, Keyes inserted himself in a slightly different though parallel historical narrative of black-white intimate relations as the righteous agent of retribution. His words recall Mollena Williams's facetious yet cogent remark linking race play to reparations: "Yes. Payback, you see. We aren't getting reparations, so go beat up some White [person] and get yours."[12] Playing into his apocryphal Africanity, Keyes enacts revenge pornography. His assessment of the sex scene reinforces pornography as a stage for the eroticized play of race in which racial humiliation takes a starring role. This historic performance of revenge porn cues both the power of slavery in our erotic imaginary and the imbrication of pleasure, race, and humiliation that is so central to interracial pornography.

We might understand that one black male pornography star "fucking the hell out of [one] white chick" may do little to account for "the great-still unfolding massive crime of official and unofficial America against Africa, African slaves, and their descendants," in the words of African American lawyer, scholar, and activist Randall Robinson.[13] However, Keyes clearly imagines himself as engaged in some sort of quest for reparations for the institutionalized rape of black women, "his mothers and aunts," that took place as a result of transatlantic slavery. Lacking the "repair" fundamental to most modern definitions of African American reparations, like that, for example, of the National Coalition of Blacks for Reparations in America (N'COBRA), Keyes's act is less one of remedy and more one of reprisal.[14] Nevertheless, amid renewed conversations about reparations, pornography reemerges as a critical, if unconventional, space to interrogate the lingering erotic aftershocks of slavery and the negotiation of its memory—its complex physical and psychic settlements.[15] In a seemingly supernatural feat, Keyes summons the power of "ten thousand Africans" to fuel his sexual redress. Ironically perhaps, it is this same colorfully conjured African heritage that impels his casting as a virile black buck ravishing a blond white woman. This history is the source of both his sexual liberation and his ensnarement, his pleasure and his pain—an erotic tension familiar within BDSM.

Keyes' self-professedly noble description of his sexual performance is problematic for a number of reasons. First, he was financially compensated for his role in the film that launched his acclaimed career as a pornographic actor.[16] Second, he imagined white men's rape of black women to be atoned by another sexual crime: a black man's ravishment of a white woman. In the film, crimes against the flesh were avenged with crimes against the flesh. Women's passive, objectified bodies thus become the battlefield for male revenge fantasies. Third, Keyes frames the act as one of revenge and not something done for his own personal pleasure. The pleasure of both Keyes and Chambers is obfuscated through the framing of the sex act as a one-way violent act of vengeance that Keyes carries out against Chambers. The audience's pleasure in watching is similarly complicated. For example, how do we reconcile our own pleasure in this supposedly sadistic act? How might we become complicit through the voyeuristic act of spectatorship? Finally, in the (hetero)sexist androcentric tradition of men's policing of women's sexuality, the black male is responsible for adjudicating the crimes against the flesh of black women.

However vexed Keyes's commentary is, it conveys a lust for revenge that speaks to the explicit fantasies of racist violence that animate performances of black-white interracial sex in modern pornography.[17] His remarks signal the slippages between collective and subjective diasporic memory, desire and antagonism, sexual gratification and retribution, labor and pleasure, intention and reception, anxiety and arousal, past and present. If revenge seethes in the performances of Vanessa Blue and Skin Diamond, here it suppurates. Keyes's revenge-porn reflection serves as an entry into this chapter's exploration of the narratives of racialized aggression that script performances of black-white interracial intimacy in contemporary pornography and how these narratives problematically jettison the black female body. As I signaled in the previous chapter, pornography presents a contemporary staging of racialized sexualized violence wherein the retaliatory rhetoric of interracial aggression is enacted.

Canonical black feminists have long critiqued what they have argued to be the harmful racism that operates within and is perpetuated by pornography, specifically its treatment of black women. Anti-pornography feminists have also identified pornography's "racist" treatment of black women in their overall contention that pornography causes gender-specific harms.[18] While these scholars pioneered a feminist critique of pornography that considers black female sexuality, the concepts of racism, sexism, exploitation, and victimization that buttress this body of work prevent a more nuanced, radical analysis of the polyvalence of pornography, its vital narration of the complexities of black female sexuality, and the productive opportunities it presents for black female sexual pleasure and power. I am less interested in racism and more interested in the complex relationship between racialization and pleasure and how interracial pornography reveals both our libidinal investments in racial-sexual alterity and the history of chattel slavery. Like Linda Williams, I believe the label of "racism" is too simple and insufficient to describe the intricate web of anxiety, fear, desire, and ambivalence that powers performances of interracial intimacy in pornography.[19]

Too often when racism is the charge against interracial pornography, it impedes a deeper critical analysis. Gloria Cowan and Robin Campbell's study of interracial pornography is an important exception.[20] Cowan and Campbell's analysis of the entanglement of racism and sexism in commercial interracial video pornography illuminates how gender informs the expression of racism in pornography.[21] Their overall argument is that interracial sex in pornography manifests greater levels of aggression than intraracial sex: while black men exhibit higher rates of aggression and less intimate behavior than white men, black women are increasingly treated with more aggression than white women. Though they do not explicitly analyze interracial pornography's scripts of racial-sexual aggression, such as the script of (inter)racial-sexual revenge, they evoke Keyes and his legacy, referring to the pornographic icon of the prodigiously endowed black male whose role is to "punish erring White women and reduce their status."[22]

Black feminists and anti-pornography feminists paved the way for a critique of racism in interracial pornography, typically from the arena of film and media studies.[23] Linda Williams argues that more than other genres of porn, interracial pornography depends on an explicit awareness of racial taboo driven by fear: it is "the fear once generated by white masters to keep white women and black men apart—that gives erotic tension to interracial sex acts which in 'ordinary' nonracialized pornography have become rote."[24] Although Williams does not analyze black women's sexuality within interracial pornography, she directs our attention to the "missing figures" beyond the frame of the camera who energize and "haun[t]" the scene of interracial desire:

> When the black woman and the white man recognize and desire one another across their differences, this recognition is nevertheless haunted and erotically animated by the missing figure of the black man, who finds his very masculinity and virility jeopardized by his exclusion. It is also haunted by the missing figure of the white woman deprived of a partner because of the white male's interest in the "othered" woman. Similarly[,] in the sexual-racial recognition of the white woman and the black man, it is the jealous white man who represents the absent third term and who has his masculinity (and mastery) put in jeopardy by his exclusion. To a lesser degree, the second scenario is also haunted by the black woman who loses a potential partner to the myth of superior white womanhood.[25]

In this shifting configuration of exclusion and inclusion, black women occupy an exceedingly ambivalent space in the imaginary of interracial pornography. While they perform as foils to white masculinity, their exclusion is also informed by their imagined difference from white female sexuality. Yet even as absent figures, black women are disempowered. Williams argues "the white man has much more power in his absence to structure the scene in which he does not act than does the black man, the white woman, or the black woman," concluding that the black male–white woman pairing is more transgressive and therefore "more erotic."[26] While Williams's analysis gestures toward how powerful these missing figures can be in their absence, I find this reading problematic because it privileges white masculinity and further jettisons the "others." If we continue to see and think like this, then we continue to invest a kind of totemic power and control in white men as the authors and primary architects of *the* interracial fantasy while viewing interracial pornography as only a repetition of familiar hetero-gendered, racial-sexual stereotypes, rather than perhaps, as I suggest here, a kind of queer parody of these stereotypes.

I am not interested in reinforcing hierarchies of eroticism but rather in unveiling the ways that pornography shows how the pleasures in traversing the binary of black and white are often also informed by the pleasures of crossing and recrossing the borders of heterosexual and homosexual. Williams's reading does not account for the queer desire that I argue is central in "heterosexual" interracial pornography that manifests the "queering" of the color line, the historical entanglement of the black-white border with the homosexual/heterosexual binary.[27] Interracial sex enacted in pornography might best be imagined as a fantastic queer orgy wherein a panoply of figures—anxiously animated by the unsettled binaries between black and white, man and woman, past and present, gay and straight—people the erotic scene. Furthermore, as I discuss here, the anxious begrudging white male is no longer an "absent third term" or a simple voyeur but is rather an active partner in the spectacle of sex between black men and white women. BDSM, I argue, allows us to make better sense of his role and the labyrinthine pleasures of these dramatized illicit encounters.

As is the case in race play, racialized debasement is vital in interracial pornography. According to Daniel Bernardi, pornography scholars have failed to address how interracial pornography reflects and perpetuates "the coercive power of whiteness" and the devaluing of people of color.[28] He deems interracial porn a form of "hate speech" that reduces people of color to perverse phenotypical and physiological fetishistic parts, familiar fragments in the labor of sexual desire.[29] He critiques anti-porn feminists for their overly simplistic, essentialized critiques of pornography as violence and radical sex scholars, such as Williams, for their failure to comprehensively address race and racism as integral to pornography's pleasures.[30] Indeed, what is powerful about Bernardi's argument is that an explicit admission of pornography's hateful racism does not preclude a more comprehensive, rigorous, and nuanced analysis of the complex dynamics of racialized pleasures and power.[31]

Like Bernardi, Gail Dines critiques both pornography scholarship's standpoint of whiteness and the heteropatriarchal pornographic fantasy that scripts performances of black-white intimacy in interracial pornography.[32] For Dines, interracial pornography is an instantiation of one of the foundations of the radical feminist anti-pornography argument: that pornography's (male) pleasure is constitutive of (female) debasement. Dines writes, "It is hard to conceive of a better way to degrade white women, in a culture with a long and ugly history of racism, than having them penetrated again and again by a body that has been constructed, coded, and demonized as a carrier for all that is sexually debased, namely the black male."[33] While black women are left out of this interracial equation, black men exist in and for their rendering of white womanhood. Dines's reading of interracial pornography excludes both pleasure and black agency: blackness labors in service of the production of white female sexuality. Natalie Purcell rightly identifies chattel slavery and its legacies of racialism as a wellspring of black-white interracial pornographic fantasy.[34] Unfortunately, while making an important case for the "realness" and materiality of pornographic fantasy, Purcell, like Dines, reads blackness as a sign of "degradation and inferiority" in a way that neglects the multifaceted perverse pleasures that interracial pornography reflects and engenders. Indeed, our problem with pornography is akin to our trouble with BDSM: we register the eroticized domination and submission in both as perverse, aberrant, harmful, and often nonconsensual, while failing to interrogate the pleasure and agency potentially experienced in these power dynamics. Yet, a politics of perversion unveils the imbrication of pornography's perverse pleasures—queer, BDSM, and interracial.

I argue that queer race pleasures—a simultaneous pleasure in race and queerness—are essential in interracial pornography. BDSM enables us to read performances of interracial intimacy more comprehensively and with an eye for the perverse queer race pleasures they enact not outside but rather in the context of the gendered and racialized degradation they perform. The lens of BDSM facilitates a more inventive and nuanced reading of the complex dynamics of racialized pleasure, power, and agency in interracial pornography, which is more complicated than a reiteration of the stereotyped performance of excessive black masculinity as the "spoiler of white womanhood."[35] BDSM elucidates the pornographic narratives of interracial revenge, illuminating the genre as a *play* of erecting and transgressing the eroticized boundaries of race, a dynamic scripted by the memory of chattel slavery. BDSM performs a critical queering of interracial "heterosexual" pornography—one that reads across the gendered and racialized subject positions of pleasure, power, and desire to recognize the homoerotic pleasures and anxieties, as well as the eroticization of racial-sexual alterity that anchors contemporary American interracial pornography.

Historically scripted narratives of racialized sexualized discipline are important in more than just "straight" interracial pornography. In their analyses of the genre of gay male interracial pornography, both David McBride and Tim Dean have recognized the significance of the revenge narrative for the pornographic power play of sex across the black-white color line. McBride identifies "retributive sex" as a common element of gay interracial pornography—a kind of "pleasure/labor" energized by the taboo of interracial sex.[36] Similarly, Dean recognizes the "established porn convention of representing interracial sex as a punishment meted out by blacks to whites."[37] For Dean, racial difference, specifically black and white difference, makes it possible to visualize other differences that are more concealed, like the difference between HIV-negative and HIV-positive partners. Race thus serves to compound the eroticized transgression operating in bareback pornography, the subject of Dean's analysis, so that "a black man fucking a white man without protection adds salience to the idea of revenge."[38] Like other scholars, Dean acknowledges the haunting presence of chattel slavery in the imaginary of interracial gay male pornography and how it fuels narratives of retribution that black and white play protagonists with/in.[39]

The linkages between black-white interracial sex and revenge have, of course, a long convoluted history in these United States. In the wake of Ida B. Wells-Barnett's bold reporting of the connections between interracial sexuality and lynching, "our country's national crime," numerous scholars have documented how anxiety about and the policing of interracial sex motivates lynching, rape, and other modes of racialized sexual violence.[40] For example, T. Denean Sharpley-Whiting interrogates the hypocrisy of the Ku Klux Klan's "anti-interracial sex ideology" because the political economic program of its members was (and still is) tethered to interracial sex.[41] She borrows the anti-pornography feminist theory of thanatic pornography as a framework for reading the dynamics of black-white interracial desire and sexual violence that metaphorically cultivate the fraternity of Klan culture.[42] Like Sharpley-Whiting, I treat pornography as a lens. However, here I am interested in how that lens reveals the politics of interracial sex and the queer pleasures and violence that mark this transgression. Interracial pornography brings into high relief the still-animated charge of sex across the color line.

Cuckolding at the Color Line

Sex becomes in this popular theory the principle around which the whole structure of segregation of the negroes—down to disfranchisement and denial of equal opportunities on the labor market—is organized. The reasoning is this: "For, say what we will, may not all the equalities be ultimately based on potential social equality, and that in turn on intermarriage? Here we reach the real *crux* of the question." In cruder language, but with the same logic, the Southern man on the street responds to any plea for social equality: "Would you like to have your daughter marry a Negro?"
-Gunnar Myrdal[43]

Perversely reiterating "the 'Negro' question," contemporary American interracial pornography plays in and with the anxiety that Myrdal's incisive mid-twentieth-century query revealed. In *An American Dilemma* (1944), Myrdal's landmark study interrogating black-white race relations and the quandary of an American democracy that founds itself on principles of racial exclusion and discrimination, he argues that the "anti-amalgamation doctrine," or the miscegenation taboo, provided the epistemological foundation for black-white segregation, particularly in the American South. For Myrdal, sex is at the core of discrimination against African Americans and of interracial relations. Though pornography does not carry the same threat of interracial progeny or social enervation that historically have characterized rhetoric against marriage across the color line, Myrdal's articulation of the menacing power of black-white intimacy resounds in interracial pornography while summoning the proverbial family drama in this play of race. In interracial pornography, the anti-amalgamation doctrine is evoked not as a reason for keeping the races at a definitive distance from each other but as a perverse technique of queer carnal intimacy. While interracial porn exploits the miscegenation taboo in its marketing and making of black-white sex, it reveals interracial intimacy as a queer fantasy. This fantasy is further elucidated by BDSM, which illuminates the dynamics of racialized shame, humiliation, pleasure, and power that are imperative within the genre. The homoeroticism at play galvanizes the hyperbole about and illicitness of interracial intimacy while the purported deviance of BDSM further compounds the power of taboo.

The gendered language of Myrdal's study, which frames the problem of miscegenation as an issue between black men and white women, reverberates in today's commercial interracial pornography, which, from a mainstream commercial standpoint, features black men and white women. As I discuss later in this chapter, black women's exclusion from the niche of interracial pornography speaks to not only pornography's resuscitation of the miscegenation taboo as a phenomenon between black men and white women but also to the exclusion of black women from the categories of race and gender and from the larger economy of sexual desire and the discrimination against them from within the pornography industry. Signaling a historical disavowal of black women as daughters of the nation, Myrdal's description of the problem of miscegenation as an issue between (white) daughters and "Negroes" prefigured the shape of contemporary hard-core interracial pornography. While "nigger" is a powerful ambivalent signifier of eroticized black abjection that is vital to the play of race and its pornographic renderings, "negro" and its various iterations also possess a particular valence within pornography.

In 2005 Andrew S., a white male, started the website mydaughtersfucking anigga.com (which has since changed to mydaughtersfuckingablackdude. com), an interracial pornography website that features sex between black men and white women.[44] Andrew S., whose background is in theatre and who admits that he had no experience or real interest in pornography at the time he entered the industry, owns Hush Hush Entertainment, an interracial pornography production company that is recognized across the industry as a pioneer on the cutting edge of American interracial hard-core porn.[45] His description of his entry into the industry is tellingly laconic; he states, "I [directed] for a while, [and then] I had an idea to start the website Mydaughtersfuckinganigga.com. That took off, and I built my own company."[46] There are conflicting stories about the true "mastermind" behind the site: Andrew S., black male porn star and lead actor Shane Diesel, and/or a collaboration between the two.[47] Nevertheless, Andrew S.'s vague description of the creative process (or lack thereof) that led to Mydaughtersfuckinganigga.com suggests that after being in the porn industry for just a short time, he became acutely aware of the commercial potential of racial stereotypes in pornography, specifically the taboo of black-white interracial sex. The site relies on stock racial-sexual stereotypes, mainly the mythical, monstrous black cock, a trope numerous scholars have identified as a predominate motif of black masculinity in pornography, specifically interracial pornography.[48]

Mydaughtersfuckingablackdude.com is part of a trend of contemporary interracial pornography that focuses on the hyperbolic eroticization of the transgressive pairing of the black male with the white female. The website boasts,

> Famous for inspiring nervous breakdowns around the globe, My Daughter's Fucking a Black Dude is like no other site on the Net! The dinner bell is ringing and inside this hardcore interracial site, teen white girls are the main course. The legendary Blackzilla brings his 1 foot of solid monster cock to the table, where the appetizer is black sausage and desert is cum pudding.[49]

This description positions white women against black men in a highly legible relationship of pure, youthful white female sexuality with a monstrous, violent black male sexuality. Though Hush Hush specializes in interracial pornography, much of its pornography capitalizes on the phenomenon of the cuckolded white male who desires to watch "his" woman—daughter, wife, and/or mother—have sex with a black man. Cram Johnson, the co-proprietor of and director/producer of a similar brand of interracial cuckold porn that features the Oh No! There's a Negro in My Mom/Daughter/Wife series and the video *I Can't Believe You Sucked a Negro: A Cuckold's POV*, recognizes the pornographic currency of the mythology of white womanhood. He states, "When white people fuck white people it's *whatever*; the same is true of black-on-black sex. But when the races mix, especially if the purity of the sacred white woman is compromised, it gets a lot of attention—even if the white girl is as dirty and disease-riddled as humanly possible."[50] Though this vein of pornography strategically evokes the same fears Myrdal identifies as fueling the anti-amalgamation doctrine, in its parroting of this scene it reveals these anxieties—and their concurrent pleasures—to be more complex than the conventional framing of beastly black masculinity versus chaste white femininity. As *Cuckold Stories 2* shows (and as Johnson suggests), white womanhood is not universally configured as an icon of purity or passivity in interracial pornography but is rather complicit in both interracial and queer desire.

I am interested less in pornography's recapitulation of racial-sexual fantasies—the sanctity of white female sexuality and fetishized mythologization of the black "monster cock"—than in the dynamics of queer desire that animate these recitals and how BDSM sheds light on this queer desire, specifically, the dynamics of white male humiliation and debasement that are so vital to the pleasures of the genre. For Andrew S., his website is a kind of satire of racism: "It just hit a nerve, because it was irreverent and it was about making fun of racism. It was a fine line, but somehow people got it. To this day, we haven't gotten one letter or email that was negative about our site. We were wondering if people got it and—obviously—they did."[51] Echoing Andrew, I am interested in expanding our thinking of pornography as a venue of race play, a stage upon which the pleasures of race and racism are enacted while the queer pleasures in the erotic project of race are recognized.

An important *Adult Video News* (*AVN*) cover story, "Black Humor: The Marketing of Racial Stereotypes in Interracial Porn" (2009), discusses the lucrative, popular, and controversial brand of interracial cuckold pornography. *AVN* positions interracial pornography as a solution to the decline in industry sales as a result of both technological shifts (i.e., the increasing availability of free Internet porn) and the larger economic decline.[52] Interracial sales have continued to grow, as evidenced by the fact the genre is no longer merely the domain of specialized studios.[53] Pornographers and distributors cross the country recognize the currency of this formula of interracial sex. The article quotes Allison Miller, a white woman who owns a pornography retail store in Richmond, Virginia, aptly named Taboo:

My customers seem to enjoy black men 'taking advantage of' white women; seducing their white daughters and wives. The *Blackzilla* line is one of my best-selling series. *Oh No! There's a Negro in My Mom* is also one that sells as soon as it hits the shelves. The more 'wrong' a title is, the more appealing it is. My customers don't want to see a loving interracial couple; they want to see massive black dicks satisfying or defiling pretty white girls.[54]

Assembling the diverse voices of top black male performers/producers, white male directors/producers, and industry sales and marketing professionals, the article replicates the industry's exclusionary rendering of interracial pornography that it gestures toward critiquing. One black male performer/director contends that the industry's narrow framing of interracial pornography reflects an "economic imperialism practiced by the white owners of distribution companies, talent agencies, and others in this industry who perpetuate the idea of the black man being the only male species to be considered 'interracial.'"[55] Black male performers and producers in this niche wrestle with a complex "burden of representation" in their negotiation of a slippery space hemmed in by racism—its stifling reproduction and its productive possibilities for pleasure and parody.[56] This conflicted terrain is the stage of pornography's play of race.

Black male performers in the lucrative niche of interracial porn describe different personal boundaries with regard to performing the stereotypes of excessive black male sexuality that are scripted by the miscegenation taboo. Award-winning black male performer Jack Napier recognizes the "power of taboo as a marketing tool."[57] However, in his own work he is not in favor of using racial stereotypes. Acknowledging the interracial brand pioneered by Hush Hush and black male performer Shane Diesel as "the furthest plateau," Napier states, "I am not trying to knock another man's hustle—I am not trying to knock a pork chop off his plate—but I just don't see how perpetuating negative stereotypes turns into a positive thing."[58] Napier describes black men's contradictory position in the industry: it rewards them for performing their hyperracialized blackness, yet simultaneously prompts them to feel that race becomes *the* factor through which they are not merely remunerated but also seen.

Lexington Steele, one of the most recognizable black male performers in not only interracial commercial porn but also in the industry as a whole, is similarly wary of the industry's construction of racial-sexual images and identities. He holds the white male imaginary responsible for what he views as porn's problematic commodification of stereotypes and ultimate dehumanization of the black male body:

> It's the white producer that tends to hold on to those elements of age-old taboo. I would never put out something like *Blackzilla*. I believe it's disrespectful because you're saying the black male performer is a monster. Is he a monster because his dick is bigger than yours? Is a guy who is 7-foot-6 a monster because he's a tall guy? I happen to have a large dick—does that make me a monster?[59]

However, Steele, a lead actor in pornography's play of race, concedes that he "choose[s] to play with stereotypes too."[60] He says, "As a producer, it behooves me to maximize my earning potential by strategically taking advantage of the black male as taboo."[61] His interracial Silverback Attack series evidences such play. Released January 1, 2006, the first video in the series, *Silverback Attack*, depicts sex between various white female performers and Steele, who performs a bestial and primitive black male sexuality. In referencing the silverback gorilla as a symbol for the black male, the series title evokes the deep histories of both scientific racism and visuality as a technology of racialization wherein pseudo-scientific practices such as craniology, physiognomy, and phrenology linked black men to apes.

The taboo of interracial pornography is manifold, emanating from larger sociohistorical conventions regarding intimacy between black men and white women and from interdictions from within the porn industry. In 2001, porn industry lawyer Paul Cambria created an informal list of sex acts that he advised producers to avoid.[62] While neither the acts themselves nor their representations were illegal, Cambria flagged them as presenting a high risk for prosecution. He included interracial sex, which he referred to as "black men-white women themes," within a diverse range of actions that ranged from "tight bondage" to "menstruation" to "fisting." Paradoxically, this list marked the dawn of the burgeoning niche of interracial pornography.

Like Andrew S., Shane Diesel, the longtime lead performer in Hush Hush's interracial cuckold porn, imagines pornography as a comedic site in which to play with racial-sexual stereotypes. Recalling a signing where a group of young white male fans with swastika tattoos asked him to sign DVD covers, Diesel states: "I love 'em—to me it's comedy. Most stereotypes are rooted in some truth. You can make fun of it and put on a good scene. Performers just need to set boundaries that they are comfortable with."[63] When Diesel retired from his role as Blackzilla with Hush Hush in 2008 to work with other production companies, he communicated a desire to move on from the part, stating "I've been doing the Blackzilla series for almost four years, and I got to the point where it was repetitious and routine, and I wanted to do something more."[64] Nevertheless, haunted by the Blackzilla of his past, he continues to perform in a similar vein of interracial porn premised on his "monster cock" and has become even further entrenched in the genre of interracial cuckold porn, regularly playing the role of "bull," a term used within the cuckold lifestyle and pornography to refer to the male lover in a cuckold relationship.

Cuckold pornography, which depicts the eroticized humiliation of a male figure, typically a husband, father, or boyfriend as he watches his wife, girlfriend, or daughter engage in sexual relations with another man, is a perverse rendering and satire of the normativity—indeed fantasy—of the institution of (white) heteropatriarchal monogamy. Though it features narratives of racialized humiliation, a major component of the genre's financial success and popularity is the fantasy of racialized desire that depends upon a queer valence of black sexuality. The cuckold fantasy is not limited to the realm of pornography. Network reality television shows in the United States such as *Wife Swap* (Lifetime) and *Celebrity Wife Swap* (ABC) and the increased visibility of the cuckold lifestyle on social media attest to the mainstream currency of the cuckolding fantasy and the collective anxieties regarding monogamy and the institution of marriage. Both interracial and same-sex desire compound the anxiety cuckold pornography reflects and produces about the viability and pleasure of monogamy. Hence I suggest that pornography might be instrumental in queering interracial desire in that it permits us to see the "Mandingo" archetype of black masculinity as less an incarnation of white female desire or a threat to the cult of white womanhood and more a product of white and black male desire and the insecurity of white heteropatriarchal mononormativity.

Diesel is the star of Digital Sin's interracial series Cuckold Stories (1–11, 2009–2013), whom *Cosmopolitan* magazine recently called an "empire."[65] Premised on the narrative of a horny white wife who is unsatisfied with her white husband and desires a "big black monster cock" to satisfy her libido, the series exemplifies the interracial cuckold niche.[66] The DVD covers of these titles illustrate the repetitiveness of this fantasy, the queerness of the genre, and its coupling with BDSM sexuality. Staging the triad of interracial queer BDSM desire, the covers often depict a white woman gazing at the camera with a look that is a combination of arousal and anxiety. The often-truncated penis of the black male is typically stuffed into, but unable to be accommodated by, her hyperextended mouth. An angst-ridden white male figure— husband, boyfriend, father, or son—hovers nearby, usually behind this interracial transgression. As his gaze locks in on the two figures, his agitation manifests in a gaping mouth, hands placed on his head or covering his eyes, and/or a strong grimace.

Though this image reveals the centrality and absolute participation of the white male in this drama, it reifies the intimacy of the black and white male. Interracial cuckold pornography eroticizes the failure of monogamy and the incestuous perversion of familial desire (mother-son, father-daughter). In interracial cuckold pornography, the illicitness of cross-race desire is as an ambiguous signifier; it compounds the transgressions of the hetero-nuclear family while obscuring the salience of queerness and BDSM. Nevertheless, the narratives of BDSM and queerness are, like the white man who is seemingly suspended in the backdrop of these images, peripheral yet important. Here the margins are actually the center: queer desire and BDSM take their seat in this perverse family play.

Pornography plays on and with the intimate entanglement of miscegenation and shame.[67] Many scholars have suggested that pornography is an apt place for enacting taboo interracial-sexual fantasies. Williams argues that "pornography and sexploitation cinema have at least been willing to explore what more polite forms do not."[68] Dwight McBride envisions pornography, specifically Internet pornography, as intervening in the politics of respectability to make possible the private consumption of what we would be "publically ashamed" of. [69] Similarly, Miller-Young posits that interracial video pornography intervenes in our shame over black-white interracial desire, enabling us to privately consume these fantasies: "People are ashamed of interracial desire. White people do not want to admit having desire for black sexuality, and what video does is allow them to enjoy this in the privacy of their own homes with no one knowing."[70] Dines imagines interracial pornography as a "safe peephole" for the white heteropatriarchal male gaze.[71] Jarrett Neal analyzes the dynamics of shame in interracial gay pornography, arguing that in "viewing interracial gay porn, gay white men who purposely distance themselves from genuine relationships with African-American men can indulge their private sexual fantasies while allowing racist and stereotypical beliefs regarding black men to persist."[72] While pornography permits the consumption of fantasies that one might not otherwise gratify, making the pleasure of interracial gay porn a white gay male's pleasure problematically disavows the unspeakable pleasures that guide this book. What about black pleasures—across genders and sexualities—in shame and the enactment of racial stereotypes that the play of interracial sex so easily lends itself to? What do we make of our libidinal investments in the history of chattel slavery and our rapture in race itself? These shameful pleasures are complex and include BDSM and homoerotic desire. BDSM and queer pleasure imbue the eroticized racialized shame that is integral to interracial pornography, specifically the cuckold niche. Thinking about pornography as a safe or ideal space for playing with taboo (inter)racial sexual fantasies bolsters the reality/ fantasy dichotomy that, like BDSM, undergirds pornography to reinforce a problematic view of pornography as the province of fantasy that is detached from our "real," "true," sexualities.[73]

Many of Diesel's scenes in the Cuckold Stories series begin with an interview between "husband" and "wife" that functions as a confession of both interracial and queer desire. Cuckold Stories 2, for example, commences with a husband and wife sitting next to each other on a living-room couch.[74] The "home" setting of private living rooms and bedrooms that serves as the mise-en-scène for many interracial cuckold videos accentuates the illicitness of this queer encounter in which the black male violates the sanctity of the marriage, the purity and size of the white female body (and the while male's policing of this corporeal site of white female sexuality), the protected space of the home, and metaphorically through that, the nation. The husband's introductory statement, "I personally love watching my wife get fucked by another guy. I like watching her get fucked by a big fat black cock, something about it turns me on so fucking much," immediately foregrounds white male desire for the black male body. While the husband introduces Diesel after this brief introductory remark as a "present" for his wife, Diesel equally performs for the pleasure of the white male. The casting of gay male porn star Derrick Paul's as the husband contributes to the homoerotic currency of the scene.

This queer instantiation and denial becomes a profound erotic tension in this kind of pornography. Cuckold pornography brings into relief the queerness of heterosexual male desire within pornography. Samuel Delaney has compellingly identified the salience of this blurred eroticized boundary between heterosexual and homosexual in contemporary American pornography as "the sine qua non" of a male porn star's career success.[75] Delaney writes, "The heterosexual male audience was fascinated by this guy in whom the usual boundary between desire to be him and the desire to possess him was set so intriguingly (in male heterosexual terms) askew."[76] Interracial cuckold pornography irradiates these boundaries. Diesel joins the couple on the couch, sitting down to form a sandwich in which the white male is in the center. He leans over the husband, who retreats into the back of the couch, and begins to kiss the wife on the mouth. This triangular spatial configuration is central to the power dynamics in the scene. The white male is visible yet set a little ways behind his wife and Diesel. He is often present in the visual frame of the camera when he is not physically part of the scene and vice versa. For example, later we can see only his hand grasping his wife's hand as Diesel fucks her from behind or just his knee in the edge of the frame as he sits in a nearby chair, watches the cuckoldry, and touches himself. Even when he is invisible, his voice performs as an active partner in the troilism.

After this kiss it is the proverbial big black cock that takes center stage—what both husband and wife "have to see." This urgent need to see, of course, is a metaphor for the need for sexual consumption. The sight of Diesel's cock (which, as extraordinarily large and "black," has already been well set up as a metonym for black male racial-sexual alterity) is just one facet of a complex prism of white male pleasure in this play of race. The husband is further aroused as he watches his wife's pleasure and debasement (he says, "I want him to wreck that pussy. Stretch it all out"). He imagines his wife sucking his own cock and fantasizes about sucking Diesel's cock as he stimulates himself. His wife's fellatio with Diesel evinces interracial homoerotic desire and its policing while providing the setting for the husband's important role as the narrator of the cuckold fantasy. As the wife fellates Diesel, it is the husband, not Diesel, who utters the dirty talk, commanding: "Suck that big-ass black cock!" and praising his wife's skills.

The labyrinthian layers of pleasure, identification, and denial are stratified by race, gender, and sexual orientation. While the husband serves as the mouthpiece, Diesel functions as a kind of director. He orders the wife to kiss her husband and tell her she loves him. Yet once she follows Diesel's command she is reprimanded; Diesel scolds, "You can't kiss him. He can't taste my cock! Go wipe his lips off. Wipe it off." White male pleasure in the black male body is acknowledged as it is desired, engaged as it is forbidden. This is a moment where the heterosexual brakes come on yet fail to halt the profound queerness of the interracial cuckold fantasy. Though Diesel prohibits the husband from tasting his cock, the camera undermines this edict, framing the husband as not merely the witness but also as a cocksucker himself. As he sits directly behind the couple on the couch, the husband's lips are situated on the same horizontal line as the wife's "cocksucking" lips. With one slight slippage of the spectators' gaze or of Diesel's hips, the "big black cock" could be inserted in the husband's ("wrong") mouth. This implied line mirrors the tension throughout the Cuckold Stories series between the recognition and disavowal of interracial homoerotic male desire.

If the husband is not allowed to taste Diesel's cock, touching him is also off limits. Diesel maintains a strict no-touching rule for the white male performer in these cuckold scenes. This rule reflects what Williams identifies as what governs heterosexual hard-core pornography: the prohibition of male-male physical contact and, presumably, male-male pleasure.[77] Diesel states, "I let the husband or boyfriend watch me have sex with his wife or girlfriend, and sort of play with his bisexual tendencies without letting him touch me."[78] Like many of the audio and visual devices at work in the Cuckold Stories series, this no-touching rule reveals the presence of homoerotic desire and pleasure, reifying the queer fantasy it attempts to quash. In many videos the near-contact of black and white male bodies undermines the authority of this rule. The absurdity of such a dictate is underscored when, in *Cuckold Stories 11* (2013), the tips of each man's naked erect penis are inches away from and pointed toward one another in a spectacle of size comparison that mirrors the video's larger juxtaposition of black and white masculinity. The contrast between the magnitude of black masculinity and white male feebleness is an unfailing trope of this type of pornography. This contest demonstrates the queer pleasures in and of white male humiliation that are so central to the interracial cuckold narrative.

In the absence of physical contact between black and white males in these interracial cuckold fantasies, the white female body becomes a fetishistic stage for the enactment of cross-racial homoerotic desire. Her body serves as a conduit for their prohibited touch. She mediates the hesitantly disavowed homoerotic desire. For example, often both men will have their hand on her head as she is giving Diesel a blow job, or she will "take" his dick while she kisses her husband. The white female as intermediary for queer black-white interracial anxiety and desire is a familiar figure. The cult of white womanhood has historically functioned as fodder for a white male phobia about black male sexuality that can only be understood as queer. White male desire for the male black body hovers amid these profound anxieties about black male desire for the white female and vice versa.

The rhetoric of BDSM intervenes in interracial cuckold pornography's tentative denial of homoerotic pleasure. The diegesis, marketing, and sales of the genre obfuscate the queer aspect of this niche of pornography, but Diesel is well aware of it. He estimates that "70 percent of [his] fans are white gay or bisexual fans."[79] Similarly, black male performer Sean Michaels, star of the Evil Cuckold series, says that his primary audience consists of couples and gay and bisexual fans.[80] In a similar vein of slippage between categories, although interracial cuckold porn is typically not marketed or sold under the banner of BDSM pornography, the language of BDSM is used in the service of softening a conflicted homoerotic desire. Marketing materials cast the male audience for interracial cuckold pornography as reflecting a "submissive" but not a queer desire. *AVN* describes one cuckold series as "push[ing] psychological buttons to emasculate and excite the legion of submissive males that enjoys the rap-idly growing cuckold fetish."[81] It also identifies white male viewers of the I Can't Believe You Sucked a Negro series as having a desire for "emas-culation" and "self-loathing" but does not specifically mention them as desiring the black male body.[82] Nevertheless, interracial same-sex desire and BDSM script the cuckold fantasy.

BDSM throws light on the dynamics of eroticized racial humiliation to bring the question of pleasure into high relief. Interracial cuckold pornography illustrates "the seeming inescapability of the BDSM scene" in performances of black-white interracial sexuality.[83] Attesting to the complexity of BDSM humiliation, Jay Wiseman, author of SM 101, ana-lyzes not just the salience of spectatorship for the pleasure humiliation brings but also the "type of people watching."[84] In cuckold interracial pornography, the race and gender of the witnesses modulate the erotic currency of humiliation. While Wiseman warns practitioners about cer-tain types of "verbal abuse" based on race, sexual orientation, religion, and body because it "may go deeper than intended," he simultaneously recognizes the intense arousal and "the sweet shame" of precisely this type of humiliation.[85] Like Wiseman, sexologists Moser and Kleinplatz cite the "difficulty" of BDSM humiliation while evoking race as one of its techniques. They identify interracial cuckolding, "the cuck fantasy," as a common example of BDSM humiliation.[86] Using BDSM as a lens to reveal humiliation as a technique of pleasure and queer desire disrupts what I believe to the oversimplified readings of interracial porn as sim-ply indicative and productive of degradation.[87] It helps us see debase-ment differently.

Kathryn Bond Stockton analyzes the entanglement of shame, plea-sure, blackness, and queerness. My thinking of the productive possi-bility of debasement is inspired by Stockton's radical re(theorization) of it. She argues that debasement is a juncture for the crossing of the "signs" of black and queer: two identifications that have historically been defined by shame. Stockton's analysis critically reorients, recovers, and replays shame, exploring black peoples', queer peoples', and black queer peoples' embrace of "valuable, generative, beautiful shame."[88] Using the metaphor of a "switchpoint," she analyzes black and queer at the inter-section of shame. Debasement is vital, Stockton argues, to accessing this "switchpoint" and navigating the seemingly distanced signs of queerness and blackness.[89] That is, black and queer come into relief through shame. This switchpoint is the stage for cuckold interracial pornography, a fantasy of queered racial abjection that is enacted "between tabooed attractions and acts of racial punishments."[90] Analyzing BDSM and pornography as axes of eroticized shame where black and queer "meet," Stockton's theorization of debasement illuminates the unspeakable pleasures that ground this book.

The sex that ensues in *Cuckold Stories 2* is tame and predictable, particularly for a sexual escapade framed as a departure from routine, vanilla, conjugal sex. The fellatio foreplay is followed by a few seconds of cunnilingus, then a variety of different sexual positions on the couch, finished with a money shot where Diesel ejaculates on the wife's face. Throughout the video, while Diesel and the wife seem to be glued to the sexual surface of the couch, the husband enjoys greater mobility, floating in and out of the camera's frame of view, but never far, audio-visually, from the copulating couple. Beyond his verbal participation, he holds back his wife's hair so the camera can get a better view of Diesel's cock in her mouth, kisses her lips as she is being fucked doggie style by Diesel, or clasps her hand as a gesture of "support." Indeed, the "taking" of the "big black cock" seems to be a joint endeavor between husband and wife. After she confesses, "I need your support. I need your fucking support. You have no idea how fucking good this feels," the husband embraces her hand as Diesel continues to fuck her hard from behind. Seemingly empowered by the touch of his hand (and/or the pleasure of Diesel's cock) she says, "I can do it. *We* can do it *together.*" Her remark illustrates the queer collusion of the scene.

The wife positions her desire for Diesel as relative to her husband's desire for him: she confesses, "I love big cocks just as much as you do." Yet once again, the white male's desire for the black male body is interrupted—disciplined by the humiliation. The husband's humiliation is multifaceted: effected by himself, his wife, and Diesel. For example, Diesel instructs the husband to take a seat in a nearby chair and orders the wife to put her underwear on his head. Encaging his face, the thong thus becomes a tool of bondage. The wife commands him to leave it on while he sits and watches the cuckoldry. The wife's humiliation of her husband and his own self-debasement is hinged on the failure of the white male body and white male sexuality in relation to the black male.

As the husband sits in the chair behind the couple and begins to jerk off what she refers to as his "little cock," she tells him not to pull it out of his pants because it will "embarrass" her.

The familiar narrative of black excess and white inadequacy (recall Vanessa Blue's *Door 2 Door*) is put in the service of policing queer desire via humiliation. Later the husband humiliates himself, telling his wife, "That's how your pussy deserves to be fucked." Just as the black male body becomes the site of its own reiteration and performative excess, the white male body co-produces the spectacle of its own racial-sexual humiliation. Pleasure is a product of both "perversions." What we do not see here is a Keyes-like interracial fantasy of humiliation and historical redress enacted on the body of the white female. Though Diesel does not explicitly acknowledge or perform the revengeful fury of the memory of chattel slavery, that history nonetheless underlies the narratives of racialization that seethe in the interracial cuckold pornography fantasy. The black male is here less a "phobogenic" (à la Fanon and Williams) object and more a figure of desire and anticipation for both husband and wife.

Cram Johnson, co-director and producer of the Oh No! There's a Negro in My Mom/Daughter/Wife series, notes the racialized Oedipal narrative performed in the interracial cuckold fantasy: "As a child you were always scared that something would happen to your mother. And as an adult you realize that most of your early fears could be traced back to the black man."[91] Johnson touches upon the complex psychological dimensions of cuckold pornography, including an Oedipal desire for the mother as incestuous love object (configured explicitly through the mother but also symbolized through the figures of wife and daughter as proxies for the mother) and white male castration anxiety, here instantiated through the black male phallus.[92] Beyond its psychoanalytic resonance, interracial cuckold pornography reveals the profound anxiety surrounding institutions of heteronormativity, such as marriage and monogamy, and their multifaceted queer (homoerotic and BDSM) insecurities. The adulterous ruination of one family begets perhaps another. However, in this queer kinship, the black female body is absent. She is relegated to another plane of pornographic performance that the industry refers to as "reverse interracial."

Moving in Reverse: Recovering the Black Female Body in Interracial Pornography

Diana Devoe, who self-identifies as and is recognized by many as the first black female pornography director, attests to the myriad layers of discrimination black female performers in the industry face—from lower pay rates and less diverse roles (what she calls "cheap product") than those of white female performers to the insidiousness of racialized "standard[s] of beauty" that devalue them.[93] She argues that black female performers' rejection within interracial pornography is allied with these discriminations:

> When you even break down the genre of interracial, interracial should mean this race and this race. It means black men and non-black women. That's all it means. If you happen to have a title that's black women and white men, it's called reverse interracial. If you happen to have a title with an Asian girl and a white guy, it's just a scene. Through interracial movies, porn has effectively taken an X-ACTO knife and just cut black women out of that equation.[94]

Her terse remark about pornography's repudiation of the black female communicates the symbolic violence enacted in this exclusion. Within the mainstream commercial industry, interracial pornography is pornography that depicts sexual acts between a black man and a white woman, what Stuart Wall describes as "white guys banging hot sistas."[95] Wall is the vice-president of Smash Pictures, a company that produces the "reverse interracial (IR)" series Black Pie for the White Guy (2006, 2009). The exclusion of the black female from interracial porn testifies to her contested ontology as an unraced, ungendered body. In this construct, black women are rendered not merely invisible but also inhuman. This debarment and the creation of an*other* category, reverse interracial, effectively excludes them from one of the most profitable niches of contemporary American commercial pornography and from larger societal ideals of beauty and body. It also signifies the failure of systems of identification such as gender and race to speak for and to the black female body.

The fact that black women hover outside the bounds of womanhood itself, beyond "the ranks of gendered femaleness," accounts for their exclusion from the genre of interracial pornography, not just, to recall Skin, their location outside of the "normal porno look."[96] In our collective racist imaginary they do not occupy the status of daughters, wives, and mothers—figures around which interracial porn pivots. Spillers troubles the legibility of black womanhood in a way that decodes their exclusion from this important niche of American commercial pornography. She problematizes race and gender, arguing that as a result of the lingering traumas of chattel slavery and its "rule of dominance," the conventional grammar of gender fails black women.[97] The gendered subject positions of "male" and "female" have no symbolic coherence for the postslavery black body. Spillers's theorization of the failure of institutions of identity and language to recognize and speak for black female subjectivity is both historically accurate and prescient.

I suggest that we see black women's exclusion from interracial pornography in tandem with other coeval institutional "failures" in the arena of black women's sexuality. Such a move not only recognizes pornography as a central, not a marginal, space for constructing black female sexuality; it also signals the widespread nature of black women's exclusion at many social levels. For example, the low marriage rates of black women have received recent attention in the media and academia, prompting Ralph Richard Banks to ask, "Is marriage for white people?"[98] Might thinking about black women's absence from interracial pornography in light of their marriage "crisis" be a move toward considering the larger "state" of black female sexuality—its continued challenges to the heteronormative state and the state of heteronormativity—beyond exclusion from the "fantasy" of interracial pornography to more material forms of exclusion? What larger institutions and systems of representation fail to include black female sexuality, and why do they do so? Furthermore, to what extent can we understand these failures as a subverting these systems themselves and/or as more historically familiar iterations of black women's exclusion?

Though the name reverse interracial porn would seem to signify a switching of the identifications of race and gender, the genre does not offer the rich, developed diegesis of the genre of interracial pornography that the cuckold fantasy does. The dynamic characterization, plot, dialogue, comedy, and mise-en-scène of interracial pornography are not matched in reverse interracial porn, which often is instead a mere hardcore partnering of black women and white men that typically lacks a developed storyline. Reverse interracial porn performs a rather insecure reversal of traditional interracial pornography. Despite its inclusion of the black female, it remains anchored in the rhetoric of racial-sexual alterity that fuels traditional interracial pornography. While it might be tempting to view reverse interracial porn, particularly that produced by black directors, as a kind of corrective response to the genre's problematic excising of black women, it reifies that exclusion. That is, although producing reverse interracial pornography creates opportunities for black women working in the industry, it reinforces their position in an alternate racialized and gendered libidinal economy and site of representation.

Lexington Steele sees the economic potential of reverse interracial pornography. Steele views it not so much as a chance to combat the exclusion of black women from interracial porn or to provide black female performers with more diverse roles but as a business opportunity. He sees reverse interracial porn as a profitable and novel commodity, "something new" to give retailers a "heads up on [their] competition."[99] In May 2006, Steele released *White Man's Revenge*, "the first title from Mercenary to only feature scenes with black females and white males."[100] While the title promises a Keyes-like narrative of historically tinged racial revenge, it fails to deliver such theatrics. Reverse interracial porn is not a sequel of sorts in the continuing drama of the miscegenation taboo in which the violated white male seeks vengeance for the black male's sexual conquest of the white female. No such script is invoked in *White Man's Revenge* or in reverse interracial porn generally, raising the questions of for what, from whom, and why the white male is seeking revenge.

White Man's Revenge begins with a hyperbolic spectacle of white male desire for black female sexuality. Two "white" male performers walk into a house where the sex acts take place with bags of chocolate items: hot chocolate, chocolate milk, candies, and so forth.[101] When the cameraman asks them why they chose to bring chocolate instead of beer, vodka, or pizza, they confess that they "just want a little chocolate." He assures them, "Well, I got a little chocolate for ya," and the first of six black women performers in the video emerges. Yet with the exception this brief introductory scene, *White Man's Revenge* is much like many other gonzo videos in which the diegesis—already weak here—is secondary to sex. Unlike the interracial cuckold genre and in defiance of its intriguing title, *White Man's Revenge* does not dramatize the taboo of black-white sexual intimacy but rather performs a more a quotidian instance of white male access to black female sexuality. What is it about this gendered iteration of interracial sex—black women and white men—that does not require such storytelling? How does the always alreadyness of black female libidinality foreclose the dramatization of certain narratives? Does this coition need no pretext? Indeed, black women's sexual intimacy with white men has never had the same taboo currency as the "reverse."[102]

If the miscegenation taboo seems weakly enacted in this "reverse" iteration of the interracial pornographic fantasy, the queerness of the scenes are undeniable. Like interracial porn, reverse interracial porn queers white male heterosexual desire. Black sexuality again becomes the conduit for both attracting and repelling white male homoeroticism, which is also exceedingly ambivalent in this scenario. *White Man's Revenge* bucks the heterosexual hard-core porn mandate of no male-male intimacy. At the beginning of one scene, one white male performer asserts: "I mean, I am not doing anything with guys." The cameraman responds, "I wouldn't hang out with you if you did; shit with dudes, man, that's all wrong!," and both men laugh. Minutes later, the camera zooms in on two erect white penises rubbing against one another in the hyperextended mouth of black female performer Marie Luv. The casting of Mario Banderas, star of *Straight Guys for Gay Eyes* (2006), as one of the male leads further throws into question the video's heteronormative posturing and homophobic dialogue.

The difference between reverse interracial and interracial porn reveals how as, Kevin Mumford argues, the taboo of black men's sexual intimacy with white women—and not the reverse—is the "defining taboo of the margin."[103] Yet pornography has not always subscribed to this racialized and gendered norm of interracial desire. In the following section, my discussion of pornography's performance of black-white interracial sex looks back at the stag genre of the early to mid-twentieth century to further illuminate the complexity of interracial desire within pornography. Though commercial interracial pornography was first produced in the United States in the early 1980s, interracial sex occupies a primordial space in the history of moving-image pornography.[104] An early example of interracial pornography illustrates the nuances of pornography's playful rendering of the color line. Not a rendering of anxiety, threat, or phobic libidinal deviance but rather an instantiation of ameliorative, jocular amalgamation, the example I read here from the stag genre signals the historical presence of the black female in interracial pornography and the instability of the erotics of and at the color line.

Another Blend of Black and White: Racial Amalgamation in the Stag Genre

Venturing back to the stag genre to analyze this example of early interracial moving-image pornography enables us to see the shifting valence of interracial desire within pornography, uncover a space the black female formerly occupied within pornography, and analyze her absence/presence in contemporary interracial pornography. Produced from roughly 1920 up until the 1960s, stag films, silent black-and-white shorts that averaged ten to twelve minutes, are the origin of American hard-core porn.[105] Until the early 1950s, stag films were shot mostly using 16mm film.[106] Because of the existing obscenity laws, stag films were anonymously produced, performed, and consumed; they were shown to a clandestine audience of predominately white males.[107] Stag films are integral, albeit underground, elements of American visual culture.[108] The clandestine nature of the production and consumption of stag films speaks to the equivocal positioning of pornography in American society and its slippery relationship to nation and nationality. Linda Williams's term "on/scenity" communicates the paradox of pornography that stags instantiate—its liminal yet central place within American culture and its unstable location somewhere between the real and the symbolic and imaginary, between mainstream and margins, between legal and illegal, between good and bad. Stag films were urgently desired yet widely shunned.[109]

Stag films serve as an insightful point from which to interrogate performances of interracial sexual fantasy and to illuminate the function of pornography as a visual technology of sexuality, race, and gender. These films were screened covertly at underground locations such as private homes, in shops after hours, and in the meeting places of fraternal organizations such as Elks Clubs. Spectatorship of these films involved more than rudimentary sex education; they also constructed and reflected white male heteropatriarchal hegemony and exclusion.[110] Although, as Joseph Slade notes, these "amateur pursuits" made little money because of their limited audience, the currency of the "stag ritual" as a collective social force of white masculinity remains strong.[111] The communal viewing audience of stag films offered a fraternity-like brotherhood of white male heteropatriarchal power, pleasure, and privilege. While Williams rightly recognizes that women were never the "intended audience for these films," early moving-image American pornography was both mobilized by and productive of a racial exclusion that reveals the constitutive relationship of old-boy networks and white masculinity to racialized sexuality.[112]

While the audience for stag films was largely white male, the performers are somewhat more diverse. Miller-Young estimates that black performers were not prominent actors in stag films until the 1930s, although their presence was symbolically evoked through racialized themes and exoticism.[113] Her important work on stag films reveals how not only contemporary racial politics but also technology informs pornography's articulation of white male desire for black female sexuality. While the presence of black bodies in stag films is evidence of white male desire for interracial sex, Miller-Young contends that because these films were collectively viewed, interracial desire remained somewhat "policed." She writes, "Decades later, home video allowed for the proliferation of porn displaying interracial sex for white spectators in ways that were previously impermissible within the strict economy of racial segregation."[114] Kenneth Turan and Stephen Zito contend that the black presence in stag films intensified and diversified after World War II; before that, black performers were primarily symbolic participants in the genre, evoking humor through their roles as black comics or clown-like figures, servants, and lazy peeping toms. After World War II, they became explicitly sexual performers and their roles broadened slightly.[115] According to Turan and Zito, this was a result of filmmakers' capitalization on "the shock value of interracial intercourse."[116] This theory of black inclusion contrasts with historians Al Di Laurio and Gerald Rabkin's argument that an "increased tolerance of sexual diversity" was responsible for the growing numbers of black bodies on stag screens.[117] Nevertheless, Turan and Zito argue, black performers were limited by stereotypes and sub-servient roles—"old characterizations (proud, savage black men who lust after weak white women; cruel white men who abuse black women) and the old situations (black maids are seduced by white employers; black repairman come to fix the phone and fix the Vassar wife instead)."[118] I find that stag films were not quite this formulaic with regard to perfor-mances of racialized sexuality.

While racialized sexuality, particularly the black female body, dis-rupts the trite narratives that stag films clung to, however loosely; chal-lenges the rigidity of the gender roles the films depict; and disrupts the category of "woman" and "man" the films reflect and create, examples such as the ones I analyze below suggest the salience of narrative in stag-ing black sexuality and through it, interracial sex. In many stag films a trite domestic narrative serves to explain sex, reflecting a conventional heteronormative construction of gendered space. Often the female per-former waits inside a domestic space for the male to enter. His role of mechanic or deliveryman serves one function: to "bring the man into the home" so the sex acts can take place.[119] Black women, however, do not typically perform the archetypal stag female—that is, the randy, lonely housewife waiting for her husband, a messenger, a bellhop, or a maintenance man or the single woman lounging alone who is surprised by her assailant, then succumbs and then enjoys his advances. Instead, the black female performer often plays "herself," a role that speaks to the presumed libidinal nature of the black female as always already por-nographic and to her continuing exclusion from the popular image of domestic womanhood in the first half of the twentieth century. Further-more, contrary to what Turan and Zito note, black people (both men and women) performed sexually in stag films before World War II in a variety of roles and diverse characterizations. While, as Miller-Young notes, the presence of black actors is stronger in later stag films, there is evidence of black performance in stag before 1930. The biggest increase in black performers in the films in the Kinsey archive stag collection took place after 1947.

Blends (circa 1940, 8:23), depicts sex between a black female and a white male, mapping a space for the black female in pornography's vibrant (inter)racial imaginary.[120] The film plays artfully with the rhetoric of miscegenation, contrasting the polarized figures of black femininity and white masculinity. The racial-sexual alterity of the black female body as a foil for the whiteness of her male partner is the crux of the film and its erotic capital. Like many films of the genre, in the absence of sound, *Blends* relies on written text to narrate the actions of the two actors. This text provides the central storyline: a comic tale of the joys of black-white intimacy. The first frame of the text introduces the film's overarching theme of mixing: "We all know how blending improves such things as Tobaccos, Whiskeys & Spices, so we *now* show you blends in screwing!" The use of food and drink metaphors to refer to black female sexuality in pornography remains a common practice. Chocolate, cocoa, coffee, and caramel are common words that are used to signify the consumption of the black female body as a site of fetishized racial-sexual alterity within pornography. Here the use of food and drink as a metaphor for black-white amalgamation is an attempt to deproblematize interracial sex.[121] The benign, ameliorating blending of everyday American commodities—tobacco, whiskey, and spices—serves as a platform from which to explore the taboo concept of black-white intimacy.

Blends disrupts contemporary pornographic renderings of interracial intimacy to open up a space for the black female body in this line of performance. It also reveals how these fantasies and their performances are unstable and shift with the sociopolitical cultural tides. Interracial intimacy in earlier stag films is dominated by the pairing of the white male with the black female; interracial intimacy between black men and white women did not become part of the stag genre until the late 1950s.[122] Even within the imagined "safeness" and fantasy of the space of pornography, pornographers were perhaps not ready to break some racial-sexual taboos before the mid-twentieth century. The stag genre reveals the black female's historical space in the pornographic fantasy. And like contemporary interracial pornography, stag films cast interracial intimacy as heterosexual.[123]

In 1940, twenty-seven years before the landmark *Loving v. Virginia* (1967) case, in which the Supreme Court invalidated miscegenation laws, not only were marriages between black and white legally prohibited in thirty-one of the forty-eight states, but representations of interracial sex on screen were also forbidden.[124] The Production Code (also known as the Hays Code), which the Motion Picture Producers and Distributors of America (MPPDA) introduced in the 1930s, attests to the integral role of films in the invention and policing of racialized identities and whiteness as a protected category of privilege. Item number six of the "Sex" section of the code, entitled "Miscegenation," prohibited performances of black-white sexual intimacy: "sex relationships between the white and black races is forbidden." With the Hays Code's prohibition of acts of miscegenation on screen, the underground genre of stag films provided an audience, albeit a select one, with the taboo pleasure of watching black-and-white sex.

The second frame of *Blends* shows the black woman undressing in front of the camera, smiling coyly while removing her white undergarment, which contrasts with her dark skin. Rendered in black and white, the eroticized contrast of the color line becomes even more pronounced. This value heightens the performed physiological and ontological foil of the black-white interracial pairing. (Visual contrast remains an important technique of eroticized racial-sexual alterity in current interracial pornography; numerous scholars have discussed the investment of contemporary interracial pornography in the value of skin pigmentation—what Lexington Steele calls "the fascination with the color contrast."[125]) The woman turns around to display her naked backside to the camera, bends over, and begins shaking her buttocks while waving one hand through her widely parted legs. Her direct eye contact with the camera and waving motion signal her active engagement with camera and the gaze of the viewing audience. Her moves appear to be choreographed or orchestrated in compliance with the pornographic edict of revealing the body to the camera—what Williams terms hard core's "principle of *maximum visibility*."[126] This playfulness of her movement echoes the humorous text and the film's theme of harmless, if not beneficial, amalgamation. *Blends* illustrates how, as Tavia Nyong'o notes, amalgamation is not just a trope of blending; it is also a "metaphor of transformation."[127] The storylines of stag films often reflect crude humor, puns, clichés, and dirty jokes. This silliness is quickly interrupted by the explicitness of the text: "*First* you *must* have a dark, soft, luscious, black pussy. *Second* you need a long, hard Dick." Exoticized and eroticized black pussy as the synecdoche of black female sexuality is the primary ingredient—

the foundational flavor base—in the recipe of black-white interracial sex *Blends* purveys. While scholars have recognized the role of the stag film as sex pedagogy (Joseph Slade notes that "for generations of Americans, stag films provided their first unfettered view of sexual activity"), their function as a technique of racialization remains overlooked. *Blends* is a visual and textual tutorial on interracial sex in which the pedagogies of pleasure, race, and sex collide.[128]

The genitalization of the black female body works in tandem with her function as a "spice" or "flavor" to enliven the insipidity of both white sexuality and intraracial sex. This understanding of race mixing reverberates in historical European and Euro-American conceptions of miscegenation, which, contrary to popular belief, did not singularly discourage sex across the color line, at least not until the end of the nineteenth century, when (white) racial purity as imperative to the constitution of the nation became the dominant view.[129] For example, though Arthur de Gobineau recognized the attraction of miscegenation (he wrote, "It would be unjust to assert that every mixture is bad and harmful"), he believed that it would ultimately lead to the deterioration of civilization.[130] The *Blends* mentality that the exotic currency of black sexuality would improve white sexuality resonates in the very document that brought the word "miscegenation" (from the Latin *miscere* [to mix] and *genus* [race], into the national lexicon in the 1860s. Though the pamphlet *Miscegenation* (1864) was revealed to be a political hoax aimed at sabotaging Lincoln's campaign for reelection, it *played* with important extant desires and phobias surrounding black sexuality, stereotypes of racialized sexuality, and sex across the color line that interracial pornography continues to engage. In line with *Blends'* view of the dichotomous yet harmonious and productive pairing of black-white sexuality—the ameliorating property of blackness and its ability to sexually enhance—the pamphlet positions the "white American" in a state "of physical decay" for which "negro" sexuality provides an antidote.[131] Black sex intervenes in the blandness of white sexual intercourse, which is deemed "formal, ascetic, unemotional."[132] *Blends* animates the slippage between miscegenation as procreation and as merely sex in its imagining of sexual intercourse across the color line as productive, but it encourages these "blends" not so much for a progressive American civilization as for a modern sexuality.

Though *Blends* exemplifies the diversity in the pornographic rendering of black-white interracial sex, like contemporary cuckold interracial porn, it rests on the foundation of the erotic currency of black women's racial-sexual alterity. Echoing the shifting conceptions and iterations of sex across the color line, pornography serves as an important place from which to both consider the question of black-white interracial desire and to remind us that racial ideologies and their performative renderings are never fixed. *Blends* illustrates the irony of miscegenation itself— its rigidifying rather than softening of racial boundaries.[133] In blending black and white, *Blends* further reifies these racial identifications as distinct categories.

After a quick shot of the black woman sitting on a bed, legs open widely to display her genitalia to the camera, we cut to her giving a hand job to the white man, whose body is cut off by the frame so that his upper body and face are not visible.[134] He appears to push the woman's face down toward his penis but is denied. This failed attempt at fellatio— her rejection of his advance—signals the agency of the black female performer, suggesting her enforcement of firm boundaries in the context of her sexual performance. Yet the film's failure to produce fellatio merely reinforces the construction of black-white genital sexual intercourse as the ultimate blend, the most salient and pleasurable racial-sexual transgression. The text anticipates the impending intercourse: "*Now* by pushing the two thoroughly for a half hour." Always vulgarly humorous, the text narrates the acts of interracial intimacy yet never completely mirrors the happenings on screen. *Blends* plays with what Jane Gaines refers to as the "distinction between literary telling and cinematic showing," illustrating that showing and telling provide different renditions of the same "reality."[135] Multiple layers and forms of storytelling operate in tandem to convey this story of racial amalgamation.

Although the final scene of genital penetration is not the "half hour" the text promises, it is quite long, lasting almost one minute and twenty seconds of this short film. The scene seems longer because of the static nature of the shot—neither the couple nor the camera change positions. The film's emphasis on genital penetration subscribes to what Di Laurio and Rabkin identify as the stag genre's truncation of narrative and other filmic elements in favor of sex: the "raison d'être."[136] Similarly, Williams reads the stag film as a "primitive genital show" in which sex often interrupts and/or supersedes a linear narrative filmic progression.[137] *Blends* challenges this model; it provides its spectators with the spectacle of sex while simultaneously staging an elaborate story of racial amalgamation whose coherence endures throughout the entire film.

The film's penultimate line: "*So*, don't give up, just pull it a few times and it will rise again," seems to refer to the male's loss of erection as we cut to the semi-recumbent couple, smiling shyly and stimulating each other's genitals with their hands. After engaging in one final act of intercourse in the reverse cowgirl position, with the camera positioned underneath and behind their bodies to maximally capture the spectacle of genitality, the film transitions abruptly to the male with a towel in his hand, wiping his genitals before handing the towel to the woman so she can wipe hers.[138] Returning to the food metaphor that the film began with, the final text reads "After going about three or four times, then taste it and see if its blend *satisfies.*" The camera cuts to black female spreading her labia widely in front of the camera while the white male performs a brief act of cunnilingus, mirroring the abruptness with which the film finishes. We may read this act of cunnilingus, however fleeting, as signaling black female pleasure. Yet within the culinary narrative of *Blends*, this "taste" also reflects the black female pussy as an object of exoticized edibility and white male consumption (both the white male performer on screen and the stag audience at large). *Blends* sketches a historical vignette of black-white interracial intimacy that carves a space for the black female body in the landscape of early interracial pornography and instantiates the salience of black female racial-sexual alterity in early interracial pornographic fantasies.

Bright and Shiny Futures: Queering Black Female Pornographic Production

If the first part of this chapter is about the disavowal and exclusion of black females, its conclusion is invested in a project of recovery. In the previous section I began this work, leaping back to the stag genre to place the black female body in interracial moving-image pornography. Now I turn to pornography produced by black queer women as a site of intervention in the pornographic field of black female sexuality, focusing on the work on one black queer female producer/director, Shine

Louise Houston. I introduce Houston and her work not as a solution to mainstream interracial pornography's exclusion of the black female body but as a kind of modern possibility. Acutely aware of the interracial trend the cuckolding niche has pioneered, Houston frames her work as a counterpoint to mainstream commercial interracial pornography. Reflecting on her pornography production for a newspaper article that examines the trend in "racist porn," Houston states, "Sometimes I ask myself why I do it. Then I read articles like the one in AVN about the 'interracial porn market' and I remember why very quickly."[139] Although she suggests that mainstream interracial porn perpetuates dangerous myths of black sexuality, she remains reluctant "to condemn producers of racially inflammatory content."[140] Resisting the label of interracial pornography or any one of its possible iterations (such as, for example, queer reverse interracial porn), Houston's work bucks prevailing trends of interracial intimacy in pornography. Her pornography lacks the familiar stereotypes about and signifiers of excessive black female sexuality and disrupts the "historical underpinning" that stages intimate scenes of black-white sexual dominance and submission.[141] Houston's work avoids "the history of racial codes that lie in wait like traps to be sprung"; these pervasive "racial codes" of American culture make race legible and visible.[142]

We might situate both Houston's pornography and my citation of it, in what Jennifer C. Nash calls "recovery work," "black feminist representation that attempts to salvage the black female body from the violence of the visual field."[143] However, Houston, like other black queer pornographers, expresses ambivalence about the designation feminist, even though she has been acknowledged by the Feminist Porn Awards.[144] Though she does not "necessarily label [her]self a feminist" and her "intention was never to make feminist pornography," Houston believes that "pornography has a potential to be feminist or some kind of perhaps responsibility to be feminist."[145] Similarly, contemporary black queer pornographer Nenna Joiner is equivocal about the "f word." When I asked her if she identified as a feminist, she replied, "No; I wouldn't say I don't, but I don't say I do either."[146] Nevertheless, she recognizes the critical labor that the term performs for her work. In particular, the Feminist Porn Awards have "created a shelving quality or a universe in which we are able to exist." Recognizing the power of language to create a space in which not only black women's queer pornography but also the black female body itself is "able to exist," Joiner echoes Spillers, illuminating how the black female subject is hailed as subject through discourse.[147]

Transforming the field of queer pornography production, Houston produces pornography that disrupts stereotypes and the legibility of the black female body within the pornographic frame. Houston challenges "formula[s]" of normative black female sexuality in mainstream porn: "There is power in creating images, and for a woman of color and a queer to take that power . . . I don't find it exploitative; I think it's necessary."[148] Her films showcase stunning cinematography, inventive narratives, and incredibly diverse performers with respect to race, gender, and body. Houston's work critically queers representations of black female sexual desire, offering modes of pleasure outside hegemonic, heteronormative representations of black female sexuality in pornography. Houston did not fall into pornography serendipitously, nor is she a filmmaking dilettante. After earning a BA in Fine Art Film from the San Francisco Art Institute, Houston worked at the legendary San Francisco sex shop Good Vibrations (a veritable breeding ground of sex-positive pornographers since its founding in 1977) for five years before she began producing her own porn.[149] Houston discerned an urgent demand for a different type of pornography that she believed reflected the fantasies and figures of LGBT people: "That's when I'm like, there needs to be more voices. I believe in my politics. If you don't like it, do what I did. I didn't like what was going on in the porn industry in terms of representation of gay, lesbian, queer, and trans folk, so I made my own stuff."[150] This DIY impetus motivated by a profound disappointment with mainstream porn's offerings is a salient factor running through not only Houston's work but also through the work of many contemporary black queer female pornographers who desire to create and disseminate new images of black female sexuality.[151]

Houston has produced and directed a number of feature-length porn films, including *Superfreak* (2006), *The Wild Search* (2007), *Champion: Love Hurts* (2008), and *Occupied* (2013). Houston also owns and operates PinkLabel.TV, a fair-trade video-on-demand digital distribution website featuring both her own porn and the work of other independent queer pornography filmmakers. In the interest of space, here I focus on her highly critically acclaimed website crashpadseries.com, which launched in 2008 and often features interracial sexual performances.[152] Crashpad-series.com is based on Houston's first feature film, *The Crash Pad* (2005) a story about an unconnected group of couples, many of whom were couples in real life, who are given a key to a San Francisco apartment that functions as an impromptu venue for their sexual escapades. Behind the closed doors of the mysterious apartment, "a notorious hotbed of queer sex" viewers are privy, via webcam or through an actual keyhole mediated by the lens of Houston's video camera, to myriad hard-core sex acts.[153] Houston's voyeuristic gaze literally and figuratively directs the performances. She states, "I am by nature a voyeur so it's just like it's my perfect situation."[154] In many episodes the frame switches back and forth from the sexual action inside the small room to a close-up of Houston's glossy eyeball, illuminated by the light of her laptop screen, on which we see a grainy, green-filtered webcam rendition of what the primary video camera reveals inside the "crash pad." The layers of spectatorship are complex and are mediated by technology. Eight years and over 200 episodes later, the series is thriving. The Crash Pad series is not just popular with critics and viewers; performers are also eager to participate. Houston tells me that they never have to recruit performers and have a waiting list with enough models to book for approximately the next five years.

Employing the crash pad narrative of extemporaneous sex in the domestic setting of a random urban apartment, the series hinges upon a complex and contradictory performance of sexual authenticity, something critics have praised. Crashpadseries.com is framed as displaying the "real" sex of "real" lesbians. For example, a pornmoviesforwomen. com description states that "there are no gay-for-pay bottle blondes with scary fake boobs and fingernails engaged in perfunctory sex here."[155] Pink and White Productions, Houston's production company, markets crashpadseries.com as depicting more authentic expressions of queer bodies and desire:

> The premise is simple: there's an apartment, and if you're lucky enough to be given the key, you can let yourself in . . . and let yourself go. This isn't fake lesbian porn with pointless high heels and starlets barely able to conceal their distaste as they awkwardly tongue kiss. Real sex, real orgasms, real sweat, real bodily fluids, real laughter—this is the genuine

article, so utterly natural that the fact it's being filmed seems nearly incidental.[156]

The rhetoric of authenticity in Houston's work becomes an important, but problematic, strand weaving through the work of a broader wave of contemporary black female produced pornography.[157] That is, Houston is imagined and imagines herself to be making pornography that caters to the *real* fantasies of *real* black women and as work that represents *real* bodies, the kind we do not typically see in mainstream porn. The furtive locale of the crash pad provides the ground for an authentically imagined staging of queer sex. The equally mysterious mythical key opens more than the doors to the crash pad; it serves as a powerful metaphorical device that symbolizes a broader expansion of racialized sexualities in the landscape of contemporary American commercial porn, opening and unlocking a queered, destabilized deconstruction of sexual categories. Beyond depicting queer relations and sexual fantasy, the Crash Pad series is politically invested in a critique of the dichotomies of heteronormativity. As L. H. Stallings had argued in her visionary theorization of a radical black female sexual subjectivity, "Real resistance to negative stereotypes would entail more than simply reversing the binary logic of stereotypes about Black women's sexuality: it would mean destroying systems of gender and sexuality that make the stereotypes possible. Such action would aid in the initial construction of radical Black female sexual subjectivities."[158] Technology is a key to this resistance: Houston tells me that technology is "power."[159] The Internet has enabled her to "build something that [I] was going to be able to create content on a regular basis."[160] We can understand the medium facilitating not a kind of singular interruption but an ongoing process of continual permutation reflecting the dynamism and multivalence of black female sexuality itself. By providing this type of constant content, Houston deploys the technology of the Internet to make possible an ever-evolving performance of black womanhood.

Having "no fear of the technology," Houston imagines cyberspace as a laboratory for the invention of new and dynamic representational paradigms of black female sexuality.[161] As I argue elsewhere, we need to pay critical attention to pornography produced by black women as a salient force in a larger digital renaissance of black female cultural production and look toward black female pornographers as pioneers in black women's commandeering of new media as vehicles for self-representation.[162] While we need to look more closely, and certainly more seriously, at Internet pornography and the ways it allows new and different groups of people, often those who have traditionally been marginalized, to actively participate in important discourses about gender, race, sexuality this examination needs to come with a recognition of the ways this new media has buttressed existing structures of power and the ways that the Internet recycles old and discredited signifiers of black womanhood. Mireille Miller-Young has wisely cautioned us to be critical of interpretations of cyberporn that see the Internet as a site of utopian democratization. Her work exposes the ways that netporn can be "both transgressive and repressive for Black sexual politics."[163] Empowered by technology, Houston navigates a pornography cyberscape that excises black women from interracial pornography or renders their sexuality as hyperbolic, as websites such as ghettodoorway.com, ebonycumdumps.com, ghettogaggers.com, ghettobootytube.org, and hoodhunter.com do. Her work intervenes in pornography's spectacle of black female racial-sexual alterity. In the following chapter, I take up the interpretation of technology that Houston proposes, interrogating the twisted technologies of race, sexuality, gender, pleasure, and visuality in BDSM pornography.

4

Techno-Kink

Fucking Machines and Gendered, Racialized Technologies of Desire

Welcome to fucking machines.
—Tomcat[1]

A Fetish Empire

Kink.com, which was founded by Peter Acworth in 1997, is the Internet's largest producer of BDSM porn. Acworth, the son of a former Jesuit priest and sculptor, spent his youth in Derbyshire, England. In his mid- to late twenties while still in graduate school in the United States, Acworth launched his first porn website, "Hogtied," which specialized in female bondage (and is still extant).[2] In addition to his personal interest in bondage, Acworth recognized the profit potential of BDSM as an under-exploited niche.[3] Just one year later, in 1998, after running the site out of his graduate school dorm room, he left school, moved to San Francisco, which he refers to as a "fetish capital," to run full time Cybernet Entertainment, now called kink.com. Acworth is not shy about stating his financial and personal motivations for getting into the realm of Internet BDSM pornography, nor is he is mute about his political aspirations and the more pedagogical objectives of kink.com. Striving to provide "the highest quality fetish entertainment available," kink.com's primary mission is to "demystify and celebrate alternative sexualities by providing the most authentic kinky experiences."[4] Since its inception in the late 1990s, the company has evolved from Acworth's solo labor of love, where he initially did most everything himself (lighting, video, still photography, bondage, site construction, programming, and editing) in his small San Francisco apartment to a thriving company with numerous websites, employees, and a 200,000-square-foot urban castle as a company home.

In 2006, Acworth changed the company name to kink.com and began rapidly growing the business. He hired more employees, purchased more production equipment, added content to and increased the number of sites, increased its social media and digital presence, and bought and began renovating the massive historic San Francisco Armory.[5] Acworth has been strict about the types of renovation he has done to the building; he has retained and restored original period details of the Armory such as wainscoting, stone staircases, sweeping corridors, cavern access to Mission Creek, and a massive drill court spanning almost an acre, but he has been most imaginative about set design and the construction of many of kink.com's websites. From painstaking replicas of school classrooms and locker rooms to futuristic laboratories to medical examination rooms to the lavish "Upper Floor" (an Edwardian-style great house where BDSM and fetish reality shows take place in real time), kink.com is known for its elaborate sets. While hygiene, function, and safety are all critical, the design principle that drives kink.com art director Christopher Gaw is "CYFOI: Can you fuck on it?"[6] Gaw and his design team coat the wooden surfaces of desks in a mock school classroom with extra layers of polyurethane glaze to facilitate easy cleaning. They choose non-porous surfaces such as tile and vinyl to make disinfection simple. They bolster floors and other surfaces with invisible padding. The precise height of 29.5 inches, what Gaw identifies as "the ideal height for lifting someone onto it," guides their architecture.[7] The space of the armory, physically and aesthetically, has facilitated kink.com's reign as "a fetish empire" and Acworth's role as the "king of kink."[8]

Kink.com currently has thirty-six hard-core pornography websites that garner over 600,000 visitors per month.[9] In a pornography cyberscape dominated by free sites, kink.com distinguishes itself with its high-production-value BDSM and live webcam sites.[10] Site descriptions of a wide range of implements, from electrical stimulation and metal, rope, and water bondage devices to an arsenal of mechanical fucking machines, evidence the company's interest in BDSM as a technology of pleasure and its investment in authenticity. Indicative of kink.com's visibility, recently the media has both celebrated and denounced the pornography production house. It is the subject of two recent films— one a drama, *About Cherry* (2012, dir. Stephen Elliot), and the other a documentary, *Kink* (2013, dir. Christina Voros). While these films largely work to highlight the values of kink.com, which include maintaining "a safe, sane and consensual environment," "provid[ing] a fun workplace which stimulates innovation and creativity," and the principles of "honesty," "integrity," "professionalism," and "respect," recent media scandals have tempered a favorable image of the company.[11] Alleged mistreatment of sex workers, Acworth's arrest for cocaine possession, and an HIV outbreak and ensuing two-week industry moratorium in August 2013 have tarnished kink.com's reputation and raised questions about its core values.[12] In the context of these public controversies and only limited scholarly interest in kink.com, what is not being discussed are the politics of representation at play and the website's dynamic construction of race, gender, and sexuality using technology.

In this chapter, I analyze the technologies of pleasure, race, gender, sexuality, and visuality as they shape the material and ontological boundaries of the black female body and the erotic subjectivity of the black woman. These twisted technologies function as mechanisms of power that discipline black female pleasure and its performance, signaling the discursive production of black female sexuality at large. Focusing on one of kink.com's oldest websites, fuckingmachines.com, and its use of "fucking machines," mechanized phallic devices, I explore performances of racialized sexuality that are staged between human and machine, between black and white, between "man" and "woman," and between self and other. While these fucking machines most explicitly operate as technologies of pleasure, they also function as technologies of gender, race, sexuality, and visuality. My readings of these complex cyber performances come from three primary sites of analysis: the actual videos (machine and human performances), kink.com's textual description of the scenes, and the commentary of viewers. I suggest that these machines destabilize some boundaries to challenge conventional scripts of black female sexuality in pornography and reinforce others. First, I introduce the machines, staging the profound ambivalence of the human/machine binary that fuckingmachines.com erects and eroticizes. Then I discuss the machines as technologies of pleasure that signal the complexity of both pornographic pleasure and women's pleasure, a historically contested arena of sexuality. These performances engage longstanding feminist and scientific debates about women's pleasure. Finally, I explore the machines as racializing technologies that illuminate race itself as a technology. Mirroring the entanglement of these technologies, the sections of this chapter are imbricated.

Fuckingmachines.com, which launched in 2000, advertises its wares as "the first machine-specific product line ever released by any adult entertainment company." The site is devoted to mechanical sex machines that are paired with women performers.[13] It is kink.com's second oldest website and Acworth's brainchild. As such, fuckingmachines.com illustrates the company's evolution from a rudimentary independent operation to a highly financed and technologically and artistically sophisticated production company.[14] Acworth identifies the site as responsible for kink.com's fame and fortune.[15] Though it is the most popular, largest, and most visible (in the gaze of mainstream press) hard-core pornography fucking-machine site, it is not the only one, nor was it the first.[16] Fuckingmachines.com videos follow a rather repetitive structure. They begin with a short interview between machine operator and performer in which the performer is asked to share a bit about herself such as her name, age, sexual likes and dislikes. Often she is asked to state whether this is her first fucking-machine experience. The "myth" of virginity maintains a currency anchored in a heteropatriarchal invention of women's purity, which is revealed here in this pornographic scene of technosex as an ambivalent erotic commodity.[17] After the interview, the woman undresses for the camera in preparation for repeated rounds of fucking with different machine partners. The videos sometimes conclude with a post-fucking interview, providing the opportunity for the performer to narrate her experience. These post-fucking interviews function as a kind of research and development for fuckingmachines. com, enabling its developers to identify the strengths and weaknesses of different machines. On average, the women fuck four to five machines per video.[18]

Of the website's roughly 1,000 videos, which range in duration from three minutes to close to ninety minutes, approximately 4 percent feature black women.[19] Nevertheless, as I show later in this chapter, black female sexuality adds nuances to the narrative of human/machine conquest that scripts these cyborgian scenes of technosex. Fuckingmachines.com members acknowledge that black women are underrepresented on the site and often request more diverse performers.[20] Retired black adult film star Sinnamon Love corroborates this dearth of black women in kink.com's BDSM fantasy world. Love, an early performer on fuckingmachines.com, maintains that kink.com was resistant to casting black women. She writes, "They hesitated to film me because they feared the fallout of putting a black woman in bondage in their movies."[21] Love's comment recognizes—while not naming—the unique historical legacy of sexual violence against black women and the influence of that legacy on BDSM performance. Her comment conveys the historical valence of the sight of the black female in bondage and how BDSM pornography producers such as kink.com, their audiences, and black women who perform BDSM must confront this scene in both their personal and professional lives. The fact that black women are marginalized on fuckingmachines.com brings into high relief the fucking machine's operation as a technology of race.

The site's ambivalent attitude toward black female sexuality is demonstrated in its categorization of female performers. Fuckingmachines .com features both amateur performers and porn stars. Many women are "regulars" and perform in more than one video. Though originally, the site listed various statistics about female performers such as height, weight, gender, hair color, body type, measurements, and cup size, it did not initially provide information about their race, ethnicity, or nationality. Recently, the company has added a search option that allows viewers to search by various identifiers such as age, breast size, hair color, and ethnicity. While other racial categories are listed as "Caucasian," "Indian," "Latina," "Latino," and "Mixed Race," black women are tagged under the category of "Ebony." [22] The "Ebony" label signals pornography's continuing understanding of black female sexuality through skin color and the identificatory failure that black women experience and engender in the site of sexuality. This label fails to represent black women in multiple ways. First, the search term does not yield an accurate number of black female performers (the search produces only about half of the number of videos featuring black women), further obscuring black women's presence on this site. Second, it instantiates the discursive collapse of the categories used to identify the black female—the "unrelieved crisis" of the "customary lexis of sexuality" to speak to and for the black female body.[23] This slip mirrors that within the diegesis of fuckingmachines.com—that is, as I argue, black women's potential disruption of prevailing narratives of bodily-machine encounter. This chapter is concerned not just with questions of the il/legibility of black female bodies in both performance (as text) and text (as performance) but also with how technologies facilitate this il/legibility.

Meet the Fleet: Sybians, Cyborgs, and . . .

The fuckingmachines.com "arsenal" consists of a fleet of thirty-six machines that range in material, price, mechanics, and dynamics of operation, kinesis, and control. Kink.com's role as "innovators" (they use mostly custom-built machines rather than commercially produced ones) sets fuckingmachines.com apart from other sites that specialize in mechanized phallic devices.[24] The handheld Fucksall, essentially a "modified power tool" with a dildo attachment, is the least expensive and least sophisticated of the devices.[25] As a revamped power tool, it epitomizes a certain image of masculinity, embodying a heteropatriarchal male fantasy (of penetration, play, speed, control, and repair) in a dizzying oscillation that approaches a maximum of 2,400 rpm. It is shaped like a semi-automatic weapon and is typically aimed at the female performers.

Touted on the website as "the only machine that no one can out fuck," as a "champion in its own right," and as "near limitless in its speed," the Fucksall, like many of kink.com's fucking machines, is often described as triumphing over its female partner in a competitive duel between two bodies imagined in a false dichotomy—a man-made machine and a "natural" human. [26] I put natural in quotation marks to signal the fact that many of the performers' bodies are surgically augmented but also because I share Ann Balsamo's assumption that the body is "a social, cultural, and historical production" that is both a "product and process."[27] In a scene with a female performer who is a competitive gymnast, the powerhouse Fucksall emerges victorious, "put[ting] her to rest in a sweaty heap on the floor." The website proudly proclaims, "The machines win over another pussy and ass!"[28] Personified and coded as masculine, the Fucksall, like other fucking machines, succeeds in wearing out the body of its female partner, demonstrating its supremacy and sexual endurance. In this contest, dominant "machines win" and submissive women are vanquished in their frenzied orgasmic pleasure.[29] Of course, dominance and submission are key elements of BDSM practice.

This gendered technological dominance is casted in a techno-utopian imaginary that is asserted through fucking-machine performances and described by the performers and by media commentary on the machines. One female performer says that it "feels really nice, you can control the speed, the depth. You don't have to worry about it getting tired. It goes as fast as you want. It doesn't want to sleep over at night."[30] Another hails fucking machines as "absolute perfection," stating, "Guys bitch, I am too tired, not tonight, I am seeing your best friend. This, they don't talk back. You can just pull it out of the closet when you want, you can put it in any position you want."[31] Customer reviews of various machines on kink's bondage gear website, where they sell machines manufactured by outside engineers, reflect a similar techno-utopianism and sexual supremacy of machines. A customer who gives the Versa Fuk machine a star rating of five out of five raves, "It's better than ANY man!!"[32]

Though other machines have different names, designs, and functions, they similarly embody various phallocentric and violent fantasies of sexual pleasure and penetration and mechanical sovereignty, while constructing and erotizing the binary of human and machine and through it the binary of "man" and "woman." The "Intruder," kink.com's second most expensive design, is fully adjustable, has a stroke that ranges in depth from half an inch to six inches, and features a kinetic oscillation that is so powerful that the machine must be strapped down while it is in use. Techno-pastiches of existing mechanical apparatuses, the fucking machines kinetically, aesthetically, and even symbolically channel their past life in their afterlife in porn.[33] Before it was a fucking machine, for example, the Trespasser was a Kitchen Aid mixer, calling our attention to the confluence of women's domestic labor and sexual labor.

The sales narrative for the Sybian features larger sociocultural scripts of Western sexual normativity. The first commercially available fucking machine in the United States, the Sybian is not one of kink.com's inventions, although it is featured regularly in fuckingmachines.com videos. It has been "made with pride in the USA" and has been marketed in the United States since 1987, although the seeds of its genesis were planted far earlier in the mind of white male inventor David L. Lampert.[34] In the vibrant tradition of Freudian psychosexuality, fucking machines represent deviance in terms of both the "sexual aim" and the "sexual object," to use Freud's language. While Freud contended that many parts of the body and many nongenital sexual acts produced sexual pleasure beyond heterosexual penetrative genital intercourse, these acts become abnormal or pathological, he argued, when they displace heterosexual intercourse, the sine qua non of sexuality. The deviance of the Sybian, like other fucking machines, is modulated by its heterosexualization in marketing and sales narratives. Primarily marketed as a "Sexual Stimulation and Gratification Device" for facilitating a woman's journey to becoming multiorgasmic with her male partner, the Sybian is also credited with health benefits that include the alleviation of stress-related migraines and overall libido enhancement. The therapeutic benefits of orgasms is both a selling point for these fucking machines and a way to shift them out of the perverse domain of pornography and into the realm of women's sexual health.[35]

The claims that the Sybian will improve women's health is not the only way the manufacturer seeks to counteract the machine's perversity; it is also sold as a machine for couples, diluting its queerness. In this framing, fucking machines are presented as aids to heterosexual genital intercourse, thereby evading the definitive mark of sexual aberrancy—the departure from this "norm."[36] David Lampert, the inventor of the Sybian, states, "I have always thought that using the Sybian is something a couple does together in an intimate embrace."[37] One kink.com performer imagines it as "kind of like foreplay" to sex with a male partner.[38] According to the marketing, although the Sybian's purpose is to help women explore their sexuality and pleasure on their own, this is secondary to its intervention into sexual intercourse with a male partner. Another white male commercial sex machine maker enforces this heterosexual aim by requiring proof of marriage before he will sell his devices.[39] Whether billed on its website as "the ultimate alternative to a [male] partner," a tool for heightening "women's sexual responsiveness," or an accouterment to sexual intercourse with a male partner ("as a prelude or extension to lovemaking"), male sexuality is evoked, privileged in its absence, and assumed to be a salient component in women's sexual pleasure. Familiar and long-standing social, psychoanalytic, and moral conventions of sexuality are coded in these "freakish" sexual apparatuses, evidence of sexuality's continuing heterosexual discipline.

Fucking machines inhabit both the commercial and the pornographic spheres of the Internet. Though these two realms are often imagined as distinctly separate, the rhetoric of deviance is a strong force in both arenas of fucking-machine performance. For example, Lampert's objection to the pornification of his brainchild is not based on its co-optation by the adult entertainment industry but rather by that industry's perverse use of the machine. Lampert contends that pornography "Videos and DVDs Portray Sybian in Wrong Light!," stating:

> They show what the viewer wishes to see. Nearly all material shows a frontal view of the woman using Sybian alone. Occasionally it is shown with a partner behind so the viewer still sees a frontal view of her. I have always thought that using the Sybian is something a couple does together in an intimate embrace.[40]

Sans male partner, fuckingmachines.com subverts the Sybian's heteronormative design. We witness again pornography's multifaceted power to pervert.

While in the commercial realm, the potential deviancy of fucking machines is tempered by their participation in a narrative of heterosexual genital sexual intercourse, in the pornographic arena, the fact that the machines are continually compared to men reinserts them into the heteronormative framework that they, as *not* (hu)man, work to queer. For example, countless videos stage a contest between human and machine in which fucking machines succeed in delivering superhuman pleasure and record orgasms to their female partners. However, this narrative reflects not just the machines' victory over the bodies of the women they fuck but also their superiority over the male partners they have ostensibly displaced. In the domain of hard-core BDSM pornography, the machines' complex deviance—an aberrancy derived more from the excessive pleasure they produce *as* machine than from the partners they replace—is strategically heightened and eroticized.

Fuckingmachines.com is invested in demarcating the border between human and machine while eroticizing the sexual transgression of this boundary. Nevertheless, their performances render both machine and human as profoundly hybrid organisms, as cyborgs. Fucking machines are part of a myriad of cyborg bodies that inhabit, indeed dominate, the cyberspace. A recent study reveals that bots, automated data collection web services, not humans, are responsible for the increased traffic on the Internet; nearly two-thirds of global Internet activity is attributed to bots.[41] Troubling the line between "human" and "machine," Donna Haraway invokes the cyborg, which is an apropos figure here.[42] Fucking machines function as cyborgs: they exist in a liminal space between nature and culture, as "hybrid[s] of machines and organism," "creature[s] of social reality as well as a creature[s] of fiction."[43]

On fuckingmachines.com, the boundaries of the subject are ruptured as they are reified. Yet it is around the dynamic of pleasure that fucking machines most strikingly play cyborgs, providing *"pleasure* in the confusion of boundaries."[44] Countless feminist scholars have embraced the figure of the cyborg. Ann Balsamo, for example, argues that the cyborg, an "emblem of postmodern identity," presents a radical challenge to how feminists approach the body in order to disrupt the nature/culture divide that limits feminist scholarship.[45] While the trope of the cyborg is useful for theorizing the "bodies" of fucking machines and human performers and the eroticized boundaries between the two, it is not entirely adequate for analyzing race. Feminist women of color scholars have critiqued Haraway's cyborg theory for its celebratory appropriation of and alliance with the revolutionary politics of U.S. and third world women of color feminism and its failure to adequately acknowledge and theorize race and white privilege.[46] Still, despite the limitations of the cyborg trope, it is a useful theoretical device in considering how the human/nonhuman binary is erected, eroticized, and transgressed on fuckingmachines.com.

In its blurring of the boundaries between the body and the technological, the cyborg summons the posthuman. Scripted by a narrative of technosexual supremacy, fucking machines embody a posthumanist ethos in which technology augments the human body as an intervention into its sexual and physical limitations. N. Katherine Hayles argues that the posthuman is marked by fluid boundaries, a concept that brings the artificiality of the human's physical body, "the original prosthesis," into sharp relief.[47] While feminist scholars of color have interrogated the cyborg's racialization, they have also contested the white privilege that undergirds posthumanism. Alex Weheliye offers a stunning critique of posthumanist theory's elision of race. He deconstructs the hegemonic Western white liberal conception of humanity that posthumanism reflects and requires.[48] He argues that "Hayles reinscribes white masculinity as the (human) point of origin from which to progress to a posthuman state."[49] Weheliye interrogates the resonance of the posthuman for those "represented as *having* a body, but not *being* a body," those who "were never human."[50] Judith Halberstam and Ira Livingston echo this claim in a more redemptive meditation on the posthuman. They write, "You're not human until you're posthuman. You were never human."[51] While Weheliye's contestation of the posthuman is based on race, Halberstam and Livingston's critique is focused on sexuality. They postulate the posthumanness of queerness and the queerness of posthumanity—its queer fucking with sexuality itself.

As technologies of queering sexuality, fucking machines enact a posthuman fucking with fucking. Complicating conventional conceptions of fucking to subvert its reproductive foundation, fucking machines echo the posthumanist question "What is allowed to be fucking?"[52] Halberstam and Livingston suggest that "it becomes possible to assert a non-relation between fucking and reproduction—the relation upon which patriarchal humanity is predicated—partly because of the diversity of sexual practices, partly because of technological operations, but mainly because the point where they converge is no longer an adequate anchoring point for a meaningful or workable system."[53] Though fucking machines demonstrate a posthuman fucking, they mimic heterosexual human penetrative sex. "Robot style" becomes another iteration of "doggie style."[54] Beyond their technologically facilitated destabilization of the reproductive "anchor" of fucking, they queer fucking in their multiple gendered, racialized, and sexualized layers of pleasure and performance.

If You Build It, They Will Come: Fucking Machines and/as Technologies of Pleasure

Fucking machines most clearly operate as technologies of pleasure: they produce women's orgasms. In their industrious labor as technologies of women's pleasure, fucking machines bring into relief women's pleasure within pornography as a complex, multi-sited performance that includes the director, the performer, spectators, "man," "woman," and "machine." Pleasure here is configured as an elaborate encounter between different bodily agents enacted at multiple sites of the body and between two poles of desire: rapture and anxiety. The complexity of women's pleasure is revealed by the technology that mediates it. The performances on fuckingmachines.com reanimate long-standing feminist debates about the contested geography of women's orgasms (whether they are clitoral or vaginal), the question of whether women ejaculate, and the debate over the dildo question. Fucking machines both reify and contest the phallocentric, androcentric, and heteronormative ideologies of women's pleasure these feminist debates have exposed.

Tomcat, an openly transgender man who has been the director of fuckingmachines.com for eight years, was recently featured in a *Village Voice* article titled "The Man behind the Fucking Machine."[55] He is responsible for casting machines and performers. Sometimes he allows performers to choose their machine partners, but most often he selects the machines himself. In his principal role as a performer at fuckingmachines.com, Tomcat prefers the Fucksall "because it's handheld and you can kind of work with the girl."[56] His use of the preposition "with" highlights the complex layers of cooperative labor (machines, performer, director, etc.) enacted on fuckingmachines.com and implodes his own spatial positioning as "behind" the machines and/or performers. His statement requires us to think about pleasure as more than that of the kink.com audience and the female performer. Hence, the ambiguity and irony of Tomcat's designation as "The Man behind the Machine" emanates from far more than his identification as a transman. His is not just "behind the machine" as the director but also "behind" the performers so he can orchestrate the collaborative labor of machine and performer. He states, "If I leave the model in control they get so into what they are doing they forget to really work with the machines."[57] His words speak to the choreography and labor of pleasure. In many scenes he gives explicit audible directions to female performers, guiding their positioning with the machines.

Tomcat says that the central goal of fuckingmachines.com is "to create a fetish experience that causes uncontrollable orgasms" for the female performers.[58] His casting of machines is guided by the objective of giving the female performers a techno-superior orgasm, "the best orgasm ever."[59] Tomcat feels that this privileging of women's pleasure sets the site apart from conventional mainstream Internet pornography: "It's a solo site and the goal is to make you feel good. It's what makes you feel good. I think normally in porn it's not about the woman having fun and Fucking Machines changes that."[60] Isaac Leung also argues that fucking-machines.com disrupts gendered narratives of pleasure and positionality in mainstream heterosexual pornography in order to privilege "real" female pleasure: "Fucking-machines repositioned the female from the passive to active role, and the 'male/active' social construction was being deemphasized due to the lack of a biological and symbolic male."[61] However, the biological and symbolic presence of the male and the question of male pleasure remain strong throughout the fuckingmachines.com site. Contrary to what Leung argues, women are typically more *in*active while fucking the machines as they cannot move because the machines cannot follow them. Furthermore, we must problematize such a rendering of authentic female pleasure, particularly on a for-profit pornography site where, as sex worker, activist, and author Audacia Ray notes, "machines are most commonly used by women who are fucking for money."[62] Pleasure here is inextricable from its performance as sexual labor between humans and machines. Acworth reminds us that kink.com is "a commercial enterprise" whose "products gravitate towards that which sells."[63] The fact that most consumers of the videos fuckingmachines.com sells are male further raises the issue of male pleasure.

We must also problematize the idea of fuckingmachines.com as a "solo site." On the contrary, it offers a multiplex performance of various actors, including the machines themselves, which are deeply personified. Tomcat believes that his manipulation of the machines lends a sort of intimacy to the videos: "Having me drive the machine adds a human element to the inhuman."[64] Beyond physically operating many of the fucking machines as a kind of third partner in a technological ménage à trois, in many videos, Tomcat conducts before and after interviews with the performers. In these interviews, we hear but do not see him. However, Tomcat is not some Oz-like man behind the curtain of a performance between a woman and a machine; he is an important performer. Just as the performances stretch boundaries of human and machine, they also extend beyond the spatio-temporal frame of the camera. Whether it is

Acworth's English accent, masked face, and truncated, disembodied arm aiming a Fucksall into the orifices of a female performer or Tomcat's "invisible" hand or voice punctuating the scenes, fuckingmachines.com is far more than a solo site.

Fuckingmachines.com enacts a cyborgian orgy, blurring and eroticizing the lines demarcating the stages of performance and the lines between humans and machines. Ray posits that the "size and intensity of the various machines" positions them as live sexual partners, not inanimate sex toys.[65] This machine-human partnership is ideal, according to Ray, because it facilitates consumption by a homophobic heterosexual male audience. She contends that "for straight men, the images on the site represent a kind of ideal; they're able to watch girls be penetrated and fucked without the nuisance of having to look at another man's penis."[66] This theory quashes the queer pleasure it seems to want to recognize. Similarly, it disavows the homoerotic pleasure that is so salient in pornography. As cyborg "bodies," fucking machines provide complex levels of phallocentric identification and pleasure. Although the male presence is often concealed and purportedly "backstage," it is strong in the videos through the male personification of the machines, the director's performance, viewer commentaries, and the machines themselves as phallic avatars of their white male inventors.

A multivalent anxiety animates the machines' performances. While for Ray, the magnitude and potency of the fucking machines permits some to imagine them as a nonthreatening human partner without the queer-phobic visual spectacle of another male's penis, this power also serves to soothe the male ego through techno-fetishism. She contends, "The supposed mechanical superiority of the machines becomes a spectacle to behold in itself, one that no longer reflects on the man's physical or sexual capabilities."[67] For Ray, the machines engender, particularly in male spectators, "a near miasma of technophobia and technofetishism."[68] Similarly, Tomcat refers to this entanglement of fear and pleasure, asserting that it is not "technofear" but "technojoy," the "joy of tech-induced orgasms," that powers fucking machines and their performances. This fear/pleasure paradigm galvanizes the contradictory personification of the machines, which are both humanized as ideal, indeed superior, sexual partners for the women performers *and* eroticized as "pure" machine.

This tension between seeing fucking machines as quasi-human and seeing them as machines emerges at multiple sites of their performance. For example, the fuckingmachine.com website that introduces the machine "arsenal" lists detailed "tech specs" of each machine, such as maximum rpms, torque, stroke and horsepower, along with an image of the machine and a textual description.[69] This presentation resembles how fuckingmachine.com introduces female performers, who are similarly depicted with a photograph and statistics such as height, weight, gender, hair, body type, measurements, sexual role, scene role, pubic hair, and cup size. Rightly noting the humanization of the machines, Sarah Schaschek believes that fuckingmachines.com reveals "a deep skepticism about the commodification and technologization of the human body that becomes visible, among other places, in images of sexual action."[70] Like Ray and Tomcat, Schaschek notes the fear that fuckingmachines.com plays on, with, and against. For her, this fear is about the pornography performer's potential replacement by the machine in an exploitative system of capitalist efficiency and a broader technophobia related to the increasing standardization, mechanization, and commercialization of sexuality and the spectacle of the body.[71]

Anxiety mars the utopian fantasies present in Tomcat's conceptualization of the fucking machines and their tirelessness. Championing the device's indefatigability, he states, "But it doesn't stop. It never gets tired. Unless you have a power outage, that thing is going to just keep going."[72] In referring to a power outage—the electrical Achilles heel of the machines—he renders ambivalent and tempers with anxiety his own casting of the fucking machine's sexual sovereignty. This tension between possible power failure and steady performance is expressed in earlier videos in the fuckingachines.com archives. For example, Acworth asks one female performer who is excited to try the fucking machines because "guys always run out of batteries," "What makes you think that our machines are not going to run out of batteries?"[73] These moments stage the machine's slippage between techno-utopian fantasy and failure. This anxiety about the machine's performance is matched by anxiety about women's sexual pleasure. The performances on fuckingmachines.com engage long-standing debates about the contested source, expression, and site of women's sexual pleasure.

In addition to the competition staged between human and machine in these complex performances, there is competition between machine and machine. In fuckingmachines.com videos, performers use fucking machines in combination with vibrators, specifically Hitachi Magic Wands. The use of vibrators, as technologies of clitoral pleasure, in tandem with fucking machines, as technologies of vaginal penetration, speaks to the still-vexed question of the geography of women's sexual pleasure.[74] The technological supremacy and personification of the machines is reified by the use of the vibrator as foreplay. In many videos, women stimulate themselves with a vibrator to "warm up" for the "real" sex with the machines. Nevertheless, the performances on fuckingmachines.com performances disrupt the privileging of genital penetrative pleasure that the machines engineer. They thus contest problematic hierarchies of pleasure and heteronormative discourses of women's authentic pleasure that the machines, as technologies of penetration, seem to emblematize.

Dynamically reflecting historical shifts (across disciplinary domains) in understandings of women's sexual pleasure, the performances on fuckingmachines.com exhibit the simultaneity and multiplicity of women's sexual pleasure. The complex politics of pleasure played out in this battle of machines (fucking machine versus Hitachi Magic Wand) is staged at the site of woman's pleasure—whether orgasm is clitoral or vaginal, internal or external—and through the dynamics of (self-)control and agency. That is, while most fucking machines require a remote controller (whether it be human or nonhuman), the vibrator is used more as an instrument of self-titillation.[75] It enables the female performers to control their own pleasure by directing the speed and location of stimulation. The Japanese-manufactured Hitachi Magic Wand has been a best-selling vibrator for over three decades and is frequently used on pornography sets. Hailed as the "King of Vibrators," "by far the most superior wand massager in the world," an instrument with "relentless power," and a highly competitive "pleasure machine," it has two control speeds and a 6,000-rpm motor.[76] Thus, the same rhetoric of techno-utopian pleasure that is used to describe kink.com's fucking machines is also used to describe the Hitachi Magic Wand vibrator.[77] It performs here in a kind of battle, or perhaps concert, of machines—the vaginally penetrating fucking machine and clitoral stimulating vibrator—that reanimates important feminist debates about the nature of female sexual pleasure and climax.

Since the early 1970s, a diverse range of feminist scholars have been challenging phallocentric readings of women's sexual pleasure and debating whether female orgasms derive from vaginal penetration or clitoral stimulation. Such debates began in the first half of the twentieth century with Freud, who argued that the clitoral orgasm was a problematic vestige of infantile sexuality and that vaginal orgasms were the "appropriate" form of the mature woman's sexual climax. Freud believed that as women matured into adulthood, they moved away from clitoral masturbation to progress toward a mature type of pleasure produced in "*the* sexual act"—"the appropriate stimulations of an erotogenic zone (the genital zone itself in the glans penis) by the appropriate object (the mucous membrane of the vagina)."[78] According to Freud, this act produces a pleasure that is "the highest in intensity."[79] It wasn't until Dr. William Masters and Virginia Johnson's groundbreaking research at the mid-twentieth century that the clitoral orgasm gained legitimacy through the medical, and soon after that, the popular gaze.[80]

Drawing upon the legacy of Masters and Johnson's sexology, kink. com's fucking machines use technology to make visible the mystery of women's sexual "responsiveness." Indeed, through the repeated achievement of climax by performers and laboratory-like settings, the fucking-machines.com site displays Masters and Johnson's belief that the "female orgasmic experience can be visually identified as well as recorded by acceptable physiologic techniques."[81] A "fucking machine," a cylindrical motorized Plexiglas phallus device named Ulysses that was capable of intravaginal photography, was critical to Masters and Johnson's study of the elusive female orgasm as the crux of women's sexuality.[82] As instruments of women's vaginal penetration, both Ulysses and fucking machines perform a hetero-genitalization of women's sexual pleasure that the clitoris complicates as a simultaneous and (in the case of Masters and Johnson) primary site of pleasure.[83] Like the high-tech dildo Ulysses, kink.com's fucking machines reveal a technological mediation of women's sexual pleasure that makes it visible. In the wake of the televisual reincarnation of Ulysses on the Showtime network drama *Masters of Sex*, fucking machines have gained a new visibility that mirrors their function as technologies of visibility. Linda Williams has written extensively on pornography as a technology of visibility, specifically the visibility of sexual pleasure, arguing that in "speaking sex," pornography articulates sexual difference and the truth of sexual pleasure. She argues that pornography is a Foucauldian form of *scientia sexualis*—a mechanism that labors not only to produce pleasure but also "to tell the truth of sex."[84]

Evidencing the enmeshment of technologies that fucking machines evince, the video camera itself becomes a fucking machine. In some fuckingmachines.com videos beginning in the mid-2000s, the camera, always already an instrument of sexualized visibility, is fastened to the base of the fucking machine's dildo attachment, permitting an extreme close-up of the female performer's genitals and penetration. Literally hitched to the fucking machines, these cameras testify to the more symbolic grafting of technologies at play on the fuckingmachines.com site. In one video, for example, black female porn star, Jada Fire, walks into a large space-age laboratory featuring sleek gray floor tiles and bright florescent lighting paneled into silver walls toward a small table draped with white fur in the center of the room.[85] The "Bunny Fucker," a large formidable stainless-steel floor-based fucking machine with thick steel beams for legs, is aimed at the table. The bright red dildo tip of the machine pops against the white fur. As she reclines on the table, the camera switches from a long shot at the perimeter of the room to a low-angle close-up from the base of the machine to the eye of the so-called pussy cam. She waves at the camera briefly before beginning to stimulate herself with a vibrator. Before she gets up from the table to turn on the Bunny Fucker, the camera switches back, as it does periodically throughout the video, to a long shot that enables viewers to see the small black camera attached to the shaft of the machine.

These alternating views shift our angle and our proximity to the fucking and change the video's quality and color. The fucking-machine camera provides a lower resolution image with far less vibrant color. The comments posted in response to the video refer to the camera's function as a technology of visuality and of racialization. Multiple viewers complained about the "pussy cam's" failure to capture Jada's "color." In articulating the camera's failure as a technology of vision, they inadvertently reveal how it functions as a technology of racialization. Visual technologies, especially photographic technologies, remain a prime technique of racialization for the black female body.[86] The pussy cam brings into focus pornography's varied function as a visual technology of race.

The combination of the pornographic and the scientific around the question of women's pleasure is evident in moving-image pornography dating back to the mid-twentieth century—the period of Masters and Johnson's research. In a clever analysis that compares the "coloscopic" film to the "beaver" film, Eithne Johnson writes, "That so much film pornography emerged in the late 1960s must be understood in relation to Masters and Johnson's 'modernist' attempt to isolate the signs that would demonstrate female sexual 'responsiveness' and their scientific contention that the female body has the same 'natural' capacity for orgasmic performativity as the male body."[87] In these entangled technologies, the pornographic gaze meshes with the scientific gaze to reveal what Foucault has identified as the "interplay of truth and sex."[88] Though Masters and Johnson's research was anchored in a heteronormative foundation that considered women's orgasms in relation to the male body and to heterosexual relationships—very much like that of the claims about commercial fucking machines—their repositioning of the primary geographic site of women's climax from vagina to clitoris inspired feminist critiques of women's sexual pleasure.

Ann Koedt's influential article "The Myth of the Vaginal Orgasm" (1970) is an incisive critique of heterosexuality and the heteronormative dictates of female sexual pleasure. Koedt contends that the vaginal orgasm is a myth, a product of an oppressive phallocentric sexual economy that fears and negates the clitoral orgasm, which she argues is the only organ that brings women to sexual climax. She writes, "Women have thus been defined sexually in terms of what pleases men; our own biology has not been properly analyzed. Instead, we are fed the myth of the liberated woman and her vaginal orgasm—an orgasm that in fact does not exist."[89] Riffing off Koedt a few years later, Jill Johnson argued in "The Myth of the Myth of the Vaginal Orgasm" that vaginal orgasms are not only genuine but are also more intense and "profound" then clitoral ones. Her radical critique of women's sexual pleasure calls for women's complete sexual independence from men as the "sine qua non of the feminist revolution."[90]

Fuckingmachines.com reanimates the vexed question of the geography of women's sexual pleasure to underscore women's sexuality as a politicized site of discourse production. From science to feminist criticism, the female orgasm has long been a fraught event. Nancy Tuana has revealed how both cultural and scientific conceptualizations of the female orgasm reflect and perpetuate "epistemologies of ignorance within feminist epistemologies."[91] Ignorance, as is often assumed, is not a case of "not-yet-knowing" but is cultivated, practiced, and actively produced.[92] Such "epistemologies of ignorance" function to restrict our understanding of women's sexual pleasure outside the oppressive domain of heterosexual reproduction. Identifying the oppressive influence of procreation on understandings of women's sexual pleasure, Tuana is in conversation with other feminist scholars such as Gayatri Spivak, who argues that the clitoris is a key site not just of women's sexual pleasure but also of women's subjectivity and agency. Spivak contends, "The pre-comprehended suppression or effacement of the clitoris relates to every move to define women as sex object, or as means or agent of reproduction—with no recourse to a subject-function except in terms of those definitions or as 'imitators' of men."[93] Though fucking machines renegotiate the "terms of reproduction" that make female pleasure legible, they often act as "imitators' of men" and reinforce hegemonic, heteropatriarchal concepts of women's sexuality.[94]

Pornography has long demonstrated anxiety about the site of women's orgasm. Though Jane Gaines identifies the vibrator as an "off-stage" instrument, a positioning that fuckingmachines.com dynamically contests, she reads the vibrator as symbolically narrating the mystery of women's sexual pleasure, a key interest of hard-core pornography.[95] Gaines argues that the vibrator reveals the ultimate failure of mainstream heterosexual pornography to acknowledge the clitoris as a site of women's sexual pleasure:

> The vibrator is the off-stage instrument that makes up for the fact that pornography has failed to understand (and more importantly produce) women's pleasure. The vibrator is able to produce what the "spectacularised ejaculating penis" *cannot* since, unlike much of pornography which is obsessed with the relocation of the clitoris, the vibrator is designed for use on the clitoris *in its actual location* (it is not, for instance, designed to be used in the throat).[96]

Gaines's reference to the golden-age film *Deep Throat* (dir. Gerard Damiano, 1972) to illustrate pornography's uncertainty—or perhaps ignorance, to borrow from Tuana—regarding the site of women's pleasure is smart. In the film the main character (played by Linda Lovelace) visits her doctor (played by Harry Reems) because of her inability to reach orgasm, only to find that her clitoris is mysteriously located in her throat. Performing the doctor-prescribed "deep throat" fellatio is the only remedy for her sexual problem. This classic scene of phallocentric pornographic pleasure demonstrates how pornography's engagement with the question of women's authentic pleasure is often accessed geographically.

One cannot discuss pornography's authentication of pleasure without considering the money shot. Because biological male penises are absent in the videos on fuckingmachines.com, the site lacks what many have recognized as the quintessence of hard-core heterosexual pornography: the money shot. A "nearly universal" act in U.S. hard-core moving-image porn, the money shot is usually performed so that the male ejaculates not inside but on the body of his female or male partner—typically on the face, mouth, buttocks, stomach, and/or breasts.[97] Williams offers a seminal theorization of the money shot as "visual evidence of the mechanical 'truth' of bodily pleasure caught in involuntary spasm; the ultimate and uncontrollable—ultimate *because* uncontrollable—confession of sexual pleasure in the climax of orgasm."[98] This visual testimony of gendered pleasure is deeply contradictory, reflecting pornography's role as "a genre that holds out promise of women's pleasure and in the end offers not women's pleasure but spectacularised male ejaculation instead."[99] As a site purportedly devoted to women's authentic pleasure— Tomcat writes that "this site is about the IN_OUT that genuinely gets the girl off"—fuckingmachines.com is deeply invested in the spectacle of women's orgasm. Invested in the enterprise of revealing female pleasure, the site seems to have the performance of women's repetitive orgasms down to a science.

The technology of the fucking machines repeatedly puts women's capacity for orgasm to the test. Though women typically verbally confirm that they have had numerous orgasms, it is the visual technology of the camera that provides evidence of this pleasure.[100] While the machines are tasked with the exercise of relentless fucking, it is in fact spectacle of women's pleasure and women's bodies that must work harder here. No sexual match for the machines, women unfailingly lose in this contest of stamina and performance. In countless videos we see women who are physically "wiped out" from the machine's delivery of multiple orgasms. After using three fucking machines and one vibrator, Marie Luv, for example, loses exact count of how many "epic leg shaking, pussy quivering orgasms" she has had.[101] Her legs tremble so much that it is difficult for her to stand. After fucking the second machine, named The Little Guy, she lays curled up on a floor mat in a fetal position. This scenario of women's exhaustion at the "hands" of the machine recurs again and again in the site's videos. However, in this repeated performance of orgasm, the proverbial pornography money shot is absent.

Even though the machines do not deliver conventional money shots, the economic lexicon of pleasure that scripts the term "money shot" informs the way fuckingmachines.com represents women's experiences. For example, the site consistently depicts female performers as "spent" after several rounds with the indefatigable machines. Illuminating the capitalist and libidinal economies grounding the money shot, Williams analyzes the use of the concept of the fetish in both Marxian and Freudian discourse to illuminate "how commodity culture, sexual pleasure, and phallic subjectivity interpenetrate in the hard-core porno's money shot."[102] Williams echoes Steven Marcus, who argues that the fantasy of pornography is one that disrupts conventional conceptions of the body "as a productive system with only a limited amount of material at its disposal."[103] Fucking machines both test and reveal these limits, extracting pleasure to the point of bringing the bodies of female performers to the brink of exhaustion.

Yet we might read the limitless fucking of fucking machines as less a function of their mechanical technologies and more a product of the representational technologies of pornography and its narrative conventions as "a world of plenty," or what Steven Marcus refers to as pornotopia. He argues that women demonstrate an unlimited capacity for orgasm in pornotopia.[104] Modern sexology, specifically Masters and Johnson's research documenting women's potential for multiple orgasms, informs his theorization of pornographic pleasure. Marcus contends that pleasure in pornography is infinite and never fully realized: "The idea of pleasure in pornography typically excludes the idea of gratification, of cessation. Pleasure is thought of as endless and as an endless repetition."[105] From the narratives fuckingmachines.com offers to the kinesis of the machines to the machines' delivery of women's multiple orgasms, repetition is a central trope on the site. For Marcus, the "virtually unlimited female orgasm capacity" reflects a kind of socioeconomic zeitgeist:

> The notion of a multiply orgasmic female corresponds exquisitely to the needs of a society based on mass consumption. It is in effect a perfect image of mass consumption—particularly if we add to this image the further details that she is probably masturbating, alone, with the aid of a mechanical-electrical instrument—including the difficulties and anxieties involved in management and sustainment.[106]

Marcus's analysis of the socioeconomic anxieties surrounding women's orgasm annotates the complex anxieties at play in fuckingmachines.com. Beyond "anxieties about problems of accumulation, production, and excessive expenditure," women's capacity for multiple orgasms contributes to profound anxieties regarding the failure of the male body and the institution of heterosexuality itself.

Casting light upon orgasm and its spectacle, fucking machines powerfully bring to the surface anxieties about categories of identity as markers of power and difference and the stability and legibility of those categories in the face of increasing technologization. Yet the queerness of the actors in this cyborgian sexual scene and the presence of human, nonhuman, and *other* urges us to consider the question of sexual difference more broadly and intersectionally than Williams's formative male/female analysis. Consequently, I am interested in the dynamic ways the money shot has evolved and continues to evolve since Williams's formative reading and how contemporary American pornography, in the context of the increasingly diverse sexualities and bodies of its performers, producers, and consumers, challenges the notion that the money shot is "the most representative instance of phallic power and pleasure."[107]

Across genres, American hard-core pornography reveals a shift away from the money shot as we once knew it and potentially away from dominant phallocentric economies of pleasure. For example, analyzing the "visual archive" of gay male bareback porn, Tim Dean builds upon the concept of the money shot. Unlike Williams, Dean situates it outside a heteronormative framework.[108] He sees it, as it is traditionally conceptualized (visible male ejaculation on the outside surface of the body) as at odds with bareback sex, which is dependent on internal ejaculation. Thus, for Dean, in bareback sex, "non-normative sex comes up against the norms of representation."[109] That is, if the money shot depends on visual proof of pleasure in the projection of semen *on* the body and the practice of bareback sex is contingent upon ejaculate deposited *inside* the body, how can bareback porn reconcile this representational quandary—rendering visible what is invisible while remaining a kind of authentic "visual archive" of bareback sex itself?[110] Dean discusses the multiple possibilities for reconciling this conflict, all of which are adaptations of the money shot that are practiced in contemporary American bareback porn.[111] Bareback porn shares with conventional heterosexual hard-core porn a requirement of visibility that is motivated by an "intense curiosity about the body's interior."[112] Dean argues that it is "the difference between a body's exterior and its interior" that impels the visual goals of bareback pornography.[113]

Perhaps the worries of male porn performers about the money shot some two decades ago were well founded. In an article exploring pornography's changing gendered dynamics of labor in the mid-1990s, Susan Faludi exposed the rampant sexism of the industry and the anxieties male porn stars harbored about their genital performance—getting wood and ejaculating on cue—and their status within the industry in a time of shrinking pools of male talent, wage gaps that favored women, and the reign of contract girls.[114] Faludi's interviews with male performers portray the money shot as vexed, anxiety producing, and ambivalent—a symbol of dominance through the exhibition of a purportedly uniquely male power *and* a fetishized oppressive measure of men's value as performers.[115] Longtime adult entertainment figure William Margold, whom Faludi interviewed, envisioned the money shot as the final masculine stronghold in an industry that was becoming increasingly feminized, for example, by privileging female performers with higher pay rates and more opportunities to shoot and by catering to the fantasies of increasing numbers of women customers.[116] He stated, "We're the last bastion of masculinity. The one thing a woman cannot do is ejaculate in the face of her partner. We have that power."[117] However, countless female squirters have proved Margold wrong, and hard-core pornography has provided evidence of women's ability to ejaculate (and do so in the face of her partner).

While Dean asks how pornography can produce a money shot when ejaculation occurs internally, fuckingmachines.com asks how it can deliver a money shot without a biological penis. Fuckingmachines. com regularly depicts female ejaculation, which is often referred to as squirting. The subgenre of squirting in contemporary porn speaks to the continuing reign of hard core porn's "principle of visibility" and the potential destabilization of this regime from its phallocentric foundation.[118] Like the contested geography of women's sexual pleasure, female ejaculation has a vexed history in modern sexological discourse. As Shannon Bell notes, "the genealogy of female ejaculation has been one of discovery, disappearance, and rediscovery."[119] This genealogy extends back over 2,000 years. Female ejaculation was a topic of scientific, medical, and philosophic inquiry in diverse global cultures, including those of ancient China and ancient Greece. It wasn't until the nineteenth century that women's ejaculation was deemed aberrant and pathological. Key sexologists ranging from Krafft-Ebing to Freud contributed to the construction of women's ejaculation as a marker of sexual deviance.[120] The medicalization of female ejaculation persists as studies about the etiology of the controversial phenomenon continue to investigate the physiological source of the fluid, the means by which it is expelled, the biochemical composition of the ejaculate, whether or how female ejaculation is associated with orgasm, the distinction between squirting and coital incontinence, and the impact of female ejaculation on women's sexual relationships.[121]

While fucking machines renew the question of the physical location of women's sexual pleasure and the "volume" of its expression, they also raise an equally animated issue in this arena: the dildo question. As penetrative devices, kink.com's fucking machines, like commercial sex machines, have a dildo attachment that is a vital component of the machine's technique of pleasure. Numerous feminist scholars have critiqued the dildo. Participants in the so-called dildo wars remained divided about whether the dildo is a technique of radical lesbian feminist sexual intercourse; a liberation from androcentric, phallocentric, heter-onormative sex; "a parable of genderfuck"; or a totem of patriarchy that problematically instantiates women's sexual pleasure as vaginal, effac-ing the clitoris as a site of orgasm.[122] Jeanne E. Hamming for example, argues for a critical liberation of the dildo, which she reinscribes as a nonphallic signifier, from the penis.[123] She contends that lesbian and heterosexual women's use of the strap-on dildo should not be seen as an emulation of heterosexual sex.

As a profoundly queer hybrid human-machine, does the dildo-armed fucking machine present the same issues as the dildo-wielding lesbian? Coleen Lamos also calls attention to the difference between the phallus and the penis in her analysis of the dildo, which, as she notes, "can at any moment be taken (on) either as a faithful substitute for the penis or as a parodic mine of its phallic pretentions."[124] The binary of repli-cation/subversion that undergirds the dildo debates is the same binary that scaffolds discussions of race play. Just as some women practice race play as a mode of processing and pleasuring racial trauma, women use the dildo as a tool for reframing and renegotiating experiences of sexual violence. For example, Minge and Zimmerman argue for an urgent "re-signification" of the dildo "as a tool of sexual agency" that recognizes its potential as an instrument for "rescripting" the trauma of violent sexual penetration.[125] Dildos are another site where the technologies of plea-sure, gender, race, and sexuality intersect.

The question of race and the use of the dildo as a technology of ra-cialized pleasure is less present in these debates, which largely took place among white middle-class lesbians.[126] However, in a short piece published in *Black Lace*, an erotic magazine for black lesbians, Alycee J. Lane interrogates the insidious racialization of the controversial sex toy and its evasion of critique in lesbian feminist discourse: "What does it mean, exactly, when white hegemony extends to the production of dil-dos?"[127] Jane recounts her shopping trip to search for "one brown beau-tiful dildo" after a conversation with a friend left her unsatisfied with her trusty "mauve" one and her own racial authenticity in using it. This difficult customer experience enlightened Lane about the problematic racialization of dildos, which ranged from the discrimination of "flesh" color as a sales category to the Mandingo stereotypes that informed the design and marketing of brown dildos. Frustrated with these options,

Lane left the store seemingly content to return to her mauve dildo. Yet the foray was not futile. She reflected that "the entire experience forced me to more critically examine how race permeates American culture. A sex toy easily becomes the location for racial terror and desire because sex itself is that location. We confront the violence of history and its consequences. We speak out allegiances according to the color we choose."[128] Lane identifies the imbrication of "racial terror and desire" that is so central to the question of black female sexuality. Her awareness of the racial politics of sex toys hinged upon the constitutive relationship of violence and black female sexuality.

The coloring of dildos signals their complex play with race. In the videos on fuckingmachines.com, the dildos are a wide range of colors, from violet to emerald green to "flesh" tones of beige, dark brown, tan, and salmon. The colors of fucking-machine dildos are perhaps less daring. Customers who buy the Sybian, for example, can choose between two colors only, "beige" or "chocolate" dildos. In her powerful analysis of the coloring of another type of toy, the Barbie doll, Ann Ducille explores the commodification of race as a "deep play of difference" that relies upon skin color as the prototypical manifestation of difference.[129] I have already discussed skin's function as an ambivalent erotic racial signifier that is highly commodified in contemporary American hard-core pornography. Like dildos, Barbie "both produces and denies difference" through a (re)production of stereotypes and the legible signs of racial difference.[130] The coloring of dildos introduces the topic of the complex labor of fucking machines as technologies of race that similarly toy with the "discursively familiar."[131]

The Tangled Technologies of Fucking Machines: Racializing Technology, Technologizing Race

In this final section I consider the multifaceted racialization of the machines, reading their performances as imbricated technologies of racialization, sexualization, gendering, visuality, and pleasure in the context of theories of race and/as technology and "new media" discourses of race in cyberspace. While fuckingmachines.com presents complex technologies of racialization performed at the multiple, overlapping sites of machines, performers, and spectators, in the limited scholarly engagement with fucking machines, race is overlooked or undertheorized.[132] First, I read the machines as not merely extensions of their white inventors and the white male imaginary but as embodiments of white masculinity. Analyzing the machines' whiteness is critical to exposing the racialization of the bodies they fuck in order to stage the intimate relationship between white masculinity and the performance of black female sexuality. This racialization is not the conventional exoticization of black female sexuality in pornography, but operates as a technique of racial-sexual alterity nonetheless. In the previous chapters I've analyzed how race is explicitly evoked and employed as an implement or technology of BDSM, where it is used as a primary tool of eroticized humiliation, shame, pleasure, and power in pornography performance; here I engage the technologies of race in BDSM pornography while considering race itself as a technology. Finally, I consider spectatorship as a site that reveals the machines' operation as technologies of racialization, reading fuckingmachines.com user comments as discursive performances of black female sexuality. Looking toward the domain of spectatorship further reveals the tangled technologies of the machines, reinforcing how the production of black female sexuality is imbricated with that of white male sexuality.

Fucking machines are avatars of their largely white male architects.[133] Nowhere is the white heteropatriarchal lineage of the machines more clear than in Timothy Archibald's quasi-photoethnography, documentary book *Sex Machines: Photographs and Interviews*. Archibald uses interviews and photography to explore the underground community of sex machine inventors in primarily rural, small-town America. Though it is unfortunate that race is not a topic of Archibald's interview questions, the images provide evidence of the fact that going back as far as the mid-nineteenth century, white men have been *the* "practitioners of a timeless craft."[134] In his study of American sex machines, Hoag Levins identifies more than 800 patents for various sexual devices dating back to 1846, when Dr. John Beers, a white male dentist, patented a diaphragm named "Wife's Protector" that was made of gold wire and oiled silk.[135] Rachel P. Maines traces the invention of the first electromechanical vibrator to a British physician in the 1880s; its use in the hands of physicians became popular in the late nineteenth century as a treatment for women's "hysteria."[136] David Levy dates the first known sex machine, a primitive self-operated device that sprayed milk into the vagina to mimic semen, to 1900.[137] Deeply invested in the therapeutic potential of the orgasm, Marxist sexologist Wilhelm Reich, a pupil of Freud, invented a quasi–fucking machine, the "orgone energy accumulator," a box that allegedly induced orgasms to improve what Reich termed "orgastic potency."[138] It became popular in the United States in the mid-twentieth century.

I would trace the white male genealogy of fucking machines back even further. We might locate the blueprints for kink.com's twenty-first-century fucking machines in the late eighteenth century in the work of Marquis de Sade, who designed technological devices to express what Beauvoir identifies as his ethic, "the fundamental identity of coition and cruelty."[139] The engravings illustrating the 1797 edition of Sade's *L'Histoire de Juliette* prefigured kink.com's arsenal of fucking machines. They present a Sadean erotic carnival of excess: figures are linked by fingers, tongues, and genitals in patterns of contorted flesh. Voluptuous women balance on considerable erections, piled atop one another like circus elephants, and are suspended from ceilings in intricate bondage devices that facilitate a feast of penetration.[140] This history presents a genealogy of the technology-inspired, racialized, and gendered architectonics of pleasure that situate fuckingmachines.com as a product of the white male gaze.

Not a single face of color appears in the more than fifty color photographs in *Sex Machines: Photographs and Interviews*. Most of the images are portraits of inventors and their machines in their "natural" habitats: bedrooms, living rooms, garages, and tool sheds. Like the inventors, the machines are deliberately posed in various domestic spaces such as atop a tightly made bed beside the family pet, on a table littered with board games in a den, in a living room in front of an antique mahogany china hutch, or perched on a makeshift island in the middle of a kitchen. Many photographs depict the men tinkering with their machines on a workbench or posing proudly next to them. The photographs vividly capture the "on/scenity" of the fucking machines in the fabric of our national domesticity.[141] One sex machine maker, Paul, owner and founder of Sartan's BDSM Workshop, states,

Figure 4.1. Sadean fucking machines from *Sixty Erotic Engravings from Juliette* (New York: Grove Press, 1969)

The popular image of the adult industry, or anything sexual, has dark rooms and black curtains and kinda grungy nasty people behind it—people not in touch with the emotional factor. And it's not true. Look at us. We are your average neighbors. We mow our lawn, we feed our kids healthy food, we go to school meetings. I guess we are the perverts of the world. We could be next to you in the supermarket.[142]

Paul gives voice to the politics of perversion, articulating the contradictory position, image, and (in)visibility of fucking machines in American society. Simultaneously underground and out in the open, quotidian and extraordinary, these perverse and marginal amateur sexual technologies clandestinely occupy the center of the domestic spaces of "middle" America.

Archibald documents the machines as apparatuses of not just sexual but also nationalist pleasure. This pleasure—an amalgamation of an inventor's sense of achievement, machismo, fatherly pride, and sexualized gratification—is vividly conveyed in the portraits. In one photograph, Dwaine Baccus, a white middle-aged inventor from Emmett, Idaho, with thin greying hair and wire-rimmed glasses, poses, sans machine, in front of a red garage door. Baccus wears blue jeans and a white T-shirt that displays an American flag and the words "Let Freedom Ring." The red, white, and blue palette of the image reinforces its patriotic aura. This nationalism works to temper the potential shame and deviance of the labor of, in, and by these sexual technologies and their makers. In an increasingly xenophobic age of neoliberal globalization, this "made in America" visual sentiment is not subtle. In another image, Rick Van Theil of Spindoll Manufacturing and Sales in Henderson, Nevada, poses shirtless next to his invention, The Orgasmo. The pink dildo mounted on the machine's metal "arm" mimics the color and substance of his own flesh. The close proximity of Van Theil's bare torso and the dildo further collapses the boundary between man and machine in this queer family portrait. Whiteness is paradoxically represented, indeed commodified, as both essential and invented.

Fucking machines fuck with race. More than incarnations of white masculinity, fucking machines embody the technology of race as a mechanism of difference, power, and pleasure while illuminating the continuing salience and challenges of racial difference in cyberspace. As technologies of race, fucking machines perform black female sexuality as a technique of difference. However they (re)configure black female racial-sexual alterity in terms that are not entirely commonplace in pornography. That is, fuckingmachines.com videos mute the familiar hyperbolic scripts of black female sexuality, instead favoring a "colorblind" philosophy in which blackness is not typically referred to verbally or in the textual descriptions of videos. Indeed, while the machines are loud, their motors humming, hammering, clinking, and whirring, race speaks more quietly and its codes communicate more subtly. Pornographic blackness is fucked with, reconfigured in its technological mediation, its legibility disrupted and the codes of its pornographic script scrambled. Is this a kind of collapse of technology or of "blackness" (as we know it) in the face of technology?

In fucking-machine performances, technology intervenes to catalyze a productive disintegration of blackness that works to unmoor it from its stereotyped foundation. However, the reigning ideological opposition of blackness and technology is problematic. Alondra Nelson has compellingly unveiled the "binary between blackness and technology" and the ways new technologies generate and are generated from veteran racialisms.[143] Nelson argues,

> In these politics of the future, supposedly novel paradigms for understanding technology smack of old racial ideologies. In each scenario, racial identity, and blackness in particular, is the anti-avatar of digital life. Blackness gets constructed as always oppositional to technologically driven chronicles of progress."[144]

This conflict between blackness and technology reinforces the relationality of race. In chapter 1, I evoked Bernasconi's concept of race as a border concept to bring into relief how race play reveals race to be an erotic play with the binary of black and white. If race is indeed a border concept, perhaps this border is best delineated and policed by a "human" body. Although black female sexuality is ostensibly muted in the presence of the fucking machines, it nevertheless informs these techno-fucking encounters.

The concept of hysteria reflects the entangled technologies (of race, pleasure, gender, and sexuality) of fucking machines and the nuances that black female sexuality engenders in these performances. In their objective of producing maximum pleasure, kink.com's fucking machines often reduce their female performers to a kind of primitive state of orgasm overdose. Eyes rolling back in their heads, unable to speak, they become, in effect, hysterical with pleasure. In these performances we see the not-too-distant shadows of the Victorian-era pathologization of women's sexual pleasure. Here, however, the technologically induced orgasm engenders hysteria rather than providing a cure for it. These fucking machines drive women wild with pleasure, creating "insane," "uncontrollable" orgasms that make "girls," as Acworth refers to them, "pretty crazy."[145] Foucault has revealed the "hystericization of women's bodies" as an integral part of the knowledge/power system of sexuality.[146] Hysteria is even more pronounced in kink.com's brightly lit medical and scientific laboratory settings, where performers fuck machines on gynecological tables with foot stirrups. In these scenes, the fucking machines channel the vibrator as an electromechanical medical instrument. But beyond the repeated blurring of the pornographic, and scientific gazes, how does race speak in such scenes?

As technologies of women's hysterical pleasure, fucking machines produce different resonances for racialized sexuality. I have argued that the historical legacies of black female sexuality critically inform black women's BDSM performance. This history is just as resonant in the videos on fuckingmachines.com, albeit somewhat subdued. This is not the antebellum auction block or the slave cabin, but race plays dynamically here nonetheless. The racial performances here are less hyperbolic and more unfamiliar on a pornographic register. For example, well-known black female performer Sydnee Capri (who also starred in *White Men's Revenge*) fucks six machines in a dated medical laboratory setting that features a stainless steel gynecological table, a sink, a small frame on the wall representing a doctor's diploma, a shelf with various tinctures in glass bottles, and antique medical paraphernalia that include a scale and a hanging skeleton. Her black female body in such a room, re-created as a twenty-first century space of pleasure, recalls a history of the nineteenth-century pain her sisters endured. From the probing of Saartjie Baartman at the hands of Georges Cuvier to the experimental gynecological "work" of the so-called father of the speculum, J. Marion Sims, on the bodies of enslaved black

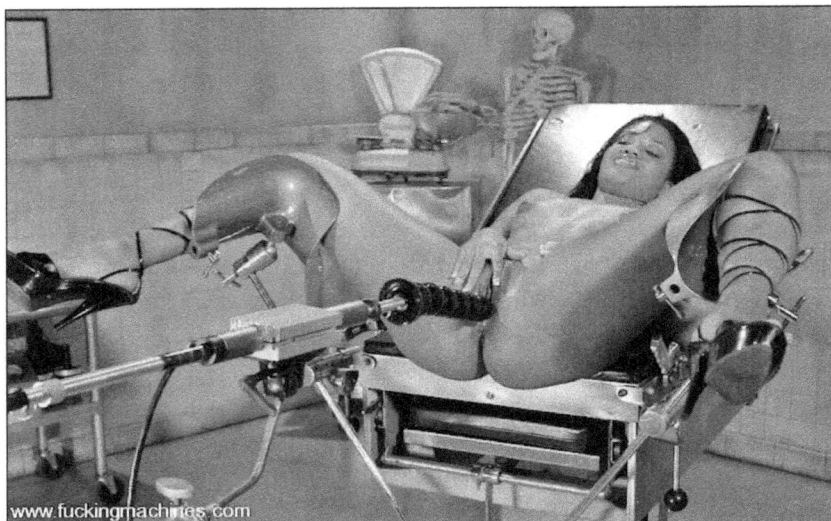

Figure 4.2. "Sydnee Capri," fuckingmachines.com

women—a series of experiments that Sims himself described as not only "complete failure[s]" but also as producing extreme agony—the history of the medical-sexual abuse of the black female body has a long reach.[147] The nineteenth-century development of gynecological surgery on the bodies of black female slaves is ineluctable in these twenty-first-century kink.com gynecological scenes of women's techno-pleasure, particularly when such scenes are inhabited by a black female body.

This scene with Capri provides evidence of the white male mediation of black female sexuality on fuckingmachines.com. A snapshot of the hand of white male engineer, G-Force, operating the power panel of the Fuckatron just meters away from Capri, who is perched on all fours on the table as she is penetrated from behind, documents the white male intervention in black female sexuality and the eroticization of this control as integral to the racialized fantasy of techno-pleasure in this video.[148] Like white male participation in the interracial cuckold pornographic fantasy, white male performance here, however noncorporeal and "behind" the machines, can only be understood as queer. Typically in fucking-machine videos, the operator's body is mostly kept out of the frame of the camera; exceptions include brief glimpses of parts of the operator's body when he makes various adjustments to the machine, hands vibrators to performers, applies more lube, and operates handheld devices. Clear and deliberate visual evidence of the presence of the behind-the-scenes (hu)man operation of the (non-handheld) fucking machines is atypical in the fuckingmachines.com archive. In the video with Capri and the Fuckatron, this lapse foregrounds the racial dynamics of the cyborgian orgy, revealing the presence of a white male who is manipulating the fucking-machine technology and through it, the body of the black female performer. These momentary ruptures of the visual frame are compounded by the audio presence of white maleness. In addition to the pre-fucking introductory interview, G-Force interacts verbally with Capri throughout her performances with different machines—from introducing a new machine and asking if she's ever ridden it to a verbal warning during her first romp with the Sybian ("Don't wear yourself out") just eight minutes into the 42-minute video. This interaction is a critical intervention into the performance of black female sexuality. Just a few minutes after Capri mounts the second machine, the Rocker (with Hitachi in hand), he yells, "Sydnee, Sydnee, Sydnee, don't wear yourself out on this one either!"

These warnings are common in fuckingmachines.com videos. They reflect the site's economy of pleasure, the investment of its purveyors in the spectacle of both the quality *and* quantity of female orgasms. In the video with Capri, however, they reflect a tradition of white males' disciplining of black female sexuality that is made more transparent by the rupture in the performative and textual (though still of course performative) production of black female sexuality. For example, in the textual description of this video, Capri is described as "NEVER get[ting] tired!" However just after fucking her first machine, the Sybian, in response to G-Force's command to not "wear [her]self out," she replies, "I already have." This tension signals the investment of the site in long-standing tropes of the excessive libidos of black women and the athleticism of the black female body. Although Capri is positioned as a tireless performer, this indefatigability is highly manipulated by the white male "hand." This disembodied hand is caught, almost eerily, rupturing the frame in many videos, contesting the machines' autonomy and manifesting white masculinity's interference in the performance of black female sexuality.

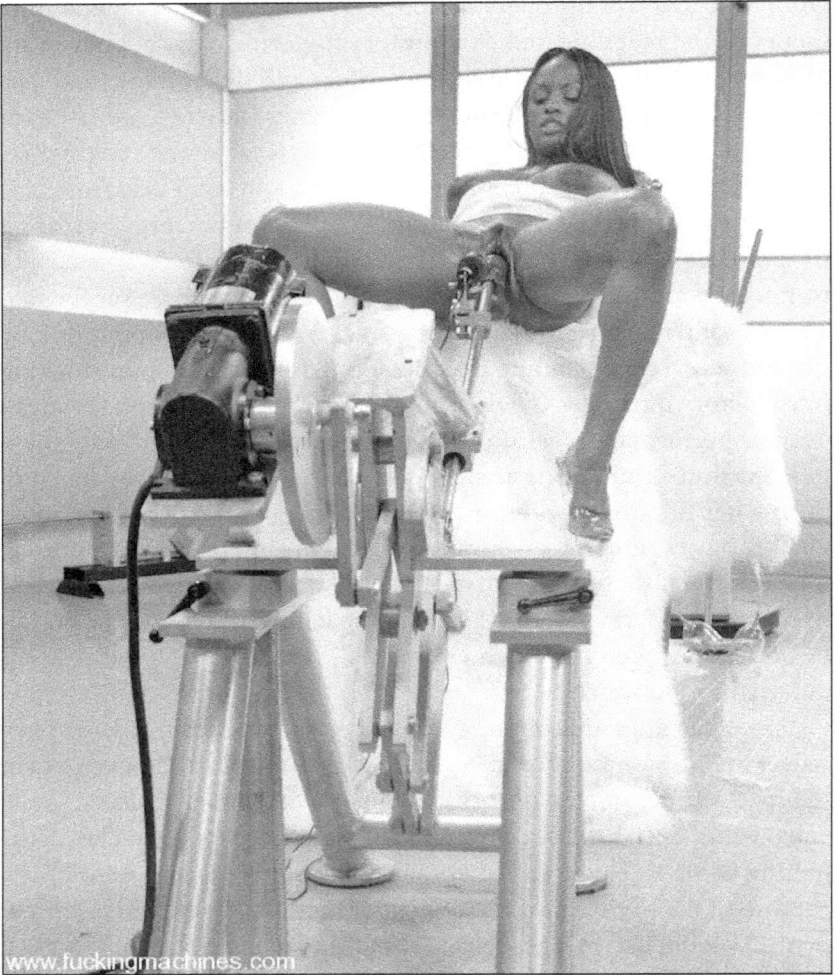

Figure 4.3. "Jada Fire," fuckingmachines.com

Technology mediates and ultimately unveils the notion of black women's hypersexuality as an artifice.

The machines' functions as technologies of race are multiplex. They are racialized themselves, they effect a racialization of their operators and partners, and they reveal the technology of race itself, which consists not merely of modes of racialized domination and submission but also of pleasures in this technique. Contemporary theorizations of race as technology draw upon feminist scholarship that theorizes gender as a technology, which, in turn, is anchored in Foucauldian discourse on sex as a technology. Considering sex as a technology, or a "set of effects," recognizes the historical function of sexuality as an apparatus of (bio) power in the service of bourgeoisie hegemony.[149] Just as the fucking machines labor simultaneously as technologies of sex, pleasure, race, and gender, the technology of sex is a composite technology. It functions concurrently as a technology of visibility. Foucault writes, "Sex became a matter that required the social body as a whole, and virtually all of its individuals, to place themselves under surveillance."[150] The medicalization of perversion I discussed in the introduction and the hystericization of women's bodies that I have argued fucking machines produce are two "mechanisms of knowledge and power" that Foucault argues constitute the technology of sex, along with the sexualization of children and the regulation of procreation.[151]

Feminist scholars have adapted Foucault's concept of the technology of sex to argue for the technology of gender. Teresa de Lauretis contends that gender is a dynamic technology of "representation and self-representation," the product of multiple discursive sociocultural technologies that include the media, institutions, ideologies, and epistemologies.[152] She critiques Foucault's theorization of the technology of sex for failing to account for gender and the nuances of sexuality for men and women. Her theory of gender as technology looks at gender outside the limits of sexual difference, which she understands to problematically universalize the category of woman and replicate Western heteropatriarchy. In her analysis of de Lauretis, Anne Balsamo more recently used the term "technologies of the gendered body" to describe the ever-deepening relationship between technology and the body. For Balsamo, "gender . . . is *both* a determining social condition and a social consequence of technological deployment."[153] Like de

Lauretis, Balsamo uses the concept of technology to reveal gender as a material and cultural "product" and "process."[154]

Just as feminists have theorized the technology of gender, critical race theorists have argued that race is a technology. This argument is presented in a special issue of *Camera Obscura* titled "Race and/as Technology." Though scholars such as Michael Omi and Howard Winant have long theorized race as a technology of domination and power, this collection critically interrogates the racialized embodiment of technology.[155] In the introductory article Wendy Hui Kyong Chun writes, "Crucially, race as technology shifts the focus from the *what* of race to the *how* of race, from *knowing* race to *doing* race by emphasizing the similarities between race and technology."[156] Looking at race as a technology is an important intervention in binary modes of racial thinking that tend to approach it either scientifically or as "purely cultural."[157] Perhaps most importantly for Chun, race and/as technology facilitates a critical reframing of the discourse of race that focuses "on modes of recognition and relation, rather than on being."[158] "Race and/as technology" recognizes the flexibility of race as a relation and set of relations rather than as an essence or entity.

Other important articles in this collection similarly argue that race is an apparatus. Like Chun, Beth Coleman highlights the "doing" of race. She writes, "In extending the function of *techné* to race, I create a collision of value systems. In this formulation, race exists as if it were on par with a hammer or a mechanical instrument; denaturing it from its historical roots, race can then be freely engaged as a productive tool."[159] She highlights the "technical agency" of race: what she perceives as a kind of productive and potentially liberating mobility for the racialized subject. Jennifer González's reading of race as technology is perhaps less hopeful. She argues that digital visual culture is a vital technology of the "oppressive regime" of race but simultaneously sees it as a site for the critique and alteration of racial discourse.[160] In González's analysis, race is a "visual system of power whose parameters have been the focus of every innovation in visual recording devices."[161] Like fucking machines, González illustrates how the technology of race conspires with technology of visuality, identifying race as a visual technique. She describes cyberspace's simultaneous imagining of itself as a site of "universal subjectivity that can escape the limitations of race" and as a space of the "proliferation of racially marked avatars and experimental hybrids."[162]

This proliferation has facilitated a digital visual lexicon of race that exploits "new" technology for the construction, distribution, and consumption of "old" racial-sexual alterity. This is the profound paradox of inter°ace. I coin this term to describe the phenomenon of digitized race and the contradictory and complex modes cyberculture uses to configure race as a commodified category of representation and power. Inter°ace speaks to the temporal and spatial places where the race and digital technology intersect to permutate race. The tension of inter°ace between reinvention and replication mirrors the tension of fucking machines, which, as "racially marked avatars and experimental hybrids," represent a recapitulation of IRL (in real life) difference and a potential disruption of their own compulsive reiteration. In the context of fuckingmachines. com, inter°ace gains another relevance, signaling what may be read as an interracial sexual performance between woman and machine.

While inter°ace describes fuckingmachines.com's illumination of race as a relation between technology and the body, it also narrates the fucking they enact as between two different categories of bodies. In the previous chapter, I analyzed interracial sex in pornography as a profoundly queer sexual performance; here I further queer the term "interracial" to extend it to sex across the boundary between machine and human. Given that the color line itself is so often a border that divides the human from the nonhuman, the inter°acial sex fuckingmachines. com performances enact is not too far of a conceptual stretch. González argues that the prevalence of miscegenation in cyborgian discourse reflects "a general tendency to link the 'otherness' of the machines with the otherness of racial and sexual difference."[163] The sexualized nature of the human-machine amalgamation that marks the cyborg summons miscegenation. Both cyborgs and racial hybrids are the product of a kind of miscegenation or illicit pairing.[164] The performances on fuckingmachines.com add the taboo of sex that crosses the border between humans and machine to illicit sex that crosses the racial divide. The eroticization of racial-sexual alterity here is profoundly multifaceted.

The tension between utopian fantasy and material reality that undergirds digital subjectivity mirrors that of the utopian techno-fetishistic tension between fucking machines as mechanical apparatuses and their racialized embodiment. While fucking machines promise a kind of techno-utopian fantasy of the machine, albeit an anxious one, they remain deeply wedded to the racialized and gendered human body. As Cameron Bailey argues, "Cybersubjectivity promises the fantasy of disembodied communication but it is firmly connected to bodies through the imaginative act required to project into cyberspace."[165] In purportedly providing a sexual experience that "no human can replicate," fucking machines are programmed by and indeed reproduce racialized and gendered codes of sexuality.[166] The genesis of fuckingmachines.com corresponds with a wave of scholarly analyses of race in cyberspace that began in the early 2000s, much of which worked to implode what Nelson calls the "founding fiction of the digital age," the myth of post-corporeal and postracial cybersubjectivity.[167] Lisa Nakamura, a leading voice in this field, reveals the salience of race in cyberspace as a domain of fantasy of racial otherness in which white is often an assumed standard. She has coined the term "identity tourism" to critique the problematic trend of "passing" in cyberspace—the use of "race and gender as amusing prostheses that [can] be donned and shed without real life consequences."[168] More recently, in pondering the question of "race after the Internet," Nakamura has argued that the digital technologies of the Internet continue to transform our conceptualizations of race while fostering new modes of racialized discrimination, inequality, privilege, and power.[169] In the post-Internet world, "race has itself become a digital medium, a distinctive set of informatic codes, networked mediated narratives, maps, images, and visualizations that index identity."[170] Understanding race as a form of encoding facilitates its recognition as a technology of power.

Nakamura is one of many scholarly pioneers who interrogates the insidious digital postracial utopianism that marked early discussions of race and cyberspace, particularly in the days of the pre-graphic Internet. Kalí Tal similarly critiques the "whitinizing of cyberspace" that operates on multiple fronts: the elision of people of color in cyberspace and the failure of scholars to recognize African American critics—who have a long, rich tradition of writing about the fracturing and multiplicity of identity, embodiment, and disembodiment—as pioneers in this field.[171] Tal expands the question of race and representation on the Internet beyond the issue of the bodies on screen to include the broader critical practices engaged in reading cyberspace. As a site that instantiates how technologies of racialization extend temporally and spatially beyond the "bodies" in our frame of view, fuckingmachines.com demands such a critique.

While race, as we are accustomed to hearing it, is quieter in these performances, it speaks more loudly in the viewers' comments on the videos. Although the black female performer's race is not typically a topic of discussion in pre- or post-performance interviews or in the descriptions of the videos, blackness is most always named—called out and called on—by one or more user.[172] These forums explicitly blacken the female performers. Just as I read Sisko's blog as an essential element of race-play performance, here I analyze these viewer's comments as vital technologies of racialization. Reading the racial performances in these liminal and often overlooked sites of analysis in pornography scholarship facilitates an urgently needed critical expansion of pornography's play of race, pushing these performances and our readings of them beyond the bodies in our immediate view. If, as I have suggested, the conventional pornographic "racial codes" of black female sexuality are challenged by the technologies that mediate it, it is in the remarks section where these codes hypostatize. In this cacophony of comments, blackness is interpellated in ways that range from simple acknowledgement to criticism to praise to requests for more black female performers. The familiar hyperbolic pornographic lexicon of black female sexuality creeps in here as users describe the black female body with words such as "chocolate," "ebony," and "brown sugar" and phrases such as "the blacker the berry the sweeter the juice." These terms resuscitate pornography's racial-sexual epidermal schema from its torpidity during the performances themselves.

The construction of race is inextricable from the metaphorical and literal policing of race in this arena. These remarks discipline the black female body in order to signify her belonging in this techno-sexual site. Black female sexuality is often summoned in relation to white male sexuality. Whiteness (white maleness) is confessed as black womanness is recognized. That is, users often refer to the black female body in relation to their own whiteness (and its confession) on this purportedly anonymous cyber site. For example, one viewer imagines his "fat white cock between those ass cheeks." Another writes "am awhite guy and want more black women," while another suggests, "USE MORE BLACK GIRLS US WHITE FOLK LIKE TO SEE THEM GETTING FUCKED." In each of these comments, the black female body is written in and through white male sexuality and its value is actualized through the white male body.[173] Kink.com's inter°acial policing operates more palpably through its regulation of member's comments. In order to promote respectful community dialogue, the company has "guidelines for posting comments." When users violate these guidelines, kink.com can delete a user's posts or suspend and/or ban his or her account. In addition to remarks that include profanity or spam, that solicit users, and that constitute phishing, posts that "contain racist or homophobic remarks" are not allowed.[174] Despite this, racialisms are frequent.

In speaking to and for the black female body, users also speak to one another. It is not uncommon to see a continuing dialogue about the quality of a performance, the authenticity of a performer's orgasms, the casting of machines, the set, and the body of the female performer. In performances with black women, blackness often is the pivot for these debates. These forums typically reflect a kind of race-"positive" position, often complimenting, albeit ambivalently, the eroticized, exoticized black female and even imploring kink.com to feature more fucking-machine videos with black women. However, they also reflect a refusal of blackness that is articulated through the policing of fucking-machines.com as a space of whiteness. This phenomenon is evidenced in the comments for a video with black female performer Melrose Foxx. Though the 43-minute video was filmed in a novel setting—kink.com's RV in San Francisco's iconic Golden Gate Park—it is rather typical. It begins with a short pre-fucking interview conducted outside on a park bench, during which Tomcat welcomes Foxx to fuckingmachines.com, asks about her knowledge of the machines, her experience in pornography, and her sexual preferences. The camera then follows Foxx inside the RV to a small bed that serves as the stage where the fucking takes place with three machines: SatisfyHer, the Intruder, and the Sybian. Like many fuckingmachines.com performers, Foxx is seemingly exhausted after multiple orgasms and requires breaks in between machine partners. The video concludes with a short post-fucking interview during which she corroborates the sexual supremacy of the machines, her "new best friend[s]," saying, "I think I am going to get rid of the boyfriend."

While the video diegetically and sequentially subscribes to fucking-machines.com's repetitive routine, the black female body disrupts this convention and is policed by the spectatorial gaze. One fuckingma-chines.com member, tsunami 69, writes, "You guys should really consider a site specific to this type of content/model. It's becoming far too common to keep my interest in a monthly membership." Other important responses function not so much as a defense of black female sexuality but as a calling out of the marginality of its presence, a peripherality that is articulated in tsunami69's failure to explicitly cite blackness as he summons it. One viewer, for example, writes:

> i liked it and i think it's bull crap that ass [sic] soon as a model is posted that is not white someone rates poor and talks about content/models they don't need a site specific because not everyone on the site like to watch white girls getting fucked by machines twenty four seven sure it's fun an good but you can only watch so many white girls before you get tired of seeing white girls getting fucked.

However, Tomcat's response is where we can see how the policing of black female sexuality on the site is yoked to the larger hegemonic ideological disciplining of black female sexuality that fuckingmachines.com displays. Tomcat's "defense" of Foxx is couched not in advocacy for the site's diversity but rather in the superior physicality of the black female body as an opponent in the contest between woman and machine: "You are all entitled to your opinion on what you personally find hot—just be fair to the model. I will say that 43 minutes of machine fucking is VERY intense—especially on high. Melrose is one of the rare few models who fucked the machines back, using her own rhythm to cum. She's hot as fuck and we all have the pleasure of watching her." The black female's contested space in this techno-sexual scene is recuperated through a resort to stereotypes. In citing Foxx's "rhythm" and athleticism with the machines (even at high speeds), Tomcat evokes her blackness. Similarly replete with stereotypes, the description for the video notes Foxx's "incredible way of fucking in time with the machines" writing, "She shakes, grinds and fucks back all the way to orgasm heaven."[175] Like tsumani69, Tomcat elides blackness as he interprets it.

As a digital platform for these cyber comments, the Internet catalyzes fuckingmachines.com's collaborative technologies of race, pleasure, and visuality. Fuckingmachines.com illuminates the myriad ways the Internet is altering the contemporary production and consumption of race. While scholars from both sides of pornography's ever-seething fault line have critiqued Internet porn, the myriad ways the Internet enables pornography to operate as a technology of race is rarely analyzed.[176] On the fucking machines.com site, the Internet facilitates a DIY mode of racialization in which multiple actors—human and nonhuman, silent and speaking, flesh and machine—collude in the performance of black female sexuality to play in and about pornography's precarious game of race. Discussions of DIY pornography often focus on the ways that "indieporn or "altporn" has creatively changed not just pornography and the industry but also our experience and knowledge of sexuality and the body.[177] Yet it is also the case that pornography facilitates a DIY racial construction, another example of how technology continues to shape the racial project.

Fuckingmachines.com requires us to think more comprehensively about the complex technologies involved in new media's reconfiguration of these relationships and to expose the many agents, components, spaces, and technologies of the digital production of race. Throughout the fuckingmachines.com site, black female sexuality is constituted from both bodily performance—human and machine—and text. The performance of black female sexuality by multiple agents reveals that our racial-sexual performances are not just our own. Beyond the machines' performances as avatars of white male inventors and white male machine operators at kink.com, fucking machines reflect the technology of race as an apparatus of power and pleasure while illuminating the continuing project of re(configuring) racial difference in cyberspace. Indeed, fuckingmachines.com attests to the ever-expanding scope of the performance of black female racial-sexual alterity.

Conclusion

Encore: A Note on Repetition

"Racist remarks" are not the only things kink.com prohibits in online comments. "Unnecessarily repetitive" posts are also prohibited, yet they are rife. If the posts are incredibly repetitive—using the same limited lexicon to describe female physicality ("hot," "hottie," "smokin' hot," "super hot," typically followed by an inordinate number of exclamation marks)—so too are the performances. In the peculiar cacophony of human and nonhuman sounds that becomes a sort of soundtrack in fucking-machine videos—moaning, groaning, slurping, sucking, clicking, droning, buzzing—it is the somnolent humming that energizes the repetitive thrusts of the machines that is most prominent. The repetition of the machines, as tangled technologies of gender, race, sexuality, pleasure, and visuality, ignite the multiple themes of this book. In this conclusion, I use the repetition of fucking machines to illuminate the larger, if less pronounced, processes of rote at work in pornography's performance of racialized sexuality and to recapitulate the motifs in this book. There is much repetition here: the repetition of tensions between the binaries of fantasy/reality, black/white, absence/presence, and inside/outside; the fact that BDSM and pornography both serve as platforms for the dynamic spectacle of race play; the repetition of the narratives of historical trauma and black abjection that script performances in both of these genres; and our own tenacious disciplining of the enactment of these performances.

Repetition is a salient black cultural motif.[1] Exploring this fundamental element on which black culture, specifically performance, hinges, James Snead engages the concept of the musical "cut": a mode of "abruptly skipping it back to another beginning which we have already heard."[2] Reflecting Derrida's concepts of iterability and difference that highlight the change, alterity, and invention in repetition, Deborah

McDowell uses the theory of the "changing same" to map key historical moments in black women's literature.[3] I am less interested in black culture as a mode of repetition than in *what* we keep retuning to, how, and *for* what. Though I focus on the memory of chattel slavery as a source of erotic pleasure, slavery has been a significant trope of cultural production, from literature, to film, to music, to visual arts. It was not until the mid- to late twentieth century, however, that its representation became a recurring cultural motif as a mode of interrogating modern black subjectivity.[4] As Christina Sharpe has so compellingly revealed, the repetition of "monstrous intimacies," the haunting racial-sexual violence of slavery, is constitutive of postslavery subjectivity.[5] Pornography and BDSM illuminate the erotic legacies of racial bondage and our "compulsion" to revisit this history in our intimate spheres.

The repetition at work in fuckingmachines.com is powerful and layered, inflecting the narrative, the kinetic technology of the machines; the spectacle of women's orgasms; and the performance of racialized sexuality. As I have shown, fuckingmachines.com subscribes to a formulaic narrative frame: the interview with the performer, the vibrator "warm-up," the sequential fucking with different machines, and (sometimes) a closing interview finale. This repetitiveness mirrors the repetition of the machine's kinetic range of motion—whether this means a stroke range from 0–20 centimeters, as the Annihilator has; a maximum rpm of 2,400, as the Fucksall has; a height range of 36–76 centimeters, as the Bunny Fucker has; a torque value of 4.86 newton meters, as the Monster has; or a stroke adjustment setting of six seconds, as the Intruder has.[6] The erotic economy of fuckingmachines.com depends upon repetition. The repetitive movement of the machines, as superhuman sexual partners, produces women's multitudinous climaxes. Fuckingmachines.com's compulsive repetition of women's orgasms is a lens through which to consider the reproduction of racialized sexuality at work in porn and BDSM.

Pornography's Generic Refrain

The multifaceted repetition at work in fuckingmachines.com reflects repetition in the genre of pornography itself. Even before the early anti-pornography critiques by radical feminists, scholars identified the salience of the convention of repetition within pornography.[7] More recently, Susanna Paasonen has approached the question of repetition within pornography from the perspective of affective power, "the power of pornographic images and texts to move their viewers and readers."[8] She argues that our pleasure in pornography is premised on our affective relation to the figures on screen and that repetition facilitates this identification.[9] I am inspired by Paasonen's push to move beyond a "literal cataloguing" of pornography's redundant iconography to think critically about "these choreographies in the modality of porn."[10] However, I believe we need to expand the critique of pornography's repetition to see it as reflective of, as contesting, and as engendering larger reiterative performances of identifications of power such as race, gender, and sexuality. Pornography's repetitive pleasure—a pleasure in repetition—is bound up with its repetition of race.

As a site that brilliantly exemplifies pornography's capitalist logic of sexuality in its spectacle of the mechanical extraction of women's multiple orgasms, fuckingmachines.com brings the "orgasm industry" of pornography into high relief.[11] Sarah Schaschek uses the term Orgasm Inc. to describe the fundamental seriality of pornography's pleasure.[12] Informed by Paasonen, Schaschek has recently argued that repetition is not just constitutive of the genre, it is also essential to pleasure in pornography.[13] Relying on philosophical theories of repetition, mainly Derrida's concept of iterability, she underscores the instability and difference in repetition: "The orgasmic formula might be reproducible, yet the images are always at risk of 'failing' to arouse or even to signify a definitive scenario."[14] I too am interested in the question of failure in repetition, not so much how pornography fails but how pornography brings into high relief the failure of categories of identity and their tired yet easily energized tropes of racialized sexuality. I want to reorient the question of pornography and bodily failure to think about how pornography renders the body as a site of racial-sexual failure to tell the truth of our race, sexuality, and gender *and* reveal the failure of these categories as truths.

All Pink on the Inside? Pornography's Changing Same

Beyond its generic repetition, pornography engages repetition as an established mode of racial performativity. This repetition brilliantly reflects our myriad insecurities about the category of race. In an interview on the topic of interracial sex, Diana Devoe rhetorically questions the role of racial categorization within the adult entertainment industry: "Why is there an interracial designation in adult at all if we are all just having sex and we are all pink on the inside? Why is there interracial? Why is there Black? Why is there Asian? There's these categories because it is about attraction. It is about selling a fantasy."[15] The specific categories within pornography—of race, fetish, sexual preference—are about, as Devoe notes, "selling a fantasy" and the need to categorize (in order to market and sell) these specific fantasies. However, the fantasy of racial-sexual alterity that pornography sells and BDSM traffics in is exceedingly ambivalent. It reifies these categories to stage their erotic transgression and performs a self-mocking hyperbole, a *play*, of race that underscores its own pleasure. As I have shown, pornography and BDSM eroticize not just the racial-sexual difference of the black female body but also the ambivalence of this difference—its instability—signaling a profound anxiety over the *sameness* of the black female body. Performances of black female sexuality in contemporary American pornography and BDSM are grounded in the shifting tectonics of desire and derision, sameness and difference. The colloquial phrase "it's all pink on the inside," which is simultaneously inclusive and discriminative and is rooted in difference and sameness, astutely encapsulates a number of contradictions at play within the spectacular repetition of black female sexuality.

The phrase signals the body as the primary site for the enactment of the fantasy of racial-sexual alterity while unveiling this otherness as fantasy. Black female sexuality prompts a critical reorienting of the questions of pornography, repetition, and bodily failure to consider how pornography and BDSM, both deeply embodied practices, paradoxically reveal the body as a critical yet unreliable site of racial determination (black on the outside, pink on the inside)—one that not only fails to tell the truth of our race but also reveals the failure of these categories as truths. Homi Bhabha sheds light on the salience of repetition for the question of otherness, the primary "discursive strategy" of which is the stereotype, a technique that requires continual rehearsal and "vacillates between what is already 'in place,' already known, and something that must be anxiously repeated."[16] Indeed, repetition is a critical modality in the construction of categories of otherness, such as race, gender, and sexuality. Butler has of course, analyzed gender as a repeated performance—"*a stylized repetition of acts*"—a practice of citation.[17] However, this repetition does not engender the same, a "univocal signification," but rather produces something different.[18] This potential for difference, Butler argues, can function subversively to critique hegemonic constructions of gender and disrupt the myth of "gender reality."[19]

Pornography and BDSM, which are fluent in the lexicon of stereotypes, disrupt the very "fixity" and "reality" of race and sexuality they labor to uphold while evincing the rapture in these repetitions. We might read this changing same as characteristic of the repetition of representation itself. Just as Bhabha encourages an understanding of repetition that foregrounds its role as a technology of racialized power that undermines the fixity of race and Butler argues that repetition contests the verisimilitude of gender, Walter Benjamin discusses repetition as a mode of inauthenticity. In his famous essay "The Work of Art in the Age of Mechanical Reproduction," Benjamin argues that instead of merely copying, mechanical reproduction fundamentally changes a work of art. Because authenticity is not duplicable, he argues, mechanical reproduction represents a kind of liberation from the burden of authenticity, "emancipat[ing] the work of art from its parasitical dependence on ritual."[20] Benjamin speaks to the anxiety of repetition in the visual sphere that is based on authenticity and its impossibility. His theorization of repetition, authenticity, and the image reinforces the concept that the reiteration of racial-sexual paradigms contests their truths. From its spectacular play on the volatile boundaries of black and white, past and present, to its queering of heterosexual monogamy to its techno-mediation of racialized sexual pleasure, blackness is naturalized and denaturalized, stabilized and mercurial in its repetitive performance in contemporary American pornography and BDSM.

Repetition as Reconciliation with Trauma

Beyond punctuating the genre of pornography and illuminating the performance of racialized sexuality in both pornography and BDSM, repetition becomes a lens for understanding the reiterative modality of eroticized black abjection that operates in both genres. Psychoanalytic theories of repetition bring to light the "perpetual returns" to the mythologized eroticized site of chattel slavery and the hold the spectacle of racial bondage maintains over our erotic imaginary.[21] Repetition is a primary component of modern trauma theory.[22] Psychoanalysis engages the phenomenon of our compulsion to return to the site of trauma. Freud's theory of repetition compulsion offers a way to understand these recurrent intimate restagings and our libidinal investments in rehearsing chattel slavery. Repetition compulsion is the phenomenon through which an individual performs a repeated, compulsive return to the primordial scene of psychic trauma as an attempt to reestablish the past and rewrite history. Freud argues that "the compulsion to repeat must be ascribed to the unconscious repressed."[23] Freud understood repetition compulsion as a negotiation of the death instinct rather than as a libidinal cathexis of Eros.

Freud's understanding of compulsive repetition sheds light on race play as a mode of engaging and making pleasurable the past traumatic history of slavery and the present strain of everyday anti-black racism. The theory of repetition compulsion serves as an exegesis of the nature of both the human psyche and trauma. Yet Freud critically remarked, as BDSM and pornography cogently reveal, "that the unpleasurable nature of an experience does not always unsuit it for play."[24] In theorizing adult repetition of distress, Freud engaged the notion of pleasure as a "motive for play."[25] He writes,

> Finally, a reminder may be added that the artistic play and artistic imitation carried out by adults, which, unlike children's, are aimed at an audience, do not spare the spectators (for instance, in tragedy) the most painful experiences and can yet be felt by them as highly enjoyable. This is convincing proof that, even under the dominance of the pleasure principle, there are ways and means enough of making what is in itself unpleasurable into a subject to be recollected and worked over in the mind.[26]

As I have discussed, race play, like other kinds of BDSM play, can be a way that some individuals work with and through various traumas, alchemizing pain into pleasure while practicing agency and mastery over the unpleasurable past. Yet emphasizing BDSM's relationship to trauma can work to reinforce its understanding as psychopathology.[27]

Thus, the lens of trauma is a useful but precarious one. I am aware of the potential risk that using the psychoanalytic lens of trauma may have in reinscribing the medicalizing rhetoric of sexuality that I have sought to dismantle in this book. In particular, I have worked to depathologize black women's non-"normative" fantasies in performances of pornography and BDSM. I also remain concerned about what happens when we think about trauma as *the* formative element of black female sexuality. On the contrary, what pornography and BDSM can foreground are black female sexuality's pleasures in the unpleasurable. Furthermore, the line of thought that conceptualizes black female sexual performance as a mechanical return to the primordial site of trauma might privilege the redemptive in black women's sexuality, further burdening black women as the primary narrative agents of such history. Throughout this book, I have problematized a way of thinking that positions black women as the guardians of this kind of historical weight in order to locate the site of trauma in the "home" (to recall nelson) of black female subjectivity. Sharon Holland interrogates this "need to subject black bodies to the rule of race," suggesting that it is in the erotic where we might indeed challenge this rule. She writes, "By thinking through our erotic commitments, we might come to think differently about the historical—we might find a grounding for racist practice that acknowledges both systematic practices and quotidian effects that far exceed our patterned understanding of how history has happened to us."[28]

Perhaps one step toward negotiating this burden of blackness is rethinking repetition as not indicative of weight but rather as a kind of vacuity. Might we imagine repetition as a psychic mechanism for engaging not just the unspeakable, that which we cannot utter, but also the unpossessable, that which we cannot grasp, or have perhaps never held? Cathy Caruth theorizes trauma as the belated interpretation of an event or image that repeatedly haunts, indeed possesses, the individual who experiences it.[29] She understands trauma as a profound present-historical burden, one that is paradoxically heavy to hold but unable to grasp: "The traumatized, we might say, carry an impossible weight of history within them, or become themselves the symptom of a history that they cannot entirely possess."[30] These ongoing historical recitals of racial-sexual violence in the landscape of the performance of modern black female sexuality reveal "that the impact of the traumatic event lies precisely in its belatedness, in its refusal to simply be located, in its insistent appearance outside the boundaries of any single place or time."[31] There might be no clearer substantiation for the sustained collective trauma of transatlantic slavery than the repetition of its "image" in cultural media across time and space.

What especially intrigues me about this psychoanalytic theory of the repetition of trauma as a lens through which to read the repetition that powers performances of black female sexuality is how it positions repetition in relationship to memory and its collapse. Freud suggests that repetition marks the failure of memory and acts as a kind of panacea for this failure.[32] Caruth reveals failure to be important to the experience of trauma—our failure to not only "entirely possess" history but also the failure of memory itself; that is, our forgetting. She writes, "The historical power of trauma is not just that the experience is repeated after its forgetting, but that it is only in and through its inherent forgetting that it is first experienced at all."[33] Similarly, in his theory of repetition, Deleuze identifies the relationship between repetition and the failure of memory, conceptualizing forgetting as more a result rather than a cause of repetition. Describing repetition as an encounter and a vital mode of experience and subjectivity, he writes, "I do not repeat because I repress. I repress because I repeat, I forget because I repeat. I repress, because I can live certain things or certain experiences only in the mode of repetition."[34] For postslavery subjects with no conventional memory of slavery, these insistent returns might become not an attempt at re-memory, but a kind of forgetting.

NOTES

INTRODUCTION

1 Samuel R. Delany, *Shorter Views: Queer Thoughts & the Politics of the Paraliterary* (Hanover, N.H.: Wesleyan University Press, 1999), 65.

2 Scholars use different terms to describe the diverse practices encompassing BDSM and its equally heterogeneous community of practitioners. In this book I will be interchanging "sadomasochism" (also abbreviated as "S/M," "S&M," and/ or "SM") with the term "BDSM." "BDSM" is a widely used umbrella term that stands in for "bondage and discipline" (B/D, B & D), "domination/submission" (D/S, DS), and "sadism and masochism." I use the contemporary term "BDSM" because of its resonance in the adult entertainment industry and its highlighting of the power exchange—the play of dominance and submission—essential to the practice. For a wonderful discussion of the terminology of BDSM, see Margot Weiss, *Techniques of Pleasure: BDSM and the Circuits of Sexuality* (Durham, N.C.: Duke University Press 2011), vii–xii.

3 Mistress Heart served as project manager of The Bay Area Women of Color BDSM Photo Project.

4 Sensuous Sade, "SCENEprofiles Interview with Mistress Heart of San Francisco," http://67.159.222.79/interviews/mistressheartinterview.htm.

5 Shilo McCabe, interview with Ariane Cruz, March 19, 2014.

6 Ibid. Similarly, Ms. Heart states: "Why is it that when I am out in the community, at events, play parties, in the images I see portrayed on web sites and BDSM printed media etc., there are not very many people like me out there? I know that the wealth of ethnic diversity this area has to offer is quite outstanding, so where are all those people in our BDSM world?" See Sensuous Sade, "SCENEprofiles Interview."

7 crystal am nelson, interview with Ariane Cruz, January 18, 2012.S

8 Ibid.

9 Ibid.

10 Ibid.

11 Ibid.

12 Ibid.

13 Lee Harrington, *Shibari You Can Use: Japanese Rope Bondage and Erotic Macramé* (Lynnwood, Wash.: Mystic Productions, 2007).

14 crystal am nelson, interview with Ariane Cruz, January 18, 2012.

15 Ibid.

16 Ibid.

17 crystal am nelson, "untitled (bound)—building me a home," n.d., http://crystal-amnelson.com/untitledbound.

18 Ibid.

19 Huey Copeland, *Bound to Appear: Art, Slavery, and the Site of Blackness in Multicultural America* (Chicago: University of Chicago Press, 2013), 14.

20 Ibid., 17.

21 Ibid., 14.

22 Andrea Dworkin, Catherine MacKinnon, and Diana Russell are three in this camp. See Andrea Dworkin, *Our Blood: Prophecies and Discourse on Sexual Politics* (New York: Harper & Row, 1976); Andrea Dworkin, *Pornography: Men Possessing Women* (New York: Penguin, 1979); Andrea Dworkin, *Intercourse* (London: Arrow, 1988); Catherine MacKinnon, *Toward a Feminist Theory of the State* (Cambridge, Mass.: Harvard University Press, 1991); Catherine MacKinnon, "Sexuality, Pornography, and Method: Pleasure under Patriarchy," *Ethics* 99 no. 2 (1989): 314–346; and Diana Russell, ed., *Making Violence Sexy: Feminist Views on Pornography* (New York: Teacher's College Press, 1993).

23 *Fifty Shades of Grey*, directed by Sam Taylor-Johnson (Universal Pictures, 2015).

24 Margot D. Weiss, "Mainstreaming Kink: The Politics of BDSM Representation in U.S. Popular Media," *Journal of Homosexuality* 50, nos. 2–3 (2006): 103–132.

25 Ariane Cruz, "Pornography: A Black Feminist Woman Scholar's Reconciliation," in *The Feminist Porn Book: The Politics of Producing Pleasure*, edited by Tristan Taormino, Constance Penley, Celine Shimizu, Mireille Miller-Young (The Feminist Press at CUNY, 2013), 215–227.

26 Freud's understanding of polymorphous perversity is useful here as a kind of degenitalization and elaboration of erotic pleasure.

27 *The New Oxford American Dictionary*, 3rd ed. (London: Oxford University Press, 2010), s.v. "pervert."

28 Patricia McFadden, "Sexual Pleasure as Feminist Choice," *Feminist Africa* 2 (2003), accessed September 27, 2010, http://www.feministafrica.org/index.php/sexual-pleasure-as-feminist-choice.

29 For the politics of respectability, see Evelyn Brooks Higginbotham, *Righteous Discontent: The Women's Movement in the Black Baptist Church, 1880–1920* (Cambridge, Mass.: Harvard University Press, 1993); Hazel V. Carby, *Reconstructing Womanhood: The Emergence of the Afro-American Woman Novelist* (Oxford: Oxford University Press, 1987); Evelynn Hammonds, "Toward a Genealogy of Black Female Sexuality: The Problematic of Silence," in *Feminist Genealogies, Colonial Legacies, Democratic Futures*, edited by M. Jacqui Alexander and Chandra Talpade Mohanty (London: Routledge, 1997), 171–181; Darlene Clark Hine, "Rape and the Inner Lives of Black Women in the Middle West," *Signs* 14, no. 4 (1989): 912–920; and Kevin K. Gaines, *Uplifting the Race: Black Leadership, Politics, and Culture in the Twentieth Century* (Chapel Hill: University of North Carolina Press, 1996).

30 *Oxford Dictionaries*, s.v. "kink," accessed June 4, 2015, http://www.oxforddiction-aries.com/us/definition/american_english/kink.

31 Polymorphous perversity references the degenitalization of erotic pleasure and its expansion to multiple sites of the body. Freud explicitly states that his use of the term "polymorphously perverse disposition" implies "no moral judgment." Sigmund Freud, "An Autobiographical Study," in *The Freud Reader*, edited by Peter Gay (New York: W. W. Norton & Company, 1989), 24 (see also 23). "On the contrary, while he identifies a polymorphously perverse degenitalization of pleasure in children and "perverse" adults, he argues that perversion is a part of "normal" human adult sexuality and "a general and fundamental human characteristic." Sigmund Freud, "Three Essays on the Theory of Sexuality," in *The Freud Reader*, edited by Peter Gay (New York: W. W. Norton & Company, 1989), 268.

32 Ibid., 258.

33 For example, Paul Moreau de Tours, *Des aberrations du sens génésique* (1877) inspired Richard Krafft-Ebing's *Psychopathia Sexualis* (1886), which informed Freud's theory of perversions in *Three Essays on the Theory of Sexuality* (1905). For more about this lineage, see Dany Nobus and Lisa Downing, eds., *Perversion: Psychoanalytic Perspectives/Perspectives on Psychoanalysis* (London: Karnac, 2006).

34 Freud, "Three Essays on the Theory of Sexuality," 240.

35 See Lisa Downing, "Perversion, Historicity, Ethics," in *Perversion: Psychoanalytic Perspectives/Perspectives on Psychoanalysis*, edited by Dany Nobus and Lisa Downing (London: Karnac, 2006), 153.

36 Jonathan Dollimore, *Sexual Dissidence: Augustine to Wilde, Freud to Foucault* (Oxford: Clarendon Press, 1991), 198.

37 Michel Foucault, *The History of Sexuality*, vol. 1, *An Introduction* (New York: Vintage Books, 1990), 48.

38 Adrienne Rich, *Blood, Bread, and Poetry: Selected Prose, 1979–1985* (New York: W. W. Norton, 1994). For more on a feminist reclamation of perversion as a mode of subverting heteropatriarchal oppression, see Linda LeMoncheck, *Loose Women, Lecherous Men: A Feminist Philosophy of Sex* (Oxford: Oxford University Press, 1997).

39 Gayle Rubin, "Thinking Sex: Notes for a Radical Theory of the Politics of Sexuality," in *Pleasure and Danger: Exploring Female Sexuality*, edited by Carol Vance (London: Routledge, 1984), 267–319.

40 Michael Warner, *Fear of a Queer Planet: Queer Politics and Social Theory* (Minneapolis: University of Minnesota Press, 1993), xxvii.

41 Michael Warner, *The Trouble with Normal: Sex, Politics, and the Ethics of Queer Life* (Cambridge, Mass.: Harvard University Press, 2000).

42 Lauren Berlant and Michael Warner, "Sex in Public," *Critical Inquiry* 24, no. 2 (1998): 558.

43 Foucault, *The History of Sexuality*, 48.

44 Evelynn Hammonds, "Black (W)holes and the Geometry of Black Female Sexuality," *differences: A Journal of Feminist Theory* 6, nos. 2–3 (1994): 138.

45 Ibid. Here Hammonds draws on Michele Wallace's black hole trope; see Wallace, *Invisibility Blues: From Pop to Theory* (London: Verso, 1990).

46 Hammonds, "Black (W)holes," 139.

47 Hammonds, "Toward a Genealogy of Black Female Sexuality," 177.

48 Cathy Cohen, "Punks, Bulldaggers, and Welfare Queens: The Radical Potential of Queer Politics?" *GLQ: A Journal of Lesbian and Gay Studies* 3, no 4: (1997): 437–465.

49 Warner, *The Trouble with Normal*, 48.

50 Cathy Cohen, "Deviance as Resistance: A New Research Agenda for the Study of Black Politics," *Du Bois Review* 1, no. 1 (2004): 37.

51 Leopold von Sacher-Masoch, *Venus in Furs* (1870), in *Masochism*, translated by Jean McNeil (New York: Zone Books, 1991). See also Marquis de Sade, *120 Days of Sodom & Other Writings*, translated by Austryn Wainhouse and Richard Seaver (New York: Grove Press, 1966); Marquis de Sade, *Justine, Philosophy in the Bedroom, and Other Writings*, translated by Richard Seaver and Austryn Wainhouse (New York: Grove, 1965); and Marquis de Sade, *Juliette*, translated by Austryn Wainhouse (New York: Grove Press, 1968).

52 Richard von Krafft-Ebing, *Psychopathia Sexualis* (Chicago: Bloat, 1999), 55–56.

53 Ellis sees sadism and masochism as complementary rather than opposed; Havelock Ellis, *Studies in the Psychology of Sex*, vol. 1 (New York: Random House, 1942), 159.

54 Deleuze refutes what he argues is "the fallacious concept of sadomasochism." In contrast to Freud, Deleuze reorients the pre-Oedipal family drama around the mother, not the father, as the central figure governing the masochistic fantasy. Additionally, he departs from Freud's clinical approach to offer a "literary approach" to analyzing masochism. I further discuss Deleuze's theory of masochism in the next chapter. See Gilles Deleuze, "Coldness and Cruelty," in Deleuze, *Masochism*, translated by Jean McNeil (New York: Zone Books, 1991), 57, 14. In this de-privileging of castration anxiety in the etiology of masochism, Deleuze is in agreement with Theodore Reik; see Reik, *Masochism in Modern Man*, translated by Margaret H. Beigel and Gertrud M. Kurth (New York: Grove, 1962).

55 Classical theories of sadism and masochism reflect disputation not only regarding the relationship between sadism and masochism but also with respect to the gendered embodiment of these perversions and their "natural" "masculinity" and "femininity." Krafft-Ebing found sadism to be more frequent in men, reflecting what he identified as the gendered pattern of (hetero)sexuality in which men are active and women are passive. Similarly, recognizing the existence of the perversions of sadism and masochism in so-called normal sexuality, Freud argued that the sexuality of the (male) "normal individual" reflects the presence of sadism. While he initially identified masochism in females, Freud's study "The Economic Problem of Masochism" focused on male subjects; Sigmund

Freud, "The Economic Problem of Masochism," (1924), in *The Standard Edition of the Complete Psychological Works of Sigmund Freud*, vol. 19, The Ego and the Id *and Other Works (1923–1925)*, translated by J. Strachey (London: The Hogarth Press, 1961). Reik argues that men are inherently more masochistic than women. Gebhard illuminates the gendered cultural scripts that inform the fantasy and practice of sadomasochism to decenter the innate, the biological, and the psychological in favor of cultural influences and scripted social behaviors. See Krafft-Ebing, *Psychopathia Sexualis*, 83, 117; Sigmund Freud, "Infantile Sexuality," in *The Basic Writings of Sigmund Freud*, translated and edited by A. A. Brill (1938; repr., New York: Random House, 1995), 569; Reik, *Masochism in Modern Man*; Paul G. Gebhard, "Fetishism and Sadomasochism," in *Dynamics of Deviant Sexuality: Scientific Proceedings of The American Academy of Psychoanalysis*, edited by Jules Masserman (New York: Grune & Stratton, 1969), 71–80.

56 Freud, "Infantile Sexuality," 569.

57 Krafft-Ebing, *Psychopathia Sexualis*, 80.

58 Freud believed that masochism was more distant from "normal" than sadism; Freud, "Three Essays on the Theory of Sexuality," 252. Fanon echoes Freud, writing, "We know how much of sexuality there is in all cruelties, tortures, beatings"; Franz Fanon, *Black Skin, White Masks* (New York: Grove Press, 1952), 59.

59 See Darren Langdridge and Meg Barker, eds., *Safe, Sane, and Consensual: Contemporary Perspectives on Sadomasochism* (Basingstoke: Palgrave Macmillan, 2007); Andrea Beckmann, *The Social Construction of Sexuality and Perversion: Deconstructing Sadomasochism* (London: Palgrave MacMillan, 2009); Thomas S. Weinberg, "Sadism and Masochism: Sociological Perspectives," *Bulletin of the American Academy of Psychiatry and the Law* 6, no. 3 (1978): 284–295; Thomas S. Weinberg, "Research in Sadomasochism: A Review of Sociological and Social Psychological Literature," *Annual Review of Sex Research* 5 (1994): 257–279; Thomas S. Weinberg, ed., *S&M: Studies in Dominance and Submission* (Amherst, N.Y.: Prometheus Books, 1995); and Thomas S. Weinberg and G. W. Levi Kamel, *S and M: Studies in Sadomasochism* (Buffalo, N.Y.: Prometheus Books, 1983).

60 For more, see "Paraphilic Disorders," American Psychological Association: DSM-5 Development, accessed August 20, 2013, http://www.dsm5.org/Documents/Paraphilic%20Disorders%20Fact%20Sheet.pdf.

61 Rubin, "Thinking Sex," 287.

62 Silverman reads the discrepancies in masochism as illuminative of perversion itself, employing masochism to complicate prevailing conceptualizations of masculinity; Kaja Silverman, "Masochism and Male Subjectivity," *Camera Obscura* 6, 2, no. 17 (1988): 32.

63 Ibid.

64 Ibid., 63.

65 Kaja Silverman, *Male Subjectivity at the Margins* (New York: Routledge, 1992), 187.

66 Stoller writes, "Psychoanalysis is a moral order trying to transform itself into an amoral order, that is, a science"; Robert J. Stoller, *Pain and Passion: A*

Psychoanalyst Explores the World of S &M (New York: Plenum Press, 1991), 36 (see also 3).

67 Robert J. Stoller, *Perversion: The Erotic Form of Hatred* (New York: Pantheon, 1975), xi.

68 Ibid.

69 Ibid.

70 Stoller, *Pain and Passion*, 35.

71 Stoller writes: "We shall not untangle the origins and dynamics of perversion unless we put aside the concept *normal*. 'Normal' stops exploration; though we need 'normal' inside us, as a rudder for our moral codes, we had best know that what we feel is eternal ('normal') is relative, culture-bound, and subject to change without notice." Stoller, *Pain and Passion*, 50 (see also 35).

72 Beckmann, *The Social Construction of Sexuality and Perversion*.

73 Stoller, *Pain and Passion*, 35.

74 Alice Walker, "Porn," in *You Can't Keep a Good Woman Down* (New York: Harcourt Brace Jovanovich Publishers, 1971), 83.

75 Alice Walker, "Coming Apart: By Way of Introduction to Lorde, Teish and Gardner," in *You Can't Keep a Good Woman Down* (New York: Harcourt Brace Jovanovich Publishers, 1971), 52.

76 Ibid., 42.

77 Patricia Hill Collins, *Black Feminist Thought: Knowledge, Consciousness and the Politics of Empowerment.* (London: Routledge, 1990), 168.

78 Jewel D. Amoah, "Back on the Auction Block: A Discussion of Black Women and Pornography," *National Black Law Journal* 4, no. 2 (1997): 204–221.

79 Collins, *Black Feminist Thought*, 167; Amoah, "Back on the Auction Block," 205.

80 Tracey A. Gardner, "Racism and the Women's Movement," in *Take Back the Night: Women on Pornography*, edited by Laura Lederer (New York: William and Morrow, 1980), 105.

81 Luisah Teish, "A Quiet Subversion," in *Take Back the Night: Women on Pornography*, edited by Laura Lederer (New York: William and Morrow, 1980), 117.

82 Audre Lorde, "Uses of the Erotic: The Erotic as Power," in *Sister Outsider: Essays and Speeches* (Berkeley: The Crossing Press, 1984), 53–59. I discuss Lorde's theory of erotic more in depth in the next chapter.

83 Carol Vance, ed., *Pleasure and Danger: Exploring Female Sexuality* (London: Routledge, 1984), 1.

84 Jennifer C. Nash, "Strange Bedfellows: Black Feminism and Antipornography Feminism," *Social Text* 26 no. 4 (2008): 51–76.

85 Mireille Miller-Young, *A Taste for Brown Sugar: Black Women in Pornography* (Durham, N.C.: Duke University Press, 2014); Mireille Miller-Young, "Hip-Hop Honeys and da Hustlaz: Black Sexualities in the New Hip-Hop Pornography," *Meridians* 8, no. 1 (2008): 261–292; Mireille Miller-Young, "Sexy and Smart: Black Women and the Politics of Self-Authorship in Netporn," in *C'lickme: A Netporn Studies Reader*, edited by Katrien Jacobs, Marije Janssen, and Matteo Pasquinelli,

([Amsterdam:] Institute of Network Cultures, 2007), 205–216, http://www.net-workcultures.org/_uploads/24.pdf.

86 Mireille Miller-Young, "Let Me Tell Ya 'bout Black Chicks: Interracial Desire and Black Women in 1980's Video Pornography," in *Pornification: Sex and Sexuality in Media Culture*, edited by Kaarina Nikunen, Susanna Paasonen, and Laura Saaren-maa (Oxford: Berg, 2007), 33.

87 Mireille Miller-Young, "The Deviant and Defiant Art of Black Women Porn Directors," in *The Feminist Porn Book: The Politics of Producing Pleasure*, edited by Tristan Taormino, Constance Penley, Celine Parrenas Shimizu, and Mireille Miller-Young (New York: The Feminist Press at the City University of New York, 2013), 111.

88 Ibid., 2.

89 Ibid., 1.

90 Nash, *The Black Female Body*, 30.

91 Linda Williams, *Hardcore: Power, Pleasure, and the Frenzy of the Visual* (Berkeley: University of California Press, 1989).

92 Williams, *Hardcore*; Linda Williams, ed., *Porn Studies* (Durham, N.C.: Duke University Press, 2004); Miller-Young, "Let Me Tell Ya 'bout Black Chicks"; Miller-Young, "Hip-Hop Honeys and da Hustlaz"; Miller-Young, Penley, Shimizu, and Taormino, *The Feminist Porn Book*; Miller-Young, *A Taste for Brown Sugar*; Constance Penley, "Whackers and Crackers: The White Trashing of Porn," in *Porn Studies*, edited by Linda Williams (Durham, N.C.: Duke University Press, 2004), 309–334; Celine Parreñas Shimizu, *The Hypersexuality of Race: Performing Asian/American Women on Screen and Scene* (Durham, N.C.: Duke University Press, 2007); Jennifer C. Nash, *The Black Body in Ecstasy: Reading Race, Reading Pornography* (Durham, N.C.: Duke University Press, 2014).

93 E. Patrick Johnson, ed., *Black Queer Studies: A Critical Anthology* (Durham, N.C.: Duke University Press, 2005); E. Patrick Johnson, *Appropriating Blackness: Performance and the Politics of Authenticity* (Durham, N.C.: Duke University Press, 2003); Thomas F. DeFrantz and Anita Gonzalez, eds., *Black Performance Theory* (Durham, N.C.: Duke University Press, 2014); Judith Butler, *Bodies that Matter: On the Discursive Limits of Sex* (New York: Routledge, 1993); Judith Butler, *Gender Trouble: Feminism and the Subversion of Identity* (New York: Routledge, 1990).

CHAPTER 1. THE DARK SIDE OF DESIRE

1 June Jordan, "Poem about My Rights" (1989), in *Directed by Desire: The Collected Poems of June Jordan* (Port Townsend, Wash.: Copper Canyon Press, 2007), 311.

2 Gwendolyn DuBois Shaw, *Seeing the Unspeakable: The Art of Kara Walker* (Durham, N.C.: Duke University Press, 2004).

3 For more about these critiques, see "Stereotypes Subverted? Or for Sale?," special issue, *International Review of African-American Art* 14, no. 3 (1997); "Reading Black through White: Kara Walker and the Question of Racial Stereotyping. A Discussion between Michael Corris and Robert Hobbs," in *Differences and Excess*

in Contemporary Art: The Visibility of Women's Practices, edited by Gill Perry (Oxford: Blackwell, 2004), 104–123.

4 Juliette Bowles, "Extreme Times Call for Extreme Heroes," *International Review of African-American Art* 14, no. 3 (1997): 4. See also Howardina Pindell, ed., *Kara Walker No/Kara Walker Yes/Kara Walker?* (New York: Midmarch Art Press, 2009), 13.

5 Bowles, "Extreme Times Call for Extreme Heroes," 5. See also Henry Louis Gates Jr., *The Signifying Monkey: A Theory of African-American Literary Criticism* (Oxford University Press, 1988).

6 Christina Sharpe, *Monstrous Intimacies: Making Post-Slavery Subjects* (Durham, N.C.: Duke University Press, 2010), 175.

7 Ibid., 154, 156.

8 Amy Tang, "Postmodern Repetitions: Parody, Trauma, and the Case of Kara Walker," *differences* 21, no. 2 (2010): 154.

9 See *Negress Notes (Brown Follies)*, 1996–1997, watercolor on paper twenty-four sheets, 9x6 inches, collection of Michael and Joan Salke, reprinted in Kara Walker, *Narratives of Negress* (New York: Rizzoli, 2007).

10 Kara Walker, *Untitled*, from the series *American Primitives*, 2001, reprinted in Kara Walker, *After the Deluge: A Visual Essay by Kara Walker* (New York: Rizzoli, 2007), 5.

11 Elizabeth Alexander, "'Can you be BLACK and Look at This?' Reading Rodney King Videos," *Public Culture* 7 (1994), 80. For a discussion of how the trauma of slavery became an imprint in the collective processes of African American identity formation, see Ron Eyerman, *Cultural Trauma: Slavery and the Formation of African American Identity* (London: Cambridge University Press, 2001).

12 In using the term "black women," I am referring to African American women for whom the history of chattel slavery in the Americas has produced the sociohistorical conditions that uniquely inform black female subjectivity and sexual politics. My use of this term is not intended to essentialize black American womanhood; rather, I use the term to gesture to a black women's standpoint influenced by the condition and experience of gendered and racialized abjection, a "common experience of being black women in a society that denigrates women of African descent"; Patricia Hill Collins, *Black Feminist Thought: Knowledge, Consciousness and the Politics of Empowerment* (London: Routledge, 1990), 22. Here, I focus on black women who practice BDSM, a small but nonetheless heterogeneous group of women in the already marginalized larger kink community.

13 Darlene Clark Hine, "Rape and the Inner Lives of Black Women in the Middle West," *Signs* 14, no. 4 (1989): 912–920. For more on sexual assaults of black female slaves and their aftermath, see Hazel V. Carby, *Reconstructing Womanhood: The Emergence of the Afro-American Woman Novelist* (Oxford: Oxford University Press, 1987); Ann DuCille, "'Othered' Matters: Reconceptualizing Dominance and Difference in the History of Sexuality in America," *Journal of the History of Sexuality* 1, no. 1 (1990): 102–127; Elsa Barkley Brown, "Imaging Lynching: African

American Women, Communities of Struggle, and Collective Memory," in *African American Women Speak Out on Anita Hill-Clarence Thomas*, edited by Geneva Smitherman (Detroit: Wayne State University Press, 1995), 100–124; Cheryl Harris, "Whiteness as Property," *Harvard Law Review* 106, no. 8 (1993): 1707–1791; and Adrienne Davis, "'Don't Let Nobody Bother Yo' Principle': The Sexual Economy of Slavery," in *Sister Circle: Black Women and Work*, edited by Sharon Harley and The Black Women Work Collective (New Brunswick, N.J.: Rutgers University Press, 2002), 103–127.

14 For more on stereotypes of black womanhood rooted in legacies of slavery, see Collins, *Black Feminist Thought*; K. Sue Jewell, *From Mammy to Miss America and Beyond: Cultural Images and the Shaping of US Social Policy* (London: Routledge, 1993); and Melissa Harris-Perry, *Sister Citizenship: Shame, Stereotypes, and Black Women in America* (New Haven, Conn.: Yale University Press, 2011). For more on the sexualization of the black female body in visual representation, see Michael D. Harris, *Colored Pictures: Race and Visual Representation* (Chapel Hill: North Carolina, University of Chapel Hill Press, 2003); Lisa Gail Collins, *The Art of History: African American Women Artists Engage the Past* (New Brunswick, N.J.: Rutgers University Press, 2002); Deborah Willis and Carla Williams, *The Black Female Body: A Photographic History* (Philadelphia: Temple University Press, 2002); and bell hooks, "Selling Hot Pussy," in *Black Looks: Race & Representation* (Boston: South End Press, 1992), 61–77.

15 Hine, "Rape and the Inner Lives of Black Women in the Middle West."

16 Hortense Spillers, "Mama's Baby, Papa's Maybe: An American Grammar Book," *Diacritics* 17, no. 2 (1987): 68.

17 "Interview with Audre Lorde: Audre Lorde and Susan Leigh Star," in *Against Sadomasochism: A Radical Feminist Analysis*, edited by Robin Ruth Linden, Darlene R. Pagano, Diana E. Russell, and Susan Leigh Star (East Palo Alto, Calif.: Frog in the Well, 1982), 68, italics in original.

18 Paul H. Gebhard, "Fetishism and Sadomasochism," in *Dynamics of Deviant Sexuality: Scientific Proceedings of the American Academy of Psychoanalysis*, edited by Jules Masserman (New York: Grune & Stratton, 1969), 71. See also Thomas S. Weinberg, "Sadomasochism and the Sciences: A Review of the Sociological Literature," in *Sadomasochism: Powerful Pleasures*, edited by Peggy J. Kleinplatz and Charles Moser (New York: Hawthorn Press, 2006), 17–40.

19 Gebhard, "Fetishism and Sadomasochism," 70, 66.

20 Lorde, "Uses of the Erotic: The Erotic as Power," in *Sister Outsider: Essays and Speeches* (Berkeley: The Crossing Press, 1984), 53. Though Lorde does not explicitly broach BDSM in "Uses of the Erotic," her brief mention of consent gains an interesting cadence in light of her earlier critique of BDSM published in *Against Sadomasochism*. She specifies that consent is vital to the erotic: "That brings me to the last consideration of the erotic. To share the power of each other's feelings is different from using another's feelings as we would use a kleenex. When we look the other way from our experience, erotic or otherwise, we use rather than rather

share the feelings of those others who participate in the experience with us. And use without consent of the used is abuse" (58). One wonders how Lorde might have responded to testimonies, scholarly and quotidian, that BDSM is an erotic practice that indeed privileges consent.

21 Ibid., 54.

22 Ibid.

23 Ibid.

24 Ibid, 70.

25 Ibid, 69.

26 Ibid, 70.

27 Portillo regards her BDSM identity as paramount, trumping not just her sexual orientation but also her racial categorization. She states: I've purposely arranged my identifying tags ("S/M dyke of color") into the order of their significance for me." See Tina Portillo, "I Get Real: Celebrating my Sadomasochistic Soul," in *Leatherfolk: Radical Sex, People, Politics, and Practice*, edited by Mark Thompson (Los Angeles: Daedalus Publishing Company, 1991), 49.

28 Ibid, 50.

29 Ibid., 51.

30 Margot D. Weiss, *Techniques of Pleasure: BDSM and the Circuits of Sexuality* (Durham, N.C.: Duke University Press, 2011), 24.

31 This debate is far more complex than a binary of for and against BDSM. As I argue in this chapter, we must interrogate this polar framing to consider the various nuances with regard to intersecting categories of identity such as race, gender, and sexuality in the context of BDSM. For the purposes of this chapter however, such polarity effectively animates the feminist exchange to demonstrate the contested space BDSM has historically occupied in women's sexuality.

32 The first meeting of SAMOIS was held June 13, 1978, in San Francisco, although its genesis can be traced back to Cardea, a BDSM support group that was formed three years earlier for women, which emerged from the long-time BDSM support and education organization the Society of Janus (1974–present). SAMOIS lasted until the spring of 1983. For more, see Pat Califia, "A Personal View of the History of the Lesbian S/M Community and Movement in San Francisco," in *Coming to Power: Writings and Graphics on Lesbian S/M*, edited by members of SAMOIS, a Lesbian/Feminist S/M Organization (Boston: Alyson Publications, 1981), 248; and Gayle Rubin, "The Outcasts: A Social History," in *The Second Coming: A Leatherdyke Reader*, edited by Pat Califia and Robin Sweeny (Los Angeles: Alyson Publications, 1996), 339.

33 See SAMOIS, *Coming to Power* (Boston: Alyson Publications, 1981). In 1979, prior to the publication of *Coming to Power*, SAMOIS self-published a 45-page booklet entitled *What Color Is Your Handkerchief? A Lesbian S/M Sexuality Reader* (Berkeley, Calif: SAMOIS, 1979).

34 For more about the radical feminist opposition to BDSM during this time, see Robin Ruth Linden, Darlene R. Pagano, Diana E. Russell, and Susan Leigh

Star, eds., *Against Sadomasochism: A Radical Feminist Analysis* (East Palo Alto, Calif.: Frog in the Well, 1982). See also Sheila Jeffreys, *The Lesbian Heresy: A Feminist Perspective on the Lesbian Sexual Revolution* (London: The Women's Press, 1994).

35 Karen Sims and Rose Mason, "Racism and Sadomasochism: A Conversation with Two Black Lesbians" in *Against Sadomasochism*, 102–103.

36 Ibid., 99.

37 There was dispute over the racial identity of this woman. While Alice Walker views the woman bottom as black, Pat Califia identifies her as a Latina. What comes to the surface here in this contention is the power of the black/white binary as the legible configuration of racial domination and submission and enactment of racism and the power of our own gazes as spectators in scripting scenes of racialized eroticism.

38 Alice Walker, "A Letter of the Times, or Should This Sado-Masochism Be Saved?," in *Against Sadomasochism: A Radical Feminist Analysis*, edited by Robin Ruth Linden, Darlene R. Pagano, Diana E. Russell, and Susan Leigh Star (East Palo Alto, Calif.: Frog in the Well, 1982), 207, italics in original.

39 Ibid.

40 Ibid., 208.

41 For Kara Walker, the slave as a "mythic," "fictional" persona enables a kind of creative self-reinvention. See Jerry Saltz, "Kara Walker: Ill-Will and Desire," *Flash Art* 29, no. 191 (1996): 86.

42 Walker, "A Letter of the Times."

43 Ibid., 206.

44 Ibid.

45 Ann McClintock, "Maid to Order: Commercial S/M and Gender Power," in *More Dirty Looks: Gender, Pornography and Power*, edited by Pamela Church Gibson (London: British Film Institute, 2004), 241.

46 Isaac Julien, "Confessions of a Snow Queen: Notes on the Making of *The Attendant*," *Critical Quarterly* 36, no. 1 (1994): 123.

47 Ibid.

48 McClintock, "Maid to Order," 241; Irene Reti, "Remember the Fire: Lesbian Sadomasochism in a Post Nazi Holocaust World," in *Unleashing Feminism: Critiquing Lesbian Sadomasochism in the Gay Nineties*, edited by Irene Reti (Santa Cruz, Calif.: HerBooks: 1993), 81.

49 Sheila Jeffreys, "Sadomasochism: The Erotic Cult of Fascism," in *The Lesbian Heresy: A Feminist Perspective on the Lesbian Sexual Revolution* (North Melbourne: Spinifex, 1993), 171.

50 Susan Sontag, "Fascinating Fascism" in *Under the Sign of Saturn* (New York: Farrar, Straus and Giroux, 1980), 83, 100.

51 Ibid., 99.

52 Ibid., 104.

53 Ibid., 103.

54 Many scholars have identified a theatricality in BDSM. Recent examples include Lynda Hart, *Between the Body and the Flesh: Performing Sadomasochism* (New York: Columbia University Press, 1998); and Danielle Lindemann, *Dominatrix: Gender, Eroticism, and Control in the Dungeon* (Chicago: University of Chicago Press, 2012).

55 Sontag's essay is reductive; does not attend to sociohistorical cultural context; relies on fragile and underdeveloped connections between fascism and sado-masochism, pornography, and other forms of cultural production (such as film and photography), sexual consent, and violence; effects historical slippages between Nazism and fascism; and lacks an informed analysis of the practice of sadomasochism. One such notorious critique is Adrienne Rich's "Femi-nism and Fascism: An Exchange. Adrienne Rich, Reply by Susan Sontag," *The New York Times Review of Books*, March 20, 1975, accessed June 1, 2013, http://www.nybooks.com/articles/archives/1975/mar/20/feminism-and-fascism-an-exchange/?pagination=false. For further critique of Sontag, see Jeffrey T. Schnapp, 'Fascinating Fascism," *Journal of Contemporary History* 31, no. 2 (April 1996): 235–244; and David Renton, "Sex Is Violence: A Critique of Susan Sontag's 'Fascinat-ing Fascism,'" in *Making Sense of Sexual Consent*, edited by Mark Cowling and Paul Reynolds (Aldershot, England: Ashgate, 2004), 243–254. For a more recent view on the relationship between sexuality and Nazism, see Elizabeth D. Heine-man, "Sexuality and Nazism: The Doubly Unspeakable?" *Journal of the History of Sexuality* 11, nos. 1–2 (2002): 22–66.

56 Reti, "Remember the Fire," 94.

57 Ibid., 89.

58 See ibid., 85. See also SAMOIS, "Handkerchief Codes: Interlude II," in *Coming to Power: Writings and Graphics on Lesbian S/M*, edited by members of SAMOIS, a Lesbian/Feminist S/M Organization (Boston: Alyson Publications, 1981), 151–153.

59 Reti, "Remember the Fire," 93.

60 Susan Griffin, *Pornography and Silence: Culture's Revenge against Nature* (New York: Harper & Row, 1981), 179, 189.

61 Ibid., 161.

62 Ibid., 160.

63 Ibid., 159.

64 Ibid.

65 Susan Leigh Star, "Swastikas: The Street and the University," in *Against Sadomasochism: A Radical Feminist Analysis*, edited by Robin Ruth Linden, Darlene R. Pagano, Diana E. Russell, and Susan Leigh Star (East Palo Alto, Calif.: Frog in the Well, 1982), 132. An archetypal sign that has been traced to many ancient civilizations such as India, China, Japan, and throughout Europe, the swastika did not become a racialized icon until the mid-nineteenth century. For the evolution and social construction of the swastika, see Malcolm Quinn, *The Swastika: Constructing the Symbol* (London: Routledge, 1994); and Steven Heller, *The Swastika: Symbol beyond Redemption?* (New York: Allworth Press, 2000).

66 Star, "Swastikas," 134.

67 Ibid., 133, 135.

68 Pat Califia, on the other hand, credits gay leathermen as being among the first (along with professional femdoms) to actually support lesbian sadomasochists. See Califia, "A Personal View of the History of the Lesbian S/M Community and Movement in San Francisco," 247.

69 Arnie Kantrowitz, "Swastika Toys," in *Leatherfolk: Radical Sex, People, Politics, and Practice*, edited by Mark Thompson (Los Angeles: Daedalus Publishing Company, 1991), 198. See also Lawrence Mass, "Nazis and Gay Men II: An Exchange with Arnie Kantrowitz," in Lawrence Mass, *Homosexuality and Sexuality: Dialogues of the Sexual Revolution*, vol. 1 (New York: Harrington Park Press, 1990), 200–212; and Lawrence Mass, "The Swastika and the Pink Triangle: Nazis and Gay Men: An Interview with Robert Plant," in *Homosexuality and Sexuality*, 189–199.

70 Dossie Easton and Janet W. Hardy, *The New Bottoming Book* (Emeryville, Calif.: Greenery Press, 2001), 8.

71 Kantrowitz, "Swastika Toys," 207.

72 Ibid., 194.

73 Ibid., 203, 208.

74 Linda Wayne, "S/M Symbols, Fascist Icons, and Systems of Empowerment," in *The Second Coming: A Leatherdyke Reader*, edited by Pat Califia and Robin Sweeny (Los Angeles: Alyson Publications, 1996), 248.

75 Ibid., 246, 249. See also Ferdinand de Saussure, *Course in General Linguistics* (New York: McGraw-Hill, 1966); Jonathan Culler, *Ferdinand de Saussure*, rev. ed. (New York: Cornell University Press, 1986); Charles Sanders Peirce, *The Essential Peirce*, vol. 2, edited by the Peirce Edition Project (Bloomington: Indiana University Press, 1998); and Thomas Lloyd Short, *Peirce's Theory of Signs* (Cambridge: Cambridge University Press, 2007).

76 Sharpe, *Monstrous Intimacies*, 129.

77 Pat Califia, "Feminism and Sadomasochism," *Heresies* 12 (1981): 32.

78 Ibid., 30.

79 Biman Basu, *The Commerce of Peoples: Sadomasochism and African American Literature* (Lanham, Md.: Lexington Books, 2012), 136.

80 Ibid., 137.

81 For Basu, "the matter of consent itself is thoroughly troubled in domination and submission"; ibid., 162.

82 Gayle Rubin, "Thinking Sex: Notes for a Radical Theory of the Politics of Sexuality," in *Pleasure and Danger: Exploring Female Sexuality*, edited by Carol Vance (London: Routledge, 1984), 267–319. For a wonderful critique of the neoliberal rendering of consent, see Cheryl Hanna, "Sex Is Not a Sport: Consent and Violence in Criminal Law," *Boston College Law Review* 42, no. 2 (2001): 239–290.

83 Rubin, "Thinking Sex," 279, 304, 291.

84 Joseph Fischel, "Against Nature, against Consent: A Sexual Politics of Debility," *differences: A Journal of Feminist Cultural Studies* 24, no. 1 (2013): 56–103.

85 See Chris White, "The Spanner Trials and the Changing Law on Sadomasochism in the UK," in *Sadomasochism: Powerful Pleasures*, edited by Peggy Kleinplatz and Charles Moser (New York: Routledge, 2006), 167–187.

86 Davis, "'Don't Let Nobody Bother Yo' Principle.'"

87 Sharpe, *Monstrous Intimacies*, 4.

88 Christina E. Sharpe, "The Costs of Re-Membering," in *African American Performance and Theater History: A Critical Reader*, edited by Harry Elam Jr. and David Krasner (New York: Oxford University Press, 2001), 322.

89 Ibid., 327.

90 Sharpe, *Monstrous Intimacies*, 141.

91 "RACK" (Risk Aware Consensual Kink) is a newer acronym the BDSM community has adopted to encapsulate the importance of both consent and individual responsibility while at the same time highlighting practicality and objectivity. The term was coined and proposed in the late 1990s by Gary Switch on The Eulenspiegel Society friend list. See Gary Switch, "From SSC to RACK," http://www.differentequals.com/ssc.html. Examples of literature that cite the salience of consent in BDSM practice include Jay Wiseman, *SM 101: A Realistic Introduction*, 2nd ed. (San Francisco, Greenery Press, 1996); Staci Newmahr, *Playing on the Edge: Sadomasochism, Risk, and Intimacy* (Bloomington: Indiana University Press, 2011); Mark Cowling and Paul Reynolds, eds., *Making Sense of Sexual Consent* (Aldershot, UK: Ashgate, 2004); Darren Langdridge and Meg Barker, eds., *Safe, Sane and Consensual: Contemporary Perspectives on Sadomasochism* (Hampshire, UK: Palgrave, 2007); Darren Langdridge, "Voices from the Margins: Sadomasochism and Sexual Citizenship," *Citizenship Studies* 10, no. 4 (2006): 373–389; Joseph W. Bean, *Leathersex* (San Francisco: Daedalus, 1994); Weiss, *Techniques of Pleasure*; Peggy Kleinplatz and Charles Moser, eds., *Sadomasochism: Powerful Pleasures* (New York: Routledge, 2006). Beyond documenting the importance of consent in BDSM practice, some scholars contend that BDSM offers a kind of exemplary ethical model of sexual consent for relationships. See Andrea Beckmann, "'Sexual Rights' and 'Sexual Responsibilities' within Consensual 'S/M' Practice," in *Making Sense of Sexual Consent*, edited by Mark Cowling and Paul Reynolds (Aldershot, UK: Ashgate, 2004), 195–196; and Hanna, "Sex Is Not a Sport."

92 Newmahr, *Playing on the Edge*, 146–147; Melanie A. Beres, "'Spontaneous' Sexual Consent: An Analysis of Sexual Consent Literature," *Feminism & Psychology* 17, no. 1 (2007): 101–102.

93 Weiss, *Techniques of Pleasure*, 228, italics in original; see also 227.

94 Judith Butler, "Lesbian S & M: The Politics of Dis-illusion," in *Against Sadomasochism: A Radical Feminist Analysis*, edited by Robin Ruth Linden, Darlene R. Pagano, Diana E. Russell, and Susan Leigh Star (East Palo Alto, Calif.: Frog in the Well, 1982), 173.

95 Sandra Lee Bartky, *Femininity and Domination: Studies in the Phenomenology of Oppression* (New York: Routledge, 1990), 48. See also Butler, "Lesbian S & M."

96 Butler, "Lesbian S & M," 172.

97 Gary Taylor and Jane Ussher, "Making Sense of S & M: A Discourse Analytic Account," *Sexualities* 4, no. 3 (2001): 293–314. See also Andrea Beckmann, "Deconstructing Myths: The Social Construction of 'Sadomasochism' versus 'Subjugated Knowledges' of the Practitioners of Consensual 'SM,'" *Journal of Criminal Justice and Popular Culture* 8, no. 2 (2001): 66–95.

98 In an attempt "to further define the line between an atypical sexual interest and disorder" and to differentiate between behavior and disorder the DSM-5 uses the term "sexual masochism disorder" instead of "sexual masochism" (DSM-IV). Upon this revision, BDSM rights and advocacy groups like the National Coalition for Sexual Freedom (NCSF) celebrated the depathologization of kink, citing a rise in the success rate of child custody cases for identified kinky parents. Vigorous debates continue in the psychiatric and BDSM arenas and beyond about whether to remove these paraphilia from the category of mental disorders. See "Paraphilic Disorders Fact Sheet," *Diagnostic and Statistical Manual of Mental Disorders*, accessed August 20, 2013, http://www.dsm5.org/Documents/Paraphilic%20Disorders%20Fact%20Sheet.pdf, and "DSM-V Revision Project," accessed June 1, 2014, http://www.dsm5.org/Documents/Paraphilic%20Disorders%20Fact%20Sheet.pdf.

99 Newmahr, *Playing on the Edge*; Weiss, *Techniques of Pleasure*; Lindemann, *Dominatrix*.

100 Though Lindemann does not make such an explicit caveat, race is marginalized in her analysis of professional female dominatrices; see Lindemann, *Dominatrix*. My critique of these important recent works differs from Camille Paglia's critique of them for their heavy reliance on theory and their failure to provide what she sees as adequate historical context; instead, my critique focuses on their undertheorization of the connections between race and BDSM and the nuances of the practice for racialized sexuality. See Camille Paglia, "Scholars in Bondage: Dogma Dominates Studies of Kink," *The Chronicle Review*, May 20, 2013, accessed June 4, 2013, http://chronicle.com/article/Scholars-in-Bondage/139251/.

101 Staci Newmahr, "Becoming A Sadomasochist: Integrating the Self and Other in Ethnographic Analysis," *Journal of Contemporary Ethnography* 37, no. 5 (2008): 628.

102 Newmahr, *Playing on the Edge*, 17.

103 Weiss, *Techniques of Pleasure*, 26.

104 Andrea Plaid, "Interview with the Perverted Negress," *Racialicious*, July 10, 2009, accessed September 7, 2010, http://www.racialicious.com/2009/07/10/interview-with-the-perverted-negress/.

105 Mollena Williams, "Race Play: Hitting the Mainstream Media . . . ?" The Perverted Negress, April 11, 2013, accessed June 2, 2013, http://www.mollena.com/2013/04/12212/.

106 Scott Daddy, "Race Play," *EdgeMediaNetwork*, April 5, 2010, accessed September 7, 2010, http://www.edgeboston.com/index.php?ch=columnists&sc=scott_daddy&sc3=&id=104189&pf=1.

107 "Racial Name Calling, and Racists['] Fantasies," group page on fetlife.com, accessed June 8, 2012, https://fetlife.com/groups/8118/about.

108 Sharon Holland, *The Erotic Life of Racism* (Durham, N.C.: Duke University Press), 26, 29.

109 Daisy Hernandez, "Playing with Race: On the Edge of Edgy Sex, Racial BDSM Excites Some and Reviles Others," *Colorlines: News for Action*, December 21, 2004, accessed June 26, 2011, http://colorlines.com/archives/2004/12/playing_with_race. html.

110 These are all group pages on fetlife.com: "Black Women Who Love to Be Called Names During Race Play," https://fetlife.com/groups/13670; "Race Play," fetlife. com/groups/9885; "Cyber Race Play," https://fetlife.com/groups/38455; "Lesbians and Bisexual Women into Race Play," https://fetlife.com/groups/43392; "Black Cum Whores for White Masters," https://fetlife.com/groups/23986;"Racial Name Calling, and Racists['] Fantasies."

111 Hernandez, "Playing with Race."

112 Weiss, *Techniques of Pleasure*, 214.

113 Ibid.

114 Adrienne D. Davis, "Bad Girls of Art and Law: Abjection, Power, and Sexuality Exceptionalism in (Kara Walker's) Art and (Janet Halley's) Law," *Yale Journal of Law and Feminism* 23 (June 2011): 102. Davis echoes Gayl Jones, who describes the slave plantation as a "sex show" wherein the violence inflicted upon the black body titillated white men, women, and children. See Gayl Jones, *Corregidora* (Boston: Beacon Press, 1975), 125.

115 Anonymous femdom, interview with Ariane Cruz, May 14, 2013. This same femdom states, "I feel I'm comfortable with certain types of race play[;] like[,] I don't ever bottom[,] obviously[,] from the femdom."

116 The Black Fuhrer, interview with Ariane Cruz, June 19, 2012. Williams confirms the difficulty of race play even within the spectrum of BDSM edge play; see Plaid, "Interview with the Perverted Negress."

117 Easton and Hardy, *The New Bottoming Book*, 148–149.

118 Viola Johnson, "Playing with Racial Stereotypes: The Love That Dare Not Speak Its Name," Leatherweb, accessed April 5, 2013, http://www.leatherweb.com/race-playh.htm. Johnson is winner of the National Leather Association's Pantheon of Leather Lifetime Achievement Award in 1995 and the National Gay and Lesbian Task Force Leather Leadership Award in 2012. She serves as Director/Senior Griot of the Carter/Johnson Library and Collection, which is dedicated to preserving the history of the SM/leather/fetish communities.

119 V. M. Johnson, *To Love, to Obey, to Serve: Diary of an Old Guard Slave* (Fairfield, Conn.: Mystic Rose Books, 1999), 276.

120 Johnson, "Playing with Racial Stereotypes."

121 Ibid.

122 Ibid.

123 Johnson, *To Love, to Obey, to Serve*, 132.

124 Deleuze contends that sadism and masochism represent two polar juridical approaches: while sadism derogates the law and/or supersedes it, masochism and its contract represent the generation of law; Gilles Deleuze, "Coldness and Cruelty," in Deleuze, *Masochism*, translated by Jean McNeil (New York: Zone Books, 1991), 76–77, 20.

125 See Johnson, *To Love, to Obey, to Serve*, 51.

126 Deleuze, "Coldness and Cruelty," 75.

127 Weinberg, "Sadomasochism and the Social Sciences: A Review of the Sociological and Social Psychological Literature," in *Sadomasochism: Powerful Pleasures*, edited by Peggy J. Kleinplatz and Charles Moser (New York: Harrington Park Press, 2006), 33.

128 Weiss, *Techniques of Pleasure*, 7 (see also 188).

129 Ibid., 188, see also 210–211.

130 Ibid., 29.

131 Ibid., 219.

132 Ibid., 17 (see also 18).

133 Ibid., 189.

134 Sharpe, *Monstrous Intimacies*, 175.

135 Butler, "Lesbian S & M: The Politics of Dis-illusion," 173.

136 My use of the term "racialism" here is informed by Peggy Pascoe's use of it to refer to a larger, broader ideological nexus of race and racism undergirded by the tension between biology and culture. See Pascoe, "Miscegenation Law, Court Cases, and Ideologies of 'Race' in Twentieth-Century America," *Journal of American History* 83, no. 1 (1996): 47–48.

137 Weiss, *Techniques of Pleasure*, 197.

138 Ibid., 199.

139 Ibid., 200.

140 Ibid.

141 The Black Fuhrer, "White on Black Race Play—My Views," Youtube.com, October 26, 2009 http://www.youtube.com/watch?v=o4W8f-xmCEE.

142 The Black Fuhrer, interview with Ariane Cruz, June 19, 2012.

143 Ibid.

144 Kevin Mumford, *Interzones: Black/White Sex Districts in Chicago and New York in the Early Twentieth Century* (New York: Columbia University Press, 1997), xi.

145 Williams recounts a time when a white woman witnessed her playing with a white man and automatically assumed she was engaged in a race-play scene. To the woman's expression of revulsion at the sight "of a white man beating and torturing a Black woman," Williams responded, "'You know what's funny? That wasn't a race-play scene. That man didn't do race play. What you saw was the man to whom I was in service playing with me. What you perceived was a race play scene. I can't warn you about your own perceptions.'" This incident gestures toward important questions about the witnessing of the spectacle of race play and the complicated dynamics of empathy and complicity that are well-synthesized

in Saidiya Hartman's profound question, "Can the white witness of the spectacle of suffering affirm the materiality of Black sentience only by feeling for himself?" See Mollena Williams, "BDSM and Playing with Race," in *Best Sex Writing 2010*, edited by Rachel Kramer Bussel (San Francisco: Cleis Press, 2010), 70. See also Saidiya Hartman, *Scenes of Subjection: Terror, Slavery, and Self-Making in Nineteenth-Century America* (London: Oxford University Press, 1997), 19.

146 Weiss, *Techniques of Pleasure*, 205–206.

147 Beckmann, "'Sexual Rights' and 'Sexual Responsibilities' within Consensual 'S/M' Practice," 203.

148 Ibid.

149 Margot D. Weiss, "Working at Play: BDSM Sexuality in the San Francisco Bay Area," *Anthropologica* 48, no. 2 (2006): 230.

150 Newmahr, *Playing on the Edge*, 163.

151 Robert Bernasconi, "Crossed Lines in the Racialization Process: Race as a Border Concept," *Research in Phenomenology* 42, no. 2 (2012): 206–228.

152 Ibid., 216.

153 Ibid., 212.

154 Abdul R. JanMohamed, "Sexuality on/of the Racial Border," in *Discourses of Sexuality: From Aristotle to AIDS*, edited by Domna C. Stanton (Ann Arbor: University of Michigan Press, 1992), 99. See also Bernasconi, "Crossed Lines in the Racialization Process," 207.

155 Bernasconi, "Crossed Lines in the Racialization Process," 227, 216.

156 JanMohamed, "Sexuality on/of the Racial Border," 99.

157 Holland, *The Erotic Life of Racism*, 2, 88.

158 Bernasconi, "Crossed Lines in the Racialization Process," 222; see also Bean, *Leathersex*, 131.

159 Plaid, "Interview with the Perverted Negress."

160 Ibid.

161 Kantrowitz, "Swastika Toys," 208; Pat Califia, *Macho Sluts*, Little Sister's Classics #10 (1988; repr., Vancouver, B.C.: Arsenal Pulp Press, 2009), 9; Simone de Beauvoir, *Must We Burn Sade?*, translated by Annette Michelson (London: John Calder, 1962), 40; Marquis de Sade, *The 120 Days of Sodom and Other Writings*, compiled and translated by Austryn Wainhouse and Richard Seaver (New York: Grove Press, 1966).

162 Leonore Tiefer, *Sex Is Not a Natural Act and Other Essays* (Boulder, Colo.: Westview Press, 2004), 98.

163 The racial epithets I recite here are examples derived from interviews with black women who practice race play, both professionally and nonprofessionally.

164 Williams, *The Toybag Guide to Playing with Taboo* (Eugene, Ore.: Greenery Press, 2010), 44.

165 For more on healing and/in BDSM, see Darren Langdridge and Trevor Butt, "A Hermeneutic Phenomenological Investigation of the Construction of Sadomasochistic Identities," *Sexualities* 7, no. 1 (2004): 31–53; Ani Ritchie

and Meg Barker, "Feminist SM: A Contradiction in Terms or a Way of Challenging Traditional Gendered Dynamics through Sexual Practice?" *Lesbian and Gay Psychology Review* 6, no. 3 (205): 227–239; and Taylor and Ussher "Making Sense of S&M: A Discourse Analytic Account." Lynda Hart explores BDSM's return to the site of sexual trauma as a mode of reinvention or (re)experience; see Hart, *Between the Body and the Flesh*. Easton and Hardy explore BDSM's potential for a kind of sexual transcendence and spiritual and physical ecstasy. See Dossie Easton and Janet W. Hardy, *Radical Ecstasy* (Emeryville, Calif.: Greenery Press, 2004). Similarly, Lee Harrington explores the intersections of the kinky and the sacred in *Sacred Kink: The Eightfold Paths of BDSM and Beyond* (Lynwood, Wash.: Mystic Productions, 2009).

166 Beckmann, "'Sexual Rights' and 'Sexual Responsibilities' within Consensual 'S/M' Practice," 204.

167 The term "rememory" is wedded to the memory of chattel slavery; see Toni Morrison, *Beloved* (New York: Plume, 1987).

168 Sharpe, *Monstrous Intimacies*.

169 Corie Hammers defines rape play as "a BDSM encounter wherein a mock rape is performed according to agreed-upon rules set out and negotiated beforehand." See Corie Hammers, "Corporeality, Sadomasochism, and Sexual Trauma," *Body & Society* 20, no. 2 (2014): 68–90.

170 Ibid., 69.

171 Ibid., 74.

172 Ibid., 70.

173 Ibid., 79.

174 Ibid., 76.

175 Ibid., 73.

176 Theodore Reik, *Masochism in Modern Man*, translated by Margaret H. Beigel and Gertrud M. Kurth (New York: Grove, 1962), 77.

177 Spillers, "Mama's Baby, Papa's Maybe," 67.

178 Sharpe, "The Costs of Re-Membering," 315.

179 Darren Langdridge, "Speaking the Unspeakable: S/M and the Eroticization of Pain," in *Safe, Sane and Consensual: Contemporary Perspectives on Sadomasochism*, edited by Darren Langdridge and Meg Barker (Basingstoke: Palgrave Macmillan, 2007), 90.

180 Ibid., 96.

181 Williams, *The Toybag Guide*, 42.

182 Lindemann, *Dominatrix*, 149.

183 Danielle Lindemann, "BDSM as Therapy?" *Sexualities* 14, no. 2 (2011): 59.

184 Weiss, *Techniques of Pleasure*, 210–211.

185 Ibid., 210–211; Lindemann, "BDSM as Therapy?," 161.

186 Williams, "BDSM and Playing with Race," 71.

187 Lindemann, "BDSM as Therapy?," 161.

188 Graydancer, "The Voice of the Oppressor Speaks," December 30, 2011, reposted as "And Now a Word from 'The Man,'" The Perverted Negress, accessed June 12, 2012, http://www.mollena.com/2011/12/and-now-a-word-from-the-man/.

189 Frantz Fanon, *Black Skin, White Masks* (New York: Grove Press, 1952), 173.

190 Lindemann, *Dominatrix*, 149.

191 Ibid., 149–150.

192 Califia, "Feminism and Sadomasochism," 32.

193 Beckman, for example, argues that "'play' with socio-culturally dominating symbols and representations of power hierarchies allows for their change"; Beckmann, "'Sexual Rights' and 'Sexual Responsibilities' within Consensual 'S/M' Practice," 203.

194 Robin Ruth Linden, for example, cites literature on both sides of the "catharsis debate" to argue for the "invalidity" of the "catharsis hypothesis." See Linden, "Introduction: Against Sadomasochism," in *Against Sadomasochism: A Radical Feminist Analysis*, edited by Robin Ruth Linden, Darlene R. Pagano, Diana E. Russell, and Susan Leigh Star (East Palo Alto, Calif.: Frog in the Well, 1982), 14, 9.

195 Meg Barker and Darren Langdridge, "Silencing Accounts of Silenced Sexualities," in *Secrecy and Silence in the Research Process: Feminist Reflections*, edited by Róisín Ryan Flood and Rosalind Gill (London: Routledge, 2010), 68.

196 Ibid., 70.

197 Ibid., 72.

198 Meg Barker, Camelia Gupta, and Alessandra Iantaffi, "The Power of Play: The Potentials and Pitfalls in Healing Narratives of BDSM," in *Safe, Sane and Consensual: Contemporary Perspectives on Sadomasochism*, edited by Darren Langdridge and Meg Barker (Basingstoke: Palgrave Macmillan, 2007), 198.

199 Ibid., 205–206, 210.

200 Goddess Sonya, interview with Ariane Cruz, November 2, 2011. Goddess Sonya has been working as a professional dominatrix for over ten years and maintains her own website, www.goddesssonya.com, specializing in "ethnic kink" featuring primarily black women. Reflecting the growth in Internet-facilitated sex work at large, professional female dominatrixes embrace the Internet as a mode of not just commerce and networking but also a place where they have access to autonomy, community, marketing, and authorship of what Anne O Nomis calls "self-crafted identity." See Anne O Nomis, *The History & Arts of the Dominatrix* (Basingstoke, UK: Anna Nomis, 2013), 180. Indicative of the ways it has radically transformed sex work as a whole, the Internet has further privatized and augmented commercial sex work in ways that have fundamentally altered the business of professional domination and facilitated the growth of independent domes. See Lindemann, *Dominatrix*; and Ronald Weitzer, ed., *Sex for Sale: Prostitution, Pornography, and the Sex Industry*, 2nd ed. (New York: Routledge, 2010).

201 Goddess Sonya, interview with Ariane Cruz.

202 Lindemann, *Dominatrix*, 54.

203 Ibid., 72–74.

204 Ibid., 62.

205 Siobhan Brooks, *Unequal Desires: Race and Erotic Capital in the Stripping Industry* (Albany, N.Y.: SUNY Press, 2010), 7.

206 Mireille Miller-Young, *A Taste for Brown Sugar: Black Women in Pornography* (Durham, N.C.: Duke University Press, 2014), 230.

207 Ibid., 9, italics in original.

208 Ibid, 10.

209 Michel Foucault, *The History of Sexuality*, vol. 1, *An Introduction* (New York: Vintage Books, 1990), 94.

210 Leo Bersani, "Is the Rectum a Grave?" *AIDS: Cultural Analysis/Cultural Activism* 43 (1987): 216.

211 Plaid, "Interview with the Perverted Negress."

212 Black people within the BDSM community maligned Williams as a "'self hating Black-woman,' a 'traitor to the race,' 'deeply disturbed and in need of serious counseling,' and 'unfit to be in the community'"; Williams, "BDSM and Playing with Race," 71.

213 Michel Foucault, *Ethics: Subjectivity and Truth*, edited by Paul Rabinow (New York: The New Press, 1994), 165.

214 See ibid. One such example of BDSM's somatic possibilities is the de-genitalization of pleasure wherein nongenital erotogenic and libidinal zones of the body are realized see ibid. BDSM, as Elizabeth Grosz suggests, "intensif[ies] particular bodily regions—the buttocks being whipped, the hand that whips, bound regions of the body in domination practices—not using pain as a displacement of or guise for the pleasure principle, but where pain serves as a mode of corporeal intensification"; Elizabeth Grosz, *Space, Time, and Perversion: Essays on the Politics of Bodies* (New York: Routledge, 1995), 199.

215 Gary Fisher, *Gary in Your Pocket: Stories and Notebooks of Gary Fischer*, edited by Eve Kosofsky Sedgwick (Durham, N.C.: Duke University Press, 1996), 231.

216 Ibid., 239.

217 Ibid.

218 Darieck Scott, *Extravagant Abjection: Blackness, Power, and Sexuality in the African American Literary Imagination* (New York: New York University Press, 2010).

219 Fisher, *Gary in Your Pocket*, 199.

220 Carol Vance, "Pleasure and Danger: Toward a Politics of Sexuality," in *Pleasure and Danger: Exploring Female Sexuality*, edited by Carol Vance, 1–27 (London: Routledge, 1984), 1–27.

CHAPTER 2. PORNOGRAPHY'S PLAY(ING) OF RACE

1 For more about Abrams, see "Abiola Abrams: Self-Love Coach, Advice Columnist, TV Personality, Transformational Speaker," Sacred Bombshell: Life with Abiola, 2015, http://www.abiolatv.com/media-kit-lifestyle-expert-tv-personality-love-columnist-speaker-inspirational-coach/.

2 Abiola Abrams, "Intimacy Intervention: My Husband Uses Racial Slurs during Sex," *Essence Magazine*, April 9, 2013, accessed September 7, 2013, http://www.essence.com/2013/04/08/intimacy-intervention-my-husband-uses-racial-slurs-during-sex/.

3 Ibid.

4 Ibid.

5 Ibid.

6 Mollena Williams, "BDSM and Playing with Race," in *Best Sex Writing: 2010*, edited by Rachel Kramer Bussel (San Francisco: Cleis Press, 2010), 70.

7 Mollena Williams, "Race Play: Hitting the Mainstream Media . . . ?" The Perverted Negress, April 11, 2013, accessed January 29, 2016. http://www.mollena.com/2013/04/12212/.

8 Beyondblackandwhite.com is a website geared toward black women in interracial relationships. See Christelyn Karazin, "Abiola Abrams and Mollena Williams Address Now-Infamous Letter that Called Interracial Relationships into Question," Beyond Black & White, April 11, 2013, accessed July September 9, 2013, http://www.beyondblackwhite.com/abiola-abrams-mollena-williams-address-now-infamous-letter-called-interracial-relationships-question/.

9 Alexis Garrett Stodghill, "Controversial Letter Goes Viral as Readers Discuss 'Race Play,' a Sexual Fetish Involving Racial Slurs," April 22, 2013, accessed September 9, 2014, http://thegrio.com/2013/04/22/controversial-letter-goes-viral-as-readers-discuss-race-play-a-sexual-fetish-involving-racial-slurs/. See also "About the Grio," the Griot, accessed September 11, 2013, http://thegrio.com/about/.

10 "Racial Slurs, and 4 Other Things You Shouldn't Say during Sex," *Clutch Magazine*, April 8, 2013, accessed September 8, 2013, http://www.clutchmagonline.com/2013/04/racial-slurs-and-4-other-things-you-shouldnt-say-during-sex/comment-page-1/#comments.

11 Andrea Plaid, "Your Sex Acts—and Partners—Aren't Uplifting the Race," Racialicious, April 3, 2009, accessed June 5, 2012, http://www.racialicious.com/2009/04/03/your-sex-acts-and-partners-arent-uplifting-the-race/; Joyce Bird, "The Ethics of Fantasy," The Art of Transgression, October 1, 2013, accessed November 7, 2013, http://theartoftransgression.com/tag/race-play/; Tracy Clark-Flory, BDSM: It's Less Transgressive Than You Think," *Salon.com*, January 18, 2012, accessed June 5, 2012, http://www.salon.com/2012/01/12/bdsm_its_less_transgressive_than_you_think/; Catherine Scott, "Thinking Kink: Playing with Race in BDSM," *Bitchmedia.com*, August 6, 2012, accessed July 17, 2013, http://bitchmagazine.org/post/thinking-kink-bdsm-and-playing-with-race-sex-sexuality; Catherine Scott, "Thinking Kink: The Right to Play with Race,"*Bitchmeda.com*, August 8, 2012, accessed July 17, 2013, http://bitchmagazine.org/post/thinking-kink-the-right-to-play-with-race-feminist-magazine-bdsm-sex; Daisy Hernandez, "Playing with Race," *Colorlines: News for Action*, December 21, 2004, accessed June 26, 2011, http://colorlines.com/archives/2004/12/playing_with_race.html; Yvette Safire, "The Naked Reader Book Club: Playing the Race Card," Sex Is Social, April 30,

2010, accessed June 5, 2012, http://www.edenfantasys.com/sexis/erotica/naked-reader-book-club-race-as-fetish-0430101/; Anna North, "When Prejudice Is Sexy: Inside the Kinky World of Race-Play," Jezebel.com, March 14, 2012, accessed June 12, 2013, http://jezebel.com/5868600/when-prejudice-is-sexy-inside-the-kinky-world-of-race-play.

12 Williams rightly acknowledges that she has "unintentionally" become "the poster child" for race play because so many others aren't willing to publically speak about it. See Mollena Williams, "The Negress Natters: On BDSM & Race Play," audiolink, November 20, 2009, http://www.mollena.com/2009/11/the-negress-natters-on-bdsm-race-play/.

13 Feminista Jones, "[TALK LIKE SEX] Race Play Ain't for Everyone," *Ebony*, July 23, 2013, accessed August 4, 2013, http://www.ebony.com/love-sex/talk-like-sex-race-play-aint-for-everyone-911#axzz2uMawpRG4

14 Lori Adelman, "How Race Plays a Dynamic Role in S&M Culture," *The Grio*, March 29, 2011, accessed April 5, 2012, http://blackinamerica.com/cgi-bin/blog.cgi?blog_id=199491

15 Kirstin West Savali, "Plantation S&M Fantasies: Would You Engage in Slave Sex Roll [*sic*] Play?" *HelloBeautiful*, November 6, 2013, accessed December 9, 2013, http://hellobeautiful.com/2013/11/06/plantation-retreats-race-play/.

16 Chauncey Devega, "Playing with Sex, Power, and Race: Did You Know that There Are 'Plantation Retreats' Where Black People Go to Serve Their White 'Masters,'?" Indomitable: The Online Home of Essayist and Cultural Critic Chauncey Devega, August 12, 2012, accessed August 29, 2012, http://www.chaunceydevega.com/2012/08/playing-with-sex-power-and-race-did-you.html.

17 Ibid.

18 Sarah Ahmed, "Feminist Killjoys (and Other Willful Subjects)," *S&F Online* 8, no. 3 (2010), http://sfonline.barnard.edu/polyphonic/ahmed_01.htm.

19 Karen Halttunen, "Humanitarianism and the Pornography of Pain in Anglo-American Culture," *American Historical Review* 110, no. 2 (1995): 303–334; Steven Marcus, *The Other Victorians: A Study of Sexuality and Pornography in Mid-Nineteenth-Century England* (New York: Basic Books, 1964). See also Marquis de Sade, *The 120 Days of Sodom & Other Writings*, trans. Austryn Wainhouse and Richard Seaver (New York: Grove Press, 1966); Marquis de Sade, *Justine, Philosophy in the Bedroom, and Other Writings*, translated by Richard Seaver and Austryn Wainhouse (New York: Grove, 1965); and Marquis de Sade, *Juliette*, translated by Austryn Wainhouse (New York: Grove Press, 1968).

20 Halttunen, "Humanitarianism and the Pornography of Pain," 317.

21 Linda Williams, *Hardcore: Power, Pleasure, and the Frenzy of the Visual* (Berkeley: University of California Press, 1989), 186.

22 Examples include Edward Donnerstein, Daniel Linz, and Steven Penrod, *The Question of Pornography: Research Findings and Policy Implications* (New York: Free Press, 1987); Attorney General's Commission on Pornography, *Attorney General's Commission on Pornography: Final Report*, 2 vols. (Washington, D.C.:

U.S. Department of Justice, 1986); Andrea Dworkin, *Intercourse* (London: Arrow, 1988); Andrea Dworkin, *Our Blood: Prophecies and Discourse on Sexual Politics* (New York: Harper & Row, 1976); Andrea Dworkin, *Pornography: Men Possessing Women* (New York: Penguin, 1979); Catherine MacKinnon, "Sexuality, Pornography, and Method: Pleasure under Patriarchy," *Ethics* 99, no. 2 (1989): 314–346; Laura Lederer, ed., *Take Back the Night: Women on Pornography* (New York: William and Morrow, 1980).

23 Williams, *Hardcore*, 188–189.

24 Ibid.

25 Andrea Dworkin argues, for example, that heterosexual intercourse itself is a kind of sadism, see Dworkin, *Intercourse*, 63. For readings of the sovereign male cinematic gaze as directed by sadistic, voyeuristic desire, see Ann E. Kaplan, *Women and Film: Both Sides of the Camera* (New York: Methuen, 1983); and Annette Kuhn, *Women's Pictures: Feminism and Cinema* (London: Routledge, 1982).

26 Laura Mulvey, "Visual Pleasure and Narrative Cinema," *Screen* 16, no. 3 (1975): 14.

27 Gaylyn Studlar, "Masochism and the Perverse Pleasures of the Cinema," in *Movies and Methods*, edited by Bill Nichols (Berkeley: University of California Press, 1985), 602–621; Gaylyn Studlar, *In the Realm of Pleasure: Von Sternberg, Dietrich, and the Masochistic Aesthetic* (New York: Columbia University Press, 1988).

28 Williams, *Hardcore*, 227.

29 Ibid.

30 Like SAMOIS, Williams sees in sadomasochism a "clearer confrontation with the oscillating poles of our gendered identities and the role of power in them"; ibid., 228.

31 Ibid., 197.

32 Ibid., 198.

33 Ibid., 199.

34 Ibid., 196.

35 Natalie Purcell, *Violence and the Pornographic Imaginary: The Politics of Sex, Gender, and Aggression in Hardcore Pornography* (Routledge, 2012), 144.

36 Ibid., 144, 196.

37 Darieck Scott, *Extravagant Abjection: Blackness, Power, and Sexuality in the Literary Imagination* (New York: New York University Press, 2010); and Tim Dean, *Unlimited Intimacy: Reflections on the Subculture of Barebacking* (Chicago: University of Chicago Press, 2009). Many scholars have discussed the black top as an erotic icon in gay and BDSM pornography; see Dwight A. McBride, *Why I Hate Abercrombie & Fitch: Essays on Race and Sexuality* (New York: New York University Press, 2005); David Savran, *Taking It Like a Man: White Masculinity, Masochism, and Contemporary American Culture* (Princeton, N.J.: Princeton University Press, 1998); and Jarret Neal, "Let's Talk about Interracial Porn," *Gay and Lesbian Review* 20, no. 4 (2103): 23–26.

38 Scott, *Extravagant Abjection*.

39 Dean unveils "the genre's persistent effort to picture what remains invisible—whether it be the virus, ejaculation inside the body, or the moment of infection"; Dean, *Unlimited Intimacy*, 113.

40 Ibid., 157.

41 Ibid., 149.

42 Ibid., 161; see also 158–159. Examples of literature that examines sexuality, desire, and racial difference include bell hooks, *Black Looks: Race and Representation* (Boston: South End Press, 1992); Kobena Mercer, *Welcome to the Jungle: New Positions in Black Cultural Studies* (New York: Routledge, 1994); Homi Bhabha, *The Location of Culture* (New York: Routledge, 1994); and Abdul R. JanMohamed, "The Economy of Manichean Allegory: The Function of Racial Difference in Colonialist Literature," *Critical Inquiry* 12, no. 1 (1985): 59–87.

43 Dean, *Unlimited Intimacy*, 162; see also 158.

44 McBride, *Why I Hate Abercrombie & Fitch*, 101.

45 Bobby Blake with John R. Gordon, *My Life in Porn: The Bobby Blake Story* (Philadelphia: Running Press, 2008), 242.

46 Ibid, 167.

47 Savran, *Taking It Like a Man*, 236.

48 See Gilles Deleuze, "Coldness and Cruelty," in Deleuze, *Masochism*, translated by Jean McNeil (New York: Zone Books, 1991), 31; Stuart Hall, ed., *Representation: Cultural and Signifying Practices* (London: Sage Publications, 1997); and Alan Blass, *Difference and Disavowal: The Trauma of Eros* (Stanford, Calif.: Stanford University Press, 2002).

49 Femdomx.com loosely interprets the BDSM title, focusing on "fetishism, domination and kink-related activities"; "Vanessa Blue Inks Exclusive Deal with Hustler, Launched Fetish Website," *Adult Video News*, November 16, 2004, accessed September 25, 2010, http://business.avn.com/articles/video/Vanessa-Blue-Inks-Exclusive-Deal-with-Hustler-Launches-Fetish-Web-Site-41181.html.

50 In 2009, Blue was inducted into the Urban X Hall of Fame.

51 Mireille Miller-Young, "Putting Hypersexuality to Work: Black Women and Illicit Eroticism in Pornography," *Sexualities* 13, no. 2 (2010): 230.

52 "FemDomX Launches Affiliate Program," *Adult Video News*, December 13, 2004, accessed September 19, 2010, http://business.avn.com/articles/video/FemDomX-Launches-Affiliate-Program-41433.html.

53 "Vanessa Blue Unleashes Fem-Dom Vision on Hustler," *Adult Video News*, February 27, 2005, accessed September 25, 2010, http://business.avn.com/articles/video/Vanessa-Blue-Unleashes-Fem-Dom-Vision-on-Hustler-42323.html.

54 Ibid.

55 Ibid. Her use of the word "girl" instead of "woman" reflects not so much her own infantilization of the female body as her adoption of the language of the adult entertainment industry that is grounded in the profitable bedrock of eroticized female infantilization.

56 Blue, e-mail to Ariane Cruz, December, 3, 2010.

57 Ibid.

58 See www.femdomx.com.

59 Larry Townsend, *The Leatherman's Handbook II* (New York: Book Surge Publishing, 2007), 43; Larry Townsend, *The Leatherman's Handbook* (New York: Freeway Press, 1972).

60 Bill Thompson, *Sadomasochism: Painful Perversion or Pleasurable Play?* (London: Cassell, 1994), 84.

61 See Chris Nieratko, "Vanessa Blue," *Bizarre Magazine*, August 2005, accessed October 19, 2010; and Gene Ross, "Conversations with Vanessa Blue," August 25, 2007, accessed October 19, 2010, http://www.adultfyi.com/read.php?ID=27452.

62 Nieratko, "Vanessa Blue."

63 Ibid.

64 "Vanessa Blue Unleashes Fem-Dom Vision on Hustler."

65 Here Blue is in conversation with Hortense Spillers, who meditates on the flesh's memory of pain. Spillers states: "I think that the generations of slavery did carry pain in the flesh, that information was passed through the body in pain or through the torn flesh"; "Hortense Spillers, Interviewed by Tim Haslett for the Black Cultural Studies Website Collective in Ithaca," February 4, 1998, accessed October10, 2010, http://www.blackculturalstudies.org/spillers/spillers_intvw.html.

66 Gary Fisher, *Gary in Your Pocket: Stories and Notebooks of Gary Fischer*, edited by Eve Kosofsky Sedgwick (Durham, N.C.: Duke University Press, 1996), xi.

67 XBIZ, a leading publisher of business information and news regarding the adult entertainment, has been hosting an annual award ceremony for over a decade.

68 Though it is not clear in the DVD, *Get my Belt*'s website says that Madison is a blacksmith as well as a slave master.

69 Scott, *Extravagant Abjection*, 214.

70 "Skin Diamond Profile," *AVN*, accessed August 14, 2013, http://www.avn.com/porn-stars/Skin-Diamond-432418.html.

71 Ibid.

72 "Bad" Brad Berkwitt, "Skin Diamond: From Audrey Hepburn to a Midsummer Night's Dream & Back—This Adult Movie Star Is as Diverse as They Come," February 22, 2012, accessed August 15, 2013, /http://www.newzbreaker.com/2012/02/22/skin-diamond-from-audrey-hepburn-to-a-midsummer-night's-dream-back---this-adult-movie-star-is-as-diverse-as-they.come.

73 "Model Spotlight: Skin Diamond," *Rap Industry Models*, 2012, accessed August 14, 2013, http://rapindustry.com/skin-diamond.htm.

74 Skin says that in her personal life for example, breath play is one of her favorite turn-ons. See "Model Spotlight: Skin Diamond."

75 Skin, a relative newcomer to porn, is not unfamiliar with the entertainment industry. Her father starred in *Balamory* (2002–2005), a BBC children's television program filmed in Scotland. Skin herself had a short appearance on the show.

76 Her mainstream modeling clients include Louis Vuitton and American Apparel. She has graced the covers of numerous magazines, ranging from *Bizarre* (October

2009) to *Hustler* (June 2013). Comic-book artist David Mack used her as a model in his Marvel Comic miniseries *Daredevil: End of Days* (issue 3, 2012). She also recently starred in B.o.B.'s hip-hop video "John Doe."

77 Jessica P. Ogilivie, "10 Porn Stars Who Could Be the Next Jenna Jameson," *LA Weekly*, March 26, 2013, accessed Aug15, 2013 http://blogs.laweekly.com/arts/2013/03/porn_stars_young_san_fernando_valley.php?page=8.

78 Jesse Capps, "Exclusive Interview: Skin Diamond," Rock Confidential, March 28, 2012, accessed August 14, 2013, http://www.rockconfidential.com/inside/interviews/exclusive-interview-skin-diamond/.

79 When asked what BDSM stands for, Skin replied, "It's uh . . . Bondage, something, sadomasochism (giggles), I don't actually know what the whole thing stands for which is kind of silly considering how much of it I do." Kassem G, "Skin Diamond Goes Deep," June 2, 2012, accessed July 1, 2013, http://www.youtube.com/watch?v=1IYwFLDwIDw.

80 This lapse could also be read as a performance of the stereotype of porn stars as unintelligent.

81 Newmahr, *Playing on the Edge*, 66, 65.

82 Ibid., 66. Here Newmahr is in disagreement with scholars such as Darren Langdridge who argue that sex is central to BDSM. See Langdrige, "Voices from the Margins: Sadomasochism and Sexual Citizenship," *Citizenship Studies* 10 no. 4 (2006): 373–389; Darren Langdridge and Trevor Butt, "A Hermeneutic Phenomenological Investigation of the Construction of Sadomasochistic Identities," *Sexualities* 7, no. 1 (2004): 31–53; and Gary W. Taylor and Jane M. Ussher, "Making Sense of S&M: A Discourse Analytic Account," *Sexualities* 4, no. 3 (2001): 293–314.

83 Ibid., 25. This observation differs from Gini Graham Scott's identification of the BDSM scene as "mostly attractive and quite ordinary-looking people" in her pioneer ethnography of BDSM; Scott, *Dominant Women Submissive Men: An Exploration in Erotic Dominance and Submission* (New York: Praeger, 1983), x.

84 Ibid.

85 Ariane Cruz, "Gettin' *Down Home with the Neelys*: Gastro-Porn & Televisual Performances of Gender, Race & Sexuality," *Women and Performance* 23, no. 3 (2013): 323–349.

86 Capps, "Exclusive Interview: Skin Diamond."

87 Richard Dyer, *White: Essays on Race and Culture* (London: Routledge, 1997).

88 "Model Spotlight: Skin Diamond."

89 "Skin Profile," *Model Mayhem*, accessed August 15, 2013, http://www.modelmayhem.com/272301.

90 "Skin Diamond Profile."

91 Capps, "Exclusive Interview: Skin Diamond."

92 Ibid.

93 "Skin Diamond Interview from 2012 Miami Beach Exxxotica," Youtube video, June 6, 2012, accessed July 2, 2013, http://www.youtube.com/watch?v=fUAZWKrzvw.

94 We might also understand the name more humorously as a pun referring to sex; "hitting the skins" is a black vernacular colloquialism for sexual intercourse.

95 Williams, "Race Play: Hitting the Mainstream Media."

96 Examples include Ebony Ayes, Sinnamon Love, Brown Sugar, and Coco Brown.

97 Frantz Fanon, *Black Skin, White Masks* (New York: Grove Press, 1952), 112, 117, 113.

98 Bhabha, *The Location of Culture*, 112; Mercer, *Welcome to the Jungle*, 176.

99 Paul Gilroy, *Against Race: Imagining Political Culture beyond the Color Line* (Cambridge, Mass.: Harvard University Press, 2000), 46.

100 Ibid., 46–47.

101 Ibid., 47.

102 Robyn Weigman, *American Anatomies: Theorizing Race and Gender* (Durham, N.C.: Duke University Press, 1995), 24, 31; Thomas F. Gossett, *Race: The History of an Idea in America* (Oxford: Oxford University Press, 1963). For the historical shifts in race thinking, see Robert Bernasconi, "The Policing of Race Mixing: The Place of Biopower within the History of Racisms," *Bioethical Inquiry* 7, no. 2 (2010): 205–216.

103 Weigman, *American Anatomies*, 8, 9.

104 Ibid., 33.

105 Samira Kawash, *Dislocating the Color Line: Identity, Hybridity, and Singularity in African-American Narrative* (Stanford, Calif.: Stanford University Press, 1997), 130.

106 Mikko Tuhkanen, *The American Optic: Psychoanalysis, Critical Race Theory, and Richard Wright* (New York: State University of New York Press, 2009), 75.

107 Margot D. Weiss, *Techniques of Pleasure: BDSM and the Circuits of Sexuality* (Durham, N.C.: Duke University Press, 2011), 193.

108 Joseph R. Roach, "Deep Skin: Reconstructing Congo Square," in *African American Performance & Theater History: A Critical Reader*, edited by Harry Elam Jr. and David Krasner (New York: Oxford University Press, 2001), 102.

109 Ibid.

110 "Hortense Spillers, Interviewed by Tim Haslett."

111 Toi Derricotte poetry reading, Pennsylvania State University, December 2, 2010.

112 Toni Morrison, *Love* (New York: Knopf, 2003), 77.

113 Ibid., 78. Morrison also writes about "emotional memory—what the nerves and skin remember as well as how it appeared"; Toni Morrison, *What Moves at the Margin*, edited by Carolyn C. Denard (Jackson: University Press of Mississippi, 2008), 77.

114 Lynda Hart, *Between the Body and the Flesh: Performing Sadomasochism* (New York: Columbia University Press, 1998), 10.

115 Ibid.

116 Amber Jamilla Musser, *Sensational Flesh: Race, Power, and Masochism* (New York: New York University Press, 2014), 20.

117 "New Pornfidelity Scene a Bit Racist? Bad Taste?" The Porn Pool Forum, 51, Adult DVD Talk, May 24, 2013, accessed December 17, 2013, http://forum.adultdvdtalk.com/new-pornfidelity-scene-a-bit-racist-bad-taste/1.

118 Ibid.

119 Adrienne Davis, "Bad Girls of Art and Law: Abjection, Power, and Sexuality Exceptionalism in (Kara Walker's) Art and (Janet Halley's) Law," *Yale Journal of Law and Feminism* (June 2011): 102. See also "New Pornfidelity Scene a Bit Racist? Bad Taste?"

120 New Pornfidelity Scene a Bit Racist? Bad Taste?"

121 See "Our Biography," *PornFidelity.com*, http://www.pornfidelity.com/bio.html; "Porn Fidelity Goes Hardcore," AVN.com, March 5, 2012, accessed June 2, 2013, http://www.avn.com/movies/111783.html.

122 Heather Namikoshi, "Movie Review, 'Get My Belt,'" *AVN*, July 15, 2013, accessed August 12, 2013, http://www.avn.com/movies/123694.html.

123 Ibid.

124 Similarly, Kelley Madison Productions clearly notes that "the women aren't submissive but willing and wanting participants expressing their desires and the many ways in which that can be expressed." Kelly Madison Media, "Get My Belt," accessed August 11, 2013, http://getmybelt.com.

125 See ibid.; Peter Warren, "Kelly Madison Media Strikes Hard with Get My Belt," *AVN*, April 19, 2013, accessed August 12, 2013, http://business.avn.com/articles/video/Kelly-Madison-Media-Strikes-Hard-With-Get-My-Belt-513777.html; and "'Get My Belt' Smacks Down on Shelves This Week," *AVN*, May 21, 2013, accessed August 12, 2013, http://business.avn.com/company-news/Get-My-Belt-Smacks-Down-on-Shelves-This-Week-518085.html.

126 Ed Guerrero, "The Slavery Motif in Recent Popular Cinema," *Jump Cut: A Review of Contemporary Media* 33 (February 1988): 52.

127 Ibid., 52, 58. Specifically, the Blaxploitation western film *The Legend of Nigger Charley* (1972, dir. Martin Goldman) inspired *Django Unchained*.

128 A. Davis, "'Don't Let Nobody Bother Yo' Principle': The Sexual Economy of Slavery," in *Sister Circle: Black Women and Work*, edited by Sharon Harley and The Black Women Work Collective (New Brunswick, N.J.: Rutgers University Press, 2002), 103–127. See also Jasmine Nichole Cobb, "Directed by Himself: Steve McQueen's 12 Years a Slave," *American Literary History* 26, no. 2 (2014): 340.

129 "New Pornfidelity Scene a Bit Racist? Bad Taste?"

130 Melvin Van Peebles, *Sweet Sweetback's Baadasssss Song: A Guerilla Filmmaking Manifesto* (New York: Thunders Mouth Press, 1971), 91.

131 Sharon Holland, *The Erotic Life of Racism* (Durham, N.C.: Duke University Press, 2012).

132 Armond White, "Can't Trust It," *City Arts*, October 16, 2013, accessed January 4, 2013, http://cityarts.info/2013/10/16/cant-trust-it/; see also Armond White, "Dud of the Week: 12 Years a Slave Reviewed by Armond White for CityArts," *New York Film Critics Circle*, October 6, 2103, accessed January 4, 2013, http://www.nyfcc.

com/2013/10/3450/#.Ul7ULiL3opU.twitter. For more on torture porn, see Dean Lockwood, "All Stripped Down: The Spectacle of 'Torture Porn,'" *Popular Communication: The International Journal of Media and Culture* 7, no 1 (2009): 40–48.

133 White, "Can't Trust It."

134 Henry Louis Gates Jr., "'An Unfathomable Place': A Conversation with Quentin Tarantino about *Django Unchained*," *Transition* 112 (2013): 62.

135 "Pornfidelity's Get My Belt Two Disc DVD Set," http://kellymadisonstore.com/pornfidelity-s-get-my-belt-two-disc-dvd-set.html, accessed June 2, 2013.

136 Though Skin plays the actual chattel slave in the scene, the term "slave" has a particular resonance in BDSM, where the terms "master" and "slave" typically refer to long-term consensual and contractual relationships of servitude, domination, and submission between two committed partners. Newmahr cautions, "I would not subsume 'master' and 'slave' (also nouns) under the terms 'top' and 'bottom,' for these terms in the community often refer to long-term, and/or contractual relationships, or to identities understood as fixed, rather than as kinds of play." See Staci Newmahr, *Playing on the Edge: Sadomasochism, Risk, and Intimacy* (Bloomington: Indiana University Press, 2011), 19. Skin's role as slave may also reverse the gender dynamics of commercial heterosexual BDSM, wherein, Anne McClintock argues, men not women are the "slaves," and "by far, the most common service paid for by men in heterosexual S/M is the extravagant display of submission"; Anne McClintock, "Maid to Order: Commercial S/M and Gender Power," in *More Dirty Looks: Gender, Pornography and Power*, edited by Pamela Church Gibson (London: British Film Institute, 2004), 239.

137 Susan Brownmiller, *Against Our Will: Men, Women, and Rape* (New York, Simon & Shuster, 1975); Catharine A. MacKinnon, "Not a Moral Issue," *Yale Law & Policy Review* 2, no. 2 (1984): 321–345; Diana Russell, *The Politics of Rape: The Victim's Perspective* (New York: Stein-Day, 1975); and Lederer, *Take Back the Night.*

138 Davis, "'Don't Let Nobody Bother Yo' Principle.'"

139 Saidiya Hartman, *Scenes of Subjection: Terror, Slavery, and Self-Making in Nineteenth-Century America* (London: Oxford University Press, 1997), 38.

140 Ibid., 22–23.

141 Hortense Spillers, "Mama's Baby, Papa's Maybe: An American Grammar Book," *Diacritics* 17, no. 2 (1987): 67.

142 Ibid., 87.

143 Scott, *Extravagant Abjection*, 221, italics in original

144 I discuss the technology of race more in depth in chapter 4.

145 Capps, "Exclusive Interview: Skin Diamond."

146 "Pornfidelity's Get My Belt Two Disc DVD Set."

147 "Model Spotlight: Skin Diamond."

148 Ibid. See also Capps, "Exclusive Interview: Skin Diamond."

149 Elaine Scarry, *The Body in Pain: The Making and Unmaking of the World* (Oxford: Oxford University Press), 53.

150 Paul H. Gebhard, "Sadomasochism," in *S & M: Studies in Dominance & Submission*, edited by Thomas S. Weinberg (New York: Prometheus), 41. See also Halttunen, "Humanitarianism and the Pornography of Pain."

151 Ibid., 304.

152 Namikoshi, "Movie Review: 'Get My Belt.'"

153 There is frequent moaning and verbalization cf phrases such as "oh fuck" and "oh yes, right there."

154 Berkwitt, "Skin Diamond."

155 Terri Francis, "Looking Sharp: Performance, Genre, and Questioning History in *Django Unchained*," *Transitions* 112 (2013): 39.

156 None of the other chapters in *Get My Belt* end in such a manner where the tables turn and the female bottom avenges her ravishment.

157 Williams, *Hardcore*, 101.

158 Cindy Patton, "Hegemony and Orgasm—or the Instability of Heterosexual Pornography," *Screen* 30, no. 2 (1989): 104.

159 Christina Sharpe, *Monstrous Intimacies: Making Post-Slavery Subjects* (Durham, N.C.: Duke University Press, 2010).

160 See Deleuze, "Coldness and Cruelty"; Studlar, *In the Realm of Pleasure*; Torkild Thanem and Louise Wallenberg, "Buggering Freud and Deleuze: Toward a Query Theory of Masochism," *Journal of Aesthetics & Culture* 2 (2010): 1–10; Sylvan Keiser, "Body Ego during Orgasm," *Psychoanalytic Quarterly* 21 (1952): 162–138; Michael M'Uzan, "A Case of Masochistic Perversion and an Outline of a Theory," *International Journal of Psychoanalysis* 54, no. 4 (1973): 455–467.

161 Danny Sisko, interview with Ariane Cruz, October 2, 2013.

162 Ibid.

163 Ibid.

164 Ibid.

165 Ibid.

166 Ibid.

167 Sisko's race-play videos range from about 20 to 75 minutes in duration. He does not have any statistical information on the demographics of his consumers but notes that a "very, very broad cross section of people buy my work." Outside the United States, he sells most of his race-play porn in the UK, Australia, and Canada. His custom race-play clients are "pretty much all men." Because he only gets customers' initials, not their full names, he is reluctant to make any assumptions about the gender of his customer base.

168 Sisko, interview with Ariane Cruz.

169 "Pudding Foot Video Introductory Post," Pudding Foot Video's Blog, October 29, 2012, accessed June 6, 2013, http://puddingfootvideo.blogspot.com/2012_10_01_archive.html.

170 Ibid.

171 Sisko, interview with Ariane Cruz.

172 Scott, *Extravagant Abjection*, 214.

173 Deleuze, "Coldness and Cruelty," 71.

174 Ibid., 72.

175 Studlar, "Masochism and the Perverse Pleasures of the Cinema," 605.

176 For example, the warning on the website of *Get My Belt*, which is not included in the DVD packaging, serves as a general caution about the physical aggressiveness of the material and does not explicitly mention race or racism. It simply reads: "WARNING—THIS DVD IS EXTREMELY AGGRESSIVE! VIEWER DISCRETION IS ADVISED!" See http://kellymadisonstore.com/pornfidelity-s-get-my-belt-two-disc-dvd-set.html.

177 Dean, *Unlimited Intimacy*, 116.

178 Ibid., 118.

179 Sisko, interview with Ariane Cruz.

180 TES Fest is an annual BDSM social, educational, and entertainment event. See TES Fest 2016, http://www.tesfest.org/tesfest/.

181 Bond also presented on race play at TES Fest 2003.

182 See David, "Race Play?" n.d., Leatherweb.com, accessed April 5, 2013, http://www.leatherweb.com/raceplayh.htm.

183 Wolf writes, "I like seeing TES on the cutting edge of edge play. And I do not want to see TES shying away from the tough topics"; Lolita Wolf, "A Letter from Lolita Wolf, TES Programming Chair for TES Fest 2004," Leatherweb.com, accessed April 5, 2013, http://www.leatherweb.com/raceplayh.htm.

184 Ibid.

185 Robert F. Reid-Pharr, *Black Gay Man: Essays* (New York: New York University Press, 2001), 135.

186 Wolf, "A Letter from Lolita Wolf."

187 Bond quoted in ibid.

188 Bond quoted in ibid.

189 Bond quoted in ibid.

190 Bond quoted in ibid.

191 Randall Kennedy, *Nigger: The Strange Career of a Troublesome Word* (New York: Pantheon Books, 2002), 27, 31–32.

192 Scott, *Extravagant Abjection*, 236.

193 Bond quoted in Wolf, "A Letter from Lolita Wolf."

194 Bond quoted in ibid.

195 Sisko, interview with Ariane Cruz.

196 Ibid.

197 Ibid.

198 Ibid.

199 "New Video 'Evil Judo Bitches,'" Pudding Foot Video's Blog, March 4, 2014, accessed March 5, 2014, http://puddingfootvideo.blogspot.com.

200 Ibid.

201 See Jeffrey Escoffier, "Gay for Pay: Straight Men and the Making of Gay Pornography," *Qualitative Sociology* 26, no. 4 (2003): 531–555; and Jenny Kangasvuo, "Insatiable Sluts and Almost Gay Guys: Bisexuality in Porn Magazines," in *Pornification: Sex and Sexuality in Media Culture*, edited by Susanna Paasonen, Kaarina Nikunen, and Laura Saarenmaa (Oxford: Berg, 2007), 139–150.

202 Sisko, interview with Ariane Cruz.

203 Bhabha, *The Location of Culture*, 113.

204 "Pudding Foot Video Introductory Post."

205 Sisko, interview with Ariane Cruz.

206 Ibid.

207 "Pudding Foot Video Introductory Post."

208 Foucault, *The History of Sexuality*.

209 Sisko, interview with Ariane Cruz.

210 Viola Johnson, "Playing with Racial Stereotypes: The Love That Dare Not Speak Its Name." *Leatherweb*, 1994, accessed April 5, 2013, http://www.leatherweb.com/raceplayh.htm.

211 Jennifer C. Nash, *The Black Body in Ecstasy: Reading Race, Reading Pornography* (Durham, N.C.: Duke University Press, 2014).

212 Hazel V. Carby, *Reconstructing Womanhood: The Emergence of the Afro-American Woman Novelist* (Oxford: Oxford University Press, 1987), 39

213 Ibid.

214 Arthur Jones, *Wade in the Water: The Wisdom of the Spirituals*, 3rd ed. (New York: Orbis Books, 1993), 54.

215 We might read this sex-tape parody as a satire of the contemporary pop culture sex tape as a perverse emblem of celebrity status and/or catalyst of stardom.

216 Hartman, *Scenes of Subjection*, 38.

217 Russell Simmons, "I Get It . . . And I Respect It. The Harriet Tubman Video Has Been Removed," Globalgrind, August 16, 2013, http://globalgrind.com/2013/08/15/i-get-it-and-i-respect-it-the-harriet-tubman-video-has-been-removed/.

218 Glenda R. Carpio, *Laughing Fit to Kill: Black Humor and the Fictions of Slavery* (London: Oxford University Press, 2008), 7.

219 Simmons initially tweeted, "It was the funniest thing I've ever seen"; see Kendrick Marshall, "Russell Simmons Continues the Marginalization of Black Women," The Negro Voice, August 16, 2013, accessed August 17, 2013, http://negrovoice.com/2013/08/16/russell-simmons-continues-the-marginalization-of-black-women/. For Simmons's apology, see Simmons, "I Get It . . . and I Respect It."

220 Jen Yamato, "Russell Simmons Pulls Controversial 'Harriet Tubman Sex Tape' after YouTube Channel Launch," *Deadline Hollywood*, August 15, 2013, accessed August 16, 2013, http://www.deadline.com/2013/08/russell-simmons-pulls-controversial-harriet-tubman-sex-tape-after-youtube-channel-launch/.

CHAPTER 3. INTERRACIAL ITERATIONS AND INTERNET IN(TER)VENTIONS

1 Jerry Saltz, "Kara Walker: Ill-Will and Desire," *Flash Art* 29, no. 191 (1996): 84.

2 Mollena Williams, *The Toybag Guide to Playing with Taboo* (Eugene, Ore.: Greenery Press, 2010), 72.

3 "About CCRI," End Revenge Porn, accessed April 24, 2014, http://www.endrevengeporn.org/welcome/.

4 Natalie Webb, "Power in Numbers," January 3, 2014, accessed April 24, 2014, http://www.endrevengeporn.org/revenge-porn-infographic/.

5 Craig Brittan's defunct revenge porn website, isanybodydown.com, charged a $250 fee to remove material; Joe Mullin, "Revenge Porn Is 'Just Entertainment' Says Owner of IsAnybodyDown," Ars Technica, February 4, 2013, http://arstechnica.com/tech-policy/2013/02/revenge-porn-is-just-entertainment-says-owner-of-isanybodydown/. Kevin Christopher Bollaert, creator and operator of the revenge porn site ugotposted.com, was arrested in December 2013 and was recently sentenced to eighteen years in state prison. The site allegedly charged up to $350 to remove materials.

6 Neal Karlinsky, Aude Soichet, and Lauren Effron, "FBI Investigates 'Revenge Porn' Website Founder," *ABC News*, May 22, 2012, accessed April 24, 2013, http://abcnews.go.com/Technology/fbi-investigates-revenge-porn-website-founder/story?id=16405425.

7 Dan Brekke, "'Revenge Porn' Site Operator Arrested: YouGotPosted, and HeGotBusted," *KQED News*, December 10, 2013, accessed April 24, 2013, http://blogs.kqed.org/newsfix/2013/12/10/revenge-porn-site-operator-arrested-ugotposted-and-hegotbusted/.

8 I use the term "mainscreen" to communicate the transformation of moving image pornography in the golden age of the 1970s from clandestinely screened stag films shown in private homes and fraternal organizations to films shown on large screens in public adult theaters nationwide.

9 Mireille Miller-Young, *A Taste for Brown Sugar: Black Women in Pornography* (Durham, N.C.: Duke University Press, 2014).

10 Legs McNeil and Jennifer Osborne, *The Other Hollywood: The Uncensored Oral History of the Porn Film Industry* (New York: HarperCollins, 2005), 93.

11 Ibid., 92.

12 Andrea Plaid, "Interview with the Perverted Negress," *Racialicious*, July 10, 2009, accessed September 7, 2010, http://www.racialicious.com/2009/07/10/interview-with-the-perverted-negress/.

13 Randall Robinson, *The Debt: What America Owes to Blacks* (New York: Plume, 2000), 8.

14 See the website of the National Coalition of Blacks for Reparations in America, http://ncobra.org.

15 Ta-Nehisi Coates, "The Case for Reparations," *The Atlantic*, May 21 2014, accessed June 1, 2014, http://www.theatlantic.com/features/archive/2014/05/the-case-for-reparations/361631/.

16 The film grossed over $1 million; Jody W. Pennington, *The History of Sex in American Film* (Westport, Conn.: Praeger, 2007), 56.

17 Fanon argued that black male intimacy with white women represents both a "lust for revenge" and a desire to be white; Franz Fanon, *Black Skin, White Masks* (New York: Grove Press, 1952), 69.

18 Catharine MacKinnon, *Women's Lives, Men's Laws* (Cambridge, Mass.: Harvard University Press, 2005); Catharine MacKinnon, *Only Words* (Cambridge: Harvard University Press, 1993); Andrea Dworkin, *Pornography: Men Possessing Women* (New York: Penguin, 1979); Alice Mayall and Diane Russell, "Racism in Pornography," in *Making Violence Sexy: Feminist Views on Pornography*, edited by Diane Russell (New York: Teachers College Press, 1993), 167–177; Aminatta Forna, "Pornography and Racism: Sexualizing Oppression and Inciting Hatred," in *Pornography: Women, Violence, and Civil Liberties*, edited by Catherine Itzin (Oxford: Oxford University Press, 1992), 102–112.

19 Linda Williams, "Skin Flicks on the Racial Border: Pornography, Exploitation and Interracial Lust," in *Porn Studies*, edited by Linda Williams (Durham, N.C.: Duke University Press, 2004), 302.

20 Gloria Cowan and Robin R. Campbell, "Racism and Sexism in Interracial Pornography: A Content Analysis," *Psychology of Women Quarterly* 18, no. 3 (1994): 323–338.

21 Cowan and Campbell define racism as physical and verbal aggression, inequality, intimacy, and racial stereotypes.

22 Cowan and Campbell, "Racism and Sexism in Interracial Pornography," 326.

23 Recognitions of pornography's racism also generate from within the industry. Christian Mann, a 30-year industry veteran and well-known interracial producer (he is the former owner of Video Team and is now general manager of Evil Angel), believes that porn is a place where "blatant racism" remains "absolutely permissible." See "Black/White: Sex, Race, & Profit/Mimi for Governor," episode of *Sex TV*, aired 9 September 2006, Marcia Martin, Executive Producer.

24 Williams, "Skin Flicks on the Racial Border," 275.

25 Ibid., 297.

26 Ibid., 287–298.

27 Siobhan B. Somerville, *Queering the Color Line: Race and the Invention of Homosexuality* (Durham, N.C.: Duke University Press, 2000).

28 Daniel Bernardi, "Interracial Joysticks: Pornography's Web of Racist Attractions," in *Pornography: Film and Culture*, edited by Peter Lehman (New Brunswick, N.J.: Rutgers University Press, 2006), 220.

29 Ibid., 225, 234.

30 Ibid., 222–224. See also Daniel Bernardi, "Racism and Pornography: Evidence, Paradigms, and Publishing," *Cinema Journal* 46, no. 4 (2007): 116–121. Bernardi argues that a number of feminist scholars studying pornography fail to analyze race. See Laura Kipnis, *Bound and Gagged: Pornography and the Politics of Fantasy in America* (Durham, N.C.: Duke University Press, 1999); and Drucilla Cornell, ed., *Feminism & Pornography* (Oxford University Press, 2000). See also James Elias, Veronica Diehl Elias, Vern L. Bullough, Gwen Brewer, Jeffrey J. Douglas, and Will Jarvis, eds., *Porn 101: Eroticism Pornography and the First Amendment* (New York: Prometheus Books, 1999).

31 Bernardi, "Interracial Joysticks," 229, 240.

32 Gail Dines, "King Kong and the White Woman: Hustler Magazine and the Demonization of Black Masculinity," *Violence against Women* 4, no. 3 (1998): 287; and Gail Dines, "The White Man's Burden: Gonzo Pornography and the Construction of Black Masculinity," *Yale Journal of Law and Feminism* 18, no. 1 (2006): 283–297.

33 Dines, "The White Man's Burden," 285.

34 Natalie Purcell, *Violence and the Pornographic Imaginary: The Politics of Sex, Gender, and Aggression in Hardcore Pornography* (New York: Routledge, 2012), 30.

35 Dines, "King Kong and the White Woman," 291.

36 Dwight A. McBride, *Why I Hate Abercrombie & Fitch: Essays on Race and Sexuality* (New York: New York University Press, 2005), 109, see also 108.

37 Tim Dean, *Unlimited Intimacy: Reflections on the Subculture of Barebacking* (Chicago: University of Chicago Press, 2009), 154.

38 Ibid.

39 Ibid., 155; Jarrett Neal, "Let's Talk about Interracial Porn," *The Gay and Lesbian Review* (July–August 2013): 23; Darieck Scott, *Extravagant Abjection: Blackness, Power, and Sexuality in the Literary Imagination* (New York: New York University Press, 2010), 214.

40 Ida Wells-Barnett, "Lynch Law in America" (1900), in *Words of Fire: An Anthology of African-American Feminist Thought*, edited by Beverly Guy-Shefthall (New York: The New Press, 1995), 70.

41 T. Denean Sharpley-Whiting, "Thanatic Pornography, Interracial Rape, and the Ku Klux Klan," in *A Companion to African-American Philosophy*, edited by Tommy L. Lott and John P. Pittman (New York: Blackwell), 408.

42 Ibid., 411. See also Rosemarie Tong, "Women, Pornography, and the Law," in *The Philosophy of Sex: Contemporary Reading*, 2nd edition, edited by Nicholas Power, Raja Halwani, and Alan Soble (Lanham, Md.: Rowman & Littlefield, 1991).

43 Gunnar Myrdal, *An American Dilemma: The Negro Problem and Modern Democracy*, vol. 2 (1944; repr., New Brunswick, N.J.: Transaction Publishers, 1996), 587, italics in original.

44 The website boasts "We are so controversial they made us change our name!"; http://tour.mydaughtersfuckingablackdude.com, accessed June 12, 2014.

45 See S. M. Gelerman, "The Quiet Storm: Newly Renamed, HushMoney Takes Interracial Porn to New Heights," *AVN*, May 9, 2007, accessed March 01, 2009, http://business.avn.com/articles/video/The-Quiet-Storm-Newly-renamed-HushMoney-takes-interracial-porn-to-new-heights-26686.html.

46 Ibid.

47 David Sullivan, "Shane Diesel Signs Exclusive with Vengeance XXX," *AVN*, February 26, 2008, accessed March 17, 2009, http://business.avn.com/articles/1973.html.

48 Examples include Tracey A. Gardner, "Racism and the Women's Movement," in *Take Back the Night: Women and Pornography*, edited by Laura Lederer (New York: William and Morrow, 1980), 105–114; Forna, "Pornography and Racism"; Dines, "King Kong and the White Woman"; Dines, "The White Man's Burden"; Gail Dines, *Pornland: How Porn Has Hijacked Our Sexuality* (Boston: Beacon Press, 2010); Linda Williams, ed., *Porn Studies* (Durham, N.C.: Duke University Press, 2004); McBride, *Why I Hate Abercrombie & Fitch*; Scott Poulson-Bryant, *Hung: A Meditation on the Measure of Black Men in America* (New York: Doubleday, 2005); Kobena Mercer, *Welcome to the Jungle: New Positions in Black Cultural Studies* (New York: Routledge, 1994); Fanon, *Black Skin, White Masks*; and Jennifer C. Nash, *The Black Body in Ecstasy: Reading Race, Reading Pornography* (Durham, N.C.: Duke University Press, 2014).

49 My Daughter's Fucking a Nigga!, accessed March 17, 2009, www.mydaughtters-fuckinganigga.com.

50 Nelson X, "Black Humor: The Marketing of Stereotypes in Interracial Porn: An AVN Discussion," *Adult Video News*, February 2009, 76.

51 Ibid.

52 See also Violet Blue, "Racist Porn and the Recession/Violet Blue: Nothing Is Recession Proof, Especially Not Your Tired Old Racist Porn," *SFgate*, February 12, 2009, accessed July 2, 2009, http://www.sfgate.com/living/article/Racist-Porn-and-the-Recession-Violet-Blue-2464322.php; Jack, "Negro Porn Recession Proof, Claims AVN," *The Sword*, February 5, 2009, accessed July 2, 2009, http://thesword.com/black-cocks-recession-proof-claims-avn.html.

53 Nelson X, "No Boundaries: A Look at the Ethnic/Interracial Markets," *XBIZ*, May 8, 2012, accessed July 22, 2012, http://www.xbiz.com/articles/147875.

54 Nelson X, "Black Humor," 76.

55 Ibid.

56 For more on the "burden of representation," see Mercer, *Welcome to the Jungle*, 248. See also W. E. B. Du Bois, "Criterion of Negro Art," *Crisis* 32 (1926): 296–98, reprinted in Henry Louis Gates Jr., "The Black Person in Art: How Should S/He Be Portrayed?" *Black American Literature Forum* 21, nos. 1–2 (1987): 3–24.

57 Nelson X, "Black Humor," 78.

58 Ibid.

59 Ibid.

60 Ibid.

61 Nelson X, "No Boundaries."

62 There was dissension in the industry over whether the list referred to box-cover guidelines, video production guidelines, or both. See "The Cambria List," *Frontline*, 2002, accessed July 2, 2009, http://www.pbs.org/wgbh/pages/frontline/shows/porn/prosecuting/cambria.html.

63 Nelson X, "Black Humor," 78.

64 Sullivan, "Shane Diesel Signs Exclusive with Vengeance XXX."

65 Anna Breslaw, "This Dad Lives a Double Life as a Porn Star," *Cosmopolitan*, March 10, 2014, accessed June 16, 2014, http://www.cosmopolitan.com/sex-love/advice/shane-diesel-dildo-model.

66 "Shane Diesel's Cuckold Stories: Product Info," Popporn, accessed January 2, 2010, http://www.tlavideo.com/popporn-shane-diesels-cuckold-stories/p-298278-4. This interracial cuckold formula is common. Other examples include Black Market's *Fuck My White Wife* series (1–4, 2009–2012), Black Ice's *Interracial Cuckold Surprise* series (1–2, 2009–20012), Robert Hill Releasing Company's *The Negro in Mrs. Jones* (1–8, 2002–2005), Evil Angel's *Evil Cuckold* series, and Cram Johnson's *Oh No! There's a Negro in My Wife!* (1–5, 2007–2010), *Oh No! There's a Negro in My Daughter!* (1–3, 2008–2009), *Oh No! There's a Negro in my Mom!* (1–3, 2008–2009), and *I Can't Believe You Sucked a Negro!* (1–9, 2008–2010).

67 Zoë Wicomb, "Shame and Identity: The Case of the Colored in South Africa," in *Writing South Africa: Literature, Apartheid, and Democracy, 1970–1995* (Cambridge: Cambridge University Press, 1998), 92.

68 Williams, "Skin Flicks on the Racial Border," 271.

69 McBride, *Why I Hate Abercrombie & Fitch*, 106, 103.

70 Miller-Young, statement in "Black/White: Sex, Race, & Profit."

71 Dines, "King Kong and the White Woman."

72 Neal, "Let's Talk about Interracial Porn," 24.

73 Natalie Purcell has recently problematized this view, interrogating pornography's precarious yet common conceptualization as fantasy. See Purcell, *Violence and the Pornographic Imaginary*.

74 Nika Noir plays the wife and Derrick Paul plays the husband.

75 Samuel R. Delaney, *Times Square Red, Times Square Blue* (New York: New York University Press, 1999), 77.

76 Ibid., 76.

77 Linda Williams, *Hardcore: Power, Pleasure, and the Frenzy of the Visual* (Berkeley: University of California Press, 1989), 220.

78 Breslaw, "This Dad Lives a Double Life as a Porn Star."

79 Ibid. Interracial cuckold pornography is not usually sold under the rubric of gay, bisexual, or queer porn, nor is the language of queer, gay, bi, bi-curious, sexual, or homoeroticism typically evoked in its marketing. While Diesel suggests that most of his fans of interracial cuckold porn are white men, other figures in the industry suggest otherwise. According to an in-house study conducted by Fairvilla Megastore, a Florida retail chain, black men purchase 75 percent of interracial porn. See Nelson X, "Black Humor," 77.

80 Nelson X, "No Boundaries."

81 "Glenn King Joins Official Evil Angel Ranks with 'Mean Cuckold,'" *AVN*, August
    15, 2013, accessed September 30, 2014, http://business.avn.com/articles/video/
    Glenn-King-Joins-Official-Evil-Angel-Ranks-With-Mean-Cuckold-525529.html.

82 Jack Daily, "Chatsworth Pictures Puts You in the Cuckold Seat," *AVN*, June 10,
    2009, accessed July 18, 2009, http://business.avn.com/articles/video/Chatsworth-
    Pictures-Puts-You-in-the-Cuckold-Seat-342969.html.

83 Scott, *Extravagant Abjection*, 220.

84 Jay Wiseman, *SM 101: A Realistic Introduction*, 2nd ed. (San Francisco: Greenery
    Press, 1996), 242.

85 Ibid., 243.

86 Charles Moser and Peggy J. Kleinplatz, "Themes of SM Expression," in *Safe, Sane
    and Consensual: Contemporary Perspectives on Sadomasochism*, edited by Darren
    Langdridge and Meg Barker (Basingstoke: Palgrave Macmillan, 2007), 48–49.

87 See Gail Dines, *Pornland: How Porn Has Hijacked Our Sexuality* (Boston: Beacon,
    2010); Dines, "King Kong and the White Woman"; Dines, "The White Man's Bur-
    den"; and Natalie Purcell, *Violence and the Pornographic Imaginary*, 30.

88 Kathryn Bond Stockton, *Beautiful Bottom, Beautiful Shame: Where "Black" Meets
    "Queer"* (Durham, N.C.: Duke University Press, 2006), 22.

89 Ibid., 8.

90 Ibid., 23.

91 See David Sullivan, "Chatsworth Pictures Presents *Oh No, There's a Negro in My
    Mom!*" *AVN*, February 6, 2008, accessed March 30, 2009, http://business.avn.
    com/articles/28758.html. Christian Mann uses the language of psychoanalysis
    to situate the interracial cuckold fantasy as generating from the "subconscious
    ID—the thing that gets men hard and women wet—[as] the last refuge of racism."
    Quoted in Nelson X, "No Boundaries."

92 Continuing in this psychoanalytic vein of thought, we might read interracial
    cuckold porn through the psychological lens of colonial trauma. Here I am think-
    ing about Fanon's critique of Mannoni's "Prospero Complex," which describes the
    inferiority complex of the colonized and the white patriarchal projection (and
    fear) of the black male rapist. See Fanon, *Black Skin, White Masks*; and Octave
    Mannoni, *Prospero and Caliban: The Psychology of Colonization*, translated by
    Pamela Powesland (New York: Praeger, 1956).

93 Anthony Springer, "Porn Week: Diana Devoe—Ladies First," *Hip Hop DX*, Janu-
    ary 4, 2009, accessed March 10, 2009, http://hiphopdx.com/interviews/id.1299/
    title.porn-week-diana-devoe-ladies-first.

94 Diana Devoe in "Black/White: Sex, Race, & Profit."

95 See "Manila Joins Smash Pictures," *AVN*, February 13, 2016, accessed June 23,
    2008, http://business.avn.com/articles/video/Manila-Joins-Smash-Pictures-47764.
    html.

96 Hortense Spillers, "Mamas Baby, Papa's Maybe: An American Grammar Book,"
    Diacritics 17, no. 2 (1987): 80.

97 Ibid., 66.

98 Ralph Richard Banks, *Is Marriage for White People? How the African American Marriage Decline Affects Everyone* (New York: Dutton, 2011). See also Hannah Brueckner and Natalie Nitsche, "Opting Out of the Family? Social Change in Racial Equality in Family Formations Patterns and Marriage Outcomes among Highly Educated Women," paper presented at the annual meeting of the American Sociological Association, San Francisco, California, August 8, 2009. For a critique of the black "single lady phenomenon" and its visual representation, see Ariane Cruz, "Gettin' *Down Home with the Neelys*: Gastro-Porn & Televisual Performances of Gender, Race & Sexuality," *Women and Performance* 23, no. 3 (2013): 323–349.

99 Chloe Bannion, "Retailers: Diversify to Maximize," *AVN*, January 1, 2006, accessed April 1, 2009, http://business.avn.com/articles/24691.html.

100 *AVN* confirms *White Man's Revenge*'s "reversal" of interracial pornography writing: "It goes the opposite way of the standard interracial scenario of a black guy and a white girl. Instead, this one features white male performers getting busy with black females." See "Mercenary Unleashes *White Man's Revenge*," *AVN*, May 5, 2006, accessed April 1, 2009, http://business.avn.com/articles/26850.html. Steele's series *Black Reign*, which won the AVN Best Ethnic-Themed Series award twice (2005, 2006), does contain a scene of reverse interracial pornography.

101 I put white in quotation marks here because the nationality of the male performers challenges the understanding of white as not diverse: Marco Banderas is Latino (born in Uruguay and raised in Barcelona) and Jerry is from the Czech Republic.

102 Hazel V. Carby, *Reconstructing Womanhood: The Emergence of the Afro-American Woman Novelist* (Oxford: Oxford University Press, 1987), 39.

103 Kevin Mumford, *Interzones: Black/White Sex Districts in Chicago and New York in the Early Twentieth Century* (New York: Columbia University Press, 1997), 153.

104 Cowan and Campbell note its entrance into the market in 1983, "produced and marketed for a white male audience"; Cowan and Campbell, "Racism and Sexism in Interracial Pornography," 325. Susie Bright locates the dawning of a market niche for black and interracial hardcore porn in the mid-1980s; her article "Interracial and Black Videos" was scheduled to be published in *Adult Video News* in December 1986, but it was never printed. I have a copy courtesy of Susie Bright. Miller-Young argues that the video *Let Me Tell Ya 'bout Black Chicks* (1985, dir. The Dark Brothers) catalyzed a mid-1980s "movement towards a genre of black porn and interracial porn"; Miller-Young, "Erotic Economies: Researching Black Women in Pornography," lecture given at the University of California Berkeley, February 18, 2009.

105 Di Laurio and Rabkin extend the genre's U.S. production period from 1915 to 1970, instantiated by what many regard as the genre's oldest American film, *A Free Ride* (1915), also known as *A Grass Sandwich*, while Alpert and Knight, like Dave Thompson, trace the first stags to just after the turn of the century in the early

1900s. See Al Di Laurio and Gerald Rabkin, *Dirty Movies: An Illustrated History of the Stag Film, 1915–1970* (New York: Chelsea House, 1976); Hollis Alpert and Arthur Knight, "The History of Sex in Cinema: Part Seventeen, The Stag Film," *Playboy*, November 1967, 154–159, 170–189; and Dave Thompson, *Black and White and Blue: Adult Cinema from the Victorian Age to the VCR* (Toronto: ECW Press, 2007). Williams argues that the genre's apex was in the 1910s and 1920s; Williams, *Hardcore*, 85.

106 Although semi-professionals shot the earliest stag films in 35mm, that was eventually replaced by 16mm, the choice of amateur stag filmmakers as the genre increased in popularity. See Joseph Slade, "Stags, Smokers, and Blue Movies: The Origins of American Pornographic Film," exhibition announcement, Museum of Sex, February 7, 2005, accessed July 22, 2008, http://www.tomoffinlandfoundation. org/FOUNDATION/Events/ev_2005–02–07_Museum-of-Sex_Stag.htm.

107 The stage genre reached its prime in the early twentieth century after the Comstock crusades and the passage of the 1873 Comstock Law that made it illegal to send obscene material though the United States Post Office. Because stag films were privately and often secretly consumed, they evaded this law. For more see Williams, *Hardcore*, 85–86. See also Walter Kendrick, *The Secret Museum: Pornography in Modern Culture* (Berkeley: University of California Press, 1996). Like the 1873 Comstock Law, *Roth v. The United States* (1957), an important federal anti-obscenity statue that ushered the term "hard core" into legal and social discourse, also made illegal the distribution of obscene material, which it declared was not protected by the First Amendment. However, in defining obscene material as "utterly without redeeming social importance," it actually opened space for the production of pornography with purported social value. Pornography producers, sellers, and distributers thus benefited from a diminished threat of prosecution and more advantageous rationale for legal defense. Prior to *Roth*, moving-image pornography was, under common law rule as articulated in the British case *Hicklin v. Regina* (1868), most likely to be deemed obscene via the Hicklin test, and its production, consumption, and distribution was banned. The Hicklin test was the legal standard cited in American court cases throughout the 1800s and early 1900s.

108 Alpert and Knight, "The History of Sex in Cinema: Part Seventeen, the Stag Film," 154.

109 Williams, *Hardcore*, 282; Linda Williams, "Porn Studies: Proliferating Pornographies On/Scene: An Introduction," in *Porn Studies*, edited by Linda Williams, (Durham, N.C.: Duke University Press, 2004), 3. The term "on/scenity" reverberates in the work of Laura Kipnis, who writes that pornography "is simultaneously entirely central and entirely marginal"; Laura Kipnis, *Bound and Gagged: Pornography and the Politics of Fantasy in America* (Durham, N.C.: Duke University Press, 1999), 181.

110 The Benevolent and Protective Order of the Elks did not accept African American members until the 1970s and did not accept women until the mid-1990s. How-

ever, in the early twenty-first century, blacks were still denied memberships. This exclusion of African American men prompted the formation of black Elks clubs in the 1920s.

111 Joseph Slade, *Pornography in America: A Reference Handbook* (Santa Barbara: ABC-CLIO, 2000), 104; see also Di Laurio and Rabkin, *Dirty Movies*, 25.

112 Linda Williams, "'White Slavery' versus the Ethnography of 'Sexworkers': Women in Stag Films at the Kinsey Archive," *The Moving Image* 5, no. 2 (2005): 113.

113 For example, references to the jungle, safaris, and the tropics become common tropes for the black body. See Mireille Miller-Young, "A Taste for Brown Sugar: The History of Black Women in American Pornography" (PhD diss., New York University, 2004), 75.

114 Mireille Miller-Young, "Let Me Tell Ya 'bout Black Chicks: Interracial Desire and Black Women in 1980's Video Pornography," in *Pornification: Sex and Sexuality in Media Culture*, edited by Kaarina Nikunen, Susanna Paasonen, and Laura Saarenmaa (Oxford: Berg, 2007), 36.

115 Kenneth Turan and Steven F. Zito, *Sinema: American Pornographic Films and the People Who Make Them* (New York: Praeger Publishing, 1974), 91.

116 Ibid., 91.

117 Di Laurio and Rabkin, *Dirty Movies*, 101.

118 Turan and Zito, *Sinema*, 91.

119 Ibid., 92. See also Pennington, *The History of Sex in American Film*, 25.

120 *Blends* is available for viewing at the Kinsey Institute for Research in Sex, Gender, and Reproduction. Dave Thompson, who briefly mentions the film yet makes no mention of the racial dynamics so important to it, dates it from the early 1930s, while the Kinsey Institute dates it to circa 1940. Thompson, *Black and White and Blue*, 105.

121 The use of humorous food references to symbolize sex dates back to some of the earliest extant stag films such as *A Les Culs d'Or*, also known as *Mousquetaire au Restaurante* (France, 1908). See Thompson, *Black and White and Blue*, 14, 16.

122 Di Laurio and Rabkin, *Dirty Movies*, 101. Two early examples of films that portray interracial intimacy between black men and white women are *Black Seducer* (1957) and *One Dark Knight* (1957).

123 An exception to this rule is the stag film *Black and White Fantasy* (1951), which features a very brief oral sex scene between a black female and a white female. Di Laurio and Rabkin identify male homosexuality as the "strongest taboo" remaining in the stag genre. Di Laurio and Rabkin, *Dirty Movies*, 101.

124 Renee Romano, *Race Mixing: Black White Marriage in Postwar America* (Cambridge, Mass.: Harvard University Press, 2003), 2.

125 Lexington Steele, statement in "Black/White: Sex, Race, & Profit." See also Williams, "Skin Flicks on the Racial Border," 276; and Dean, *Unlimited Intimacy*, 154.

126 Williams, *Hardcore*, 48.

127 Tavia Nyong'o, *The Amalgamation Waltz: Race, Performance, and the Ruses of Memory* (Minneapolis: University of Minnesota Press, 2009), 83.

128 Slade, "Stags, Smokers, and Blue Movies."

129 The prevailing view on race mixing in the United States from the mid-nineteenth century onward was that it was a threat to racial purity and a sign of degeneration, pathology, and immorality. See Robert Bernasconi and Kristie Dotson, eds., *Race, Hybridity, and Miscegenation* (London: Thoemmes Continuum, 2005); and Robert Bernasconi and Tommy L. Lott, eds., *The Idea of Race* (Indianapolis: Hackett Publishing Company, 2000).

130 Arthur Gobineau, *The Inequality of Human Races* (1853), translated by Adrian Collins (New York: G. P. Putman, 1915), 208.

131 The pamphlet states, "The white man is going to seed, the black man is adding vigour and freshness to the trunk." See "Miscegenation," *Anthropological Review* 2, no. 5 (May 1864): 119. The rhetoric of this hoax was not entirely farfetched. Just a few years later, in 1839, inspired by James Cowles Prichard's theory of monogenesis, Alexander Walker posited racial amalgamation as a way to improve the races in *Intermarriage*.

132 Ibid.

133 Stefanie Dunning, *Queer in Black and White* (Bloomington: Indiana University Press, 2009), 12.

134 It was common for males to appear anonymously in stag films. Often the use of props such as masks, fake mustaches and beards, and facial makeup and/or a camera angle that positioned the male's face outside the frame protected the identities of male performers.

135 Jane M. Gaines, *Fire & Desire: Mixed Race Movies in the Silent Era* (Chicago: University of Chicago Press 2001), 53.

136 Di Laurio and Rabkin, *Dirty Movies*, 91.

137 See Williams, *Hardcore*, 71

138 "Throwing in the towel" is common in many stag films, where someone literally throws the performers a towel from somewhere off screen in the last seconds of a film's characteristically abrupt ending.

139 Blue, "Racist Porn and the Recession."

140 Ibid.

141 Scott, *Extravagant Abjection*, 214.

142 Stockton, *Beautiful Bottom, Beautiful Shame*, 139.

143 Nash, *The Black Body in Ecstasy*, 47.

144 Originally named Vixens and Visionaries, the annual Feminist Porn Awards, which began in Toronto in 2005, has been an important force in feminist pornography. Launched by Good for Her, a sex-positive sex store, the awards continue to be instrumental in the feminist pornography movement, which began years earlier, rooted in lesbian pornography. For example, the lesbian pornography magazine *On Our Backs*, founded by Nan Kinney, Debi Sundahl, and Susie Bright in 1984, was crucial in the movement. Also, in 1985, Kinney and Sundahl started Fatale Video, a company that produces and distributes lesbian moving-image porn. For more about the awards, see the website Good for Her Presents the Fem-

inist Porn Awards, http://www.goodforher.com/feminist_porn_awards. For more about the industry, politics, and figures of feminist porn, see Tristan Taormino, Constance Penley, Celine Shimizu, and Mireille Miller-Young, eds., *The Feminist Porn Book: The Politics of Producing Pleasure* (New York: The Feminist Press at the City University of New York, 2013).

145 Shine Louis Houston, interview with Ariane Cruz, May 24, 2012.

146 Nenna Joiner, interview with Ariane Cruz, July 14, 2012.

147 Louis Althusser, *Lenin and Philosophy and Other Essays* (New York: Monthly Review Press, 1971).

148 Umayyah Cable, "Let's Talk about Pornography: An Interview with Shine Louise Houston," Feministe, April 7, 2009, accessed April 5, 2012, http://www.feministe.us/blog/archives/2009/04/07/lets-talk-about-pornography-an-interview-with-shine-louise-houston/; see also "About Pink & White Productions," http://pink-white.biz/about/.

149 Good Vibrations has been instrumental in the careers of many pioneer luminaries in sex-positive women's pornography, such as Carol Queen, Susie Bright, and Candida Royalle.

150 Jillian Eugenios, "Chatting Up Shine Louise Houston," *Curve Magazine*, September 20, 2011, accessed March 5, 2012, http://www.curvemag.com/Curve-Magazine/Web-Articles-2011/Chatting-up-Shine-Louise-Houston/.

151 Ariane Cruz, "Sisters Are Doin' It for Themselves: Black Women and the New Pornography," in *Pornography: Contemporary Perspectives*, edited by Lindsay Coleman and Jacob M. Held (New York: Rowman & Littlefield, 2014), 225–258.

152 The work of Houston and her production company, Pink & White Productions, has received many awards; see "Awards," Pink & White Productions," http://pink-white.biz/about/awards/.

153 Crash Pad Series, vol. 1, *The Top 5 Episodes of Season 1*, DVD, Pink & White Productions, directed by Shine Louise Houston, co-directed by Shae (San Francisco: Blowfish Video, 2007).

154 Houston, interview with Ariane Cruz.

155 "Shine Louis Houston and Pink and White Productions," Porn Movies for Women, 2014, accessed May 1, 2012, http://www.pornmoviesforwomen.com/shinelouisehouston.html.

156 See "The Crash Pad," Pink & White Productions, 2013, http://pinkwhite.biz/PWWP/reviews/the-crash-pad/

157 Cruz, "Sisters Are Doin' It for Themselves."

158 L. H. Stallings, *Mutha Is Half a Word: Intersections of Folklore, Vernacular, Myth, and Queerness in Black Female Culture* (Columbus: Ohio State University Press, 2007), 2–3.

159 Houston, interview with Ariane Cruz.

160 Ibid.

161 Ibid.

162 Ariane Cruz, "Mis(playing) Blackness: Black Female Sexuality in *The Misadventures of Awkward Black Girl*," in *Contemporary Black Female Sexualities*, edited by Joanne M. Braxton and Trimiko Melancon (New Brunswick, N.J.: Rutgers University Press, 2015), 73–88.

163 Mireille Miller-Young, "Sexy and Smart: Black Women and the Politics of Self-Authorship in Netporn," in *C'lickme: A Netporn Studies Reader*, edited by Katrien Jacobs, Marije Janssen, and Matteo Pasquinelli ([Amsterdam:] Institute of Network Cultures, 2007), 207, http://www.networkcultures.org/_uploads/24.pdf.

CHAPTER 4. TECHNO-KINK

1 This statement, uttered by fuckingmachine.com director Tomcat, commences countless fuckingmachine.com videos.

2 Hogtied.com launched in 1997, initially distributing only bought material.

3 "The Peter Acworth Story Unfolds," Kink.com, December 1, 2007, http://www.kink.com/shoot/4101.

4 "Who We Are," Kink.com, http://press.kink.com/who-we-are/.

5 "Cybernet Entertainment Is Now Kink," Behind Kink, February 2, 2006, http://www.behindkink.com/2006/02/21/cybernet-entertainment-is-now-kink-com/. In 2007, when Acworth moved into the armory, the company had ninety employees, fifteen websites, and ten years of production equipment; "As of Monday, Kink Can Officially Call Its Castle 'Home,'" Behind Kink, December 19, 2007, http://www.behindkink.com/2007/12/19/as-of-monday-kink-can-officially-call-its-castle-home/.

6 Mary Jo Bolling, "Setting the Stage for Sex: Inside San Francisco's kink.com," California Home + Design, November 6, 2012, http://www.californiahomedesign.com/house-tours/setting-stage-sex-inside-san-franciscos-kinkcom/slide/5850.

7 Ibid.

8 Bryan Abrams, "The King of Kink: An Interview with Bondage-Porn Power Player Peter Acworth," *Details*, September 20, 2010, http://www.details.com/sex-relationships/porn-and-perversions/201009/king-of-kink-peter-acworth-bondage-porn-empire.

9 Marlow Stern, "James Franco & Co. Discuss the BDSM-Porn Documentary 'Kink' at Sundance," *The Daily Beast*, January 21, 2013, http://www.thedailybeast.com/articles/2013/01/21/james-franco-and-co-discuss-the-bdsm-porn-documentary-kink-at-sundance.html.

10 Ibid. See also Benjamin Edelman, "Red Light States: Who Buys Adult Entertainment," *Journal of Economic Perspectives* 23, no. 1 (2009): 213.

11 "Factsheet," Kink.com, http://press.kink.com/factsheet/.

12 Other scandals include denial of workers' compensation after injuries in the workplace, pay rate issues of cam "girls," and male performers' use of performance enhancement drugs.

13 See "Fuckingmachine.com Launches," Behind Kink, January 1, 2001, accessed April 22, 2010, http://www.behindkink.com/2001/01/01/fuckingmachines-com-launches/.

14 The first fucking-machine videos depict Acworth operating various machines in makeshift settings—on a living room couch, on foam mattresses, and on the concrete floor of his garage—using rudimentary wooden structures to suspend models that he built himself. Such scenes are primitive in comparison to the sophisticated settings and technologically advanced machines of the current site. In addition to Acworth, operators Peter Rodgers and Tony Pirelli were instrumental in the site's genesis.

15 "The Peter Acworth Story Unfolds."

16 Insex.com, a BDSM porn website that specialized in bondage, female submission, and live feed sessions (interactive live video streams), influenced Acworth and Kink.com. For more about insex.com, see *Graphic Sexual Horror* (1997–2005), produced, directed, edited by Anna Lorentzon and Barbara Bell (2009). Mechanized sex machines are the focus of other contemporary porn sites, such as bangingmachines.com, and www.obsenemachines.com.

17 Jessica Valenti, *The Purity Myth: How America's Obsession with Virginity Is Hurting Young Women* (Berkeley, Calif.: Seal Press, 2009).

18 "Jada Fire," Kink VR, April, 12, 2006, http://www.fuckingmachines.com/site/clips_flash.jsp?shootId=3540.

19 Woman of color appear in approximately 10 percent of the films. These figures were collected in August 2013. The site grows and changes rapidly.

20 For example, one user writes, "The Ebony/Black women section is pitifully small. PLEASE GET A MORE ETHNICALLY DIVERSE FIELD!"; see "Iman," Kink VR, June 5, 2005, http://www.fuckingmachines.com/site/clips_flash.jsp?shootId=3042.

21 Sinnamon Love, "A Question of Feminism," in *The Feminist Porn Book: The Politics of Producing Pleasure*, edited by Tristan Taormino, Constance Penley, Celine Shimizu, and Mireille Miller-Young (New York: The Feminist Press at the City University of New York, 2013) 101. Love has performed on multiple kink.com sites. Her first video is dated September 20, 2002. Though she names herself as the first black women performer of kink.com (then called Cybernet), I found examples of black women on the kink.com site that contest this; a fucking-machine video with two black female performers is dated September 18, 2001. Love may be very have been the first black female porn star to work with kink.com.

22 More recently, in 2015, kink.com had an "ethnicity" identification for models that included the category "black."

23 Hortense Spillers, "Mama's Baby, Papa's Maybe: An American Grammar Book," *Diacritics* 17, no. 2 (1987): 76.

24 See Bonnie Ruberg, "The Man behind the Fucking Machine," *The Village Voice*, July 16, 2008, http://www.villagevoice.com/news/the-man-behind-the-fucking-machine-6391543; and "Fuckingmachines.com launches." Fucking machines are available on a number of sites, including http://www.extremerestraints.com/fucking-machines_48/. They are also available for purchase through amazon.com.

25 "Fucking Machines Do the Trick" (episode 19), *Playboy TV*, May 19, 2006.

26 "Only One Machine Can Keep Up: The Fucksall," fuckingmachines.com, September 21, 2011, http://www.fuckingmachines.com/site/shoot/14844-Only-One-Machine-Can-Keep-Up-The-Fucksall.html?c=1.

27 Ann Balsamo, *Technologies of the Gendered Body: Reading Cyborg Women* (Durham, N.C.: Duke University, Press, 1996), 3.

28 "Only One Machine Can Keep Up: The Fucksall."

29 A recent description of a Fucking Machines video says this: "Buttfucking, pussy pounding, Sybian rides, nipple clamps, fisting, HUGE cocks, & fast machines all challenge Adrianna Chechik to a dual [sic]. Machines win." See "Oct 23, 2013: The Return of the Mega-Cummer," Fuckingmachines.com, October 23, 2013, http://www.fuckingmachines.com/site/shoots.jsp?c=1.

30 "Fucking Machines Do the Trick."

31 Ibid.

32 "BondageGear by Kink.com," Kink.com, http://bondagegear.kink.com/fucking-machines_48/versa-fuk-machine_7000.html.

33 One journalist jests that "the Intruder could have been a rowing machine belonging to a good family in Greenwich, CT before it went AWOL from prep school to porn infamy"; Katherine Mieszkowski, "Battlebots in the Bedroom," *Salon*, February 12, 2002, http://www.salon.com/2002/02/12/sexbots/.

34 "Sybian Design," https://www.sybian.com/sybian/. Acworth calls the mountable and user-controlled Sybian a "glorified vibrator" and a "perennial favorite." It is capable of vibrating and rotating at high speeds, takes different attachments, and provides internal and external stimulation. The dildo attachment rotates up to 120 rpm and vibrates up to 6,500 rpm. The Sybian retails for $1,345.

35 So-called longevity orgasms allegedly help us not only look and feel younger but also live longer by strengthening our immune systems. For more on the physical benefits of sexual pleasure, see Barry R. Komisaruk, Carlos Beyer-Flores, and Beverly Whipple, *The Science of Orgasm* (Baltimore, Md.: John Hopkins University Press, 2006); and Phillip Weis, "The Best Reason to Have Sex," *Men's Journal*, October 1, 2012, http://www.mensjournal.com/health-fitness/health/the-best-reason-to-have-sex-20121001.

36 Steven Seidman, "Theoretical Perspectives," in *Introducing the New Sexuality Studies: Original Essays and Interviews*, edited by Steven Seidman, Nancy Fischer, and Chet Meeks (London: Routledge, 2007), 4.

37 Dave Lampert, "Inventor's Thoughts," https://www.sybian.com/aff/sybian/thoughts.html.

38 "Fucking Machines Do the Trick."

39 For sex-machine maker Jon Tavern, fucking machines become hazardous when they are not used for heterosexual conjugal sex. Tavern states, "I will require anyone ordering a machine from me to provide proof of marriage and a signed statement of intent to use only within that marriage. Kind of like a gun dealer that requires proof of age and proof of passage of a firearm safety test before selling

someone a firearm. Sexual arousal is a doorway to a person's very soul and isn't to be messed with lightly." Tavern quoted in Xeni Jardin, "The Sex Machines Next Door," *Wired.com*, November 16, 2005, http://archive.wired.com/culture/lifestyle/news/2005/11/69576. See also Timothy Archibald, *Sex Machines: Photographs and Interviews* (Carrboro, N.C.: Daniel, 2005), 46.

40 Lampert, "Inventor's Thoughts."

41 James Vincent, "Nearly Two Thirds of Global Web Activity Is Thanks to Bots, Say [*sic*] Study," *Independent*, December 13, 2013, http://www.independent.co.uk/life-style/gadgets-and-tech/news/nearly-two-thirds-of-global-web-activity-is-thanks-to-bots-say-study-9003034.html. See also Denver Nicks, "Robots Have Taken over the Internet," *Time*, December 13, 2013, http://techland.time.com/2013/12/13/robots-have-taken-over-the-internet/.

42 Though Haraway is most famous for her use of the term "cyborg," Manfred Clynes and Nathan Kline coined it in 1960; Pramod K. Nayar, *An Introduction to New Media and Cybercultures* (West Sussex, UK: Blackwell), 37.

43 Donna Haraway, *Simians, Cyborgs, and Women: The Reinvention of Nature* (New York: Routledge, 1991), 149.

44 Ibid., 150.

45 Balsamo, *Technologies of the Gendered Body*, 33–34.

46 Malini Johar Schueller, "Analogy and (White) Feminist Theory: Thinking Race and the Color of the Cyborg Body," *Signs* 31, no. 1 (2005): 63–92; Chela Sandoval, *Methodology of the Oppressed* (Minneapolis: University of Minnesota Press, 2000); Abby Wilkerson, "Ending at the Skin: Sexuality in Feminist Theorizing," *Hypatia* 12, no. 3 (1997): 164–173; Joan W. Scott, "Commentary: Cyborgian Socialists?" In *Coming to Terms: Feminism, Theory, Politics*, edited by Elizabeth Weed (New York: Routledge, 1989), 216–217.

47 N. Katherine Hayles, *How We Became Posthuman: Virtual Bodies in Cybernetics, Literature, and Informatics* (Chicago: University of Chicago Press, 1999), 3; see also N. Katharine Hayles, "Refiguring the Posthuman," *Comparative Literature Studies* 41, no. 3 (2004): 311–316.

48 Hayles, *How We Became Posthuman*, 291; Alex Weheliye, "'Feenin': Posthuman Voices in Contemporary Black Popular Music," *Social Text* 20, no. 2 (2002): 21.

49 Weheliye, "'Feenin,'" 23.

50 Ibid., 22.

51 Judith Halberstam and Ira Livingston, "Introduction: Posthuman Bodies," in *Posthuman Bodies*, edited by Judith Halberstam and Ira Livingston (Bloomington: Indiana University Press, 1995), 8.

52 Ibid., 12.

53 Ibid.

54 The fucking-machine pornography website www.obsenemachines.com cheekily advertised "forget doggy style, this is robot style!"; http://www.obscenemachines.com/tour/?nats=MjQzNDoyOjQx,0,0,0,0, accessed November 15, 2013.

55 Ruberg, "The Man behind the Fucking Machine."

56 Ibid.

57 Ibid.

58 Ibid.

59 Ibid.

60 Ibid.

61 Isaac Leung, "The Cultural Production of Sex Machines and Contemporary Technosexual Practices," in *Do Androids Sleep with Electric Sheep? Critical Perspectives on Sexuality Pornography in Science and Social Fiction*, edited by Johannes Grenzfurthner, Günther Friesinger, Daniel Fabry, and Thomas Ballhausen (San Francisco: RE/SEARCH, 2009), 26–27.

62 Ray notes that fucking machines are primarily used in two arenas: pornography and swing clubs; Audacia Ray, *Naked on the Internet: Hookups, Downloads, and Cashing in on Internet Sexploration* (Emeryville, Calif.: Seal Press, 2007), 251.

63 Peter Acworth, "Why Kink Matters," *Huffington Post*, January 14, 2013, http://www.huffingtonpost.com/peter-acworth/why-kink-matters_b_2460100.html. While fuckingmachines.com has primarily male consumers, in the commercial realm, fucking machines sell largely to women; Leung, "The Cultural Production of Sex Machines and Contemporary Technosexual Practices," 27.

64 Ruberg, "The Man behind the Fucking Machine."

65 Ray, *Naked on the Internet*, 249.

66 Ibid., 249–250.

67 Ibid., 250–251.

68 Ibid., 250.

69 "Arsenal," Fucking Machines, accessed August 2, 2013, http://www.fuckingmachines.com/site/fm/machines/.

70 Sarah Schaschek, "Fucking Machines: High-Tech Bodies in Pornography," in *Screening the Dark Side of Love: From Euro-Horror to American Cinema*, edited by Karen A. Ritzenhoff and Karen Randell (New York: Palgrave Macmillan, 2012), 220, 211. See also Sarah Schaschek, *Pornography and Seriality: The Culture of Producing Pleasure* (New York: Palgrave Macmillan 2014), 53.

71 Schaschek, "Fucking Machines," 214–215.

72 Ruberg, "The Man behind the Fucking Machine."

73 See "Cole Conners," May 12, 2004, http://www.fuckingmachines.com/site/clips_flash.jsp?shootId=1879.

74 Though videos feature anal penetration, here fucking machines are primarily technologies of vaginal penetration. Even the Sybian Multiple Orgasm Sex Machine, a "vibrating saddle" whose inventor touts it as the only non-"stroking" fucking machine on the market, relies on a plastic dildo; "Sybian Multiple Orgasm Sex Machine—Overview and Specifications of the Sybian Sex Machine," accessed May 8, 2014, http://www.sybian.plazadiscounts.com/page3.html. See also Archibald, *Sex Machines*, 67.

75 The Rocker and the Sybian are two exceptions here. The candy-apple-red Rocker, a nonmechanical, mountable fucking machine resembling a child's rocking horse,

is powered by the kinetic energy of the female performer. Her rocking motion propels an erect dildo, located in center of the Rocker, to pump. On fucking machines.com, the Sybian is mostly controlled by the female performers. Some other machines, such as the Bunny Fucker, have remotes that female performers can hold and control.

76 "Magic Wand," HitachiMagic.com, https://hitachimagic.com/hitachi-magic-wand/magic-wand/?gclid=CPrGg-eYmbsCFSbNOgoddWIAOQ. Manufactured in Japan, the Hitachi has been sold by California-based retailer Hitachimagic.com for ten years.

77 "About Us," https://hitachimagic.com/about-us.

78 Sigmund Freud, "Three Essays on the Theory of Sexuality," in *The Freud Reader*, edited by Peter Gay (New York: W. W. Norton & Company, 1989), 281, 287, my italics.

79 Ibid., 281.

80 William Masters and Virginia Johnson, *Human Sexual Response* (Boston: Little, Brown, and Co., 1996); and William Masters and Virginia Johnson, *Human Sexual Inadequacy* (New York: Bantam, 1970).

81 Masters and Johnson, *Human Sexual Response*, 128.

82 Masters and Johnson were not the first to use observation in the empirical study of the female sexual orgasm. Janice Irvine traces this practice within sexology back to the late nineteenth the twentieth century. See Janice Irvine, *Disorders of Desire: Sex and Gender in Modern American Sexology* (Philadelphia: Temple University Press, 1990), 53–54.

83 According to Masters and Johnson, vaginal and clitoral orgasms are not "separate anatomic entities" and the clitoris (clitoral stimulation) is the source of both the vaginal orgasm and the clitoral orgasm. See William H. Masters and Virginia E. Johnson, *Human Sexual Response* (Boston: Little, Brown, and Company, 1966), 66, 67, 63. See also John Heidenry, *What Wild Ecstasy: The Rise and Fall of the Sexual Revolution* (New York: Simon & Shuster, 1997), 17–39; and Jane M. Irvine, *Disorders of Desire: Sexuality in Modern American Sexology* (Philadelphia: Temple University Press, 2005), 120.

84 Linda Williams, *Hardcore: Power, Pleasure, and the Frenzy of the Visual* (Berkeley: University of California Press, 1989), e.g., 1–2, 30, 229, 282, 275; Michel Foucault, *The History of Sexuality*, vol. 1, *An Introduction* (New York: Vintage Books, 1990), 57.

85 See "Jada Fire."

86 Deborah Willis and Carla Williams, *The Black Female Body: A Photographic History* (Philadelphia: Temple University Press, 2002); Allan Sekula, "The Body and the Archive," *October* 39 (Winter 1986): 3–64, Shawn Michelle Smith, *Photography on the Color Line* (Durham, N.C.: Duke University Press, 2004); Brian Wallis, "Black Bodies, White Science: Louis Agassiz's Slave Daguerreotypes," *American Art* 9, no. 2 (1995): 38–61.

87 So-called beaver films, which were popular in the United States in the mid- to late 1960s, were 16 mm loops of footage, typically of the female genitals, that were screened in public theatres. The term "coloscopic film" refers to Masters and Johnson's use of scientific imaging technologies to study the female orgasmic process; Eithne Johnson, "The 'Coloscopic' Film and the 'Beaver' Film: Scientific and Pornographic Scenes of Female Sexual Responsiveness," in *Swinging Single: Representing Sexuality in the 1960s*, edited by Hilary Radner and Moya Luckett (Minneapolis: University of Minnesota Press, 1999), 309.

88 Foucault, *The History of Sexuality*, 57.

89 Ann Koedt, "The Myth of the Vaginal Orgasm," in *Sexual Revolution*, edited by Jeffrey Escoffier (New York: Thunder's Mouth Press, 2003), 101. Originally published in Ann Koedt, *Radical Feminism* (New York: Quadrangle, 1970).

90 Jill Johnson, *Lesbian Nation: The Feminist Solution* (New York: Simon and Schuster, 1973), 165.

91 Nancy Tuana, "Coming to Understand: Orgasm and the Epistemology of Ignorance," *Hypatia* 19, no.1 (2004): 194.

92 Ibid., 195.

93 Gayatri Chakravorty Spivak, "French Feminism in an International Frame," *Yale French Studies* 62 (1981): 181.

94 Tuana, "Coming to Understand," 219.

95 Jane Gaines, "Machines that Make the Body Do Things," in *More Dirty Looks: Gender, Pornography, and Power*, 2nd ed., edited by Pamela Church Gibson (London: British Film Institute, 2004), 35.

96 Ibid., italics in original.

97 Joseph W. Slade, *Pornography in America: A Reference Handbook* (Santa Barbara, Calif.: ABC-CLIO, 2000), 106.

98 Linda Williams, *Hardcore: Power, Pleasure, and the Frenzy of the Visual* (Berkeley: University of California Press, 1989), 101, italics in original. Though Williams was not the first to consider the importance of the pornographic money shot, she offers the most compelling reading of this still-significant spectacle in modern pornography. See also Steven Marcus, *The Other Victorians: A Study of Sexuality and Pornography in Mid-Nineteenth-Century England* (New York: Basic Books, 1964); and Stephen Ziplow, *The Film Maker's Guide to Pornography* (New York: Drake, 1977).

99 Gaines, "Machines that Make the Body Do Things," 35.

100 I use the term "perform" here because it speaks to the labor of pleasure while signaling that the question of women's orgasmic authenticity is never fully resolved.

101 "Marie Luv Gets Wet with Fuckingmachines," June 6, 2007, http://www.fuckingmachines.com/site/scenes.jsp?shootId=4332.

102 Williams, *Hardcore*, 106. In her Marxian analysis of the money shot, Williams builds upon the work of Steven Marcus and his identification of a capitalist framework for analyzing sexual climax. See Steven Marcus, *The Other Victorians*.

103 Marcus, *The Other Victorians*, 22.

104 Ibid.

105 Ibid., 214.

106 Ibid., xv–xvi.

107 Williams, *Hardcore*, 95.

108 Joseph W. Slade has critiqued Williams for "reduc[ing] porn films to a single heterosexual genre"; Slade, *Pornography in America*, 290.

109 Tim Dean, *Unlimited Intimacy: Reflections on the Subculture of Barebacking* (Chicago: University of Chicago Press, 2009), 104.

110 Ibid.

111 Dean argues that bareback porn offers some creative solutions to the quandary of producing a money shot when ejaculation occurs internally: the compromise money shot, the reverse money shot, and the multiple displaced money shot.

112 Dean, *Unlimited Intimacy*, 110.

113 Ibid., 111. Dean sees bareback porn as "one instance of this genre's persistent effort to picture what remains invisible—whether it be the virus, ejaculation inside the body, or the moment of infection"; ibid., 113.

114 Despite industry changes that may be read as a kind of privileging of women in the performance side of the porn industry, the production side (producers, writers, lighting and set designers, camera operators, editors, and distributers) was largely dominated by white males in the 1990s, and this is still true today; Susan Faludi, "The Money Shot," *The New Yorker*, October 30, 1995.

115 Similarly, porn historian Joseph Slade, noting the gendered ideology of power behind money shots, writes: "Since characters in a typical hard-core film succumb to the chaos of passion, cum shots symbolize restoration of sexual order through virtuoso performance"; Slade, *Pornography in America*, 106.

116 Ibid., 68.

117 Ibid.

118 Williams, *Hardcore*, 48. Women's ejaculations have been increasingly performed and eroticized in contemporary American pornography. Many popular sites, such as redtube.com, have a large selection of squirting videos and allow users to search for videos under the category of "squirting."

119 Shannon Bell, "Liquid Fire: Female Ejaculation & Fast Feminism," in *Jane Sexes It Up: True Confessions of Feminist Desire*, edited by Merri Lisa Johnson (New York: Four Walls Eight Windows, 2002), 338; see also Bell, "Feminist Ejaculations," in *The Hysterical Male: New Feminist Theory*, edited by Arthur and Marilouise Kroker (London: Macmillan, 1991), 155–169.

120 While Krafft-Ebing associated female ejaculation with neurasthenia, Freud discussed women's "abnormal secretion" in the context of their hysteria. See Richard von Krafft-Ebing, *Psychopathia Sexualis* (Chicago: Bloat, 1999), 330; and Sigmund Freud, *Dora: An Analysis of a Case of Hysteria* (New York: Touchstone, 1997), 75.

121 See Amy Gilliland, "Women's Experiences of Female Ejaculation," *Sexuality & Culture* 13, no. 3 (2009): 121–134; Joanna B. Korda, Sue W. Goldstein, and Frank

Sommer, "Sexual Medicine History: The History of Female Ejaculation," *Journal of Sexual Medicine* 7, no. 5 (2010): 1965–1975; Zlatko Pastor, "Female Ejaculation Orgasm vs. Coital Incontinence: A Systematic Review," *Journal of Sexual Medicine* 10, no. 7 (2013): 1682–1691; Alberto Rubio-Casillas and Emmanuele A. Jannini, "New Insights from One Case of Female Ejaculation," *Journal of Sexual Medicine* 8, no. 12 (2011): 3500–3504.

122 For a wonderful synthesis of the dildo wars, see Heather Findlay, "Freud's Fetishism and the Lesbian Dildo Debates," *Feminist Studies* 18, no. 3 (1992): 563–579; and June L. Reich, "Genderfuck: The Law of the Dildo," *Discourse* 15, no. 1 (1992): 112.

123 Jeanne E. Hamming, "Dildonics, Dykes, and the Detachable Machine," *European Journal of Women's Studies* 8, no. 3 (2001): 330.

124 Coleen Lamos, "Taking on the Phallus," in *Lesbian Erotics: Practices and Critiques*, edited by Karla Jay (New York: New York University Press, 1995), 111.

125 Jeanine Minge and Amber Lynn Zimmerman. "Power, Pleasure, and Play: Screwing the Dildo and Rescripting Sexual Violence," *Qualitative Inquiry* 15, no. 2 (2009): 347, 331.

126 Findlay, "Freud's Fetishism and the Lesbian Dildo Debates," 563.

127 Alycee J. Lane, "What's Race Got to Do with It?" *Black Lace* 21 (Summer 1991): 21.

128 Ibid.

129 Ann Ducille, *Skin Trade* (Cambridge, Mass.: Harvard University Press, 1996), 8.

130 Ibid., 38.

131 Ibid., 37.

132 Leung, "The Cultural Production of Sex Machines"; see also Ray, *Naked on the Internet*; Schaschek, "Fucking Machines"; and Schaschek, *Pornography and Seriality*.

133 Though many fucking-machine designers, like Lampert, credit the "collective input" of women testers, these machines manifest as products of the white male imaginary and hand. See "Sybian Design."

134 Archibald, *Sex Machines*, 7.

135 Hoag Levins, *American Sex Machines: The Hidden History of Sex at the U.S. Patent Office* (Holbrook, Mass/: Adams Media Corporation, 1996), 8.

136 Rachel P. Maines, *The Technology of Orgasm: "Hysteria," the Vibrator, and Women's Sexual Satisfaction* (Baltimore, Md.: John Hopkins University Press, 1999), 11.

137 David Levy, *Love + Sex with Robots: The Evolution of Human-Robot Relationships* (New York: Harper Collins, 2007), 253.

138 See Wilhelm Reich, *The Function of the Orgasm: Sex-Economic Problems of Biological Energy* (New York: Farrar, Straus and Giroux, 1973); Wilhelm Reich, *Early Writings* (New York, Farrar, Straus and Giroux, 1975); and Christopher Turner, *Adventures in the Orgasmatron: How the Sexual Revolution Came to America* (New York: Farrar, Straus and Giroux, 2011).

139 Simone de Beauvoir, "Must We Burn Sade?" in Marquis De Sade, *The 120 Days of Sodom & Other Writings*, compiled and translated by Austryn Wainhouse and Richard Seaver (New York: Grove Press, 1966), 20.

140 See [Richard Seaver, comp.], *Sixty Erotic Engravings from Juliette* (New York: Grove Press, 1969).

141 Linda Williams, "Porn Studies: Proliferating Pornographies On/Scene," in *Porn Studies*, ed. Linda Williams (Durham, N.C.: Duke University Press, 2004), 3.

142 Archibald, *Sex Machines*, 10.

143 Alondra Nelson, "Introduction: Future Texts," *Social Text* 20, no. 2 (2002): 6.

144 Ibid., 1.

145 "The Peter Acworth Story Unfolds." See also Ruberg, "The Man behind the Fucking Machine."

146 Foucault, *The History of Sexuality*, 104, 103.

147 J. Marion Sims, *The Story of My Life*, edited by H. Marion Sims (New York: D. Appleton and Co., 1885): 244, 238. See also Dorothy Roberts, *Killing the Black Body: Race, Reproduction, and the Meaning of Liberty* (New York: Vintage Books, 1999), 176; Deborah Gray White, *Ar'n't I a Woman? Female Slaves in the Plantation South* (New York: W. W. Norton, 1999); and Seale Harris, *Woman's Surgeon: The Life of J. Marion Sims* (New York, Macmillan Company, 1950), 82–108.

148 "G- Force," another white male operator and webmaster at Kink.com, directs this scene.

149 Foucault, *The History of Sexuality*, 127.

150 Ibid., 116.

151 Ibid., 107.

152 Teresa de Lauretis, *Technologies of Gender: Essays on Theory, Film, and Fiction* (Bloomington: Indiana University Press, 1987), ix, 2.

153 Balsamo, *Technologies of the Gendered Body*, 9.

154 Ibid., 11, 3.

155 Michael Omi and Howard Winant describe race as a "fundamental organizing principle of social relationships." See Michael Omi and Howard Winant, *Racial Formation in the United States from the 1960s to the 1990s*, 2nd ed. (New York: Routledge, 1994), 66.

156 Wendy Hui Kyong Chun, "Introduction: Race and/as Technology; or How to Do Things to Race," *Camera Obscura* 70, 24, no. 1 (2009): 8, italics in original.

157 Ibid.

158 Ibid., 9.

159 Beth Coleman, "Race as Technology," *Camera Obscura* 70, 24, no. 1 (2009): 178.

160 Jennifer González, "Race, Secrecy, and Digital Art Practice," *Camera Obscura* 70, 24, no. 1 (2009): 60.

161 González, "Morphologies: Race as a Visual Technology," in *Only Skin Deep: Changing Visions of the American Self*, edited by Coco Fusco and Brian Wallis (New York: Harry N. Abrams, 2003), 380.

162 González, "Race, Secrecy, and Digital Art Practice," 37.

163 González, "Envisioning Cyborg Bodies: Notes from Current Research," in *The Cyborg Handbook*, edited by Chris Hables (New York: Routledge, 1995), 275.

164 Here González cites Stephanie Smith's concept of miscegenation as dependent upon "illegitimate matings"; Stephanie A. Smith, "Morphing, Materialism, and the Marketing of Xenogenesis," *Genders* 18 (Winter 1993): 75. See also González, "Envisioning Cyborg Bodies," 276.

165 Cameron Bailey, "Virtual Skin: Articulating Race in Cyberspace," in *Immersed in Technology: Art and Virtual Environments*, edited by Mary Anne Moser and Douglas MacLeod (Cambridge, Mass.: MIT Press, 1996), 42.

166 "The Alien," Kink VR, accessed July 22, 2104, http://www.fuckingmachines.com/site/fm/machines/.

167 Nelson, "Introduction: Future Texts," 1. Examples include Beth E. Kolko, Lisa Nakamura, and Gilbert Rodman, eds., *Race and Cyberspace* (New York: Routledge, 2000); Alondra Nelson, Thuy Linh N. Tu, and Alicia Headlam Hines, eds., *Technicolor: Race, Technology, and Everyday Life* (New York: New York University Press, 2001); and Anna Everett, ed., *Learning Race and Ethnicity: Youth and Digital Media* (Cambridge, MA: MIT Press, 2008).

168 Lisa Nakamura, "Afterimages of Identity: Gender, Technology, and Identity Politics," in *Reload*, edited by Mary Flanagan and Austin Booth (Cambridge: MIT Press, 2002), 323. See also Lisa Nakamura, "Race in/for Cyberspace: Identity Tourism and Racial Passing on the Internet," in *CyberReader*, 2nd ed., edited by Victor Vitanza (New York: Allyn and Bacon 1999). Mark B. Hansen, seeming to redeem cyberspace as a transgressive site of and for racial identity, has argued that Nakamura's "passing" has productive potential; Mark B. Hansen, *Bodies in Code: Interfaces with Digital Media* (New York: Routledge, 2006), 143, 147, 156.

169 Lisa Nakamura and Peter A. Chow-White, *Race after the Internet* (New York: Routledge, 2012), 2.

170 Ibid., 5.

171 Kali Tal, "The Unbearable Whiteness of Being: African American Critical Theory and Cyberculture," October 1996, http://kalital.com/Texts/Articles/whiteness.html, originally published in *Wired*, October 1996.

172 One exception is an older video (the first in the fuckingmachine.com archive to feature black women) for which the description reads: "Latoya and Tierra in a Black machines fuck fest of an update. Four big swinging tits and too many dongs to count." See "Latoya and Tierra," Fucking Machines, September 8, 2011, http://www.fuckingmachines.com/site/clips_flash.jsp?shootId=270. Another example is the description of Sydnee Capri as "all brown, smooth, and yummy"; "Sydnee Capri," Fucking Machines, May 24, 2005, http://www.fuckingmachines.com/site/clips_flash.jsp?shootId=2956.

173 "Jada Fire"; "Africa," April 12, 2002, http://www.fuckingmachines.com/site/clips_flash.jsp?shootId=424; "Andrea Renee," Fucking Machines, March 19, 2003, http://www.fuckingmachines.com/site/clips_flash.jsp?shootId=988.

174 "Guidelines for Posting Comments," Kink.com, accessed July 22, 2014, http://www.fuckingmachines.com/site/comment_guidelines.jsp.

175 "Melrose Foxx," May 6, 2009, Fucking Machines, http://www.fuckingmachines. com/site/scenes.jsp?shootId=6512.

176 For a synthesis of these critiques, see Feona Attwood, "Introduction: From Social Problem to Cultural Practice," in *Porn.Com: Making Sense of Online Pornography*, edited by Feona Attwood (New York: Peter Lang, 2010), 1–13.

177 Katrien Jacobs, *Netporn: DIY Web Culture and Sexual Politics* (New York: Rowman & Littlefield. 2007), 12. See also Mireille Miller-Young, "Sexy and Smart: Black Women and the Politics of Self-Authorship in Netporn," in *C'lickme: A Netporn Studies Reader*, edited by Katrien Jacobs, Marije Janssen and Matteo Pasquinelli ([Amsterdam:] Institute of Network Cultures, 2007), 205–216, http:// www.networkcultures.org/_uploads/24.pdf; and Ariane Cruz, "Sisters Are Doin' It for Themselves: Black Women and the New Pornography," in *Pornography: Contemporary Perspectives*, edited by Lindsay Coleman and Jacob M. Held (New York: Rowman & Littlefield, 2014), 225–258.

CONCLUSION

1 James A. Snead, "Repetition as a Figure of Black Culture," in *Black Literature and Literary Theory*, edited by Henry Louis Gates Jr. (New York: Routledge, 1990), 68.

2 Ibid., 69.

3 Deborah E. McDowell, *"The Changing Same": Black Women's Literature, Criticism, and Theory* (Bloomington: Indiana University Press, 1995). See also Jacques Derrida, *Limited Inc*, translated by Samuel Weber (Evanston, Ill.: Northwestern University Press, 1988); and Jacques Derrida, *Margins of Philosophy*, translated by Alan Bass (Chicago: University of Chicago Press, 1982).

4 McDowell, *"The Changing Same,"* 4–5.

5 Christina Sharpe, *Monstrous Intimacies: Making Post-Slavery Subjects* (Durham, N.C.: Duke University Press, 2010).

6 "Arsenal," Fucking Machines, accessed July 22, 2014, http://www.fuckingmachines. com/site/fm/machines/.

7 Susan Sontag, "The Pornographic Imagination" (1967), in Sontag, *Styles of Radical Will* (New York: Picador, 2002), 35–73; Andrea Dworkin, *Pornography: Men Possessing Women* (New York: Penguin, 1979); Linda Williams, *Hardcore: Power, Pleasure, and the Frenzy of the Visual* (Berkeley: University of California Press, 1989); Elizabeth Grosz, "Naked," in *The Prosthetic Impulse: From a Posthuman Present to a Biocultural Future*, edited by Marquard Smith and Joanne Morra (Cambridge, Mass.: MIT Press, 2006), 197.

8 Susanna Paasonen, *Carnal Resonance: Affect and Online Pornography* (Cambridge, Mass.: MIT Press, 2011), 75.

9 Susanna Paasonen, "Repetition and Hyperbole: The Gendered Choreographies of Heteroporn," in *Everyday Pornography*, edited by Karen Boyle (London: Routledge, 2010), 68.

10 Paasonen, *Carnal Resonance*, 159.

11 Sarah Schaschek, *Pornography and Seriality: The Culture of Producing Pleasure* (New York: Palgrave Macmillan, 2014), 7.

12 Ibid., 11.

13 Schaschek expands pornography's seriality beyond the genre to include the production and reception of the industry and the field of study; ibid., 3.

14 Ibid., 11.

15 Diana Devoe as quoted in "Black/White: Sex, Race, & Profit," *SexTV*, aired September 2006, www.sextelevision.net.

16 Homi Bhabha, *The Location of Culture* (New York: Routledge, 1994), 95.

17 Judith Butler, *Gender Trouble: Feminism and the Subversion of Identity* (New York: Routledge, 1990), 191, italics in original.

18 Ibid, 140.

19 Butler writes, "Genders can be neither true nor false, neither real nor apparent, neither original nor derived"; ibid., 192–193.

20 Walter Benjamin, *Illuminations*, edited by Hannah Arendt, translated by Harry Zohn (New York: Schocken, 1968), 224.

21 Huey Copeland and Krista Thompson, "Perpetual Returns: New World Slavery and the Matter of the Visual," *Representations* 113, no. 1 (2011): 1–15.

22 Jerrold R. Brandell and Shoshana Ringel, eds., *Trauma: Contemporary Directions in Theory, Practice and Research* (London: Sage, 2011).

23 Freud, "Beyond the Pleasure Principle," in *The Freud Reader*, edited by Peter Gay (New York: W. W. Norton, 1989), 603.

24 Ibid., 601.

25 Ibid.

26 Ibid.

27 Meg Barker and Darren Langdridge, "Silencing Accounts of Silenced Sexualities," in *Secrecy and Silence in the Research Process: Feminist Reflections*, edited by Róisín Ryan Flood and Rosalind Gill (London: Routledge, 2010), 67–80.

28 Sharon Holland, *The Erotic Life of Racism* (Durham, N.C.: Duke University Press, 2012), 52.

29 Cathy Caruth, "Trauma and Experience: Introduction," in *Trauma: Explorations in Memory*, edited by Cathy Caruth (Baltimore, Md.: Johns Hopkins University Press, 1995), 5.

30 Ibid.

31 Ibid., 9.

32 Snead, "Repetition as a Figure of Black Culture," 74.

33 Caruth, "Trauma and Experience," 8.

34 Gilles Deleuze, *Difference and Repetition*, translated by Paul Patton (New York: Columbia University Press, 1994), 18.

BIBLIOGRAPHY

Abrams, Abiola. "Intimacy Intervention: My Husband Uses Racial Slurs during Sex." *Essence Magazine*, April 9, 2013. Accessed September 7, 2013. http://www.essence.com/2013/04/08/intimacy-intervention-my-husband-uses-racial-slurs-during-sex/.

Abrams, Bryan. "The King of Kink: An Interview with Bondage-Porn Power Player Peter Acworth." *Details*, September 20, 2010. http://www.details.com/sex-relationships/porn-and-perversions/201009/king-of-kink-peter-acworth-bondage-porn-empire.

Acworth, Peter. "Why Kink Matters." *Huffington Post*, January 14, 2013. http://www.huffingtonpost.com/peter-acworth/why-kink-matters_b_2460100.html.

Ahmed, Sarah. "Feminist Killjoys (and Other Willful Subjects)." *S&F Online* 8, no. 3 (2010). http://sfonline.barnard.edu/polyphonic/ahmed_01.htm.

Alexander, Elizabeth. "'Can You be BLACK and Look at This?': Reading Rodney King Videos." *Public Culture* 7 (1994): 77–94.

Alpert, Hollis, and Arthur Knight. "The History of Sex in Cinema: Part Seventeen, the Stag Film." *Playboy*, November 1967, 154–159, 170–189.

Althusser, Louis. *Lenin and Philosophy and Other Essays* (New York: Monthly Review Press, 1971). (Ch03)

Amoah, Jewel D. "Back on the Auction Block: A Discussion of Black Women and Pornography." *National Black Law Journal*. 14, no. 2 (1997): 204–221.

AMOIS. "Handkerchief Codes: Interlude II." In *Coming to Power: Writings and Graphics on Lesbian S/M*, edited by members of SAMOIS, a Lesbian/Feminist S/M Organization. Boston: Alyson Publications, 1981.

Archibald, Timothy. *Sex Machines: Photographs and Interviews*. Carrboro, N.C.: Daniel, 2005.

Attorney General's Commission on Pornography. *Attorney General's Commission on Pornography: Final Report*. 2 vols. Washington, D.C.: U.S. Department of Justice, 1986.

Attwood, Feona. "Introduction: From Social Problem to Cultural Practice." In *Porn.Com: Making Sense of Online Pornography*, edited by Feona Attwood, 1–13. New York: Peter Lang, 2010.

Bailey, Cameron. "Virtual Skin: Articulating Race in Cyberspace." In *Immersed in Technology: Art and Virtual Environments*, edited by Mary Anne Moser and Douglas MacLeod, 29–50. Cambridge, Mass.: MIT Press, 1996.

Balsamo, Ann. *Technologies of the Gendered Body: Reading Cyborg Women*. Durham, N.C.: Duke University, Press, 1996.

Banks, Ralph Richard. *Is Marriage for White People? How the African American Marriage Decline Affects Everyone.* New York: Dutton, 2011.

Bannion, Chloe. "Retailers: Diversify to Maximize," *AVN*, January 1, 2006. Accessed April 1, 2009, http://business.avn.com/articles/24691.html.

Barker, Meg. "Consent Is a Grey Area? A Comparison of Understandings of Consent in *Fifty Shades of Grey* and on the BDSM Blogosphere." *Sexualities* 16, no. 8 (2013): 896–914.

Barker, Meg, Camelia Gupta, and Alessandra Iantaffi. "The Power of Play: The Potentials and Pitfalls in Healing Narratives of BDSM." In *Safe, Sane and Consensual: Contemporary Perspectives on Sadomasochism*, edited by Darren Langdridge and Meg Barker, 197–216. Basingstoke: Palgrave Macmillan, 2007.

———. "Kinky Clients, Kinky Counseling? The Challenges and Potentials of BDSM." In *Feeling Queer or Queer Feelings? Radical Approaches to Counseling Sex, Sexualities and Genders*, edited by Lyndsey Moon, 106–124. London: Routledge, 2008.

Barker, Meg, and Darren Langdridge. "Silencing Accounts of Silenced Sexualities." In *Secrecy and Silence in the Research Process: Feminist Reflections*, edited by Róisín Ryan Flood and Rosalind Gill, 67–79. London: Routledge, 2010.

Barker, Meg, and Ani Ritchie. "Feminist SM: A Contradiction in Terms or a Way of Challenging Traditional Gendered Dynamics through Sexual Practice?" In *Lesbian & Gay Psychology Review* 6, no. 3 (2005): 227–239.

Barthes, Roland. *Mythologies.* New York: Noonday Press, 1992.

Bartky, Sandra Lee. *Femininity and Domination: Studies in the Phenomenology of Oppression.* New York: Routledge, 1990.

Basu, Biman. *The Commerce of Peoples: Sadomasochism and African American Literature.* Lanham, Md.: Lexington Books, 2012.

Bataille, Georges. *Eroticism: Death and Sensuality.* San Francisco: City Lights, 1986.

Bazin, André. "The Ontology of the Photographic Image." In *Classic Essays on Photography*, edited by Alan Trachtenberg, 237–244. New Haven, Conn.: Leete's Island Books, 1980.

Bean, Joseph W. *Leathersex.* San Francisco: Daedalus, 1994.

———. *Leathersex Q & A: Questions about Leathersex and the Leathersex Lifestyle Answered.* San Francisco: Daedalus, 1996.

Beauvoir, Simone de. "Must We Burn Sade?" In *The Marquis de Sade*, edited by Paul Dinnage, 9–82. Translated by Annette Michelson. New York: Grove Press, 1953.

Beckmann, Andrea. "Deconstructing Myths: The Social Construction of 'Sadomasochism' versus 'Subjugated Knowledges' of the Practitioners of Consensual 'SM.'" *Journal of Criminal Justice and Popular Culture* 8, no. 2 (2001): 66–95.

———. "'Sexual Rights' and 'Sexual Responsibilities' within Consensual 'S/M' Practice." In *Making Sense of Sexual Consent*, edited by Mark Cowling and Paul Reynolds, 195–208. Ashgate: Aldershot, England, 2004.

———. *The Social Construction of Sexuality and Perversion: Deconstructing Sadomasochism.* London: Palgrave MacMillan, 2009.

Bell, Shannon. "Feminist Ejaculations." In *The Hysterical Male: New Feminist Theory*, edited by Arthur and Marilouise Kroker, 155–169. London: Macmillan, 1991.

———. "Liquid Fire: Female Ejaculation & Fast Feminism." In *Jane Sexes It Up: True Confessions of Feminist Desire*, edited by Merri Lisa Johnson, 327–345. New York: Four Walls Eight Windows, 2002.

Benjamin, Walter. *Illuminations*. Edited by Hannah Arendt. Translated by Harry Zohn. New York: Schocken, 1968.

Beres, Melanie A. "'Spontaneous' Sexual Consent: An Analysis of Sexual Consent Literature." *Feminism & Psychology* 17, no. 1 (2007): 101–102.

Berlant, Lauren, and Michael Warner. "Sex in Public." *Critical Inquiry* 24, no. 2 (1998): 547–566.

Bernardi, Daniel. "Cyborgs in Cyberspace: White Pride, Pedophilic Pornography, and Donna Haraway's Manifesto." In *Reality Squared: Television Discourse and the Real*, edited by James Friedman, 155–181. New Brunswick, N.J.: Rutgers University Press.

Bernardi, Daniel. "Interracial Joysticks: Pornography's Web of Racist Attractions." In *Pornography: Film and Culture*, edited by Peter Lehman, 220–243. New Brunswick, N.J.: Rutgers University Press, 2006.

———. "Racism and Pornography: Evidence, Paradigms, and Publishing." In *Cinema Journal* 46, no. 2 (2007): 116–121.

Bernasconi, Robert. "Crossed Lines in the Racialization Process: Race as a Border Concept." *Research in Phenomenology* 42, no. 2 (2012): 206–228.

———. "The Policing of Race Mixing: The Place of Biopower within the History of Racisms." *Bioethical Inquiry* 7, no. 2 (2010): 205–216.

Bernasconi, Robert, and Kristie Dotson, eds., *Race, Hybridity, and Miscegenation*. London: Thoemmes Continuum, 2005.

Bernasconi, Robert, and Tommy L. Lott, eds., *The Idea of Race*. Indianapolis: Hackett Publishing Company, 2000.

Bersani, Leo. "Is the Rectum a Grave?" *AIDS: Cultural Analysis/Cultural Activism* 43 (Winter 1987): 197–222.

Bernstein, Elizabeth. *Temporarily Yours: Intimacy, Authenticity, and the Commerce of Sex*. Chicago: University of Chicago Press, 2007.

Bernstein, Elizabeth, and Laurie Schaffner, eds. *Regulating Sex: The Politics of Intimacy and Identity*. New York: Routledge, 2005.

Bhabha, Homi. *The Location of Culture*. New York: Routledge, 1994.

Black/White: Sex, Race, & Profit, DVD. Produced by SexTV, Sep. 2006, Canada. www.sextelevision.net.

Blake, Bobby, with John R. Gordon. *My Life in Porn: The Bobby Blake Story*. Philadelphia, Pa.: Running Press, 2008.

Blass, Alan. *Difference and Disavowal: The Trauma of Eros*. Stanford, Calif.: Stanford University Press, 2002.

Blue, Violet. "Racist Porn and the Recession /Violet Blue: Nothing Is Recession Proof, Especially Not Your Tired Old Racist Porn." *SFgate*, February 12, 2009. Accessed

July 2, 2009, http://www.sfgate.com/living/article/Racist-Porn-and-the-Recession-Violet-Blue-2464322.php.

Brandell, Jerrold R., and Shoshana Ringel, eds. *Trauma: Contemporary Directions in Theory, Practice, and Research*. London: Sage, 2011.

Brekke, Dan. "'Revenge Porn' Site Operator Arrested: YouGot-Posted, and HeGotBusted." KQED News, December 10, 2013. Accessed April 24, 2013, http://blogs.kqed.org/newsfix/2013/12/10/revenge-porn-site-operator-arrested-ugotposted-and-hegotbusted/.

Breslaw, Anna. "This Dad Lives a Double Life as a Porn Star." *Cosmopolitan*, March 10, 2014. Accessed June 16, 2014, http://www.cosmopolitan.com/sex-love/advice/shane-diesel-dildo-model.

Brueckner, Hannah, and Natalie Nitsche. "Opting Out of the Family? Social Change in Racial Equality in Family Formations Patterns and Marriage Outcomes among Highly Educated Women." Paper presented at the annual meeting of the American Sociological Association, San Francisco, California, August 8, 2009.

Bright, Susie. "Inter-racial and Black Videos." Unpublished paper in author's possession.

Brooks, Siobhan. *Unequal Desires: Race and Erotic Capital in the Stripping Industry*. Albany, N.Y.: SUNY Press, 2010.

Brown, Elsa Barkley. "Imaging Lynching: African American Women, Communities of Struggle, and Collective Memory." In *African American Women Speak Out on Anita Hill-Clarence Thomas*, edited by Geneva Smitherman, 100–124. Detroit: Wayne State University Press, 1995.

Brownmiller, Susan. *Against Our Will: Men, Women, and Rape*. New York, Simon & Shuster, 1975.

Butler, Judith. *Bodies that Matter: On the Discursive Limits of Sex*. New York: Routledge, 1993.

———. *Gender Trouble: Feminism and the Subversion of Identity*. New York: Routledge, 1990.

———. "Lesbian S & M: The Politics of Dis-illusion." In *Against Sadomasochism: A Radical Feminist Analysis*, edited by Robin Ruth Linden, Darlene R. Pagano, Diana E. Russell, and Susan Leigh Star, 169–175. East Palo Alto, Calif.: Frog in the Well, 1982.

Cable, Umayyah. "Let's Talk about Pornography: An Interview with Shine Louise Houston." Feministe, April 7, 2009. Accessed April 5, 2012, http://www.feministe.us/blog/archives/2009/04/07/lets-talk-about-pornography-an-interview-with-shine-louise-houston/.

Califia, Pat. "Feminism and Sadomasochism." *Heresies* 12 (1981): 30–34.

———. *Macho Sluts*. Little Sister's Classics #10. Vancouver, B.C.: Arsenal Pulp Press, 2009.

———. "A Personal View of the History of the Lesbian S/M Community and Movement in San Francisco." In *Coming to Power: Writings and Graphics on Lesbian S/M*, edited by members of SAMOIS, a Lesbian/Feminist S/M Organization, 243–281. Boston: Alyson Publications, 1981.

Carby, Hazel V. *Reconstructing Womanhood: The Emergence of the Afro-American Woman Novelist*. Oxford: Oxford University Press, 1987.

Carpio, Glenda R. *Laughing Fit to Kill: Black Humor and the Fictions of Slavery*. London: Oxford University Press, 2008.

Caruth, Cathy. "Trauma and Experience: Introduction." In *Trauma: Explorations in Memory*, edited by Cathy Caruth. Baltimore, Md.: Johns Hopkins University Press, 1995.

Chancer, Lynn S. *Sadomasochism in Everyday Life: The Dynamics of Power and Powerlessness*. New Brunswick, N.J.: Rutgers University Press, 1992.

———. "From Pornography to Sadomasochism: Reconciling Feminist Differences." *Annals of the American Academy of Political and Social Science* 571 (September 2000): 77–88.

Chun, Wendy Hui Kyong. "Introduction: Race and/as Technology; or, How to Do Things to Race." *Camera Obscura* 70, 24, no. 1 (2009): 7–35.

Coates, Ta-Nehisi. "The Case for Reparations." *The Atlantic*, May 21 2014. Accessed June 1, 2014, http://www.theatlantic.com/features/archive/2014/05/the-case-for-reparations/361631/.

Cobb, Jasmine Nichole. "Directed by Himself: Steve McQueen's *12 Years a Slave*." *American Literary History* 26, no. 2 (2014): 339–346.

Cohen, Cathy. "Deviance as Resistance: A New Research Agenda for the Study of Black Politics." *Du Bois Review* 1, no. 1 (2004): 27–45.

———. "Punks, Bulldaggers, and Welfare Queens: The Radical Potential of Queer Politics?" *GLQ: A Journal of Lesbian and Gay Studies* 3, no. 4 (1997): 437–465.

Coleman, Beth. "Race as Technology." *Camera Obscura* 70, 24, no. 1 (2009): 177–207.

Collins, Lisa Gail. *The Art of History: African American Women Artists Engage the Past*. New Brunswick, N.J.: Rutgers University Press, 2002.

Collins, Patricia Hill. *Black Feminist Thought: Knowledge, Consciousness and the Politics of Empowerment*. London: Routledge, 1990.

Copeland, Huey. *Bound to Appear: Art Slavery, and the Site of Blackness in Multicultural America*. Chicago: University of Chicago Press, 2013.

———"In the Wake of the Negress." In *Modern Women: Women Artists at the Museum of Modern Art*, edited by Cornelia Butler and Alexandra Schwartz, 480–497. New York: The Museum of Modern Art, 2010.

Copeland, Huey, and Krista Thompson. "Perpetual Returns: New World Slavery and the Matter of the Visual." *Representations* 113, no. 1 (2011): 1–15.

Cornell, Drucilla, ed. *Feminism & Pornography*. Oxford University Press, 2000.

Cowan, Gloria, and Robin Campbell. "Racism and Sexism in Interracial Pornography." *Psychology of Women Quarterly* 18 (1994): 323–38.

Cowling, Mark, and Paul Reynolds, eds. *Making Sense of Sexual Consent*. Ashgate: Aldershot, England, 2004.

Cruz, Ariane. "Gettin' *Down Home with the Neelys*: Gastro-Porn & Televisual Performances of Gender, Race & Sexuality." *Women and Performance* 23, no. 3 (2013): 323–349.

———. "Mis(playing) Blackness: Black Female Sexuality in *The Misadventures of Awkward Black Girl*." In *Contemporary Black Female Sexualities*, edited by Joanne M. Braxton and Trimiko Melancon, 73–88. New Brunswick, N.J.: Rutgers University Press, 2015.

———. "Pornography: A Black Feminist Woman Scholar's Reconciliation." In *The Feminist Porn Book: The Politics of Producing Pleasure*, edited by Tristan Taormino, Constance Penley, Celine Shimizu, and Mireille Miller-Young, 215–227. New York: The Feminist Press at the City University of New York, 2013.

———. "Sisters Are Doin' It for Themselves: Black Women and the New Pornography." In *Pornography: Contemporary Perspectives*, edited by Lindsay Coleman and Jacob M. Held, 225–258. New York: Rowman & Littlefield, 2014.

Culler, Jonathan. *Ferdinand de Saussure*. Rev. ed. Ithaca, N.Y.: Cornell University Press, 1986.

Daddy, Scott. "Race Play." *Edge Magazine*, April 5, 2010. Accessed September 7, 2010, http://www.edgeboston.com/index.php?ch=columnists&sc=scott_daddy&sc3=&id=104189&pf=1.

Daily, Jack. "Chatsworth Pictures Puts You in the Cuckold Seat." *AVN*, June 10, 2009. Accessed July 18, 2009, http://business.avn.com/articles/video/Chatsworth-Pictures-Puts-You-in-the-Cuckold-Seat-342969.html.

Davis, Adrienne. "Bad Girls of Art and Law: Abjection, Power, and Sexuality Exceptionalism in (Kara Walker's) Art and (Janet Halley's) Law." *Yale Journal of Law and Feminism* (June 2011): 102–154.

———. "'Don't Let Nobody Bother Yo' Principle': The Sexual Economy of Slavery." In *Sister Circle: Black Women and Work*, edited by Sharon Harley and The Black Women Work Collective, 103–127. New Brunswick, N.J.: Rutgers University Press, 2002.

Dean, Tim. *Unlimited Intimacy: Reflections on the Subculture of Barebacking*. Chicago: University of Chicago Press, 2009.

DeFrantz, Thomas F., and Anita Gonzalez, eds., *Black Performance Theory*. Durham, N.C.: Duke University Press.

Delany, Samuel. *Shorter Views: Queer Thoughts and the Politics of the Paraliterary*. Hanover, N.H.: Wesleyan University Press, 1999.

———. *Times Square Red, Times Square Blue*. New York: New York University Press, 1999.

Deleuze, Gilles. "Coldness and Cruelty." In Deleuze, *Masochism*, 9–138. Translated by Jean McNeil. New York: Zone Books, 1991.

———. *Difference and Repetition*. Translated by Paul Patton. New York: Columbia University Press, 1994.

Derrida, Jacques. *Limited Inc*. Translated by Samuel Weber. Evanston, Ill.: Northwestern University Press, 1988.

———. *Margins of Philosophy*. Translated by Alan Bass. Chicago: University of Chicago Press, 1982.

Di Laurio, Al, and Gerald Rabkin. *Dirty Movies: An Illustrated History of the Stag Film, 1915–1970*. New York: Chelsea House, 1976.

Dines, Gail. "King Kong and the White Woman: Hustler Magazine and the Demonization of Black Masculinity." *Violence against Women* 4, no. 3 (1998): 291–307.

———. *Pornland: How Porn Has Hijacked Our Sexuality*. Boston: Beacon, 2010.

———. "The White Man's Burden: Gonzo Pornography and the Construction of Black Masculinity." *Yale Journal of Law and Feminism* 18, no. 1 (2006): 283–297.

Dines, Gail, Robert Jensen, and Ann Russo, *Pornography: The Production and Consumption of Inequality*. New York: Routledge, 1998.

Doane, Mary Ann. *Femmes Fatales: Feminism, Film Theory, Psychoanalysis*. New York: Routledge, 1991.

Dollimore, Jonathan. *Sexual Dissidence: Augustine to Wilde, Freud to Foucault*. Oxford: Clarendon Press, 1991.

Donnerstein, Edward, Daniel Linz, and Steven Penrod. *The Question of Pornography: Research Findings and Policy Implications*. New York: Free Press, 1987.

Downing, Lisa. "Perversion, Historicity, Ethics." In *Perversion: Psychoanalytic Perspectives/Perspectives on Psychoanalysis*, edited by Dany Nobus and Lisa Downing. London: Karnac, 2006.

Du Bois, W. E. B. "Criterion of Negro Art," *Crisis* 32 (1926): 296–98.

DuCille, Ann. "'Othered' Matters: Reconceptualizing Dominance and Difference in the History of Sexuality in America." *Journal of the History of Sexuality* 1, no. 1 (1990): 102–127.

———. *Skin Trade*. Cambridge, Mass.: Harvard University Press, 1996.

Dunning, Stefanie. *Queer in Black and White*. Bloomington: Indiana University Press, 2009.

Dworkin, Andrea. *Intercourse*. London: Arrow, 1988.

———. *Our Blood: Prophecies and Discourse on Sexual Politics*. New York: Harper & Row, 1976.

———. *Pornography: Men Possessing Women*. New York: Penguin, 1979.

Dyer, Richard. *White: Essays on Race and Culture*. London: Routledge, 1997.

Easton, Dossie, and Janet W. Hardy. *The New Bottoming Book*. Emeryville, Calif.: Greenery Press, 2001.

———. *Radical Ecstasy*. Emeryville, Calif.: Greenery Press, 2004.

Edelman Benjamin. "Red Light States: Who Buys Adult Entertainment?" *Journal of Economic Perspectives* 23, no. 1 (2009): 209–220.

Elias, James, Veronica Diehl Elias, Vern L. Bullough, Gwen Brewer, Jeffrey J. Douglas, and Will Jarvis, eds. *Porn 101: Eroticism Pornography and the First Amendment*. New York: Prometheus Books, 1999.

Ellis, Havelock. *Studies in the Psychology of Sex*. Vol. 1. New York: Random House, 1942.

Escoffier, Jeffrey. "Gay for Pay: Straight Men and the Making of Gay Pornography." *Qualitative Sociology* 26, no. 4 (2003): 531–555.

Eugenios, Jillian. "Chatting Up Shine Louise Houston." *Curve Magazine*, September 20, 2011. Accessed March 5, 2012, http://www.curvemag.com/Curve-Magazine/ Web-Articles-2011/Chatting-up-Shine-Louise-Houston/.

Everett, Anna Everett, ed. *Learning Race and Ethnicity: Youth and Digital Media*. Cambridge, Mass.: MIT Press, 2008.

Eyerman, Ron. *Cultural Trauma: Slavery and the Formation of an African American Identity*. Cambridge: Cambridge University Press, 2001.

Faludi, Susan. "The Money Shot." *The New Yorker*, October 30, 1995.

Fanon, Frantz. *Black Skin, White Masks*. New York: Grove Press, 1952.

Findlay, Heather. "Freud's Fetishism and the Lesbian Dildo Debates." *Feminist Studies* 18, no. 3 (1992): 563–579.

Fischel, Joseph. "Against Nature, against Consent: A Sexual Politics of Debility." *Differences: A Journal of Feminist Cultural Studies* 24, no. 1 (2013): 56–103.

Fisher, Gary. *Gary in Your Pocket: Stories and Notebooks of Gary Fischer*. Edited by Eve Kosofsky Sedgwick. Durham, N.C.: Duke University Press, 1996.

Flanagan, Mary, and Austin Booth. *Reload: Rethinking Women & Cyberculture*. Cambridge: MIT Press, 2002.

Forna, Aminatta. "Pornography and Racism: Sexualizing Oppression and Inciting Hatred." In *Pornography: Women, Violence, and Civil Liberties*, edited by Catherin Itzin, 102–112. Oxford: Oxford University Press, 1992.

Foucault, Michel. *Ethics: Subjectivity and Truth*. Essential Works of Foucault, 1954–1984, Vol. 1. New York: The New Press, 1997

———. *The History of Sexuality*. Vol. 1, *An Introduction*. New York: Vintage Books, 1990.

Francis, Terri. "Looking Sharp: Performance, Genre, and Questioning History in *Django Unchained*." *Transitions* 112 (2013): 32–45.

Freud, Sigmund. "An Autobiographical Study." In *The Freud Reader*, edited by Peter Gay, 3–43. New York: W. W. Norton, 1989.

———. *The Basic Writings of Sigmund Freud*. Translated and Edited by. A. A. Brill. New York: Modern Library, 1938.

———. *Case Histories I: "Dora" and "Little Hans."* Translated by Alix and James Strachey. Harmondsworth: Penguin, 1983.

———. "The Economic Problem of Masochism." (1924). In *The Standard Edition of the Complete Psychological Works of Sigmund Freud*. Vol. 19, The Ego and the Id *and Other Works (1923–1925)*. Translated by J. Strachey. London: The Hogarth Press, 1961.

———. "Infantile Sexuality." In *The Basic Writings of Sigmund Freud*, translated and edited by A. A. Brill, 548–571. 1938; repr., New York: Random House, 1995.

———. "Three Essays on the Theory of Sexuality." In *The Freud Reader*, edited by Peter Gay, 239–292. New York: W.W. Norton & Company, 1989.

Gaines, Jane M. "Competing Glances: Who Is Reading Robert Mapplethorpe's Black Book?" *New Formations* 16 (Spring 1992): 24–39.

———. *Fire & Desire: Mixed-Race Movies in the Silent Era*. Chicago: University of Chicago Press, 2001.

———. "Machines that Make the Body Do Things." In *More Dirty Looks: Gender, Pornography and Power*, edited by Pamela Church Gibson, 31–44. 2nd ed. London: British Film Institute, 2004.

Gaines, Kevin K. *Uplifting the Race: Black Leadership, Politics, and Culture in the Twentieth Century*. Chapel Hill: University of North Carolina Press, 1996.

Gardner, Tracey A. "Racism and the Women's Movement." In *Take Back the Night*, edited by Laura Lederer, 105–114. New York: William and Morrow, 1980.

Gates, Henry Louis, Jr. *The Signifying Monkey: A Theory of African-American Literary Criticism*. Oxford University Press, 1988.

———. "'An Unfathomable Place': A Conversation with Quentin Tarantino about *Django Unchained*." *Transition* 112 (2013): 47–66.

Gebhard, Paul H. "Fetishism and Sadomasochism." In *Dynamics of Deviant Sexuality: Scientific Proceedings of the American Academy of Psychoanalysis*, edited by Jules Masserman, 71–80. New York: Grune & Stratton, 1969.

———. "Sadomasochism." In *S & M: Studies in Dominance & Submission*, edited by Thomas S. Weinberg, 41–45. New York: Prometheus, 1995.

Gelerman, S. M. "The Quiet Storm: Newly Renamed, HushMoney Takes Interracial Porn to New Heights." *AVN*, May 9, 2007. Accessed March 1, 2009, http://business. avn.com/articles/video/The-Quiet-Storm-Newly-renamed-HushMoney-takes-interracial-porn-to-new-heights-26686.html.

Gilliland, Amy. "Women's Experiences of Female Ejaculation." *Sexuality & Culture* 13, no. 3 (2009): 121–134.

Gilroy, Paul. *Against Race: Imagining Political Culture beyond the Color Line*. Cambridge, Mass.: Harvard University Press, 2000.

Gobineau, Arthur. *The Inequality of Human Races*. Translated by Adrian Collins. 1853; repr., New York: G. P. Putman, 1915.

González, Jennifer. "Envisioning Cyborg Bodies: Notes from Current Research." In *The Cyborg Handbook*, edited by Chris Hables Gray, 267–279. New York: Routledge, 1995.

———. "Morphologies: Race as a Visual Technology." In *Only Skin Deep: Changing Visions of the American Self*, edited by Coco Fusco and Brian Wallis, 379–393. New York: Harry N. Abrams, 2003.

———. "Race, Secrecy, and Digital Art Practice." *Camera Obscura* 70, vol. 24, no. 1 (2009): 37–65.

Griffin, Susan. *Pornography and Silence: Culture's Revenge against Nature*. New York: Harper & Row, 1981.

Gossett, Thomas F. *Race: The History of an Idea in America*. Oxford: Oxford University Press, 1963.

Grosz, Elizabeth. "Naked." In *The Prosthetic Impulse: From a Posthuman Present to a Biocultural Future*, edited by Marquard Smith and Joanne Morra, 187–202. Cambridge, Mass.: MIT Press, 2006.

———. *Space, Time, and Perversion: Essays on the Politics of Bodies*. New York: Routledge, 1995.

Guerrero, Ed. "The Slavery Motif in Recent Popular Cinema." *Jump Cut: A Review of Contemporary Media* 33 (February 1988): 52–59.

Halberstam, Judith, and Ira Livingston. "Introduction: Posthuman Bodies." In *Posthuman Bodies, edited by Judith Halberstam and Ira Livingston*. Bloomington: Indiana University Press, 1995.

Hall, Stuart, ed., *Representation: Cultural and Signifying Practices*. London: Sage Publications, 1997.

Halttunen, Karen. "Humanitarianism and the Pornography of Pain in Anglo-American Culture." *American Historical Review* 110, no. 2 (1995): 303–334.

Hammers, Corie. "Corporeality, Sadomasochism, and Sexual Trauma." *Body & Society* 20, no. 2 (2014): 68–90.

Hamming, Jeanne E. "Dildonics, Dykes, and the Detachable Machine." *European Journal of Women's Studies* 8, no. 3 (2001): 329–341.

Hammonds, Evelynn M. "Black (W)holes and the Geometry of Black Female Sexuality." *Differences* 6, nos. 2–3 (1994): 127–45.

———. "Toward a Genealogy of Black Female Sexuality: The Problematic of Silence." In *Feminist Genealogies, Colonial Legacies*, edited by M. Jacqui Alexander and Chandra Talpade Mohanty, 170–182. New York: Routledge, 1997.

Hanna, Cheryl. "Sex Is Not a Sport: Consent and Violence in Criminal Law." *Boston College Law Review* 42, no. 2 (2001): 239–290.

Hansen, Mark B. *Bodies in Code: Interfaces with Digital Media*. New York: Routledge, 2006.

Haraway, Donna. *Simians, Cyborgs, and Women: The Reinvention of Nature*. New York: Routledge, 1991.

Harrington, Lee. *Sacred Kink: The Eightfold Paths of BDSM and Beyond*. Lynwood, Wash.: Mystic Productions, 2009.

———. *Shibari You Can Use: Japanese Rope Bondage and Erotic Macramé*. Lynnwood, Wash.: Mystic Productions, 2007.

Harris, Cheryl. "Whiteness as Property." *Harvard Law Review* 106, no. 8 (1993): 1707–1791.

Harris, Michael D. *Colored Pictures: Race and Visual Representation*. Chapel Hill, N.C.: University of North Carolina Press, 2003.

Harris, Seale. *Woman's Surgeon: The Life of J. Marion Sims*. New York, Macmillan Company, 1950.

Harris-Perry, Melissa. *Sister Citizenship: Shame, Stereotypes, and Black Women in America*. New Haven, Conn.: Yale University Press, 2011.

Hart, Lynda. *Between the Body and the Flesh: Performing Sadomasochism*. New York: Columbia University Press, 1998.

Hartman, Saidiya. *Scenes of Subjection: Terror, Slavery, and Self-Making in Nineteenth-Century America*. London: Oxford University Press, 1997.

Hasslet, Tim. "Interview with Hortense Spillers." *Black Cultural Studies*, February 4, 1998.

Hayles, N. Katherine. *How We Became Posthuman: Virtual Bodies in Cybernetics, Literature, and Informatics*. Chicago: University of Chicago Press, 1999.

———. "Refiguring the Posthuman." *Comparative Literature Studies* 4, no. 3 (2004): 311–316.

Hernandez, Daisy. "Playing with Race: On the Edge of Racy Sex, BDSM Excites Some and Reviles Others." *Colorlines: News for Action*, December 21, 2004. Accessed June 26, 2011. http://colorlines.com/archives/2004/12/playing_with_race.html.

Heineman, Elizabeth D. "Sexuality and Nazism: The Doubly Unspeakable?" *Journal of the History of Sexuality* 11, nos. 1–2 (2002): 22–66.

Heller, Steven. *The Swastika: Symbol beyond Redemption?* New York: Allworth Press, 2000.

Higginbotham, Evelyn Brooks. *Righteous Discontent: The Women's Movement in the Black Baptist Church, 1880–1920*. Cambridge, Mass.: Harvard University Press, 1993.

Hine, Darlene Clark. "Rape and the Inner Lives of Black Women in the Middle West." *Signs* 14, no. 4 (1989): 912–920.

Holland, Sharon. *The Erotic Life of Racism*. Durham, N.C.: Duke University Press, 2012.

hooks, bell. *Black Looks: Race and Representation*. Boston: South End Press, 1992.

"Interview with Audre Lorde: Audre Lorde and Susan Leigh Star." In *Against Sadomasochism: A Radical Feminist Analysis*, edited by Robin Ruth Linden, Darlene R. Pagano, Diana E. Russell, and Susan Leigh Star, 66–71. East Palo Alto, Calif.: Frog in the Well, 1982.

Irvine, Janice M. *Disorders of Desire: Sexuality and Gender in Modern American Sexology*. Philadelphia: Temple University Press, 2005.

Jack. "Negro Porn Recession Proof, Claims AVN." *The Sword*, February 5, 2009. Accessed July 2, 2009, http://thesword.com/black-cocks-recession-proof-claims-avn.html.

Jacobs, Katrien. *Netporn: DIY Web Culture and Sexual Politics*. New York: Rowman & Littlefield, 2007.

JanMohamed, Abdul. "The Economy of Manichean Allegory: The Function of Racial Difference in Colonialist Literature." *Critical Inquiry* 12, no. 1 (1985): 59–87.

———. "Sexuality on/of the Racial Border: Foucault, Wright and the Articulation of 'Racialized Sexuality.'" In *Discourses of Sexuality: From Aristotle to AIDS*, edited by Donna Stanton, 94–116. Ann Arbor: University of Michigan Press, 1992.

Jardin, Xeni. "The Sex Machines Next Door." *Wired.com*, November 16, 2005, http://archive.wired.com/culture/lifestyle/news/2005/11/69576.

Jeffreys, Sheila. *The Lesbian Heresy: A Feminist Perspective on the Lesbian Sexual Revolution*. London: The Women's Press, 1994.

———. "Sadomasochism: The Erotic Cult of Fascism." In *The Lesbian Heresy: A Feminist Perspective on the Lesbian Sexual Revolution*. North Melbourne: Spinifex, 1993.

Jewell, K. Sue. *From Mammy to Miss America and Beyond: Cultural Images and the Shaping of US Social Policy*. London: Routledge, 1993.

Johnson, E. Patrick. *Appropriating Blackness: Performance and the Politics of Authenticity*. Durham, N.C.: Duke University Press, 2003.

———ed. *Black Queer Studies: A Critical Anthology*. Durham, N.C.: Duke University Press, 2005.

Johnson, Eithne. "The 'Coloscopic' Film and the 'Beaver' Film: Scientific and Porno-graphic Scenes of Female Sexual Responsiveness." In *Swinging Single: Representing Sexuality in the 1960s*, edited by Hilary Radner and Moya Luckett, 301–324. Min-neapolis: University of Minnesota Press, 1999.

Johnson, Jill. *Lesbian Nation: The Feminist Solution*. New York: Simon and Schuster, 1973.

Johnson, Viola. "Playing with Racial Stereotypes: The Love That Dare Not Speak Its Name." *Leatherweb*, 1994. Accessed April 5, 2013. http://www.leatherweb.com/race-playh.htm.

Johnson, V. M. *To Love, to Obey, to Serve: Diary of an Old Guard Slave*. Fairfield, CT: Mystic Rose Books, 1999.

Jones, Arthur. *Wade in the Water: The Wisdom of the Spirituals*. 3rd ed. New York: Orbis Books, 1993.

Jones, Feminista. "[TALK LIKE SEX] Race Play Ain't for Everyone." *Ebony*, July 23, 2013. Accessed August 4, 2013, http://www.ebony.com/love-sex/talk-like-sex-race-play-aint-for-everyone-911#axzz2uMawpRG4.

Jones, Gayl. *Corregidora*. Boston: Beacon Press, 1975.

Julien, Isaac. "Confessions of a Snow Queen: Notes on the Making of *The Attendant*." *Critical Quarterly* 36, no. 1 (1994): 120–126.

Jordan, June. "Poem about My Rights" (1989). In *Directed by Desire: The Collected Poems of June Jordan*. Port Townsend, Wash.: Copper Canyon Press, 2007.

Julien, Isaac. "Confessions of a Snow Queen: Notes on the Making of *The Attendant*." *Critical Quarterly* 36, no. 1 (1994): 120–26.

Kangasvuo, Jenny. "Insatiable Sluts and Almost Gay Guys: Bisexuality in Porn Maga-zines." In *Pornification: Sex and Sexuality in Media Culture*, edited by Susanna Paasonen, Kaarina Nikunen, and Laura Saarenmaa. Oxford: Berg, 2007.

Kantrowitz, Arnie. "Swastika Toys." In *Leatherfolk: Radical Sex, People, Politics, and Practice*, edited by Mark Thompson, 193–209. Los Angeles: Daedalus Publishing Company, 1991.

Kawash, Samira. *Dislocating the Color Line: Identity, Hybridity, and Singularity in African-American Narrative*. Stanford, Calif.: Stanford University Press, 1997.

Keiser, Sylvan. "Body Ego during Orgasm." *Psychoanalytic Quarterly* 21 (1952): 162–138.

Kendrick, Walter. *The Secret Museum: Pornography in Modern Culture*. Berkeley: Uni-versity of California Press, 1996.

Kennedy, Randall. *Nigger: The Strange Career of a Troublesome Word*. New York: Pantheon Books, 2002.

Kerr, Dara. "Bots Now Running the Internet with 61 Percent of Web Traffic." *CNET*, December 12, 2103, http://www.cnet.com/news/bots-now-running-the-internet-with-61-percent-of-web-traffic/.

Kipnis, Laura. *Bound and Gagged: Pornography and the Politics of Fantasy in America*. Durham, N.C.: Duke University Press, 1999.

Kleinplatz, Peggy, and Charles Moser, eds. *Sadomasochism: Powerful Pleasures*. New York: Routledge, 2006.

———. "Themes of SM Expression." In *Safe, Sane and Consensual: Contemporary Perspectives on Sadomasochism*, edited by Darren Langdridge and Meg Barker, 35–54. Basingstoke: Palgrave Macmillan, 2007.

Koedt, Ann. "The Myth of the Vaginal Orgasm." In *Sexual Revolution*, edited by Jeffrey Escoffier, 100–109. New York: Thunder's Mouth Press, 2003.

Kolko, Beth E., Lisa Nakamura, and Gilbert Rodman, eds. *Race and Cyberspace*. New York: Routledge, 2000.

Komisaruk, Barry R., Carlos Beyer-Flores, and Beverly Whipple. *The Science of Orgasm*. Baltimore, Md.: John Hopkins University Press, 2006.

Korda, Joanna B., Sue W. Goldstein, and Frank Sommer. "Sexual Medicine History: The History of Female Ejaculation." *Journal of Sexual Medicine* 7, no. 5 (2010): 1965–1975.

Krafft-Ebing, Richard von. *Psychopathia Sexualis*. Chicago: Bloat, 1999.

Kuhn, Annette. *Women's Pictures: Feminism and Cinema*. London: Routledge, 1982.

Lamos, Coleen. "Taking on the Phallus." In *Lesbian Erotics: Practices and Critiques*, edited by Karla Jay, 101–124. New York: New York University Press, 1995.

Lane, Alycee J. "What's Race Got to Do with It?" *Black Lace* (Summer 1991): 21.

Langdridge, Darren. "Speaking the Unspeakable: S/M and the Eroticization of Pain." In *Safe, Sane and Consensual: Contemporary Perspectives on Sadomasochism*, edited by Darren Langdridge and Meg Barker. Basingstoke: Palgrave Macmillan, 2007.

———. "Voices from the Margins: Sadomasochism and Sexual Citizenship." *Citizenship Studies* 10, no. 4 (2006): 373–389.

Langdridge, Darren, and Meg Barker, eds. *Safe, Sane and Consensual: Contemporary Perspectives on Sadomasochism*. Basingstoke: Palgrave Macmillan, 2007.

Langdridge, Darren, and Trevor Butt. "A Hermeneutic Phenomenological Investigation of the Construction of Sadomasochistic Identities." *Sexualities* 7, no 1 (2004): 31–53.

Lauretis, Teresa de. *Technologies of Gender: Essays on Theory, Film, and Fiction*. Bloomington: Indiana University Press, 1987.

Lederer, Laura, ed. *Take Back the Night*. New York: William and Morrow, 1980.

Lehman, Peter. *Pornography: Film and Culture*. New Brunswick, N.J.: Rutgers University Press, 2006.

LeMoncheck, Linda. *Loose Women, Lecherous Men: A Feminist Philosophy of Sex*. Oxford: Oxford University Press, 1997.

Leung, Isaac. "The Cultural Production of Sex Machines and Contemporary Technosexual Practices." In *Monochrom's Arse Elektronica Anthology*, edited by Johannes Grenzfurthner, Günther Friesinger, Daniel Fabry, and Thomas Ballhausen, 16–34. San Francisco: RE/SEARCH, 2009.

Levins, Hoag. *American Sex Machines: The Hidden History of Sex at the U.S. Patent Office*. Holbrook, Mass.: Adams Media Corporation, 1996.

Levy, David. *Love + Sex with Robots: The Evolution of Human-Robot Relationships*. New York: HarperCollins, 2007.

Lindemann, Danielle. "BDSM as Therapy?" *Sexualities* 12, no. 2 (2011): 151–172.

———. *Dominatrix: Gender, Eroticism, and Control in the Dungeon*. Chicago: University of Chicago Press, 2012.

Linden, Robin Ruth. "Introduction: Against Sadomasochism." In *Against Sadomasochism: A Radical Feminist Analysis*, edited by Robin Ruth Linden, Darlene R. Pagano, Diana E. Russell, and Susan Leigh Star. East Palo Alto, Calif.: Frog in the Well, 1982.

Lockwood, Dean. "All Stripped Down: The Spectacle of 'Torture Porn.'" *Popular Communication: The International Journal of Media and Culture* 7, no 1 (2009): 40–48.

Lorde, Audre. "Uses of the Erotic: The Erotic as Power." In *Sister Outsider: Essays and Speeches*, 53–59. Berkeley: The Crossing Press, 1984.

Love, Sinnamon. "A Question of Feminism." In *The Feminist Porn Book: The Politics of Producing Pleasure*, edited by Tristan Taormino, Constance Penley, Celine Shimizu, and Mireille Miller-Young. New York: The Feminist Press at the City University of New York, 2013.

M'Uzan, Michael. "A Case of Masochistic Perversion and an Outline of a Theory." *International Journal of Psychoanalysis* 54, no. 4 (1973): 455–467.

MacKinnon, Catherine. "Not a Moral Issue." *Yale Law & Policy Review* 2, no. 2 (1984): 321–345.

———. *Only Words*. Cambridge: Harvard University Press, 1993.

———. "Sexuality, Pornography, and Method: Pleasure under Patriarchy." *Ethics* 99, no. 2 (1989): 314–346.

———. *Towards a Feminist Theory of the State*. Cambridge, Mass.: Harvard University Press, 1991.

———. *Women's Lives, Men's Laws*. Cambridge, Mass.: Harvard University Press, 2005.

MacKinnon, Catherine, and Andrea Dworkin, eds. *In Harm's Way: The Pornography Civil Rights Hearings*. Boston: Harvard University Press, 1998.

———. *Pornography and Civil Rights: A New Day for Women's Equality*. New York: Women against Pornography, 1988.

Maines, Rachel P. *The Technology of Orgasm: "Hysteria," the Vibrator, and Women's Sexual Satisfaction*. Baltimore, Md.: John Hopkins University Press, 1999.

Mannoni, Octave. *Prospero and Caliban: The Psychology of Colonization*. Translated by Pamela Powesland. New York: Praeger, 1956.

Marcus, Steven. *The Other Victorians: A Study of Sexuality and Pornography in Mid-Nineteenth-Century England*. New York: Basic Books, 1964.

Marshall, Kendrick. "Russell Simmons Continues the Marginalization of Black Women." The Negro Voice, August 16, 2013, http://negrovoice.com/2013/08/16/russell-simmons-continues-the-marginalization-of-black-women/.

Masters, William, and Virginia Johnson. *Human Sexual Inadequacy*. New York: Bantam, 1970.

———. *Human Sexual Response*. Boston: Little, Brown, and Co., 1996.

Mayall, Alice, and Diane Russell. "Racism in Pornography." In *Making Violence Sexy: Feminist Views on Pornography*, edited by Diane Russell. New York: Teachers College Press, 1993.

McBride, Dwight A. *Why I Hate Abercrombie & Fitch: Essays on Race and Sexuality*. New York: New York University Press, 2005.

McClintock, Anne. "Maid to Order: Commercial S/M and Gender Power." In *More Dirty Looks: Gender, Pornography and Power*, edited by Pamela Church Gibson, 237–253. London: British Film Institute, 2004.

McDowell, Deborah E. *'The Changing Same,' Black Women's Literature, Criticism and Theory*. Bloomington: Indiana University Press, 1995.

McFadden, Patricia. "Sexual Pleasure as Feminist Choice" *Feminist Africa* 2 (2003). Accessed September 27, 2010. http://www.feministafrica.org/index.php/sexual-pleasure-as-feminist-choice.

McNeil, Legs, and Jennifer Osborne, *The Other Hollywood: The Uncensored Oral History of the Porn Film Industry*. New York: HarperCollins, 2005.

Mercer, Kobena. "Skin Head Sex Thing: Racial Difference and the Homoerotic Imaginary." In *How Do I Look? Queer Film and Video*, edited by Bad Object Choices, 169–222. Seattle: Bay Press, 1991.

———. *Welcome to the Jungle: New Positions in Black Cultural Studies*. New York: Routledge, 1994.

Mieszkowski, Katherine. "Battlebots in the Bedroom." *Salon*, February 12, 2002, http://www.salon.com/2002/02/12/sexbots/.

Miller-Young, Mireille. "The Deviant and Defiant Art of Black Women Porn Directors." In *The Feminist Porn Book: The Politics of Producing Pleasure*, edited by Tristan Taormino, Constance Penley, Celine Parrenas Shimizu, and Mireille Miller-Young. New York: The Feminist Press at the City University of New York, 2013.

———. "Erotic Economies: Researching Black Women in Pornography." Lecture given at the University of California Berkeley, February 18, 2009.

———. "Hip-Hop Honeys and da Hustlaz: Black Sexualities in the New Hip-Hop Pornography." *Meridians* 8, no. 1 (2008); 261–292.

———. "Let Me Tell Ya 'bout Black Chicks: Interracial Desire and Black Women in 1980's Video Pornography." In *Pornification: Sex and Sexuality in Media Culture*, edited by Kaarina Nikunen, Susanna Paasonen, and Laura Saarenmaa, 33–44. Oxford: Berg, 2007.

———. "Putting Hypersexuality to Work: Black Women and Illicit Eroticism in Pornography." *Sexualities* 13, no. 2 (2010): 219–235.

———. "Sexy and Smart: Black Women and the Politics of Self-Authorship in Netporn." In *C'lick Me: A Netporn Studies Reader*, edited by Katrien Jacobs, Marije Janssen and Matteo Pasquinelli, 205–216. [Amsterdam] Institute of Network Cultures, 2007. http://www.networkcultures.org/_uploads/24.pdf.

———. "A Taste for Brown Sugar: The History of Black Women in American Pornography," PhD dissertation. New York University, 2004.

———. *A Taste for Brown Sugar: Black Women in Pornography*. Durham, N.C.: Duke University Press, 2014.

Minge, Jeanine, and Amber Lynn Zimmerman. "Power, Pleasure, and Play: Screwing the Dildo and Rescripting Sexual Violence." *Qualitative Inquiry* 15, no. 2 (2009): 329–349.

Morrison, Toni. *Beloved*. New York: Plume, 1987.

———. *Love*. New York: Knopf, 2003.

———. *What Moves at the Margin*. Edited by Carolyn C. Denard. Jackson: University Press of Mississippi, 2008.

Moser, Charles, and Peggy J. Kleinplatz. "Themes of SM Expression." In *Safe, Sane and Consensual: Contemporary Perspectives on Sadomasochism*, edited by Darren Langdridge and Meg Barker. Basingstoke: Palgrave Macmillan, 2007.

Mullin, Joe. "Revenge Porn Is 'Just Entertainment' Says Owner of IsAnybodyDown." Ars Technica, February 4, 2013, http://arstechnica.com/tech-policy/2013/02/revenge-porn-is-just-entertainment-says-owner-of-isanybodydown/.

Mulvey, Laura. "Visual Pleasure in Narrative Cinema." *Screen* 16, no. 3 (1975): 6–18.

Mumford, Kevin. *Interzones: Black/White Sex Districts in Chicago and New York in the Early Twentieth Century*. New York: Columbia University Press, 1997.

Musser, Amber Jamilla. *Sensational Flesh: Race, Power, and Masochism*. New York: New York University Press, 2014.

Myrdal, Gunnar. *An American Dilemma: The Negro Problem in Modern Democracy*. Vol. 2. New Brunswick, N.J.: Transaction Publishers, 1944.

N.a. "Extreme Times Call for Extreme Heroes." *International Review of African-American Art* 14, no. 3 (1997): 3–14.

Nakamura, Lisa. "Afterimages of Identity: Gender, Technology, and Identity Politics." In *Reload*, edited by Mary Flanagan and Austin Booth, 321–331. Cambridge: MIT Press, 2002.

———. Cybertypes: *Race, Ethnicity, and Identity on the Internet*. New York and London: Routledge, 2002.

———. *Digitizing Race: Visual Cultures of the Internet*. Minneapolis: University of Minnesota Press, 2007.

———. "Race in/for Cyberspace: Identity Tourism and Racial Passing on the Internet." In *CyberReader*, 2nd ed., edited by Victor Vitanza, 442–453. New York: Allyn and Bacon, 1999.

Nakamura, Lisa, and Peter Chow-White, eds. *Race after the Internet*. New York: Routledge, 2011.

Nakamura, Lisa, Beth Kolko, and Gilbert Rodman, eds. *Race in Cyberspace*. New York: Routledge, 2000.

Namikoshi, Heather. "Movie Review: 'Get My Belt.'" *AVN*, July 15, 2013. Accessed August 12, 2013, http://www.avn.com/movies/123694.html.

Nash, Jennifer C. *The Black Body in Ecstasy: Reading Race, Reading Pornography*. Durham, N.C.: Duke University Press, 2014.

———. "Strange Bedfellows: Black Feminism and Antipornography Feminism." *Social Text* 26, no. 4 (2008): 51–76.

Nayar, Pramod K. *An Introduction to New Media and Cybercultures*. West Sussex, UK: Blackwell.

Neal, Jarrett. "Let's Talk about Interracial Porn." *The Gay and Lesbian Review* (July–August 2013): 23–26.

Nelson, Alondra. "Introduction: Future Texts." *Social Text* 20, no. 2 (2002): 1–15.

Nelson, Alondra, Thuy Linh N. Tu, and Alicia Headlam Hines, eds. *Technicolor: Race, Technology, and Everyday Life*. New York: New York University Press, 2001.

Newmahr, Staci. "Becoming a Sadomasochist: Integrating the Self and Other in Ethnographic Analysis." *Journal of Contemporary Ethnography* 37, no. 5 (2008): 619–643.

———. *Playing on the Edge: Sadomasochism, Risk, and Intimacy*. Bloomington: Indiana University Press, 2011.

Nicks, Denver. "Robots Have Taken Over the Internet." *Time*, December 13, 2013, http://techland.time.com/2013/12/13/robots-have-taken-over-the-internet/.

Nieratko, Chris. "Vanessa Blue." *Bizarre Magazine*, August 2005.

Nobus, Dany, and Lisa Downing, ed. *Perversion: Psychoanalytic Perspectives, Perspectives on Psychoanalysis*. London: Karnac, 2006.

Nomis, Anne O. *The History & Arts of the Dominatrix*. Hampshire, UK: Anna Nomis Ltd/Da Vinci House, 2013.

Nyong'o, Tavia. *The Amalgamation Waltz: Race, Performance, and the Ruses of Memory*. Minneapolis: University of Minnesota Press, 2009.

Ogilivie, Jessica P. "10 Porn Stars Who Could Be the Next Jenna Jameson." *LA Weekly*, March 26, 2013. Accessed August 15, 2013. http://blogs.laweekly.com/arts/2013/03/porn_stars_young_san_fernando_valley.php?page=8.

Omi, Michael, and Howard Winant. *Racial Formation in the United States from the 1960s to the 1990s*. 2nd ed. New York: Routledge, 1994.

Paglia, Camille. "Scholars in Bondage: Dogma Dominates Studies of Kink." *The Chronicle Review*, May 20, 2013. Accessed June 4, 2013, http://chronicle.com/article/Scholars-in-Bondage/139251/.

Pascoe, Peggy. "Miscegenation Law, Court Cases, and Ideologies of 'Race' in Twentieth-Century America." *Journal of American History* 83, no. 1 (1996): 44–69.

Paasonen, Susanna. *Carnal Resonance: Affect and Online Pornography*. Cambridge, Mass.: MIT Press, 2011.

———. "Repetition and Hyperbole: The Gendered Choreographies of Heteroporn." In *Everyday Pornography*, edited by Karen Boyle, 63–76. London: Routledge, 2010.

Pastor, Zlatko. "Female Ejaculation Orgasm vs. Coital Incontinence: A Systematic Review." *The Journal of Sexual Medicine* 10, no. 7 (2013): 1682–1691.

Patton, Cindy. "Hegemony and Orgasm—or the Instability of Heterosexual Pornography." *Screen* 30, no. 2 (1989): 100–113.

Peirce, Charles Sanders. *The Essential Peirce*. Vol. 2. Edited by the Peirce Edition Project. Bloomington: Indiana University Press, 1998.

Penley, Constance. "Whackers and Crackers: The White Trashing of Porn." In *Porn Studies*, edited by Linda Williams, 309–334. Durham, N.C.: Duke University Press, 2004.

Pennington, Jody W. *The History of Sex in American Film*. Westport, Conn.: Praeger, 2007.

Pindell, Howardina, ed. *Kara Walker No/ Kara Walker Yes/ Kara Walker?* New York: Midmarch Art Press, 2009.

Plaid, Andrea. "Interview with the Perverted Negress." *Racialicious*, July 10, 2009. Accessed September 7, 2010. http://www.racialicious.com/2009/07/10/interview-with-the-perverted-negress/.

——. "Your Sex Acts—and Partners—Aren't Uplifting the Race." *Racialicious*, April 3, 2009. Accessed June 5, 2012, http://www.racialicious.com/2009/04/03/your-sex-acts-and-partners-arent-uplifting-the-race/.

Portillo, Tina. "I Get Real: Celebrating my Sadomasochistic Soul." In *Leatherfolk: Radical Sex, People, Politics, and Practice*, edited by Mark Thompson, 49–55. Los Angeles: Daedalus Publishing Company, 1991.

Purcell, Natalie. *Violence and the Pornographic Imaginary: The Politics of Sex, Gender, and Aggression in Hardcore Pornography*. New York: Routledge, 2012.

Quinn, Malcolm. *The Swastika: Constructing the Symbol*. London: Routledge, 1994.

Ray, Audacia. *Naked on the Internet: Hookups, Downloads, and Cashing in on Internet Sexploration*. Emeryville, Calif.: Seal Press, 2007.

"Reading Black through White: Kara Walker and the Question of Racial Stereotyping. A Discussion between Michael Corris and Robert Hobbs." In *Differences and Excess in Contemporary Art: The Visibility of Women's Practices*, edited by Gill Perry, 104–123. Oxford: Blackwell, 2004.

Reich, June L. "Genderfuck: The Law of the Dildo." *Discourse* 15, no. 1 (1992): 112–127.

Reich, Wilhelm. *Early Writings*. New York, Farrar, Straus and Giroux, 1975.

——. *The Function of the Orgasm: Sex-Economic Problems of Biological Energy*. New York: Farrar, Straus and Giroux, 1973.

Reid-Pharr, Robert F. *Black Gay Man: Essays*. New York: New York University Press, 2001.

Reik, Theodore. *Masochism in Modern Man*. Translated by Margaret H. Beigel and Gertrud M. Kurth. New York: Grove, 1962.

Reti, Irene. "Remember the Fire: Lesbian Sadomasochism in a Post Nazi Holocaust World." In *Unleashing Feminism: Critiquing Lesbian Sadomasochism in the Gay Nineties*, edited by Irene Reti. Santa Cruz, Calif.: HerBooks: 1993.

——, ed. *Unleashing Feminism: Critiquing Lesbian Sadomasochism in the Gay Nineties*. Santa Cruz, Calif.: HerBooks, 1993.

Rich, Adrienne. *Blood, Bread, and Poetry: Selected Prose, 1979–1985*. Norton: New York, 1994.

——. "Feminism and Fascism: An Exchange. Adrienne Rich, Reply by Susan Sontag." *The New York Times Review of Books*, March 20, 1975. Accessed June 1, 2013, http://www.nybooks.com/articles/archives/1975/mar/20/feminism-and-fascism-an-exchange/?pagination=false.

Ritchie, Ani, and Meg Barker. "Feminist SM: A Contradiction in Terms or a Way of Challenging Traditional Gendered Dynamics through Sexual Practice?" *Lesbian and Gay Psychology Review* 6, no. 3 (2005): 227–239.

Roach, Joseph R. "Deep Skin: Reconstructing Congo Square." In *African American Performance & Theater History: A Critical Reader*, edited by Harry Elam Jr. and David Krasner, 101–113. New York: Oxford University Press, 2001.

Roberts, Dorothy. *Killing the Black Body: Race, Reproduction, and the Meaning of Liberty*. New York: Vintage Books, 1999.

Robinson, Randall. *The Debt: What America Owes to Blacks*. New York: Plume, 2000.

Romano, Renee. *Race Mixing: Black White Marriage in Postwar America*. Cambridge, Mass.: Harvard University Press, 2003.

Ruberg, Bonnie. "The Man behind the Fucking Machine." *The Village Voice*, July 16, 2008, http://www.villagevoice.com/news/the-man-behind-the-fucking-machine-6391543.

Rubin, Gayle. "The Outcasts: A Social History." In *The Second Coming: A Leatherdyke Reader*, edited by Pat Califia and Robin Sweeny. Los Angeles: Alyson Publications, 1996.

———. "Thinking Sex: Notes for a Radical Theory of the Politics of Sexuality." In *Pleasure and Danger: Exploring Female Sexuality*, edited by Carol Vance, 267–319. London: Routledge, 1984.

Rubio-Casillas, Alberto, and Emmanuele A. Jannini. "New Insights from One Case of Female Ejaculation." *Journal of Sexual Medicine* 8, no. 12 (2011): 3500–3504.

Russell, Diana, ed. *Making Violence Sexy: Feminist Views on Pornography*. New York: Teachers College Press, 1993.

———. *The Politics of Rape: The Victim's Perspective*. New York: Stein-Day, 1975.

Sacher-Masoch, Leopold von. *Venus in Furs*. [1870]. In *Masochism*. Translated by Jean McNeil. New York: Zone Books, 1991.

Sade, Marquis de. *The 120 Days of Sodom & Other Writings*. Translated by Austryn Wainhouse and Richard Seaver. New York: Grove Press, 1966.

———. *Juliette*. Translated by Austryn Wainhouse. New York: Grove Press, 1968.

———. *Justine, Philosophy in the Bedroom, and Other Writings*. Translated by Richard Seaver and Austryn Wainhouse. New York: Grove, 1965.

———. *Sixty Erotic Engravings from Juliette*. New York: Grove Press, 1969.

Saltz, Jerry. "Kara Walker: Ill-Will and Desire." *Flash Art* 29, no. 191 (1996): 82–86.

SAMOIS. *Coming to Power: Writings and Graphics on Lesbian S/M*. 2nd ed. Boston: Alyson Publications, 1981.

———. *What Color Is Your Handkerchief? A Lesbian S/M Sexuality Reader*. Berkeley, Calif: SAMOIS, 1979.

Sandoval, Chela. *Methodology of the Oppressed*. Minneapolis: University of Minnesota Press, 2000.

Saussure, Ferdinand de. *Course in General Linguistics*. New York: McGraw-Hill, 1966.

Savali, Kirstin West. "Plantation S&M Fantasies: Would You Engage in Slave Sex Roll [*sic*] Play?" *HelloBeautiful*, November 6, 2013. Accessed December 9, 2013, http://hellobeautiful.com/2013/11/06/plantation-retreats-race-play/.

Savran, David. *Taking It Like a Man: White Masculinity, Masochism, and Contemporary American Culture*. Princeton, N.J.: Princeton University Press, 1998.

Scarry, Elaine. *The Body in Pain: The Making and Unmaking of the World*. Oxford: Oxford University Press.

Schaschek, Sarah. "Fucking Machines: High-Tech Bodies in Pornography." In *Screening the Dark Side of Love: From Euro-Horror to American Cinema*, edited by Karen A. Ritzenhoff and Karen Randell, 211–223. New York: Palgrave Macmillan, 2012.

———. *Pornography and Seriality: The Culture of Producing Pleasure*. New York: Palgrave Macmillan, 2014.

Schnapp, Jeffrey T. 'Fascinating Fascism." *Journal of Contemporary History* 31, no. 2 (April 1996): 235–244.

Schueller, Malini Johar. "Analogy and (White) Feminist Theory: Thinking Race and the Color of the Cyborg Body." *Signs* 31, no. 1 (2005): 63–92.

Scott, Darieck. *Extravagant Abjection: Blackness, Power, and Sexuality in the Literary Imagination*. New York: New York University Press, 2010.

———"Jungle Fever? Black Gay Politics, White Dick, and the Utopian Bedroom." *GLQ* 1, no. 3 (1994): 299–321.

Scott, Gini Graham. *Dominant Women, Submissive Men: An Exploration in Erotic Dominance and Submission*. New York: Praeger, 1983.

Scott, Joan W. "Commentary: Cyborgian Socialists?" In *Coming to Terms: Feminism, Theory, Politics*, edited by Elizabeth Weed. New York: Routledge, 1989.

Seidman, Steven. "Theoretical Perspectives." In *Introducing the New Sexuality Studies: Original Essays and Interviews*, edited by Steven Seidman, Nancy Fischer, and Chet Meeks. London: Routledge, 2007.

Sekula, Allan. "The Body and the Archive." *October* 39 (Winter 1986): 3–64.

Sharpe, Christina. "The Costs of Re-Membering." In *African American Performance and Theater History: A Critical Reader*, edited by Harry Elam Jr. and David Krasner, 306–327. New York: Oxford University Press, 2001.

———. *Monstrous Intimacies: Making Post-Slavery Subjects*. Durham, N.C.: Duke University Press, 2010.

Sharpley-Whiting, T. Denean, "Thanatic Pornography, Interracial Rape, and the Ku Klux Klan." In *A Companion to African-American Philosophy*, edited by Tommy L. Lott and John P. Pittman, 407–412. New York: Blackwell, 2006.

Shaw, Gwendolyn DuBois. *Seeing the Unspeakable: The Art of Kara Walker*. Durham, N.C.: Duke University Press, 2004.

Shimizu, Celine Parreñas. *The Hypersexuality of Race: Performing Asian/American Women on Screen and Scene*. Durham, N.C.: Duke University Press, 2007.

Short, Thomas Lloyd. *Peirce's Theory of Signs*. Cambridge: Cambridge University Press, 2007.

Silverman, Kaja. *Male Subjectivity at the Margins*. New York: Routledge, 1992.

———. "Masochism and Male Subjectivity." *Camera Obscura* 6, 2, no. 17 (1988): 30–67.

Simmons, Russell. "I Get It . . . And I Respect It. The Harriet Tubman Video Has Been Removed." Globalgrind, August 16, 2013, http://globalgrind.com/2013/08/15/i-get-it-and-i-respect-it-the-harriet-tubman-video-has-been-removed/.

Sims, J. Marion. *The Story of My Life*. Edited by H. Marion Sims. New York: D. Appleton and Co, 1885.

Slade, Joseph. *Pornography in America: A Reference Handbook*. Santa Barbara: ABC-CLIO, 2000.

———. "Stags, Smokers, and Blue Movies: The Origins of American Pornographic Film." The Museum of Sex Exhibition Announcement, February 7, 2005. Accessed July 22, 2008. http://www.tomoffinlandfoundation.org/FOUNDATION/Events/ev_2005-02-07_Museum-of-Sex_Stag.htm.

Smith, Shawn Michelle. *Photography on the Color Line*. Durham, N.C.: Duke University Press, 2004.

Smith, Stephanie A. "Morphing, Materialism, and the Marketing of Xenogenesis." *Genders* 18 (Winter 1993)

Snead, James A. "Repetition as a Figure of Black Culture." in *Black Literature and Literary Theory*, edited by Henry Louis Gates Jr. New York: Routledge, 1990.

Somerville, Siobhan B. *Queering the Color Line: Race and the Invention of Homosexuality*. Durham, N.C.: Duke University Press, 2000.

Sontag, Susan. "Fascinating Fascism." In Sontag, *Under the Sign of Saturn*. New York: Farrar, Straus and Giroux, 1980.

———. "The Pornographic Imagination." In Sontag, *Styles of Radical Will*, 35–73. New York: Picador, 2002.

Snead, James A. "Repetition as a Figure of Black Culture." In *Black Literature and Literary Theory*, edited by Henry Louis Gates Jr., 59–79. New York: Routledge, 1990.

Spillers, Hortense. "'All the Things You Could Be by Now, If Sigmund Freud's Wife Was Your Mother': Psychoanalysis and Race." In *Female Subjects in Black and White: Race, Psychoanalysis, Feminism*, edited by Elizabeth Abel, Barbara Christian, and Helene Moglen. Berkeley: University of California Press, 1997.

———. "Mama's Baby, Papa's Maybe: An American Grammar Book." *Diacritics* 17, no. 2 (1987): 64–81.

Springer, Anthony. "Porn Week: Diana Devoe—Ladies First." *Hip Hop DX*, January 4, 2009. Accessed March 10, 2009, http://hiphopdx.com/interviews/id.1299/title.porn-week-diana-devoe-ladies-first.

Stallings. L. H. *Mutha Is Half a Word: Intersections of Folklore, Vernacular, Myth, and Queerness in Black Female Culture*. Columbus: Ohio State University Press, 2007.

Staples, Robert. "Blacks and Pornography: A Different Response." In *Men Confront Pornography*, edited by Michael S. Kimmel, 111–114. New York: Crown, 1990.

Star, Susan Leigh. "Swastikas: The Street and the University." In *Against Sadomasochism: A Radical Feminist Analysis*, edited by Robin Ruth Linden, Darlene R. Pagano, Diana E. Russell, and Susan Leigh Star, 131–135. East Palo Alto, Calif.: Frog in the Well, 1982.

Stern, Marlow. "James Franco & Co. Discuss the BDSM-Porn Documentary 'Kink' at Sundance." *The Daily Beast*, January 21, 2013, http://www.thedailybeast.com/articles/2013/01/21/james-franco-and-co-discuss-the-bdsm-porn-documentary-kink-at-sundance.html.

Stockton, Kathryn Bond. *Beautiful Bottom, Beautiful Shame: Where "Black" Meets "Queer."* Durham, N.C.: Duke University Press, 2006.

Stoller, Robert. *Observing the Erotic Imagination*. New Haven, Conn.: Yale University Press, 1985.

———. *Pain and Passion: A Psychoanalyst Explores the World of S &M*. New York: Plenum Press, 1991.

———. *Perversion: The Erotic Form of Hatred*. New York: Pantheon, 1975.

———. *Sexual Excitement: Dynamics of Erotic Life*. New York: Pantheon, 1979.

Studlar, Gaylyn. *In the Realm of Pleasure: Von Sternberg, Dietrich, and the Masochistic Aesthetic*. New York: Columbia University Press, 1988.

———. "Masochism and the Perverse Pleasures of the Cinema." In *Movies and Methods*, edited by Bill Nichols, 602–621. Berkeley: University of California Press, 1985.

Sullivan, David. "Chatsworth Pictures Presents *Oh No, There's a Negro in My Mom!*" *AVN*, February 6, 2008. Accessed March 30, 2009, http://business.avn.com/articles/28758.html.

———. "Shane Diesel Signs Exclusive with Vengeance XXX." *AVN*, February 26, 2008. Accessed March 17, 2009, http://business.avn.com/articles/1973.html.

Tal, Kali. "The Unbearable Whiteness of Being: African American Critical Theory and Cyberculture." October 1996. Accessed July 8, 2009. http://kalital.com/?s=The+Unbearable+Whiteness+of+Being%3A+African+American+Critical+Theory+and+Cyberculture.

Tang, Amy. "Postmodern Repetitions: Parody, Trauma, and the Case of Kara Walker." *Differences* 21, no. 2 (2010): 142–172.

Taormino, Tristan, Constance Penley, Celine Shimizu, and Mireille Miller-Young, eds. *The Feminist Porn Book: The Politics of Producing Pleasure*. New York: The Feminist Press at the City University of New York, 2013.

Taylor, Gary W. "The Discursive Construction and Regulation of Dissident Sexualities: The Case of SM." In *Body Talk: The Material and Discursive Regulation of Sexuality, Madness and Reproduction*, edited by Jane M. Ussher, 106–130. London: Routledge, 1997.

Taylor, Gary W., and Jane M. Ussher. "Making Sense of S&M: A Discourse Analytic Account." *Sexualities* 4, no. 3 (2001): 293–314.

Teish, Luisah. "A Quiet Subversion." In *Take Back The Night: Women on Pornography*, edited by Laura Lederer, 115–118. New York: William and Morrow, 1980.

Thanem, Torkild, and Louise Wallenberg. "Buggering Freud and Deleuze: Toward a Query Theory of Masochism." *Journal of Aesthetics & Culture* 2 (2010): 1–10.

Thompson, Bill. *Sadomasochism: Painful Perversion or Pleasurable Play?* London: Cassell, 1994.

Thompson, Dave. *Black and White and Blue: Adult Cinema from the Victorian Age to the VCR*. Toronto: ECW Press, 2007.

Thompson, Mark, ed. *Leatherfolk: Radical Sex, People, Politics, and Practice*. Los Angeles: Daedalus Publishing Company, 1991.

Tiefer, Leonore. *Sex Is Not a Natural Act and Other Essays*. Boulder, Colo.: Westview Press, 2004.

Tong, Rosemarie. "Women, Pornography, and the Law." In *The Philosophy of Sex: Contemporary Reading*. 2nd ed. Edited by Nicholas Power, Raja Halwani, and Alan Soble. Lanham, Md.: Rowman & Littlefield, 1991.

Townsend, Larry. *The Leatherman's Handbook*. New York: Freeway Press, 1972.

———. *The Leatherman's Handbook II*. New York: Book Surge Publishing, 2007.

Tuana, Nancy. "Coming to Understand: Orgasm and the Epistemology of Ignorance." *Hypatia* 19, no. 1 (2004): 194–232.

Tuhkanen, Mikko. *The American Optic: Psychoanalysis, Critical Race Theory, and Richard Wright*. New York: State University of New York Press, 2009.

Turan, Kenneth, and Stephan F. Zito. *Sinema: American Pornographic Films and the People Who Make Them*. New York: Praeger Publishing, 1974.

Turner, Christopher. *Adventures in the Orgasmatron: How the Sexual Revolution Came to America*. New York: Farrar, Straus and Giroux, 2011.

Valenti, Jessica. *The Purity Myth: How America's Obsession with Virginity Is Hurting Young Women*. Berkeley, Calif.: Seal Press, 2009.

Vance, Carol. "Pleasure and Danger: Toward a Politics of Sexuality." In *Pleasure and Danger: Exploring Female Sexuality*, edited by Carol Vance, 1–27. London: Routledge, 1984.

———, ed. *Pleasure and Danger: Exploring Female Sexuality*. New York: Harper Collins, 1993.

Van Peebles, Melvin. *Sweet Sweetback's Baadasssss Song: A Guerilla Filmmaking Manifesto*. New York: Thunder's Mouth Press, 1971.

Vincent, James. "Nearly Two Thirds of Global Web Activity Is Thanks to Bots, Say Study." *Independent*, December 13, 2013, http://www.independent.co.uk/life-style/gadgets-and-tech/news/nearly-two-thirds-of-global-web-activity-is-thanks-to-bots-say-study-9003034.html.

Walker, Alice. "Coming Apart: By Way of Introduction to Lorde, Teish and Gardner." In *You Can't Keep a Good Woman Down*. New York: Harcourt Brace Jovanovich Publishers, 1971.

———. "A Letter of the Times, or Should This Sado-Masochism Be Saved?" In *Against Sadomasochism: A Radical Feminist Analysis*, edited by Robin Ruth Linden, Darlene R. Pagano, Diana E. Russell, and Susan Leigh Star, 205–208. East Palo Alto, Calif.: Frog in the Well, 1982.

———. "Porn." In *You Can't Keep a Good Woman Down*. New York: Harcourt Brace Jovanovich Publishers, 1971.

Walker, Kara Walker, *After the Deluge: A Visual Essay by Kara Walker*. New York: Rizzoli, 2007.

———. "Extreme Times Call for Extreme Heroes." *International Review of African-American Art* 14, no. 3 (1997): 2–15+.

Wallace, Michele. *Invisibility Blues: From Pop to Theory*. London: Verso, 1990.

Wallis, Brian. "Black Bodies, White Science: Louis Agassiz's Slave Daguerreotypes." *American Art* 9, no. 2 (1995): 38–61.

Warner, Michael. *Fear of a Queer Planet: Queer Politics and Social Theory*. Minneapolis: University of Minnesota Press, 1993.

———. *The Trouble with Normal: Sex, Politics, and the Ethics of Queer Life*. Cambridge, Mass.: Harvard University Press, 2000.

Warren, Peter. "Kelly Madison Media Strikes Hard with Get My Belt." *AVN*, April 19, 2013. Accessed August 12, 2013, http://business.avn.com/articles/video/Kelly-Madison-Media-Strikes-Hard-With-Get-My-Belt-513777.html.

Wayne, Linda. "S/M Symbols, Fascist Icons, and Systems of Empowerment." In *The Second Coming: A Leatherdyke Reader*, edited by Pat Califia and Robin Sweeny, 242–251. Los Angeles: Alyson Publications, 1996.

Webb, Natalie. "Power in Numbers." January 3, 2014. Accessed April 24, 2014, http://www.endrevengeporn.org/revenge-porn-infographic/.

Weheliye, Alexander G. "'Feenin': Posthuman Voices in Contemporary Black Popular Music." *Social Text* 20, no. 2 (2002): 21–47.

Weigman, Robyn. *American Anatomies: Theorizing Race and Gender*. Durham, N.C.: Duke University Press, 1995.

Weinberg, Thomas S. "Research in Sadomasochism: A Review of Sociological and Social Psychological Literature." *Annual Review of Sex Research* 5, no. 1 (1994): 257–279.

———. "Sadism and Masochism: Sociological Perspectives." *Bulletin of the American Academy of Psychiatry and the Law* 6, no. 3 (1978): 284–295.

———. "Sadomasochism and the Social Sciences: A Review of the Sociological Literature." In *Sadomasochism: Powerful Pleasures*, edited by Peggy J. Kleinplatz and Charles Moser, 17–40. New York: Harrington Park Press, 2006.

———, ed. *S&M: Studies in Dominance & Submission*. New York: Prometheus Books, 1995.

Weinberg, Thomas, and G. W. Levi Kamel. *S and M: Studies in Sadomasochism*. Buffalo, N.Y.: Prometheus Books, 1983.

Weis, Phillip. "The Best Reason to Have Sex." *Men's Journal*, October 1, 2012, http://www.mensjournal.com/health-fitness/health/the-best-reason-to-have-sex-20121001.

Weiss, Margot D. "Mainstreaming Kink: The Politics of BDSM Representation in U.S. Popular Media." *Journal of Homosexuality* 50, nos. 2–3 (2006):103–132.

———. *Techniques of Pleasure: BDSM and the Circuits of Sexuality*. Durham, N.C.: Duke University Press, 2011.

———. "Working at Play: BDSM Sexuality in the San Francisco Bay Area." *Anthropologica* 48, no. 2 (2006): 229–245.

Weitzer, Ronald, ed. *Sex for Sale: Prostitution, Pornography, and the Sex Industry*. 2nd ed. New York: Routledge, 2010.

Wells-Barnett, Ida. "Lynch Law in America" (1900). In *Words of Fire: An Anthology of African-American Feminist Thought*, edited by Beverly Guy-Sheftall. New York: The New Press, 1995.

White, Armond. "Can't Trust It," *City Arts*, October 16, 2013. Accessed January 4, 2013, http://cityarts.info/2013/10/16/cant-trust-it/.

———. "Dud of the Week: 12 Years a Slave Reviewed by Armond White for CityArts." *New York Film Critics Circle*, October 6, 2103. Accessed January 4, 2013, http://www. nyfcc.com/2013/10/3450/#.Ul7ULiL3opU.twitter.

White, Chris. "The Spanner Trials and the Changing Law on Sadomasochism in the UK." In *Sadomasochism: Powerful Pleasures*, edited by Peggy Kleinplatz and Charles Moser, 167–187. New York: Routledge, 2006.

White, Deborah Gray. *Ar'n't I a Woman? Female Slaves in the Plantation South*. New York: W. W. Norton, 1999.

Wicomb, Zoë. "Shame and Identity: The Case of the Coloured in South Africa." In *Writing South Africa: Literature, Apartheid, and Democracy, 1970–1995*, edited by Derek Attridge and Rosemary Jolly, 91–107. Cambridge; Cambridge University Press, 1998.

Wilkerson, Abby. "Ending at the Skin: Sexuality in Feminist Theorizing." *Hypatia* 12, no. 3 (1997): 164–173.

Williams, Linda. "Film Bodies: Gender, Genre and Excess." *Film Quarterly* 44, no. 4 (1991): 2–13.

———. *Hardcore: Power, Pleasure, and the Frenzy of the Visual*. Berkeley: University of California Press, 1989.

———. "Porn Studies: Proliferating Pornographies On/Scene." In *Porn Studies*, edited by Linda Williams. Durham, N.C.: Duke University Press, 2004.

———. "'White Slavery' versus the Ethnography of 'Sexworkers': Women in Stag Films at the Kinsey Archive." *The Moving Image* 5, no. 2 (2005): 107–134.

Williams, Linda, ed. *Porn Studies*. Durham, N.C.: Duke University Press, 2004.

Williams, Mollena. "BDSM and Playing with Race." In *Best Sex Writing: 2010*, edited by Rachel Kramer Bussel, 60–78. San Francisco: Cleis Press, 2010.

———. "The Negress Natters: On BDSM & Race Play." Audiolink, November 20, 2009, http://www.mollena.com/2009/11/the-negress-natters-on-bdsm-race-play/.

———. *Playing with Taboo*. Eugene, Ore.: Greenery Press, 2010.

———. "Race Play: Hitting the Mainstream Media . . . ?" The Perverted Negress, April 11, 2013. http://www.mollena.com/2013/04/12212/.

———. *The Toybag Guide to Playing with Taboo*. Eugene, Ore.: Greenery Press, 2010.

Willis, Deborah, and Carla Williams. *The Black Female Body: A Photographic History*. Philadelphia: Temple University Press, 2002.

Wiseman, Jay. *SM 101: A Realistic Introduction*. 2nd ed. San Francisco: Greenery Press, 1996.

Wolf, Lolita. "A Letter from Lolita Wolf, TES Programming Chair for TES Fest 2004." Leatherweb.com. Accessed April 5, 2013, http://www.leatherweb.com/raceplayh. htm.

X, Nelson. "Black Humor: The Marketing of Stereotypes in Interracial Porn: An AVN Discussion." *Adult Video News*, February 2009, 76.

———. "No Boundaries: A Look at the Ethnic/Interracial Markets." *XBIZ*, May 8, 2012. Accessed July 22, 2012, http://www.xbiz.com/articles/147875.

Yamato, Jen. "Russell Simmons Pulls Controversial 'Harriet Tubman Sex Tape' after YouTube Channel Launch." *Deadline Hollywood*, August 15, 2013. Accessed August 16, 2013, http://www.deadline.com/2013/08/russell-simmons-pulls-controversial-harriet-tubman-sex-tape-after-youtube-channel-launch/.

Ziplow, Stephen. *The Film Maker's Guide to Pornography*. New York: Drake, 1977.

INDEX

ABOUT THE AUTHOR

Ariane Cruz is Assistant Professor of Women's, Gender, and Sexuality Studies at Pennsylvania State University.

www.ingramcontent.com/pod-product-compliance
Lightning Source LLC
Chambersburg PA
CBHW022137020426
42334CB00015B/940